Crime through Time

Oxford in India Readings
Themes in Indian History

Available in the Series

* These and some earlier titles in this series were commissioned by an editorial board comprising C.A. Bayly, Neeladri Bhattacharya, and Basudev Chatterji.

For
Leela Dube (1923–2012)
Feminist and Anthropologist Extraordinaire

Contents

Series Note

The series focuses on important themes in Indian history, on those which have long been subject of interest and debate, or which have acquired importance more recently.

Each volume in the series consists of, first, a detailed Introduction; second, a careful choice of the essays and book-extracts vital to a proper understanding of the theme; and, finally, an Annotated Bibliography.

Using this consistent format, each volume seeks as a whole to critically assess the state of the art on its theme, chart the historiographical shifts that have occurred since the theme emerged, rethink old problems, open up questions which were considered closed, locate the theme within wider historiographical debates, and pose new issues of inquiry by which further work may be made possible.

Preface

Not so long ago, as we planned *Crime through Time*, our minds moved not to the past but to the present, to literature rather than history. We were struck by the manner in which Aravind Adiga's recent, prize-winning novel, *The White Tiger*, posed provocative questions about crime as the practice of social critique. This was reminiscent of our own conversations about the centrality of law, violence, and the state to projects of collective action and self-making. Put simply, in Adiga's work, we found an exploration of the violence of caste hatred and class hostility in globalizing India, and of the reproduction of privilege through the distinct, if related, registers of 'feudal' and 'modern' modes of power in these terrains. Such concerns resonate powerfully with our own attempts to understand crime and criminality as historical constructions. Produced within the interstices of state–society relations and governed by shifting ideas about normative conduct and legitimate punishment, these constructions ever entail pasts that continue into the present.

Now, the focal concern of Adiga's literary ethnographic gaze is the contemporary violence of everyday life, alongside the amorality of India's emergent middle classes, more generally. With their crude penchant for conspicuous consumption, here are social groups that continue to rely on a large service class of domestic workers—drivers, ayahs, *chaukidars*—whose labour sustains them. Rather more than their ownership of the latest dishwashers and plasma TVs, what is distinctive about this globalizing elite is their power over *living* labour, the latter often relegated to servants' quarters, forced to register with the police, issued passes to enter gated-communities, routinely under-paid, and frequently corporeally-disciplined.

It follows that even as cultural forms of hierarchical subordination are increasingly redefined and legitimized as salaried work, what is noteworthy is the fear among the middle-classes of subaltern vio-lence provoked by disparities of wealth. This fear coexists with the middle-classes' (necessarily unmet, ever deferred) aspirations sus-tained by seductions of endless consumer goods and the good life. At the same time, the mutual hostility between domestic workers and their employers incites a range of behaviors on the part of the former, from petty thievery to class violence.

Recall that in the novel, Balram Halwai, an intimate witness to his master's ethical degeneration, engages in turn in an act of 'purifying violence'. Balram kills his master. This fight-unto-death between master and servant is also a struggle for social recognition. Here, Adiga suggests that the servant's brutalization is produced by, and equally enables, the further brutalization of society. At the same time, rather than remake the social order through revolutionary violence, the fixer, the trickster, and the scamster of urban India now stands in the place of the state, including especially the latter's monopoly over legitimate violence.

Adiga's dystopic vision replicates broader trends in Indian popular and political cultures today, which turn on the mimetic interchange between law and violence. For example, such mutual begetting of the licit and the illicit significantly structures popular films about Bombay's underworld, which were inaugurated by Ram Gopal Verma's *Satya*, and that now inform sub-metro variants of underworlds such as *Omkara*. And so, too, the symmetries and asymmetries of order and excess produced within the blockbuster *Rang de Basanti* are incorporated into the more indie *No One Killed Jessica*, each as cinema and reality. The point is that even as the Indian state retreats from its earlier commitments to social welfare and collective enfranchisement, violence, instead of pedagogical transformation, appears to be the mode of political communication between social classes, while the middle-classes oppose the state through their innate entitlements.

Unsurprisingly, even the globally popular *Slumdog Millionaire*, a sort of morality play where the underdog gets the money and the girl, insistently poses questions of social relations between the elite and the subaltern. Unlike earlier models of collective rebellion or class struggle, however, the problem of social intimacy is now seen to involve escalating levels of everyday violence in urban South Asia, provoked by the potent combination of growing economic disparity and the democratization of consumer desire. And so, too, from everyday discussions of the endless scams today—involving politicians, bureaucrats, corporates, and powerbrokers—through to the politics both of India *Incorporated* and Team Anna (Hazare), contemporary representations of criminality gesture to an unstable social order predicated on the permeability of (state) law and (popular) violence. In one or another way, crime is on every Indian mind today.

To point to the topicality of a theme, however, is not to overlook that putting together a volume of essays on so broad a topic as crime and its relation to pre-colonial, colonial, and postcolonial legalities is a perilous task. The selections are unavoidably limited, and must omit a great deal of important work. Our constraints have been those of space as well as those of securing permissions for texts to be included in the volume. We seek the understanding of authors whose work we have been unable to include in this volume. It is our hope that, together with other readers, they will find that *Crime through Time* works toward disclosing certain key dynamics regarding the changing place of crime in the socio-political order, rather than making totalizing claims to represent a field so complex and generously explored as law, crime, and the state on the subcontinent.

Anupama would like to thank Riyad Koya for his comments and suggestions. She is grateful to the directors of the Centre for Modern Indian Studies (Goettingen), Ravi Ahuja and Rupa Viswanath, as well as to Srirupa Roy and Peter van der Veer for helping to create the intellectually salubrious environment in which this volume was completed.

Saurabh would like to thank Arvind and Anu for the endless hours of fun, mirth, and hospitality in their lovely Manhattan apartment, all of which went into the planning of this volume during the last two (of many) stays there.

Both of us wish to thank Francisco Figueroa Medina for all his help, from scanning proofs to correcting references, and especially for putting together the bibliography. We also acknowledge the efforts of the editorial department of Oxford University Press, New Delhi, as well as the help and patience of the contributors to *Crime through Time*. We are deeply grateful to Sudhir Patwardhan for graciously and generously allowing us to use his oil-on-canvas, *The Fall*, for the cover.

At the end, Anu proposed and worded the dedication of this volume to Leela Dube, and Saurabh concurred.

December 2012   ANUPAMA RAO, New York
                                           SAURABH DUBE, Mexico City

Acknowledgements

The editors and the publisher would like to thank the following for permission to include these articles in the volume:

Cambridge University Press for excerpts from Scott Kugle, 'Framed, Blamed and Renamed: The Recasting of Islamic Jurisprudence in Colonial South Asia', *Modern Asian Studies*, vol. 35, no. 2, 2001, pp. 257–313, and for excerpts from Rajnarayan Chandavarkar, *Imperial Power and Popular Politics: Class, Resistance and State in India, 1850–1950*, Cambridge, Cambridge University Press, 1998.

Sage Publications India Pvt. Ltd. for excerpts from 'Disciplining and Policing the "Criminals by Birth", Part 2: The Development of a Disciplinary System, 1871–1900', *The Indian Economic and Social History Review*, vol. 27, no. 3, 1990, pp. 257–87, New Delhi/Newbury Park/London, Sage.

Taylor and Francis, and *South Asia* for Anand Yang 'Disciplining "Natives": Prisons and Prisoners in Early Nineteenth Century India', vol. X, no. 2, December 1987, pp. 29–45.

Permanent Black for David Arnold, 'The Self and the Cell: Indian Prison Narratives as Life Histories' in *Telling Lives in India: Biography, Autobiography and Life History*, Delhi, Permanent Black, 2004, pp. 29–53.

History Workshop Journal for 'The Emergence of the Female Criminal in India: Infanticide and Survival under the Raj,' *History Workshop Journal*, Spring, vol. 53, 2002, pp. 73–93.

Duke University Press for Rajeswari Sunder Rajan, 'Outlaw Woman: The Politics of Phoolan Devi's Surrender, 1983' in *Scandal of the State: Women, Law, and Citizenship in Postcolonial India*, Duke University Press, 2003.

Abbreviations

ABVP	Akhil Bharatiya Vidyarthi Parishad
AGG	Agent to Governor General
AIDWA	All India Democratic Women's Association
AllD	Allahabad Division
BCJC	Bengal Criminal Judicial Consultations
BCRR	Bilaspur Collectorate Record Room
BD	Bajrang Dal
BDVSR	Bilaspur District Village Settlement Records
BISM	*Bharatiya Itihasa Samshodhaka Mandala*
BM	British Museum
BRJC	Bengal Revenue Judicial Consultations
BSP	Bahujan Samaj Party
CC	Court Case
CI	Central India
CIA	Central India Agency
CLWCB	*The Correspondence of Lord William Cavendish Bentinck* (C.H. Philips ed., 1977)
CR	Crime Record
CWMG	*Collected Works of Mahatma Gandhi*
DIGP	Deputy Inspector General of Police
DPW	Deposition of Prosecution Witness

DSCRR	District and Sessions Court Record Room, Raipur
DSP	Deputy Superintendent of Police
FD	Foreign Department
FIR	First Information Report
FPC	Foreign Political Consultations
GG in C	Governor General in Council
GG	Governor General
GOB	Government of Bengal
GOI	Government of India
GoI, Leg. Progs	Government of India, Legislative Proceedings
GSTD	General Superintendent for Thugi and Dacoity
IESHR	*Indian Economic and Social History Review*
IGP	Inspector General of Police
J	Judgement
JCERR	Jhansi Collectorate English Record Room
JCOERR	Jhansi Commissioner's English Record Room
JD	Jhansi Division
JD	Judicial Department
JRAS	*Journal of the Royal Asiatic Society*
LG	Lieutenant Governor
MSA	Maharashtra State Archives
NAI	National Archives of India
NDA	National Democratic Alliance
NWP	North-Western Provinces
NWPO, Jud. (Cr) Progs	North Western Provinces and Oudh, Judicial (Criminal) Proceedings
NWPO, Police Progs	North Western Provinces and Oudh, Police Proceedings
NWPP	North-Western Provinces Police Report
PCR	Protection of Civil Rights
PCRA	Protection of Civil Rights Act

P-D Reports	Report of the Committee on Prison Discipline
POA	Prevention of Atrocities Act
RB	Resident of Benaras
RSS	Rashtriya Swayamsevak Sangh
SDOB	Superintendent for the Suppression of Dakaiti Operations in Bundelkhand
SDPO	Sub-Divisional Police Officer
SIH	*Studies in History*
SNT	Sagar and Narbada Territories
SP	Superintendent of Police
SSRPD	*Selections from the Satara Raja's Pershwa Diaries*
ST	Sessions Trial
SWJN	*Selected Works of Jawaharlal Nehru*
T&D/ TDD	Thuggee and Dacoity Department
TADA	Terrorist and Disruptive Activities (Prevention) Act
TDP	Telugu Desam Party
UPRAA	Uttar Pradesh Regional Archives, Allahabad
VHP	Vishwa Hindu Parishad
WH	Warren Hastings
WHS	William H. Sleeman
WP	Western Provinces

Questions of Crime

An Introduction

Anupama Rao and *Saurabh Dube*

This volume explores the relationship between crime and culture, in order to better understand the changing terms, tactics, and textures of disciplinary authority, social control, and their several subversions in South Asia—from the eighteenth to the twenty-first centuries. The exploration of crime and the construction of the criminal as it relates to shifting domains of law is a particularly fruitful avenue of inquiry considering pervasive representations, in the past and the present, of South Asian peoples as peculiarly prone to conflict. On the one hand, it is easy to dismiss relentless stereotypes of endlessly conflictive subcontinental subjects as mere caricature, overlooking thereby the critical questions at stake here, including the epistemic violence of state categorization. On the other, it would be only too easy to concur with governmental orderings of crime and criminality as routine requirements of law and order, the business-as-usual of administration that defines states of civility and the civility of the state. Reaching beyond both these tendencies, this volume traces the diverse histories that are contained by everyday public descriptions and governmental configurations of conflict and crime, of deviance and criminality.

The critical place of crime in official archives and governmental discourses barely requires emphasis. Unsurprisingly, this pervasive

presence has equally led to imaginative uses of 'records of incrimination'—setting to work Simon Schama's condescending phrase toward
our own purposes—in innovative reconstructions of the past and the
present.[1] In this twin context, we seize upon crime as a point of entry
not only to unravel the dynamic between states and subjects but to
understand as well the ways in which intimate social lives have been
shaped by these encounters.

Here, crime appears at once as a category produced by legal
regimes and governmental registers as well as a practice intimating the intersections of social experience and state power. At stake,
then, are multiple articulations between governmental categories,
formations of state authority, and structures of everyday life. These
articulations themselves suggest that far from constituting a settled
fact, questions of crime are better approached as problems of knowledge and of knowing.

What constitutes crime, when, and to whom? In terms of social
space, where does crime appear as a politically powerful or/and a
culturally critical expression of aberrance? How has crime entailed a
definitional apparatus as well as a disciplining one? What do divergent
perceptions and incommensurable articulations of crime tell us about
historical actors and social institutions? Which sorts of histories are
possessed by crime and how are we to narrate these pasts?

To raise these questions is to no less register that we give crime
its due. On the one hand, we understand crime as meaning-making
activity, including as a comment about the world on the part of the dispossessed who have challenged their social exclusion through a range
of actions including violence, individual or collective. On the other
hand, we acknowledge that crime is compelling, entailing strange
desires, hidden motives, curious conflicts, spectacles of competition, and seductions of violence. Taken together, our focus on crime
learns from the sensibility that only those concepts which 'compel
our desire as well as our resistance receive and deserve the most sustained critique.'[2]

Eschewing its apparent innateness, the focus of this volume is on
the social production of crime. Indeed, located within recent depar-
tures in anthropology and history as well as in cultural and legal
studies, *Crime through Time* raises wider questions of social theory

and critical scholarship. Here are queries concerning the mutual binds between gendered bodies and sexual scandals, colonial legalities and subaltern illegalities, imperial power and modern law, coercion and consent, and the nation-state and the citizen-subject. This volume thinks such linkages—of modern justice and competing legalities and of the state and the subaltern—down to the ground, in order to illuminate shifting construal(s) of crime, criminality, and the criminal in South Asia over the past three centuries.

SUBJECTS OF LAW, POWER, AND VIOLENCE

In an important sense, the history of crime is the history of law. Under modern state formations, at the very least, it is the institutionalization of a domain of power and practice called the 'law' which creates distinctions between 'normal' and 'criminal' behaviour. At stake here are longer-term historical processes through which the state, rather than individuals or communities, was valorized as the legitimate agency for inflicting punishment. Needless to say, of course, that each of these terms, 'law', 'punishment', and the 'state' requires greater, context-bound exposition.

These issues framed critical considerations of crime and criminality in historical scholarship from the 1960s onwards. Such scholarship was intimately associated with wider expressions of the 'histories from below' tradition, while drawing in related tendencies. Resisting the dominant assumption that cast ostensibly criminal actions of the ordinary folk as already known truths, a new generation of historians went on to tease out the distinct implications of criminality in the making and unmaking of social worlds.

A case in point concerns E.P. Thompson's remarkable studies of eighteenth-century England. As part of a variety of wide-ranging scholarship, he focused on crime as a site for exploring the clash of social sensibilities between the communitarian concerns of peasant–artisan society, on the one hand, and an emerging social and political order defined by forces of the market, themselves predicated on 'possessive individualism', on the other. Exploring the discrete yet overlaying terrains of the 'patrician' rulers and the 'plebian' public, Thompson unraveled the place of political authority and state forms

as these impinged upon the 'crowd's autonomy' and its 'moral economy'. In the process he showed how changing conceptions of crime and
punishment—and social control through official law—were bound up
with the rise of capitalism and the presence of the eighteenth-century
Whig state as an instrument for protecting private property, which
entailed the demise of earlier forms of social cohesion and moral
critique.[3] The influence of these tendencies extended to non-Western
history writing, including historical studies of crime and criminality
in South Asia, a few represented in this volume.

At the same time, it is also important to note that such scholarship, despite its considerable accomplishments, could not escape
the association of historical progress with capitalist modernity. The
linkages could include the assumption of an evolution from 'status'
to 'contract', as Henry Maine argued.[4] They could extend to visions of
the centralization of authority, entailing control over technologies of
violence and forming a defining characteristic of the modern state, as
Weber suggested.[5] Such projections each presumed a universal *telos* to
the emergence of the law, the state, and the subject.

Now, to think through the modular character of this developmental narrative is crucial, especially for the study of crime and law in
colonial and postcolonial societies. Toward this end, our attempt
now is to outline a newer disposition to issues of law and crime, state
and subject, and violence and power. It is an indicative rather than
an exhaustive discussion, which presents a single (albeit exemplary)
rethinking of these questions, a tendency that bears import not only
for our own arguments ahead but also for ongoing and future work on
crime and culture.

Among the most important contemporary considerations of the
dynamic between law, crime, subject, and power are those to be found
in the writings of Michel Foucault. At stake especially are his analysis
of the interplay between, on the one hand, the power of categories
and the state's ability to define behaviour, and, on the other, the social
consequence of ideas regarding the 'normal' and the 'deviant' subject.
Now, it is worth exploring Foucault's argument in some detail. This is
particularly the case considering the challenge issued by his analyses
to realist conceptions of law and punishment—realist projections that

derive, ultimately, from liberal notions of the 'subject' and static conceptions of the 'state'.

Foucault argued that eighteenth-century Europe saw a shift away from the exercise of sovereign power, which was principally visual and often excessive in its application. Instead, modern states now deployed a more dispersed form of power, which quietly monitored subjects and included them in the project of self-surveillance. In his important texts on the modernity of madness as well as on the emergence of the criminal as a discrete social type,[6] Foucault contends that the emergence of specialized knowledge(s) in the form of the disciplines was consonant with a new understanding of the subject (and its social control) in eighteenth century Europe.[7] Indeed, he linked the new disciplines of the human sciences with bureaucratic innovation, further claiming that the emergence of the *medico-juridical complex*—which addressed the problem of the subject from the different ends of the 'therapeutic' and the 'rehabilitative' models—was a defining character of the soft power of the modern state.

What did Foucault mean? His argument was that European modernity was characterized by a discrepant set of temporal shifts and improving innovations, which nonetheless shared a central assumption. The presumption remains with us to this day: the individual is the locus of agency in society; and this individual is, following Nietzsche, a 'promise-making animal' who enters into binding relations of obligation and responsibility with other individuals.[8] Now, if the heroic individual was placed at the core of mainstream accounts of secular, scientific progress, Foucault's 'subject' was rather differently produced. The philosopher contended that autonomy and individuality were not end results of a developmental process, but rather, the *effect* of the process of *subjectification*, a complex set of mediations by which power acted upon human beings to make them subject *to* and subject *of* the state.

Clearly, Foucault refused the idea of an individual as posited against the state (or nature), but he also refused the idea of the state as a unitary locus from which power operates upon 'society' (as a collection of individuals). Instead, he argued that power is most effective when it works across the state/society divide.[9] Thus, subjectification occurs at the interstitial intersections of liberal categories of 'individual', 'state', and 'society'. Put differently, subjectification is the effect of the combined exercise of externalized power and its internalization (as an improving force), such that the apparently intimate and external aspects of power coincide.

Here are two well-known examples. The first concerns the curing of 'pathologies' such as madness or homosexuality that 'subject subjects' to manipulation and other forms of intervention in their own interest, such that the 'subjects subject' themselves to their own care. The second entails Foucault's discussion of how under modern regimes the punishment of prisoners shifted from displaying signs of sovereign power on their body, involving the infliction of brutal violence, to efforts instead to rehabilitate and integrate them back into the social order as a productive member. Each of these examples conveys the indistinguishable attributes of power as an improving force and power as a disciplining one. And both instances are also predicated on challenging the idea of the speaking subject—the one who responds and answers when s/he is asked about intention (as with criminal acts), experience (as in the medical exam), or to having sinned (as in the Christian confessional)—as the individual who possesses autonomy and the ability to speak truth before power. Rather, as Foucault famously argued, one is always within power even when one thinks that one is challenging it.

By rendering power as that which breaks down divisions between state and society—as well as that which undoes distinctions between the just and the unjust use of authority—Foucault was equally issuing another invitation. Here was a provocation to think beyond both, normative understandings of the state as that which is/must be necessarily resisted as well as commonplace notions of the state as a trans-historical entity with concrete existence in social space. Instead, by arguing for the complicity between discipline and improvement as the defining characteristic of European modernity, Foucault was also probing the distinctive place of the law as a repressive force. Now, rather more than the fear of penal sanction, itself implying a turn away from speech altogether, it was the proliferation of discourses and the constant incitement to speak that marked power.

For Foucault, power is productive, fecund, and promiscuous, at once constitutive of and constituted by political forces, institutional sites, and their demands for organizing and presenting scientific knowledge in a distinctive manner. Power produces social types and definitional categories—each appearing to have an analytical power of their own—that contain both evaluation and cure and which require constant surveillance. Put concretely, the criminal was to be incarcerated and made subject to a physical routine under the gaze of the prison guard; the homosexual was to be visually categorized, invited to speak about her abnormality, and made subject to the constant vigilance of the community; and the sexuality of the child was to be regulated through her monitoring in the bedroom while her body was to be disciplined in the classroom. Foucault's focus on re-training the body and its embodiment through the spatialization of power—the school, the prison, the courtroom—is thus an integral aspect of his descriptions of how modern power operates.[10]

As implied earlier, this somewhat strenuous exegetical account of Foucault's writing on modern power has particular purposes. First, it underscores the wide-ranging, critical implications of focusing on crime, criminality, and the (criminal) subject as these come to be entwined with regimes of discipline and improvement, pedagogy and propriety, and the law and the state under modernity—Western or non-Western. Second, it is precisely such recognition that has led a newer body of scholarship to imaginatively articulate questions of crime, which becomes clear from several of the chapters that constitute this book. Third and finally, it warrants emphasis that such efforts do not simply follow Foucault, seeking to fit his insights into mere case studies. Rather, as we shall see, learning from the spirit of the philosopher-historian, recent writings have rethought questions of crime, law, state, and subject, including by accessing and exceeding—and testing and contesting—the work not only of Foucault but also of other critical thinkers.[11] Indeed, taken together, scholars of South Asia have productively engaged with, often creatively transforming, European theory as they have construed new accounts of law, crime, and society on the subcontinent. Such concerns and engagements are the locus of this volume.

Pre-colonial Premonitions

For sometime now, scholars of South Asia have been preoccupied with questions of the 'transition' or 'rupture' from a pre-colonial society to a colonial regime. On the one hand, salient writings on the eighteenth and nineteenth centuries on the subcontinent have made a case for—indeed, accorded an innate heuristic privilege to—continuities between pre-colonial regimes and the colonial order. Such scholarship, which has revised our historical understanding of the period, has nonetheless predicated questions of colonial formations on issues of political economy, including imperatives of state.[12] On the other hand, a variety of scholarship at the heart of subaltern studies and postcolonial perspectives has emphasized that the break between the pre-colonial and the colonial was not merely a change from one mode of socio-political organization to the other, as earlier nationalist and Marxist narratives of historical development had implied. Rather, the externality of the colonial state to native society meant that the imposition of a new mode of organizing society (and knowledge about that society) was accomplished through a distinctive form of conquest, which involved not only the brute violence of colonial extraction but also the epistemic violence of colonial categorization. This is to say, the simultaneous processes of British colonization, global transformations of political economy, and changing ideas of governance through culture, caste, and religion meant that the colonial order was experienced as a distinctively foreign practice of rule.[13]

All of this brings up at least two critical questions: First, at what level of analysis are we to approach issues of colonial transition and/or rupture? Second, what is the transition or rupture 'from', and what is it 'to'? Rather than casting matters on a resolutely overarching scale, this book considers the continuities and transformations at stake from the perspectives of crime and law. Toward this end, our efforts begin with explorations of eighteenth-century Indian conceptions and practices of crime and punishment.

It is widely acknowledged today that the Indian subcontinent experienced major changes between the sixteenth and eighteenth centuries, alongside the wider onset of European colonization of 'new' and 'old' worlds. Pre-colonial political economies and state formations on the subcontinent were predicated upon control over territory, especially through the ability to garner tax or gather tribute. At the same time, these regimes were redistributive in nature, based on terms of incorporation: power/profit was understood to be most effective when it was distributed across, rather than concentrated in, one centre. Thus, during this period, flexible models of political incorporation allowed social groups of 'questionable' status to enter militarized service, which functioned in turn as conduits of social mobility. Indeed, the military market was an engine of social dynamism that enabled new caste formations.

Unsurprisingly, large parts of the subcontinent saw the rise of new social groups such as Jats, Rajputs, and Marathas whose identities were deeply bound up with region and locality, on the one hand, and with military service for the Mughal state (1526–1707), on the other. Actually, the models of incorporation were equally the instruments of localization. The exact dependence of early modern polities on the distribution of land tenures in recognition of military service enabled the localization of social groups that hastened the demise of the empire. This is to say that although localized identities of caste and community were intimately tied to, indeed emerged out of, imperial patterns of governance, they eventually played a key role in the practices of regionalization, which saw the breakdown of the Mughal imperial polity.

In this larger scenario, political legitimacy and territorial expansion appeared enabled by loot, plunder, guerilla warfare, and revenue farming. But this should not be seen to imply a situation of social chaos and political anarchy.[14] Rather, as part of a wider system that Frank Perlin has characterized as 'proto-industrialization', at stake were layered intersections between political enterprise, mercantile capital, revenue farming, military entrepreneurship, and the development of bureaucracy and recordkeeping.[15] In the context of broad hierarchies of power marked by conflicting interests, here were to be found structures defined by sophisticated mechanisms of revenue contracts (and collection); extensive monetization of services; a market in patrimonial tenures; an expansion of agriculture, especially through revenue farming, in the interest of settled revenue collection; and, finally, an elaborate legal-bureaucratic regime distinguished by a system of fines and punishments.[16]

This broader context frames the two chapters in the first section of the volume. We begin our considerations with Sumit Guha's discussion of the legal regime that operated under the Peshwai, the 'Brahminical state' ruled by the Chitpavans from the eighteenth century.[17] One of the distinctive aspects of Maratha rule in western India was the political conflict, from the mid-seventeenth century, between Maratha Kshatriya rulers and their Chitpavan Brahmin ministers, the Peshwas, who had begun to make autonomous claims for power. At the height of Peshwa rule in the mid-eighteenth century, this conflict was transformed into an antagonism between Brahmin and non-Brahmin.[18] So far as the disciplining of crime was concerned, the Peshwas claimed to follow the *dandaniti* or penal law prescribed by Sanskrit texts. However the punishments administered by them bore little resemblance to those sanctioned by Sanskrit texts. Rather, punishment appears to have been decentralized under the Peshwai, with caste and community norms regulating social behavior and the administration of justice. Punishment was thus caste and context-specific, but open to bargaining and negotiation. Two points warrant emphasis: on the one hand, here was a regime of severe and spectacular corporal punishment such as scarring, beatings, mutilation, and disfigurement, including of women;[19] and, on the other, it was also a system that allowed crimes against the body to be quantified through an elaborate system of fines. Money equivalence allowed corporal violence to be abstracted into monetary fines.

In the chapter that follows, Malavika Kasturi highlights processes of social mobility and caste formation *through* plunder, brigandage, and extraction. In tune with the work of Stuart Gordon, she reveals how 'crime' and extraction were not only critical to the territorial expansion of empire but argues that such practices equally aided identity-formation for social groups. Indeed, questioning the influential analytical separation between the 'social' and the 'political' in discussions of banditry, Kasturi puts the spotlight on how brigandage, or social crime, was essential to processes of state-formation in central India, also implicitly revealing the entanglements between the pre-colonial and the colonial as heterogeneous yet overlapping temporalities. Crime was neither merely social nor simply political. Rather, it was the process through which territories were conquered, political sovereignty was asserted, and identities were expressed.

COLONIAL CONCERNS

The colonization of the subcontinent by the British led to the uneasy transformation of legal regimes from more localized, region-bound practices of authority and discipline through to formations based on legal codification and centralization. Arguably, the two-fold effect was to 'culturalize' crime and to 'criminalize' social practice, an issue that will be discussed here later. The point now is that colonial authorities abhorred the idea of full convertibility of bodily harm into 'blood money' as well as practices of oath-taking and vengeance, attributing to them the status of primitive, 'law-like' institutions.[20] Unsurprisingly, in the early years of the Company state, colonial officials derided the decentralization of punishment, sought to produce law codes, and, eventually, to codify 'Hindu' and 'Muhammedan' law.

Indeed, the project of codification—as part of the institutionalization of the law— was a major preoccupation of the Company State in the aftermath of territorial conquest.[21] In a path-breaking essay, of which we provide brief extracts here, Scott Kugle illustrates the radical reinterpretation of crime, intention, and culpability that ensued from colonial efforts to codify Islamic law.[22] In the wider work, Kugle explores how a complex body of textual prescription, political intervention, and (non-binding) *fatwa* proclamations—what he calls 'Islamic law'—was rationalized into a compact body of procedural law called 'Anglo-Muhammedan' law. The British assumed that Hindu and Islamic legal systems—themselves misnomers based on the assumption of a theocratic origin to regionally specific regimes of law—did not subscribe to secular notions of social contract and natural law. Rather, Islamic law was thought to rely on what was called *substantive law*, or the malleability of textual interpretation and the right of the rulers to intervene in specific cases. This was opposed to *procedural law*, which was organized around abstract rules of jurisprudence.

The effort by the British Orientalists to find (and translate) legal codes had at its basis the intention of ultimately doing away with colonial reliance on native intermediaries. Such efforts to uncover legal codes also produced an interest in 'schools of law'—Dayabhaga and Mitakshara for Hindus, and Hanafi, Malliki, Shafi'i, and Hanbali for Muslims.[23] Codes and digests were prepared to allow English magistrates to frame case proceedings on their own, with minimal help from native intermediaries. The ultimate effect of these institutional transformations was that elements of context-dependence and judicial elasticity were stripped from Islamic law to render Muhammedan law into a partial, reified version of its more capacious twin, Islamic law. This enabled colonial judges to claim that they were capable of adjucating cases involving Muhammedan law.

As colonial courts began to impose the authority of the British judge over native intermediaries, a body of precedent was also created. It was this body of work that was redefined as procedural law, while everything else was described as 'custom'. We may thus note that the distinction, indeed opposition, between custom versus law was itself the product of a colonial legal system. This is to say, 'custom' had no identity outside its relation to procedural law, since customary law was also often decided on the basis of regional precedent.[24] Ultimately, 'British courts effectively erased the record of their own intervention, and allowed 'the shari'a' to stand on its own, bounded by the frame they had provided.'[25] This was later further re-defined as 'Muslim personal law', a similar process occurring for Hindu law, albeit with accommodation for caste and regional specificities: together, these processes were consequences of the British preoccupation with legal management of property, inheritance, marriage, maintenance, and adultery.[26] Put simply, legal codification was partial, though it came to have the force of law. The excision of these complex legal worlds points to the subordination of sophisticated traditions of legal debate and interpretation, that is, the *practice* of law, to the project of legal codification.[27]

Law played a central role in Utilitarian philosophy, which exerted a strong ideological force on projects of social engineering undertaken by the colonial state in the first half of the nineteenth century.[28] At stake here were acts of standardization enabled by racialized assumptions regarding Indian backwardness. It is no wonder, therefore, that the colonial concern with crime could focus intensely on 'bizarre' or 'barbaric' practices, such as sati, hook-swinging, and human sacrifice that were thought to reflect the religious and cultural beliefs of the natives.[29]

The notion of 'culture' had a central place in justifying colonial discipline: by devolving on to culture and religion an agency that the natives were seen to lack, colonial officials did not merely castigate native practices such as sati, but they associated them with Indian culture and Hindu religion *in toto*. It is this set of moves that allowed them to justify the exercise of coercive state power as a requirement for protecting vulnerable groups like women, thus linking law's violence with the social improvement (and the moral edification) of native society. Culture provided the alibi for colonial control, now redefined as 'improvement'. It is in this sense that the 'scandal of colonialism' might be said to lie in the 'scandal of culture'. At the same time, political exigencies made it imperative that new legal structures resemble, or mimic, native forms.[30] As colonial officials tried to transform extant practices of personhood—based on highly differentiated caste and community specific notions of honor and status—into those governed by the principles of possessive individualism, they found themselves forced to counter tradition through the despotism of (colonial/modern) law.

While criminal law was concerned with questions of physical integrity, civil law was centered on the protection of property. An early instance was the 'improving' legislation of the Permanent Settlement of Bengal (1793). Yet, as Ranajit Guha has eloquently argued, the efforts here to produce an investment in the idea of private property backfired rather drastically. They led to a market in land that enabled speculation and usury instead of agrarian improvement and prosperity.[31] And so, too, subsequent models of the Ryotwari and (later), Mahalwari settlements—which sought to directly tax peasant proprietors—indexed forms of colonial intervention through direct engagement with peasant cultivators and agrarian communities, respectively.

Law was a potent force of intervention and impoverishment—as well as objectification and stigmatization—across diverse tenurial landscapes throughout the long nineteenth century. Here, in addition to the devices of military conquest, the 'subsidiary alliance' system,

and the 'doctrine of the lapse', the British sought to establish paramount status over regions that were outside Company control through
practices of 'authoritarian reform'. This involved the use of draconian
laws to bring nomadic and otherwise itinerant communities under the
regime of agrarian production and revenue extraction through efforts
to sedentarize them as well as to demilitarize certain communities.
Peasant soldiers, nomadic communities, itinerant petty-traders, and
the so-called 'criminal tribes' (with an allegedly hereditary procliv-
ity for violent crime) all came under intense surveillance.[32] Indeed,
territorial acquisition in the early decades of the nineteenth century
was often accomplished under the guise of entering the territories of
princely states in search of Thugs and dacoits.[33]

There were acute complicities between civil and criminal law.
The challenges British officials encountered in their efforts to govern recalcitrant native subjects was visible in their administration of
colonial law, which paid scant attention to judicial procedure while
legitimizing excessive violence. It is not only that the practice of Sati
was shorn of its ritual sanction and redefined as murder. It is also that
communities understood to be habituated or addicted to crime were
prosecuted collectively, assumed to be driven by the singular intent of
a 'caste mind', as Radhika Singha reminds us in her essay in this volume.[34] Together with territorial acquisition and an enhanced revenue
demand, legal standardization functioned as an important instrument
of political pacification.

Now, legal codification has a distinctively colonial genealogy.
British law was not codified, but existed as a legal mosaic produced
by the co-existence of ecclesiastical law, common law traditions, and
statutory law. In this sense, India provided a fertile ground for legal
experimentation. As a nineteenth-century project that grew out of
Jeremy Bentham's preoccupation with shifting English law away from
the tradition of legal commentaries of Coke and Blackstone, codification consisted of *minimizing* a complex set of processes into a single
process (of adjudication) and of *systematizing* these processes so that
they reflected a unitary logic.[35] Here, the subcontinent was a focal site
as well as an experimental laboratory. At the same time, debates about
codification were deeply contentious, and the period of the mid-nine-
teenth century saw a putative reversal of the Utilitarian experiments

in social engineering that had defined earlier decades (especially the 1830s) due to the political exigencies of native revolt inaugurated by the 1857 rebellion.

It followed that the passage of a Draft Penal Code in 1837 only saw light of day in 1861 with the passing of the Indian Penal Code and the reorganization of the courts after 1864.[36] Now Presidency High Courts replaced the dual legal structure (Supreme Courts in the Presidency, an Adalat system in the muffasil) that had existed until then. Hindu and Muslim legal officers (*qazis, pundits*), who were part of the colonial legal system in a proto-juridical capacity, were disbarred, and Court Reporters were made mandatory. Finally, the 1872 Evidence Act removed the last trace of Islamic elements from procedures of testimony and evidence.[37] This is to say that the final acts of codification were preceded by the Mutiny of 1857, which placed the colonial state in a very different relationship to Indian society and its elites.[38] Elsewhere, Singha has argued that the Victorian infrastructural state was distinguished by the ubiquity of technologies of communication and identification—railways and the telegraph, photography and fingerprinting, tattooing and the Imperial Census—together with their organization and reach.[39] The visualization and visibilization of power gave it added potency, even as the infrastructure served to more efficiently extend colonialism's extractive regime.

Sanjay Nigam's essay in this volume on the implementation of the Criminal Tribes Act (1871) addresses the potent link between surplus extraction and colonial categorization. He argues that, unlike earlier models of control, the Criminal Tribes Act focused on the moral transformation of criminal communities through labor. Nigam analyzes how the Act's stated goal—to refashion footloose communities into sedentary, profit-maximizing peasants through the institution of a pass system as well as the construction of high-surveillance residence camps—instead produced a set of unanticipated, if deeply pernicious, effects. Local landowners forced members of the so-called Criminal Tribes to undertake projects of land reclamation and agrarian improvement that enhanced the value of land while dispossessing vulnerable communities from them. Ironically, colonial rhetoric— that associated physical labour with moral improvement—was used instead to justify wealthy landowners' exploitation of the 'free' labor of communities who were categorized as 'criminal.' The effect of the Criminal Tribes Act was to push vulnerable groups into new cycles of occasional crime for the sake of survival.

The association of communities with religious laws and with 'criminal cultures' was complemented by a contrasting set of processes, which aimed to *remove* women from the clutches of community and religious laws.[40] Here, colonial paradigms of social reform sometimes intersected and elsewhere conflicted with Brahmanical, elite, and often textual models of sexual and caste purity across the nineteenth century. The results were complex and contradictory. The colonial state's relentless interest in crimes of intimacy produced uneven results: there was the hardening of domestic ideology, on the one hand, and the emergence of new conceptions of female enfranchisement and sexual freedom, on the other.[41] Thus, the significance of colonial law lay in its ambivalent effects: gendered tradition justified earlier forms of patriarchal control, but ongoing forms of social life were also transformed through new conceptions of agency, consent, and individuality. If legal assumptions of individual consent and agency appeared to be antithetical to religious law, women also used them strategically to enlarge spaces of independent action.[42] Across the nineteenth century, the social emancipation of upper-caste women was coterminous with, indeed constitutive of, new modes of stigmatizing lower-caste women.[43] Meanwhile, upper and lower-caste women were impacted, albeit differentially, by new regimes of masculinity. Together, this defined the compelling yet fraught logic of gender reform in the period.

In retrospect, nineteenth-century gender reform through colonial law appears to have addressed itself solely to the lives upper-caste Hindu women, thus normalizing their social experience.[44] Beginning with the debates that culminated in the abolition of sati in 1829, reformers' attention to practices such as child marriage, the education of women, and the maintenance of widows as domestic drudges was focused solely on upper-caste women's lives. At the same time, these efforts at gender reform through legal measures had the effect of taking away existing rights. As Lucy Carroll has shown, the 1856 Widow Remarriage Act, which was formulated to enlarge the rights of upper-caste women, also homogenized the legal status of Hindu marriage. The Act protected women's right to remarry, but it did so by stating that women who remarried lost any claim upon the property of their previous spouse. The Act thus reproduced a bourgeois Victorian strategy of empowering women in terms of choices of (re)marriage, while dispossessing them materially. This could further produce new forms of dependence for lower-caste women, many of whom had the right to remarry while claiming inheritance and maintenance from a prior spouse. Women's freedom to remarry thus accompanied the Act's dispossession of rights: Presidency courts often aligned the new rights accrued under the Act with foreclosures upon female property rights, instead of following the more progressive entitlements that lower-caste women possessed under 'customary' practices.[45]

At the end, examining the disciplining of crime across the nineteenth century, straddling the division that was introduced by1857, allows for four interlinked observations. In the first place, distinctions between Hindu and Muhammedan law were produced through acts of translation and approximation to British legal terminology; and these in turn enabled new ideas of individual agency and criminal culpability. Second, projects of colonial improvement inadvertently politicized culture and community by holding them responsible for native un-freedom. Third, while caste, gender, and religion had once operated in relatively decentralized regimes of sociality, they now gained recognition as legal-political categories of cultural difference. Fourth and finally, direct intervention into Indian society that preceded the Mutiny was followed in the decades after by indirect, though no less invasive, forms of identification and control such as the census, the tenurial survey, and codified law. Taken together, colonial law and native crime not only became mutually intelligible, but were co-constituted across the long nineteenth century.

SURVEILLANCE AND SUBVERSION

The *event of crime* occurs at the interstices of competing social forces, bringing into play entwined matrices of kinship, community, state, and subject. Once convicted, however, the criminal appears in a dual, even agonistic, relationship to the state, viewed at once as intimating social danger *and* proof of the state's efficiency in controlling crime.

Two practices of colonial discipline, incarceration and transportation, played out the contradictions of criminal reform in a colonial context.[46] Each produced its own forms of subversion, also enabling new practices of collective and personal self-fashioning. As a tangible instantiation—at once material and symbolic—of colonial law, the prison thus became an experimental site for criminal reform and improvement as well as a space for resisting and subverting colonial discipline.

Arguments for incarceration were claims against corporal punishment. Imprisonment was justified through two sets of logics: the first derived from a belief in the possibility of reform and rehabilitation through social engineering; the other entailed humanitarian considerations regarding what Michael Ignatieff calls a 'just measure of pain', or the idea of *proportionality* in administering punishment.[47] The criminal's humanity was discovered at the cost of the sovereign's right to punish the criminal through violent spectacle, as Michel Foucault argued long ago.[48] The anthropologist and social theorist Talal Asad, has elaborated how changing conceptions of punishment were affected by transformations of sovereignty. He argues that against the backdrop of wide-ranging alterations in the medical sciences, especially the development of forensic medicine, the quantification of pain, that is, the idea that one could measure pain (and, therefore, human suffering) produced a significant shift in practices of punishment. The idea of calibrating punishment to fit the crime derived from the growing belief in bodily integrity as a necessary condition of being human.[49]

Yet, the colonial context of prison reform produced its own contradictions. Even as the 1835 Law Commission addressed legal codification and prison reform as interconnected issues, the colonial prison system nonetheless operated under the belief that natives responded best to excessive violence. Prisoners were brutalized through flogging, sexual violence, withholding of food, hard labour, and the use of their bodies for medical experimentation. Figuratively and literally, the prison *wore down* the prisoner's body. This was justified through arguments regarding natives' inadequacy: bodily violence was necessary when disciplining not rational subjects but collectivities bound by tradition. (Indeed, from colonial India to contemporary Abu Ghraib we can see a *mimetic* relationship between the presumed barbarism of colonial/native subjects *and* the acts of violence and terror used to contain them.) The necessity for violence was justified by using arguments about traditional culture against universal rights.

Prison discipline was a continued preoccupation. The Prison Discipline Committee's Report of 1838 was followed by related exercises in 1864, 1877, 1889, 1892, and 1919–20. At issue were sanitation and overcrowding in prisons; efforts to create distinct classes of prisoners; bids to segregate women; and endeavors to substitute the use of prisoners on public works with intramural labor. Rather than a singular focus on their 'content', however, the form of these accounts is instructive. For at stake here are practices of 'plausible deniability'. Haunted by visions of excess of colonial power, these records of incrimination stage imperial authority as an improving force, ever responsible to its subjects.[50]

Anand Yang's chapter in *Crime through Time* explores forms of resistance against colonial discipline. Yang argues that social difference *outside* prison walls (caste, religion) was reproduced within the prison as a status marker that militated against efforts to homogenize the prison population.[51] Protests around 'messing' (or common dining) underscored the political salience of food. Prison protest ultimately challenged the very idea of incarceration:[52] from efforts to protect the porosity between life inside and outside the prison through to the use of social identity against the anonymity of colonial discipline.[53] Indeed, Yang's chapter shows us that criminals politicized precisely those aspects of daily life—food, toilets, and clothing—through which they were dehumanized.

At the same time, the colonial response to political crime was different. By the 1890s, political prisoners, especially those engaged in 'revolutionary terror', were being transported. The 1905 Swadeshi movement saw assassinations and violent attacks against colonial officials and government property. In its aftermath, Bal Gangadhar Tilak was transported to Mandalay and Veer Savarkar to Port Blair. Increasingly, from revolutionary terrorists to M.K. Gandhi, a stint in prison, the ultimate symbol of the illegitimacy of colonial power, would become *de rigeur* for the political vocation of a nationalist disposition.[54]

In tune with these considerations, David Arnold examines the life of the nationalist as political prisoner. Unlike the common prisoner, political prisoners came from middle- or upper-class backgrounds.[55] They were allowed access to newspapers, ink, and paper, while being housed in proximity to one another. Ironically, the genre of 'jail writings'—political memoirs, journals, autobiographies, meditations on Indian culture and history—was enabled by the fact that the colonial prison provided a space for reflection and retreat away from anti-colonial agitation. Middle-class nationalists first experienced prison life with the intensification of anti-colonial activism, and many engaged in long and bitter battles to improve prison life. However, Arnold reminds us that they were familiar with the prison through literary and popular culture. Here, the prison was represented as a dangerous place where social hierarchy was levelled and physical vulnerability enhanced. Middle-class incarceration normalized the jail experience, but it also poses questions about the fidelity of memory: though incarcerated in South Africa between 1908 and1913, Gandhi wrote *Satyagraha in South Africa* in the Yeravda prison in 1923–4.[56] By then, his prison experience had been folded into a conversion narrative about the benefits of prison austerity. Like the ascetic and the monk, the prisoner too underwent a process of radically losing and remaking the self through bodily discipline: human suffering was transformative, and so one could witness the wasting away of one's body as the sign of a deeper, ethical transformation.

Preceding understandings of resistant subject-hoods and political self-hoods within the prison, Raj Chandavarkar unravels the spatialization of colonial power in the urban locales of Bombay in the inter-war period. His short excerpt on the police in *Crime through Time* underscores a social institution sandwiched between colonial bureaucratic authority and the informal power of the neighborhood. Chandavarkar argues that the liminality of the police meant that they were able to exercise arbitrary power against the people, while simultaneously siding with them against the state and encouraging 'informal social networks [and] local power structures'. Such processes of localization as well as the racialized structure of command within the police hierarchy produced the problem of 'policing the police'.[57] If colonial difference became an alibi for the focus on punishment rather than rehabilitation, as Yang argues, it also defined the police as awkward representatives of power, who were both within and without the state.[58]

LEGALITIES AND ILLEGALITIES

Through its long and chequered career, the collection of land revenue and the maintenance of law and order together constituted the fulcrum of the interest of the colonial state in India.[59] It was by means of ordered grids of property relations and the mechanisms of law and order—each touched by the prior emphases of Indian political regimes in these arenas—that the colonial state primarily gained access to its subjects, also attempting through these measures to contain and control, define and discipline, and normalize and naturalize Indian peoples. These matrices framed and articulated distinct notions of the person and the subject, of the individual and the community, drawing upon 'alien' and 'indigenous' schemes as well as their conjunctions.

All over India, the varieties of revenue settlements carried out by colonial regimes tended to view persons as part of social collectivities that structured tenurial and proprietary arrangements within the agrarian order. In contrast, the images mediating the notion of the 'individual' in the criminal law courts were at once clearer and more complex. Arguably, the processes and discourses of modern law operated with an inherited notion of the 'person'. Here the individual was envisioned as an integrated 'whole', detachable from the matrix of social relationships, and definable in terms of a discrete set of needs. Such a notion has a strong normative element. A construction of modern regimes of power, it is a way of distinguishing pathologies, extending control over diffuse and intimate domains of social life, and producing normalized subjects, all issues that were explored earlier. The point now is that in inherently diverse and chequered ways, the discourses and practices generated by such a notion underlay the constitution of crime, criminality, and the criminal under colonial law in South Asia.

At the same time, however, this inherited notion of the 'person', and its attendant rhetoric of the 'rule of law', stood compromised and qualified in several ways in the Indian colony. We reiterate three such sites. First, there were the intractable issues of race in legal scenarios, not only manifest as propositions of the 'backwardness' of the native but especially underscored in criminal 'cases' involving the conjoint presence of the European and the Indian. Second, in the production of the figure of the criminal, rather than exclusively accessing the 'individual', colonial law could categorize an entire community as a 'criminal' tribe/caste. In inherently tension-ridden ways, this rendered the community as at once a collective individual and an individuated collectivity. Finally, the vexed matter of 'political' crimes could throw up its own complexities concerning state legitimacy, even as it revealed varieties of counter-ideologies—from anti-colonialism, to trade-unionism, to Marxism, to Hindu nationalism—in promoting new repertoires of public protest in the twentieth century.

None of this should be surprising. After all, heroic self-representations of imperial law were in constant tension with, and often exceeded by, the routine administration of colonial justice. Indeed, in determining crime and forging the criminal, colonial law frequently attended to 'indigenous' understandings, now and again drew on the schemes of rank and honor of castes and communities, and restlessly seized on local norms and practices—all of course unto its own purposes. The establishment of crime and constructions of the criminal within the procedures and discourses of colonial-modern law were inescapable parts of imperial entanglements and their mutual histories, involving both the colonizer and the colonized.

To discuss everyday legalities/illegalities—always, alongside their interplay with state law/justice—requires that we rethink the figure of the 'criminal'. Recall now that according to the dictates of colonial/modern jurisprudence the interests, emotions, and motivations at work within a dispute, a conflict, or a trespass of the law are thought to emerge from the dynamic centers of awareness of 'individuals'. Such is the conceit of the law. At the same time, however, the emotions, motivations, and interests at work in disputes and conflict need to be approached instead as integrated elements of social experience and quotidian relationships. Thus, the contours of experience resonate with the force of cultural contingencies and critical circumstances.

Moreover, while considering legalities and illegalities from the eighteenth to the twenty-first centuries, the diverse infractions of law turned upon relationships of power that were structured by kinship and gender, caste and community, and age and race—apparently 'local' matrices that were yet inflected by governmental authority and state law in multiple manners. To act upon interests-emotions and redress problems by entering into acts of solidarity and/or by attacking the 'enemy' has always meant to negotiate or/and reassert these wide-ranging, diffuse yet intimate relationships of power.[60] This is not all. For such reprisals and solidarities have ever appeared as far removed from that striking phrase invoked by the law, 'a momentary lapse of reason'. Rather, the solidarities and reprisals have resonated with meanings that undergird the everyday objects and quotidian conventions of the social order in multiple ways: they have variously endorsed and upheld them, but often also contradicted and exceeded them.

Finally, it warrants emphasis that the symbols, metaphors, and practices of colonial-modern law were not simply external schemes, principally removed from the worlds of Indian subjects. Rather, such schemes simultaneously formed an alien legality, a strategy of settlement and revenge, and a pool of resources that were deployed selectively by peoples. It was through such overlapping yet distinct measures that sub-continental subjects came to define new pathologies and fashion novel legalities within the domain of everyday life, often also enabling other articulations of social order within communities. Such 'native' practices that at once accessed and exceeded the law in imperial India continue to find distinct configurations in the Indian post-colony.

The foregoing deliberations have all drawn upon recent developments in the anthropology of law, which have themselves been read together with social theory, critical thought, and imaginative histories. Four points stand out about legal anthropology, a field that we shall not survey at length in this Introduction. First, the dominant division in considerations of law within ethnography typically entailed an emphasis on 'rules' as against an articulation of 'processes': while the former looked for law-like analogues in all cultures, the latter sought to embed legalities and illegalities in the concrete working out of social procedures.[61] Second, these apparently distinct tendencies could nonetheless occlude the critical interplay between practice, power, and process by restricting social conflict to an attenuated articulation of locality, as a bounded and innately 'traditional/local/customary' unit.[62] Third, this is quite like the manner in which the opposition between unchanging, traditional disputing processes and dynamic, modern systems of law governed much writing on the subject, including concerning legal pluralism.[63] Fourth and finally, in tune with wider transformations in anthropology, there are now rather different stories being told of the entanglements between state law and popular legalities, the (trans-)national and the local, temporality and spatiality, and authority and alterity.[64]

Such considerations come alive in the chapters ahead. Each of the essays in this section, discussing legalities and illegalities, rescues the figure of the 'criminal' and the form of 'crime' from the impersonal determinations of state law. In place of reified abstractions of colonial justice, they focus diversely on the embedding of crime and the criminal in everyday relationships and quotidian networks of meaning and power, severally inflected by imperial law and governmental authority. Here are to be found, then, routine pathways of legalities and illegalities that were shaped by distress and hunger, gender and sexuality, and caste and community.

Our deliberations begin with a short excerpt from Ranajit Guha's classic text, *Elementary Aspects of Peasant Insurgency in Colonial India*.[65] In the book, Guha's aim is to situate the peasant as a conscious, political subject-agent of history. To this end, he examines peasant rebellions on the subcontinent across the long nineteenth century, identifying the common forms and the general ideas—or, the 'elementary aspects'—of insurgency, the consciousness that informed the activities of rebellious peasant subalterns. Among the many contributions made by Guha's wider work to the study of crime and culture, we point to two overlapping issues. On the one hand, Guha's analyses and emphases reveal possibilities of newer articulations of legalities and illegalities—in the colony and the post-colony. On the other, by rendering the peasant insurgent as an exact contemporary of, entirely coeval with, colonial domination, *Elementary Aspects* pointed to the salience of thinking through the pervasive, hierarchical dualities between subaltern 'tradition' and middle-class 'modernity'. This carries immense import for critically probing the oppositions that have characterized the historical and anthropological studies of crime and

law, the former obsessed with the colonial state and the latter enam-
oured of Indian tradition. In the tiny excerpt reproduced here, Guha
puts the spotlight on the enmeshments between poverty and crime,
legality and illegality, and distress and defiance.

Next, Padma Anagol focuses on the broader trend of derogating
'criminal women'. She offers many instances of women who had
been raped by close relatives, especially their brothers-in-law. She
also offers examples of lower-caste women, from the day labourer,
Rakhuma, who was raped on her way to the paddy fields and subsequently accused of infanticide, to the Mahar woman who was turned
out of her home by her lover when she became pregnant. In many
cases, women who committed infanticide were either transported for
life or faced rigorous imprisonment, thus challenging assumptions
of female fragility and weakness. Anagol argues that the criminalization of women was a response to anxieties around female freedom
inaugurated by the rise of women's activism, from writing autobiographies through to demands for political rights. Her chapter draws
attention to the intersections between the disciplining power of the
state—especially, the surveillance of female reproduction through
the system of birth and death registration—and community morality,
even as colonial officials routinely claimed to protect women from
their communities. At stake here is the uneasy resemblance between
the violence of the community and the violence of the state.

In the final chapter of this section of *Crime through Time*, Saurabh
Dube explores the intersection between colonial-state law and pop-
ular-coeval legalities. His work is based on a rich and rare archive of
village disputes, which were tried in the lower rungs of the imperial
court hierarchy. Dube works in the breach between the limited range
of facts required by the judgment and the abundance of information
offered by the depositions. This makes it possible to trace the play
between the concerns of ordered state legalities and the processes
of signification within village relationships. The essay is thus able
to challenge the insidious, hermetic division between unchanging
'traditional-folk-popular' disputing processes and dynamic 'colonial-
modern-state' legal systems, in order to reveal rather a formidable
interplay of everyday norms, familiar desires, and alien legalities.
On the one hand, the imaginings and actions of colonial law were

refracted and reworked to define new pathologies and fashion novel legalities within the quotidian lives of communities. On the other hand, the already-framed notions of crime and emotion, property and the person within the discourse(s) and practice(s) of modern law were quietly inflected by the recalcitrant presence of native 'customs' and 'traditions'—the unsanctioned practices of subaltern subjects.

POSTCOLONIAL PREDILECTIONS

The postcolonial period presents a problem for our efforts. It is not only that the terms and transformations of crime, violence, and law in independent India constitute complex and vast themes. It is also that there are several ways of approaching and exploring these questions regarding contemporary transformations of state and society. Anything resembling a comprehensive survey of such issues is outside the scope of this Introduction. Below we provide a schematic account of critical events and policy transformations, and evaluate their impact on law, crime, and everyday life in the post-colony.

Recall now that anti-colonialism challenged the 'legality' of colonial government, and sought to render the subcontinent ungovernable through collective action: popular agitation and the politics of the street were posited against the illegitimacy of colonial law. The years preceding the Partition and Independence saw violence against the state accompanied by violence between religious communities. This produced the problem of accounting for mass violence, and the lack of legal mechanisms through which to prosecute perpetrators, whether Hindu or Muslim. Scholars of Partition have thus focused on the question of how communities survive the aftermath of historical trauma when faced by the lack of remediation.[66]

The period after 1947 has witnessed two distinctive and apparently divergent tendencies. On the one hand, we see the successful demobilization of popular activism through the institution of constitutional protections and safeguards.[67] Thus, legal protection against social crimes such as the practice of untouchability and violence against women is an important social fact of the postcolonial Indian landscape, and a major site of struggle and activism.[68] On the other, the region has simultaneously witnessed a growing militarization of the state, rule by resort to exceptional laws, and the growing influence of political secessionism and parastate violence.[69]

One way to explain these processes is to locate them in the transformative period of the 1970s, when Zia ul-Haq's Islamicization project in Pakistan coincided with Indira Gandhi's declaration of National Emergency in India (1975–7). Each enabled the entry of new political actors onto the national stage, whether it was the rise of what is commonly referred to as 'political Islam' in Pakistan, or anti-Congress forces such as the the Janata Party (that included the Jana Sangh) in India. Trade unions and women's mobilization appear to have suffered a decisive blow in Pakistan.[70] In India, the post-Emergency period witnessed the rise of non-party people's endeavors as well as the rise of a civil liberties movement that took up issues of state violence, from custody death to army massacre of civilians.[71]

Now, people's movements in India have highlighted the contradiction between popular democracy and state forces in a number of ways. These include struggles against mass displacement for state infrastructure, of which the Narmada Bachao Andolan is perhaps best known; demands for justice by the victims of the Bhopal Union Carbide disaster in national and international fora; Dalit demands for international recognition of caste discrimination; urban struggles against demolition and eviction in almost all Indian cities today; legal struggles for the decriminalization of homosexuality; recognition of sex work as labour; and efforts by politicized adivasi communities to challenge patterns of aggressive accumulation by state and private industry in the mineral-rich regions of middle India. These struggles—many aided by the rise of public interest litigation and the intervention of progressive lawyers—have expanded the domain of legal activism by holding the state culpable of *crimes against the people*.[72] Though state forces have been often succeeded in crushing popular initiatives, alternative legalities nevertheless remain a potent force for indicting the anti-people policies of the Indian state.

A final and noteworthy set of contemporary transformations concerns the effects of pro-market, neoliberal reform on legal governance.[73] India's middle classes—the term is an aspirational category more than a descriptor of social fact, we should note—appear to be retreating from society into their privatized enclaves, while simultaneously espousing their support for anti-poor policies such as slum eviction, anti-hawking, and residential zoning for parks and green cover.[74] Simultaneously, shifts in the countryside such as the contraction of farmers' access to credit as well as land grabs for the creation of Special Economic Zones [SEZs] are rendering agriculture nonviable while pushing large numbers of migrants into urban areas. These communities in crisis seek refuge in illicit or underworld economies and criminalized existence, even as they also organize around religious and ethnic identities that have become potent sites of violent conflict.

Our selection of readings on the postcolonial period meditates on the contradictory co-existence of state protection and state culpability in the postcolonial period. This last section of *Crime through Time* explores once more how the impersonal determinations of the law, now with their clearly articulated projections of the caste-inflected citizen and the gendered subject (as well their unspoken reliance on divisions between the 'majority' and the 'minority'), continue to produce new paradoxes for the administration of justice in contemporary India. Put differently, these chapters mark the peculiar intimacies between vulnerable communities—Dalits, Muslims, women—and the postcolonial state, in order to underscore the importance of law and crime as key domains of political engagement between citizens and the state.

To begin with, Anupama Rao's essay addresses the re-inscription of Dalit vulnerability through the very laws and constitutional protections meant to protect Dalits from upper-caste violence. By analyzing a case of 'caste atrocity', the murder of a Dalit kotwal on the steps of a Hanuman temple in rural Maharashtra in 1991, Rao analyses the unexpected manner in which stringent laws such as the Prevention of Atrocities Act of 1989 can be rendered useless. Here, she focuses on two aspects of judicial failures of Dalit protection. The first entails local alliances, which enable police cover-up and bureaucratic mishandling. The second involves, more significantly, a contradiction in the articulation of anti-atrocity laws. The latter assume the workings of a collective caste consciousness as the 'cause' behind anti-Dalit violence, even though atrocities cases are adjudicated like any other case, that is, through the individuation of crime. Rao argues that the contradiction between collective cause and individuated punishment reproduces the exceptional status of Dalits as vulnerable citizen-subjects at risk.

Next, Rajeswari Sunder Rajan focuses on Phoolan Devi and her surrender, in order to challenge standard representations of female vulnerability, especially by exploring the power of the female outlaw in her negotiations with the postcolonial state. When Phoolan Devi justified her turn to banditry as a form of revenge for upper-caste violence against the lower-castes, particularly the women of these communities, she articulated a narrative that bore startling similarities with early-modern paradigms of decentralized punishment. Here, Sunder Rajan notes the equivalence between structural exclusion by caste elites and the state, on the one hand, and the dacoits' production of a reign of terror through the use of targeted violence in the Chambal Valley, on the other. The latter utilizes a model of people's justice that is deeply unsettling because it explicitly challenges the state's exclusive right over punishment but through resort to popular vengeance. In the case of Phoolan Devi's negotiated surrender, it is additionally the case that her gender was at once ignored and over-symbolized, indicating thereby the difficulty of apprehending the female outlaw as a 'killing woman' rather than as the dead or dying subject.

Finally, Tanika Sarkar's essay addresses the isomorphism of women with community, in order to parse the politics of death, or the necropolitical logic of the Gujarat pogroms of 2002. Combining critical reportage, academic analysis, and a literary sensibility, the chapter highlights the importance of sexual violence by focusing on how women's bodies were used, defaced, and discarded during the carnage in western India. Sarkar argues that the symbolic forms and logics of violence expressed chilling fantasies of Hindu revenge and historical annihilation of the Muslim other. Here, the intimacy of sexual violence, as a specifically gendered form of terror, was a violation of the Muslim community as a whole.

As others have noted, Gujarat's status as a developmental 'miracle' depends on its deep history of communal divisiveness, expropriation of Muslim property, and the exclusion of Muslims from public life in the state. Thus, neoliberalism has provided an effective cover for bids toward ethnic cleansing.[75] In this scenario, Sarkar's chapter allows us to mark a broader set of critical shifts in crime, law, and politics in contemporary India.[76] Now, new repertoires of crime, including by state functionaries, are novel claims on public visibility—and, hence, also demands for social recognition—as much as they are the indicators of deeper transformations of postcolonial politics. Increasingly, the spectacles of violence and crime are themselves sites of politics and governance, rather than just the latter's aberrant excess.

NOTES

1. Simon Schama, *The Embarrassment of Riches: An Interpretation of Dutch Culture in the Golden Age* (New York 1988).

2. William Mazzarella, 'Affect: What is it Good for?' in Saurabh Dube (ed.) *Enchantments of Modernity: Empire, Nation, Globalization* (London and New Delhi 2009), p. 291.

3. See, for example, E.P. Thompson, *Customs in Common: Studies in Traditional Popular Culture* (New York 1993) and E.P. Thompson, *Whigs and Hunters* (Harmondsworth 1977).

4. For an account of Maine's place within broader, 'developmental' accounts of the modern, patriarchal state, see Rosalind Coward, *Patriarchal Precedents: Sexuality and Sexual Relations* (London 1983). For an argument about the role of colonial governance in the development of social theory, especially in the thinking of Henry Maine, see Karuna Mantena, *Alibis of Empire: Henry Maine and the Ends of Liberal Imperialism* (Princeton 2010).

5. See, for instance Philip Abrams, 'Notes on the Difficulty of Studying the State', *Journal of Historical Sociology*, vol. 1, no. 1, 1988, pp. 58–89.

6. Michel Foucault, *Discipline and Punish: The Birth of the Prison* (New York 1979); Michel Foucault, *Madness and Civilization: A History of Insanity in the Age of Reason* (London 1967).

7. Foucault wanted to address the manner in which institutions, ideologies, and identities intersect, while he himself eschewed these terms because he saw them as products of reigning assumptions about how power operates and where it is to be located, a problem with which his entire oeuvre is concerned. We use these terms as a matter of convenience, in order to demarcate distinct domains of social life.

8. Of course, this notion of the individual was itself the result of a long revolution in ideas that ultimately saw the world as a place shorn of God and the tight embrace of community, a site where human beings now controlled and manipulated nature for secular, scientific, historical progress.

9. Such is the case since this bifurcation, according to Foucault, is itself predicated on a prior divide between the domains of public vs private or interest vs ethics, which derives from liberal projections of power as a formidable danger to spaces of intimacy and interiority. This separation of interest and power from private intimacy reflects the uneasy combination of two distinct ideas of

personhood embedded in classical liberalism. One is the history of political rights as they relate to the right to private property; the other is story of the transformation of moral sentiments in the growth of human freedom. In its narrative of political subject-formation, classical liberalism typically aligns the subject of rights with the subject of freedom and rationality.

10. For an important critique of Foucault's elision of colonialism as well as an argument about the centrality of the colonial theater for the development of the sexual politics of race see, Ann Stoler, *Race and the Education of Desire: Foucault's History of Sexuality and the Colonial Order of Things* (Durham, NC 1995).

11. Unsurprisingly, all of this has allowed scholars to raise newer questions, re-visit older arguments, and juxtapose distinct (theoretical) propositions. To illustrate this let us briefly turn to the relationship between violence and the law. Several decades ago, Walter Benjamin argued that the institutionalization of the law was predicated on forgetting the law's basis in violence. His distinction between law-making and law-preserving violence is crucial here. Law-making violence refers to an original moment, when law and society are founded on violence, and not on the social contract. Law-preserving violence is the banal, regularized violence that passes for law, as a sort of 'legitimate violence', or a violence that has been euphemized as law. Now, law-making and law-preserving forms are both manifestations of violence. But the temporal distance that separates law-preserving violence from its origins in a founding violence of law-making allows the law to appear legal, rather than as a species of violence. This is one way in which law is experienced as 'not violence'. Violence is thus rendered intrinsic, rather than external, to state power. Thus, we are able to recognize transacted violence, while structural violence remains invisible. Walter Benjamin, 'Critique of Violence', in Walter Benjamin, *Reflections: Essays, Aphorisms, Autobiographical Writings* (New York 1978), pp. 277–300.

Recently, scholars have tried to conjoin Benjamin's analysis of the relationship of law and violence with insights from the work of Foucault as well as from the writings of the Italian philosopher, Giorgio Agamben. Especially important here is Agamben's understanding of 'biopolitics' as the sovereign's right to kill, while excluding himself from the laws he makes. Such 'sovereign exception'—the right to grant oneself immunity from the laws of the land—is retained in democratic regimes, where populations such as those of the terrorist, the alien, and the refugee are dehumanized, and thus rendered capable of being killed or excised from the body politic *without cost*. When read together, thinkers such as Benjamin, Foucault, and Agamben foreground the fraught relationship between law and violence, thus throwing into question the legitimacy of modern forms of punishment while marking uncomfortable resemblances between law and revenge. Giorgio Agamben, *Homo Sacer: Sovereign Power and Bare Life*, Daniel Heller-Roazen (trans.) (Stanford 1998). For the distinction between Foucault's focus on the right to live and Agamben's concern with sovereign exception see Steven Pierce and Anupama Rao, 'On the Subject of Governance', in Edward Murphy, David William Cohen, D. Chandra Bhimull, Fernando Coronil, Monica Eileen Patterson, and

Julie Skurski (eds), *Anthrohistory: Unsettling Knowledge, Questioning Discipline* (Ann Arbor 2011), pp. 240–51. For a critical reading of the relationship between postcolonial states and the politics of death, see Achille Mbembe. 'Necropolitics', *Public Culture*, vol. 15, no. 1, 2003, pp. 11–40.

12. See, for instance, C.A. Bayly, *Rulers, Townsmen, and Bazaars: North Indian Society in the Age of Expansion, 1770-1870* (Cambridge 1983); C.A. Bayly, *Indian Society and the Making of the British Empire* (Cambridge 1988); C.A. Bayly, *Empire and Information: Intelligence Gathering and Social Communication in India, 1770–1870* (Cambridge 1997); and Norbert Peabody, 'Cents, Sense, Census: Human Inventories in Late Precolonial and Early Colonial India', *Comparative Studies of History and Society*, vol. 43, no. 1, 2001, pp. 819–50.

13. Frederick Cooper and Ann Laura Stoler, 'Between Metropole and Colony: Rethinking a Research Agenda', in Frederick Cooper and Ann Laura Stoler (eds), *Tensions of Empire: Colonial Cultures in a Bourgeois World* (Berkeley 1997), pp. 1–58.

14. Andre Wink, *Land and Sovereignty in India: Agrarian Society and Politics under the Eighteenth-century Maratha Svarajya* (Cambridge 1986).

15. Frank Perlin, 'Protoindustrialization and Precolonial South Asia', *Past and Present*, vol. 98, 1983, pp. 30–95; V. Narayan Rao, David Shulman, and Sanjay Subrahmanyam, *Textures of Time: Writing History in South India* (New York 2003).

16. Perlin, 'Protoindustrialization'.

17. H.K. Fukazawa, *The Medieval Deccan: Peasants, Social Systems and States, Sixteenth to Eighteenth Centuries* (Delhi 1991).

18. While Brahmin/non-Brahmin conflict also holds true for South India, the inter-relation between temple and agrarian economies, not to mention the far greater variety of dominant castes with links to landed power, makes the situation there rather different from the Maratha case.

19. Prisoners, including women, were transported or incarcerated in forts where they performed manual labour. Pre-colonial regimes rarely resorted to penal incarceration, however. Fukazawa, *Medieval Deccan*; Sumit Guha, 'An Indian Penal Regime: Maharashtra in the Eighteenth Century', *Past and Present*, vol. 147, 1995, pp. 101–26; and V.S. Kadam, 'The Institution of Marriage and the Position of Women in Eighteenth Century Maharashtra', *Indian Economic and Social History Review*, vol. 25, no. 3, 1988, pp. 341–70.

20. See, for example, V.T. Gune, *The Judicial System of the Marathas* (Poona 1953); Arthur Steele, *The Hindu Castes: Their Law, Religion and Customs* (Delhi 1826, reprinted 1986).

21. Radhika Singha, *A Despotism of Law* (New Delhi 1998); David Skuy, 'Macaulay and the Indian Penal Code of 1862: The Myth of the Inherent Superiority and Modernity of the English Legal System Compared to India's Legal System in the Nineteenth Century', *Modern Asian Studies*, vol. 32, no. 3, 1998, pp. 513–57.

22. Now, Kugle's discussion of what came to be called 'Anglo-Muhammedan' or 'Muhammedan' law is important, not only since scholars have tended to

principally focus on the implementation of Hindu law by colonial courts, but because Islamic law was the underlying template for legal decision-making in most parts of northern India. Thus, almost all legal terminology and revenue terms in use across the subcontinent today are of Arabic-Persian origin.

23. The Hanafi school predominated in subcontinent, as did Mitakshara among the Hindus, except in Bengal where the Dayabhaga school was dominant. Indeed, the stricter adherence to the Hedaya in the early nineteenth century, followed by reliance on case law, meant that non-Hanafi law was all but excluded from Anglo-Muhammedan law. For an account of Ashraf Ali Thanwai's turn to Maliki law to support women's right to divorce in the 1930s, see Rohit De, 'Mumtaz Bibi's Broken Heart: The Many Lives of the Dissolution of the Muslim Marriages Act', *India Economic and Social History Review*, vol. 46, no. 1, 2009, pp. 105–30.

24. The body of scholarship on relationship between law and custom in colonial India is too vast to be addressed here in any detail, though it is worth noting that caste and gender issues were typically framed as falling under the domain of customary practice. The classic text on customary law is Sripati Roy, *Customs and Customary Law in British India* (Calcutta 1911). For a salient account of the ideological role of 'custom' in postcolonial legal debate see, Marc Galanter, 'The Aborted Restoration of Indigenous Law in India', *Comparative Studies in Society and History*, vol. 14, 1972, pp. 53–70. A particularly important recent study of the policing of inter-caste marriage and relationships is to be found in Prem Chowdhry, *Contentious Marriages, Eloping Couples: Gender, Caste and Patriarchy in Northern India* (New Delhi 2007). We discuss the relationship between custom and the anthropology of law later in this Introduction.

25. Scott Alan Kugle, 'Framed, Blamed and Renamed: The Recasting of Islamic Jurisprudence in Colonial South Asia', *Modern Asian Studies*, vol. 35, no. 2, 2001, p. 310.

26. There is a large literature on the politics and history of personal law, much of it rediscovered in the context of renewed debates over the Uniform Civil Code that was set in motion by the (in)famous Shah Bano case of 1985. This is briefly discussed in Note 68. Here, we will restrict ourselves to making mention of the following important texts: Flavia Agnes, *Law and Gender Inequality: The Politics of Women's Rights in India* (New Delhi 1999); Flavia Agnes, *Family Law*, 2 vols. (New Delhi 2011); Vasudha Dhagamwar, *Law, Power, and Justice: The Protection of Personal Rights in the Indian Penal Code* (New Delhi 1992); Gregory C. Kozlowski, 'Muslim Personal Law and Political identity in Independent India', in Robert D. Baird (ed.), *Religion and Law in Independent India* (Delhi 2003), pp. 103–20.

27. Three further points warrant emphasis. First, together with other scholars, Kugle underscores the powerful impact of colonial translation in transforming living law into lifeless procedure. Second, Kugle also goes one step further to show how Muhammedan law, which was the product of colonial knowledge-production, came to be identified with 'authentic' religious personal law by twentieth century Muslim nationalists whose only access to a fuller body of Islamic law was through the detour, ironically if inevitably, of colonial mediation. Third and finally, this

detour does not merely signal the unavailability of a legal past outside colonial intervention. Rather, it alerts us to the contemporary socio-political consequence of colonial pasts of comparison and commensuration: the translation of legal terminology was nothing less than an effort to bring Islamic legal thinking in line with British conceptions regarding intention, (legal) agency, and culpability. The translation of terms was also a transformation of legal ideology.

28. See Bernard Cohn, *An Anthropologist Among The Historians and Other Essays* (Delhi 1990); Ranajit Guha, *A Rule of Property for Bengal: An Essay on the Idea of Permanent Settlement* (Paris 1963); Eric Stokes. *The English Utilitarians and India* (Oxford 1959); and David Washbrook, 'Law, State and Agrarian Society in Colonial India', *Modern Asian Studies*, vol. 15, no. 3, 1981, pp. 649–721.

29. Nicholas Dirks, 'The Policing of Tradition: Colonialism and Anthropology in Southern India', *Comparative Studies in Society and History*, vol. 39, no. 1, 1997, pp. 182–212; Lata Mani, *Contentious Traditions: The Debate on Sati in Colonial India* (Berkeley 1998); Gayatri Chakravorty Spivak, 'Can the Subaltern Speak?' in Cary Nelson and Lawrence Grossberg (eds), *Marxism and the Interpretation of Culture* (Urbana 1988), pp. 271–313.

30. See Nicholas Dirks, *Scandal of Empire: India and the Creation of Imperial Britain* (Cambridge, MA 2006) for a discussion of how critiques of colonial corruption enabled new ideas of colonial responsibility and improving government. For an account of the dual idioms of sovereignty under which the early Company State operated, see Sudipta Sen, *Distant Sovereignty: National Imperialism and the Origins of British India* (London and New York 2002). For a discussion of the East India Company's institutional form and imperial logic, see Philip Stern, *The Company-State: Corporate Sovereignty and The Early Modern Origins of the British Empire in India* (New York 2011).

31. Guha, *Rule of Property*.

32. See Singha, this volume: Nigam, this volume; and Meena Radhakrishnan, *Dishonoured by History: Criminal Tribes and British Colonial Policy* (Hyderabad 2008).

33. Colonial encroachment on native territories in pursuit of 'criminal gangs' under the stewardship of the infamous William Sleeman—who headed the Thuggee and Dacoity Department, the forerunner of the Criminal Intelligence Department (CID)—ought to be seen as part of a broader strategy of political pacification in the early years of Company rule. It is interesting to contrast efforts to justify the use of arbitrary and excessive power through transformations in legal procedure with the continued practice (and justification) of privatized violence by white settlers. See, for example, Elizabeth Kolsky, *Colonial Justice in British India: White Violence and the Rule of Law* (Cambridge 2010).

34. Also see the important essay by Sandria Freitag, 'Crime in the Social Order of North India', *Modern Asian Studies*, vol. 25, no. 2, 1991, pp. 227–61. It is worth noting the significant continuities between the colonial state's reliance on informal practices of surveillance through spies and paid informants and its later legal sanction for the figure of the 'approver', who could gain amnesty by

giving evidence against himself and his criminal co-conspirators. See Shahid Amin, *Event, Metaphor, Memory: Chauri Chaura, 1922–1992* (Berkeley 1995).

35. In this sense, codification at once homogenized and rationalized social difference.

36. The Criminal Procedure Code, the Civil Procedure Code, and the Indian Contract Act were also codified, in addition to more minor legislation such as the Negotiable Instruments Act as well as the Transfer of Property Act, among others.

37. We should not forget that legal codification was an exercise in *comparison*: Hindu and Islamic laws were compared against natural law paradigms of 'justice, equity, and good conscience'. Institutionally, this could be seen in the fact that British colonial officials and civil servants exercised a supervisory role over native authorities, such as *maulvis*, *pundits*, and *qazis*, to produce a hybrid legal order.

38. Let us recall that in the aftermath of the Mutiny, the colonial state maintained a strict policy of non-interference in matters concerning religion, since missionization and other forms of social intervention during the early nineteenth century were understood to have been one of the main causes of native disaffection. Policing and revenue-gathering functions were particular targets of bureaucratic reorganization. As well, culture and civil society were politicized in the aftermath of the Mutiny, with caste and religion becoming sites of political conflict and competition that required the arbitration of the colonial state. Nicholas Dirks, *Castes of Mind: Colonialism and the Making of Modern India* (Princeton, NJ 2001).

39. Radhika Singha, 'Settle, Mobilize, Verify: Identification Practices in Colonial India', *Studies in History*, vol. 16, no. 2, 2000, vol. 151–98. Also see Clare Anderson, *Legible Bodies: Race, Criminality and Colonialism in South Asia* (London 2004). Photography was first used in India in 1840. Fingerprinting technology, developed in Bengal by William Herschel, was in place by 1891. A system for matching fingerprints from a mass of fingerprint cards was also in place by 1897. Convinced that the capture of external traits provided a significant indication of deeper structures of vice and depravity, the pseudo-science of anthropometry extended the reach of this 'scopic' regime. For an account of the hegemony of vision for colonial knowledge, see Christopher Pinney, *Camera Indica: The Social Life of Indian Photographs* (Chicago 1997). For the importance of forensic medicine for the development of colonial jurisprudence, see the classic text, Norman Chevers, *A Manual of Medical Jurisprudence in India: Including the Outline of a History of Crime Against the Person in India* (Calcutta 1870).

40. This section relies on the introduction to Anupama Rao (ed.), *Gender and Caste: Issues in Indian Feminism* (New Delhi 2003), pp. 1–47.

41. For an extended discussion of the manner in which narratives of sexual violation organized caste masculinity, see Anupama Rao, *The Caste Question: Dalits and the Politics of Modern India* (Berkeley, CA 2009).

42. Tanika Sarkar, 'Enfranchised Selves: Women, Culture and Rights in Nineteenth-Century Bengal', *Gender and History*, vol. 13, no. 3, 2001, pp. 546–65.

43. The ritual dedication of young girls, or *devadasis*, became an important site of colonial and native reformist intervention through its association with prostitution. It is important to bear in mind that dedicated women were often from the lower-caste and 'Dalit' communities. Kunal Parker, 'A Corporation of Superior Prostitutes: Anglo-Indian Conceptions of Temple Dancing Girls, 1800–1914', *Modern Asian Studies*, vol. 32, no. 3, 1998, pp. 559–633; Lucinda Ramberg. 'When the Devi Is Your Husband: Sacred Marriage and Sexual Economy in South India', *Feminist Studies*, vol. 37, no. 1, 2011, pp. 28–60; Mytheli Sreenivas, 'Creating Conjugal Subjects: Devadasis and the Politics of Marriage in Colonial Madras Presidency', *Feminist Studies*, vol. 37, no. 1, 2011, pp. 63–92; Ashwini Tambe, *Codes of Misconduct: Regulating Prostitution in Late Colonial Bombay* (Minneapolis 2009); Priyadarshini Vijaisri, *Recasting the Devadasi: Patterns of Sacred Prostitution in Colonial South India* (Delhi 2004).

44. For an important argument about the implications of the differential status of Hindu marriage as sacrament, and Islamic marriage as contract for conceptions of women's rights, see Flavia Agnes, 'Interrogating "Consent", and "Agency" across the Complex Terrain of Family Laws in India', in Lila Abu-Lughod and Anupama Rao (eds). *Social Difference Online, Volume 1*, 2011: (http://www.socialdifference. org/files/SocDifOnline-Vol12012.pdf). Also see Tanika Sarkar, *Rebels, Wives, and Saints: Designing Selves and Nations in Colonial India* (Calcutta 2010).

45. Lucy Carrol, 'Law, Custom, and Statutory Social Reform: The Hindu Widows' Remarriage Act of 1856', *Indian Economic and Social History Review*, vol. 20, no. 4, 1983, pp. 363–88. Two further points bear emphasis. On the one hand, expressed in broad strokes, even as British policy exacerbated social differences of caste and religion in numerous ways, colonial intervention into the domain of the Indian intimate was justified by a singular, peculiar logic. In contrast to bourgeois conceptions of the private sphere as the realm of freedom and interiority, the colonial state in India understood the native private sphere as the domain of traditional barbarism. Thus, the gendered private sphere was made available to the colonizers' public scrutiny through the form of the 'scandal', of discovering the persistence of native crimes against 'their' women. This is the structure of colonial protectionism that Gayatri Chakravorty Spivak famously described as, 'white men saving brown women from brown men'. Spivak, 'Can the Subaltern Speak?' On the other hand, it is also the case of course that this interpretive frame was not the sole property of the colonial state. Anti-caste radicals such as Jotirao Phule, his wife Savitribai, and the Satyashodak activist Tarabai Shinde routinely portrayed Brahmanism as sanction for male criminality. Enforced widowhood was an important target of their critique and focused on the inhuman treatment of the widow who was tonsured, subject to severe sartorial codes, prohibited from wearing jewelry, and forced to observe dietary restrictions to control her passions. Tarabai Shinde wrote *Stri-Purush Tulana* (A Comparison between Women and Men) in 1882 in response to the court's conviction of an upper-caste widow, Vijayalakshmi, for infanticide. In this text, Shinde attacked the hypocritical stance of criminalizing women, rather than curbing male sexuality. Unlike her male colleagues, who used gender critique in the interest of anti-caste reform,

Shinde argued that all men, and not merely Brahmans, were implicated in the ill treatment of women.

46. Clare Anderson, *Convicts in the Indian Ocean: Transportation from South Asia to Mauritius, 1815–53* (London 2000); Satadru Sen, *Disciplining Punishment: Colonialism and Convict Society in the Andaman Islands* (New Delhi 2000). The social experience of transported convicts and, later, of indentured laborer is not the focus of this volume. Nonetheless, it is worth noting how domestic violence was mapped onto the violent spatial dislocations of indenture. Prabhu Mohapatra, 'Restoring the Family: Wife Murders and the Making of a Sexual Contract for Indian Indentured Labourers in the British Caribbean Colonies', *Studies in History*, vol. 10, no. 2, 1995, pp. 225–60. The use of jail labour for public works and commodity production is also well known, including a discussion by Nigam in the extended version of his essay in this volume. See also Chitra Joshi, 'Fettered Bodies: Labouring on Public Works in Nineteenth Century India', in Marcel van der Linden and Prabhu Mohapatra (eds), *Labour Matters: Towards Global Histories* (New Delhi 2009), pp. 3–21; and Padmini Swaminathan, 'Prison as Factory: A Study of Jail Manufacture in the Madras Presidency', *Studies in History*, vol. 11, no. 77, 1995, pp. 77–100.

47. Michael Ignatieff, *A Just Measure of Pain: The Penitentiary in the Industrial Revolution 1750–1850* (New York 1978).

48. Foucault, *Discipline and Punish*.

49. Talal Asad, 'On Torture, or Cruel, Inhuman, and Degrading Treatment', in Arthur Kleinman, Veena Das, and Margaret Lock (eds), *Social Suffering* (Delhi 1998), pp. 285–308.

50. Instances of corruption, torture, and bureaucratic negligence illuminate the complicity between colonial regimes and liberal polities: each relied on an infrastructure of accountability—the 'chain of command'—that attempted to override (yet implicate) excess by individuating it. For an exploration of colonial liberalism and its structures of plausible deniability, see Anupama Rao, 'Problems of Violence, States of Terror: Torture in Colonial India', in Steven Pierce and Anupama Rao (eds), *Discipline and the Other Body: Correction, Corporeality, Colonialism* (Durham 2006), pp. 151–85.

51. For an important essay on gender segregation in the prison, see Satadru Sen, 'The Female Jails of Colonial India', *Indian Economic and Social History Review*, vol. 39, no. 4, 2002, pp. 417–38.

52. Recall that a major shift had taken place in the period from non-custodial to custodial punishment, marked by the use of gaols, where under-trials were held, to the prison as a site of correction *after* conviction.

53. For a brilliant, anti-Foucauldian reading of popular resistance to incarceration see, Peter Linebaugh, *London Hanged: Crime and Civil Society in the Eighteenth Century* (Cambridge 1993). For recent subcontinental studies, see the ethnography of a Calcutta prison by Mahua Bandhyopadhyaya, *Everyday Life in a Prison: Confinement, Surveillance, Resistance* (Hyderabad 2010); and Sumanta Banerjee's classic study, *The Wicked City: Crime and Punishment in Calcutta* (Hyderabad 2009).

54. In addition to studies of individuals from M.N. Roy and Bhagat Singh to Subhas Chandra Bose and V.D. Savarkar, there is a large body of scholarship on the Jugantar and Anushilan initiatives associated with the Bengal Swadeshi movement. As well, there is a valuable (and growing) literature on the global itineraries of anti-colonial terrorism with focus on the influences here of: Mazzini and the Young Italy movement; the Irish Fenians; the French, German, and Russian anarchists; and the American Ghadar Party. Despite their divergent political ideologies, these suggest a significant, if under-explored, domain of anti-colonial thought and activism that has tended to be obfuscated by the association of Indian nationalism with Gandhian non-violence. Select studies of such global, revolutionary ideologies and practices would include: C.A. Bayly, *Recovering Liberties: Indian Thought in the Age of Liberalism and Empire* (Cambridge 2012); Arun Coomer Bose, *Indian Revolutionaries Abroad, 1905–1922: In the Background of International Developments* (Patna 1971); Sugata Bose and Kris Manjapra (eds), *Cosmopolitan Thought Zones: South Asia and the Global Circulation of Ideas* (New York 2010); Partha Chatterjee, 'Terrorism: State Sovereignty and Militant Politics in India', in Carol Gluck and Anne Loenhaupt Tsing (eds), *Words in Motion: Toward a Global Lexicon* (Durham 2009), pp. 240–62; Isaac Land (ed.), *Enemies of Humanity: The Nineteenth Century War on Terrorism* (New York 2008); Nicholas Owen, *The British Left and India: Metropolitan Anti-Imperialism, 1885–1947* (Oxford 2007); Maia Ramnath, *Haj to Utopia: How the Ghadar Movement Charted Global Radicalism and Attempted to Overthrow the British Empire* (Berkeley, CA 2012); Tilak Raj Sareen, *Indian Revolutionary Movement Abroad, 1905–1921* (New Delhi 1984); Michael Silvestri, *Ireland and India: Nationalism, Empire and Memory* (New York 2009); Nico Slate, *Colored Cosmopolitanism: The Shared Struggle for Freedom in the United States and India* (Cambridge, MA 2012); and A.G. Noorani, *Indian Political Trials, 1775–1947* (Delhi 2007).

55. On the incarceration of female nationalists, see Kamala Visweswaran. 'Small Speeches, Subaltern Gender: Nationalist Ideology and Its Historiography', in Shahid Amin and Dipesh Chakrabarty (eds), *Subaltern Studies IX: Writings on South Asian History and Society* (New Delhi 1996), pp. 83–125.

56. As would be clear, in this volume we have refrained from including texts on Gandhi's philosophy and his discussions of non-violent *satyagraha* or soulforce; studies of Gandhi's technologies of the self; as well as work on Gandhian protest as the practice of discipline, of which the classic text is perhaps Ranajit Guha, 'Discipline and Mobilize: Hegemony and Elite Control in Nationalist Campaigns', in *Dominance Without Hegemony: History and Power in Colonial India* (Cambridge, MA 1997).

57. David Arnold, *Police Power and Colonial Rule in Madras, 1859–1947* (New Delhi 1986).

58. Chandavarkar's writings on the political culture of Bombay also constitute an important departure for registering the infrastructural transformations of the inter-war period, when dyarchic government encouraged processes of 'localization' by devolving power over education, sanitation, and municipal governance to native elites. As is well known, this racially bifurcated structure

of government produced the 'effect' of representative government, even as it left provincial authorities without the finances to produce 'improving' legislation. The putative retreat of the colonial state and the regionalization of political power produced an expanded domain of action for native elites, while ultimately rendering them subservient to the military might and fiscal powers of the Centre. However, localization (together with the limited franchise of the 1919 Montford reforms) produced a new politics of the street, the neighborhood, and the city. Crime and policing played a central role in this evolving landscape.

59. This section draws upon arguments initiated in Saurabh Dube, *Stitches on Time: Colonial Cultures and Postcolonial Tangles* (Durham 2004).

60. This enemy could/can be, for example, a relative or a neighbour or the spouse's paramour, a witch or a shaman, the modern state or the lower-caste subject.

61. See, for instance John Comaroff and Simon Roberts, *Rules and Process: The Cultural Logic of Dispute in an African Context* (Chicago 1981). This work not only provides an incisive understanding of the state of legal anthropology, from the work of Malinowski and Radcliffe-Brown through till the 1970s, but breaks new ground in the ethnography of legalities and illegalities, especially exploring the dynamics between social structure and individual action. Yet, for other, earlier articulations of such questions see Max Gluckman, *Custom and Conflict in Africa* (London 1955); and Max Gluckman, *Judical Processes Among the Barotse of Northern Nigeria* (Manchester 1955). See also, Victor Turner, *Schism and Continuity in an African Society: A Study of Ndembu Village Life* (Oxford 1996; originally published in 1956). Some of the wider issues at stake in this discussion are explored in Saurabh Dube, 'Anthropology, History, Historical Anthropology', in Saurabh Dube (ed.), *Historical Anthropology* (New Delhi 2007), pp. 1–73.

62. This becomes clear from Joan Vincent's extensive survey of legal anthropology as part of her remarkable analysis of anthropology, politics, and political anthropology. Joan Vincent, *Anthropology and Politics: Visions, Traditions, and Trends* (Tucson 1990). It is also highlighted by June Starr and Jane Collier (eds), *History and Power in the Study of Law: New Directions in Legal Anthropology* (Ithaca 1988); and Sally Engle Merry, 'Anthropology, Law, and Transnational Processes', *Annual Review of Anthropology*, vol. 21, 1992, pp. 357–79. See also, Laura Nader, *Harmony Ideology: Justice and Control in a Zapotec Mountain Village* (Stanford 1991); and Comaroff and Roberts, *Rules and Processes*. In the context of the anthropology of South Asia, questions of conflict and power often found rather singular, even curious, articulations through notions of the 'dominant caste' and of the 'faction'. See, for instance, M.N. Srinivas, 'The Dominant Caste in Rampura', *American Anthropologist*, vol. 61, no. 1, 1959, pp. 1–26; T.K. Oomen, 'The Concept of Dominant Caste', *Contributions to Indian Sociology*, vol. 4, no. 1, 1970, pp. 73–83; M.N. Srinivas, *Collected Essays* (New Delhi 2002); Henry Orenstein, *Gaon: Conflict and Cohesion in an Indian Village* (Princeton 1965); David Hardiman, 'The Indian "Faction": A Political Theory Re-examined', in R. Guha (ed.) *Subaltern Studies I: Writings on South Asian History and Society* (Delhi 1982); Oscar Lewis, *Village Life in Northern India* (Illinois 1958); and S.C. Dube,

'Caste Dominance and Factionalism', *Contributions to Indian Sociology*, vol. 2, 1968, pp. 58–81. See also Bernard S. Cohn's landmark essay, 'Some Notes on Law and Change in North India', in Cohn, *An Anthropologist among the Historians*, pp. 554–74. For material on panchayat justice, see Upendra Baxi, 'Panchayat Justice: An Indian Experiment in Legal Access', in M. Cappelletti and B. Garth (eds), *From Access to Justice, Volume III: Emerging Issues and Perspectives* (Milan and Alphen aan den Rijn 1979), pp. 341–86; and Robert M. Hayden, *Disputes and Arguments Amongst Nomads: A Caste Council in India* (New Delhi 1999).

63. This is clarified by Sally Engle Merry, *Colonizing Hawai'i: The Cultural Power of Law* (Princeton 2000); Merry, 'Anthropology, Law, and Transnational Processes'; and Starr and Collier (eds) *History and Power*. See also, Patricia Ewick and Susan Silbey, *The Common Place of Law: Stories from Everyday Life* (Chicago 1998); Vincent, *Anthropology and Politics*; and Pratiksha Baxi, 'Feminist Contributions to Sociology of Law: A Review', *Economic and Political Weekly*, vol. 43, no. 43, 2008, pp. 79–85.

64. Concerning South Asia see, for instance, Pratiksha Baxi, 'Justice is a Secret: Compromise in Rape Trials', *Contributions to Indian Sociology*, vol. 44, no. 3, 2010, pp. 207–33; Erin P Moore, 'Gender, Power, and Legal Pluralism', *American Ethnologist*, vol. 20, no. 3, 1993, pp. 522–42; Leela Dube, 'Conflict and Compromise: Devolution and Disposal of Property in a Matrilineal Muslim Society', *Economic and Political Weekly*, vol. 29, no. 21, 1994, pp. 1273–84; Saurabh Dube, 'Idioms of Authority and Engendered Agendas: The Satnami Mahasabha, Chhattisgarh, 1925–50', *The Indian Economic and Social History Review*, vol. 30, no. 4, 1993, pp. 383–411; Ishita Banerjee Dube, 'Taming Traditions: Legalities and Histories in Twentieth Century Orissa', in Gautam Bhadra, Gyan Prakash, and Susie Tharu (eds), *Subaltern Studies X: Writings on South Asian History and Society* (Delhi 1999), pp. 98–125: and Dube, *Stitches of Time*. See also, Upendra Baxi. '"The State's Emissary": The Place of Law in Subaltern Studies', in Partha Chatterjee and Gyan Pandey (eds), *Subaltern Studies VII: Writings on South Asian History and Society* (Delhi 1992), pp. 257–64; Veena Das, 'Subaltern as Perspective', in Ranajit Guha (ed.), *Subaltern Studies VI: Writings on South Asian History and Society* (Delhi 1989), pp. 310–24; Saurabh Dube, *Untouchable Pasts: Religion, Identity, and Authority among a Central Indian Community, 1780–1950* (Albany 1998); and Rao, *The Caste Question*, especially chapters 4–7 on postcolonial India.

65. Ranajit Guha, *Elementary Aspects of Peasant Insurgency in Colonial India* (Delhi 1983).

66. There is a large and growing literature on the Partition, from political history to personal memoirs. A small sample of the kind of work we have in mind includes: Urvashi Butalia, *The Other Side of Silence: Voices from the Partition of India* (New Delhi 1998); Veena Das, *Life and Words: Violence and the Descent into the Ordinary* (Berkeley, CA 2006); Ritu Menon and Kamla Bhasin, *Borders and Boundaries: Women in India's Partition* (New Brunswick, NJ 1998); Gyanendra Pandey, *Remembering Partition: Violence, Nationalism and History in India* (Cambridge 2002); Vazira Fazili-Yacoobali Zamindar, *The Long Partition and the Making of Modern South Asia: Refugees, Boundaries, Histories* (New York 2007).

67. It bears emphasis that there are numerous historical studies relating India's Constitution with the Government of India Act of 1935. There is also a large jurisprudential literature on the ideas of rights and duties as these were articulated in the Indian Constitution; studies of the relationship between the apex and lower courts; considerations of the shifting balance of power between executive and judiciary; and studies of quasi-juridical forms such as the Committees of Inquiry that follow revelations of political and economic scams or large-scale sociopolitical violence such as communal riots. We are aware of these studies, including especially their potential for engaging questions of crime and postcolonial legality from other angles, but cannot include them here.

68. As we know, caste, which is at the center of constitutional commitments to social justice, was rendered into a 'class-like' indicator of socio-economic deprivation requiring affirmative action. Meanwhile the practice of untouchability has been abolished, and its practice/practitioners criminalized. For a discussion of the relationship between caste and affirmative action policies in post-independence India see, Marc Galanter, *Competing Equalities: Law and the Backward Classes in India* (Delhi 1984). For a complete list to Galanter's long and sustained engagements with the practice and history of Indian law see: http://marcgalanter.net/cv.htm

Issues of gender carry their own complexities, especially since they bear directly on the linkages between community and identity as well as the relationship between community and state. Personal laws are differentiated by religious community and govern the conduct of marriage, divorce, maintenance, and adoption for each of these communities. (When conversion is not at issue, interreligious marriages come under the domain of the Special Marriage Act of 1954, which replaced the earlier Act of 1872.) In the twentieth century, the Shari'a Act of 1937 and the passage of the Muslim Dissolution of Marriage Act of 1939 as well as the piecemeal reform of Hindu personal law in the 1950s, beginning with the passage of the Hindu Marriage Act of 1955, sought to remove customary and sectarian differences *within* these communities, in the interest of codifying the personal law for these religious communities. More recently, minority communities, especially Muslims, have found that community identity is challenged (and asserted) around crises concerning 'women's rights'. On the issue of Muslim women's rights, including a discussion of how these have been historically constituted in opposition to the rights of upper-caste Hindu women, see: Flavia Agnes, *Law and Gender Inequality: The Politics of Women's Rights in India* (Delhi 1999); Mary E. John, 'Alternate Modernities? Reservations and Women's Movement in 20th Century India', *Economic and Political Weekly*, vol. 35, nos 43–4, 2000, WS22-WS29; Nivedita Menon, 'State/Gender/Community: Citizenship in Contemporary India', *Economic and Political Weekly*, vol. 33, no. 5, 1998, PE3–PE10; Mrinalini Sinha, *Specters of Mother India: The Global Restructuring of an Empire* (Durham 2006); Rajeswari Sunder Rajan, 'Shah Bano', *Signs: Journal of Women in Culture and Society*, vol. 14, no. 3, 1989, pp. 558–82; Rajeswari Sunder Rajan. 'The Ameena "Case": The Female Citizen and Subject', in *Scandal of the State: Women, Law and Citizenship in Postcolonial India* (Durham 2003), pp. 41–71. For

studies of minority rights as these appear in the Constitution more generally see, Shefali Jha, 'Secularism in the Constituent Assembly Debates, 1946–
1950', *Economic and Political Weekly*, vol. 37, no. 30, 2002, pp. 3175–80; Neera
Chandoke, *Beyond Secularism: The Rights of Religious Minorities* (Delhi 1999);
Ralph Retzlaff, 'The Problem of Communal Minorities in the Drafting of the
Indian Constitution', in R.N. Spann (ed.), *Constitutionalism in Asia* (London
1963).

69. See, for example, Ujwal Kumar Singh, *The State, Democracy, and Anti-
Terror Laws* (New Delhi 2007).

70. See Asma Jahangir and Hina Jillani, *The Hudood Ordinances: A Divine
Sanction? A Research Study of the Hudood Ordinances and their Effect on the
Disadvantaged Sections of Pakistan Society* (Lahore 1990); Ayesha Jalal, 'The
Convenience of Subservience', in Denis Kandiyoti (ed.), *Women, Islam and
the State* (London 1991), pp. 77–114; Ian Talbot, *Pakistan: A Modern History*
(London 2009); and Saadi Toor, *The State of Islam: Culture and Cold War Politics
in Pakistan* (London and New York 2011).

71. Consider the fact-finding reports of the People's Union for Democratic
Rights (Delhi), the remarkable activities of the Andhra Pradesh Civil Liberties
Committee (APCLC), and finally, the writings and activism of APCLC mem-
ber and Human Rights Forum founder, K. Balagopal (http://balagopal.org/).
Consider, too, Singh, *Political Prisoners in India*.

72. Here one may think of: the work of a scholar we consider to be the
founder of critical legal studies in India, Upendra Baxi (http://upendrabaxi.net/
documents.html); the writings of legal scholar Rajeev Dhavan; and the work of
the Lawyers' Collective and some of the lawyers associated with this initiative
over the years including Indira Jaisingh, Colin Gonsalves, and Mihir Desai. The
contemporary field of legal activism—including the turn towards international
human rights law—succeeds this earlier moment, which grew out of the
Emergency and Naxalbari experiences of the 1970s.

73. Drawing on Sudipta Kaviraj's characterization of postcolonial transition
as exhibiting the logic of 'passive revolution', Partha Chatterjee has argued that
Indian neoliberalism is marked by divisions between 'civil' and 'political' society.
Chatterjee further engages the economist Kalyan Sanyal's theorization of 'primi-
tive accumulation' to address transformations of political economy in this period.
See Partha Chatterjee, 'Classes, Capital and Indian Democracy', *Economic and
Political Weekly*, vol. 43, no. 46, 2008, pp. 89–93; Sudipta Kaviraj, 'A Critique of
Passive Revolution', *Economic and Political Weekly*, vol. 23, nos 45–7, 1988, pp.
2429–33, 2436–41, 2443–4; and Kalyan Sanyal, *Rethinking Capitalist Development:
Primitive Accumulation, Governmentality, and Postcolonial Capitalism* (Delhi
2007).

74. There are many studies on the new politics of the urban middle-classes
in India. For Delhi and Mumbai, respectively, see, for example, Amita Baviskar,
'Urban Exclusions: Public Spaces and the Poor in Delhi', in Bharati Chaturvedi
(ed.), *Finding Delhi: Loss and Renewal in a Megacity* (New Delhi 2010), pp.
3–15. Arvind Rajagopal, 'The Violence of Commodity Aesthetics: Hawkers,

Demolition Raids, and a New Regime of Consumption', *Social Text*, vol. 16, no. 368, pp. 91–113.

75. See Nalin Mehta and Mona G. Mehta (eds), 'Gujarat Beyond Gandhi: Identity, Conflict and Society', *South Asian Culture and Society*, special issue, vol. 1, no. 4, 2010. Also see the recent study of spatial segregation of Muslims in urban India, Laurent Gayer and Christophe Jaffrelot (eds), *Muslims in Indian Cities: Trajectories of Marginalization* (London 2012).

76. This is especially the case given South Asia's geopolitical centrality for the United States War on Terror. On this issue, the politically sensitive reportage by Ahmed Rashid bears mention as do the theoretical provocations in Faisal Devji, *Landscapes of the Jihad: Militancy, Morality, Modernity* (Ithaca 2005). The current conjuncture also illustrates the local impact of global concerns regarding 'Muslim terror', for instance, with regard to the migration of impoverished Bangladeshi immigrants to India, or the politicization of Muslim women's rights in the region. As we know, such interventions extend from global rights discourses that claim to 'save' Muslim women, to crimes of honor and public discipline that use women's bodies as performative sites for enacting anxieties around social status, community identity, and masculine privilege.

I

Precolonial Premonitions

1

Wrongs and Rights in the Maratha Country

Antiquity, Custom, and Power in Eighteenth-century India*

Sumit Guha

INTRODUCTION

There are few areas as beset with problems of evidence and interpretation as that of the study of conceptions of rights in past societies. In complex literate societies with written codes of law, the problem might be approached via an analysis of those codes, but even so there would remain the problem of determining how far the codes encapsulate the extant conceptions of various social groups at the time, and the more difficult issue of establishing the extent to which the codes actually governed social practices. This would be the case in a territory with

* This essay was originally published in Michael Anderson and Sumit Guha (eds), *Changing Conceptions of Law and Justice in South Asia* (Delhi: Oxford University Press, 1997). An earlier version of this paper was read at the seminar on 'Changing Conceptions of Rights and Justice' held at the Nehru Memorial Museum and Library (NMML) from 13 to 17 March 1994. I am grateful to the participants for their many helpful suggestions, and to Michael Anderson for detailed written comments on the paper. The responsibility for any surviving errors or inaccuracies is exclusively mine.

defined boundaries and a unified legal system, but the issue becomes vastly more complicated when we consider a region of shifting political boundaries, often indefinite jurisdictions, in which several unwritten and written bodies of law and custom could be invoked or set aside as the case might be—and this was the situation in eighteenth-century Maharashtra.

The notional monarch, the *chhatrapati*, was increasingly allowing his powers to be exercised by his principal minister, the *peshwa*, but various subordinate chiefs also claimed parity with, or autonomy from, the latter and administered justice according to their lights.

So, for example, in 1771 there was a theft in the temple of Mahadev in the Western Ghats; the temple priests traced the thieves, and informed Babuji Naik of Baramati, a great man at the peshwa's court, who came, recovered the stolen property, and despatched the thieves to Pune for trial. Thereupon, the Ghatge *deshmukh* of Malavdi, within whose lands the temple was located, arrested the Brahmans and confined them, beating them daily 'like thieves', because they had sent thieves from 'our realm' to the peshwa.[1] Finally, in some areas there was even a jurisdiction shared with another sovereign—and the Maratha records exhibit cases in which the fees and fines levied in such places were duly shared with another power.[2] The state itself was tolerant of adjudication or arbitration by unofficial authority, provided the revenue arising thereby was remitted back to the state. So one Satvoji Gavde, a commander of the government cavalry, was addressed in 1783–4 as follows: 'You consider and settle people's quarrels and disputes. The fines, fees and debt-recovery charges that have accrued, and will accrue, you will credit to the account of the unit in your charge.'[3]

It must be evident that there was a considerable range of authorities offering some type of justice, and fortunate litigants might be able to choose between them. With the multiplicity of legal authorities, there was also a multiplicity of scriptural and customary sources of right, which might be invoked or set aside as the case might be. Even after the Mughal administration had been dislodged, the Marathas generally allowed the hereditary Muslim law-officers (*qazi*) to remain in office, though their authority may well have been reduced. A Marathi proverb collected in the nineteenth century runs: 'The king speaks—an army moves; the qazi speaks—his beard moves.'[4] But in the middle of the eighteenth century, we still find a woman appealing to the qazi of Ahmadnagar for justice, and then appealing from his verdict to the peshwa.[5] Even when in office, however, we cannot presume that the qazis were either sufficiently learned, or sufficiently independent of local opinion, to adhere to the strict letter of one of the various schools of Islamic jurisprudence as defined by modern scholarship. An Islamic scholar wrote disgustedly of them in the later eighteenth century: 'What shall be said of the hereditary qazis of the townships, for to be in touch with science is the lot of enemies [that is, is a misfortune] and the registers of the *despandya* [district accountants] and the words of *zamindars* [gentry] are their law and holy books.'[6]

There was probably an even wider range of authorities available to those who did not appear before the qazis, and one of the most frequently invoked authorities was custom or usage. When Steele carried out his enquiry in 1825–6,

> Fifty-six castes stated that they have no written documents or books to which they might refer as authority in points of disputed custom. Ancient usage as determined by the caste on creditable evidence is the general guide. In cases of extraordinary difficulty, Brahmuns are called in, who decide according to the written law of the Dhurmasastru.
>
> In disputes among Brahmuns, the assembled caste profess to be guided by the decision of Sastrees. The Konkne and Kanure Sonars, and the Kayusth Prubhoos have latterly made the same assumption.[7]

From Satara, Steele received the opinion that custom 'has sanctioned many things in opposition to Sastru.'

It must be evident, therefore, that many difficulties beset the effort to recover the conceptions of right from such a milieu, and I make no claim to have solved any or all of them. I shall, however, bypass some of them by abandoning the high ground of scriptural law and global conceptions of rights, and move directly into cases where rights were invoked or affirmed, thus trying to tease the broader conceptions out of the tangled narratives, the bitter complaints, and the complex investigations that we find in the sources.[8]

It is perhaps necessary at the outset to specify whose voices we have on record and in what context. The statements that we shall consider were almost all made in situations of conflict—sometimes by a complainant denied some right, more frequently enunciated by a powerful arbiter deciding a dispute, or checking a transgression. The instances themselves are taken from a variety of sources and cover a period of more than a century. It is not, therefore, to be presumed that we are recording the functioning of a homogenous, or even a consistent, system of rights: rather we are trying to catch the general conceptions that lurk behind the concrete plaints that the plaintiff thinks may be invoked in his favour, as also those that the powerful choose to cite in justification of their decisions.

THE SOURCES OF RIGHT

Antiquity itself was a source (perhaps the chief source) of right: the old way was by definition right and innovation wrong. In a land dispute, the villagers of Malegaon reproached the men of Peth—'Why do you seize the ploughs of Malegaon? And why have you broken the old and done the new?'[9] Antiquity of tenure or practice was therefore a strong prima facie evidence of its rightness, and many plaints began with an assertion of such antiquity. Thus the headman (*patil*) of Chichvad came before the court, and deposed:

> … the headmanship of the aforesaid village has been our hereditary property for generations as follows: Jauji Patil's son was Ramji Patil, my grandfather, whose son was Navji Patil my father … he died and as the heir I functioned as patil for many days, but now Keroji and Kamlaji of Chichvad have come and deny that I am entitled to the headmanship …[10]

A more emphatic assertion of age in another suit runs: 'There were twelve villages which have grown to forty villages; from that time our family has held the headmanship.'[11] A similar invocation of old usage in confirming rights is evident in an award of AD 1723, which stated: 'Enjoy the third share and seniority of headmanship of the aforesaid village *according to the old way* and bequeath it to your sons and grandsons from generation to generation, and live happily.'[12] The same respect for ancient practice is found in an order from Manaji Angre to Bal Patil, Amboji Patil, and Ram Patil; he supports their claim, because 'Your headmanship is ancient, and you have been in

enjoyment of it from the time of the late Shrimant Aba Sarkhel ...'[13]
The *shet* was the head of the merchants in a town or village, and had
certain perquisites as well—here also old practice was to be preserved:
'The rules and customs of the office of shet have been handed down
from ancient times, and they are hereby confirmed.'[14]

The transition from antiquity to genealogy is an obvious one, as
some of the citations above exemplify, and many claimants sought
to substantiate claims by proving genealogical connection with an
acknowledged holder. Genealogical enquiry often determined the
outcome of a suit. For example, two families were in contention for
the hereditary preceptorship of the caste of Sonars and Panchals in
several subdivisions of south Maharashtra. The matter was handed
over to a *panchayat,* which asked the litigants of their enjoyment of the
right in question. 'It was then agreed by the whole assembly that "you
come from the same root, and are of the same fraternity" ...' and the
right would therefore be equally shared.[15] Genealogical connections,
however, were not biological but social—adopted heirs were entirely
legitimate, while sons born of secondary marriage or concubinage
had definitely inferior rights.[16] The destruction of ancient rights was
clearly wrong, and even the highly centralizing text on politics, the
Ajnapatra, attributed to Ramachandra Pant and dated to the early
eighteenth century, while strongly warning the king against allowing
patrimonial claims to increase at his own expense, also cautioned
against the seizure of existing ones.[17]

The king was, of course, permitted to innovate by creating new claims
at his own expense; indeed he must frequently have been importuned
to do so. However, even royal grants improved with age, so much so
that ousted dynasties were cited as the sources of grants in preference
to currently ruling ones. Thus, Thomas Coats commented in the early
nineteenth century that the holders of patrimonial rights preferred to
claim that they had been awarded by the Emperor of Delhi or the Raja
of Satara who preceded them rather than by the peshwas.[18] Similarly,
a late-seventeenth-century petition to the Maratha king Rajaram asks
him to reconfirm various rights as they had existed under the Adilshahi
dynasty, which had preceded his own.[19] Indeed, in one instance he is
explicitly told that the arrangement made by his father should be set
aside, and the practice that had existed under the Adilshahi dynasty

restored.[20] Such tactlessness on the part of the petitioner indicates the significance of antiquity as a source of legitimacy.

RIGHTS TO LAND, OFFICE, AND SERVICE

The rights that have appeared so far have been rights to land and office. Disputes over these matters are frequently found in the records, but many other rights also existed. So for example, certain mendicants came and petitioned the governor of Pune in 1722 that they went from village to village exhibiting performing animals, and were supposed to receive four coppers from each house annually, as well as some bread and unpaid labour to transport their goods. They were found to have orders to this effect from previous governments, and so their rights were reconfirmed and an order issued to the headmen of villages in the tract specified.[21] *Watans*[22] could exist in a highly incorporeal form: the hereditary astrologer–priest of a village had the right to inform its residents of the auspicious moment (*muhurta*) for weddings, and claim fees (*hak* meaning right) for the service. However, in one village another Brahman told the local Mahars what the moment was, whereupon he was challenged 'you destroy the *watandar*'s hak, what is this?'[23]

Hak itself is a term worth considering. Molesworth's Dictionary[24] gives us this entry: '1 Right, title, justness of claim or pretension; 2 The share or portion due (of the revenue or of the crops ...); 3 Province, peculiar office or business. Ex. [trans. mine] Climbing trees is the monkey's hak.' This illustrates how quick the transition was from right to income from that right; and the example of the monkey shows that certain kinds of persons might have rights by virtue of their generic nature. This would determine eligibility: but not everyone who was eligible could possess any specific right. So, for example, accountants were almost everywhere Brahmans and village watchmen Mahars; this would not prevent specific members of those castes from excluding others from the duties and emoluments of their watans.[25]

RIGHTFUL HONOUR

Emoluments have figured largely in the various claims that we have considered so far, but many other claims to right were made, and on occasion, upheld. An important component of these was honour, and its active expression through such acts as being the first to receive betel leaf (*paan*) on ceremonial occasions. This was not a notion confined to the upper ranks of society: a village blacksmith had his honour, and when dishonoured by a charge of theft, left the village and settled else-where.[26] When a share of a village headmanship (*patilki*) was sold, the honours (*man-pan*) attached to the office were partitioned as scrupu-lously as the pay and perquisites. These are enumerated in practically every deed of sale that I have seen, and I cite one of the shorter lists as an example. Two-thirds of the office was sold to Pilaji Gaikwad in 1728, and one-third retained by Gadge. The former received ten rights beginning with the right to put his name and the patil's identifying mark—the plough—on official papers, to receive the first honorific turban from the state, to be greeted with the consecrated flame from the temple, and so on, while Gadge had precedence at the Holi festival to water from the water-carrier, and also shared the right to have the musicians play before him.[27]

Honour and the display of honourable status were important not only for the landholding classes, but for artisans and traders, who on occasion came to blows over the parading of bridegrooms through the public space of the market. They were ordered not to go through the market, but to confine themselves to their own streets.[28] Nor were the lower castes outside the competition for relative status, and at least one document sets out the steeds that bridegrooms of the different castes were permitted to ride upon in their marriage proces-sions in Mungi Paithan; so, for example, the Brahman's bridegroom was allowed on horseback, as also the deshmukh's, the shepherd's, the farmer's, the Muslim's and so on, but the oilman, the Jain, the leather-worker, the barber, the potter, the stone-worker, etc. had to ride a bullock, while wanderers, hunters, basket-makers, and others had to go on foot. The document was intended to define certain rights of the Mahars, and it asserts that they were also entitled to go on horseback.[29] Affronts to personal honour could bring down punishments from the state: so, for example, when the conversation between Yeshwant Shivaji and Vishwanathbhatt grew heated, the former struck the lat-ter on the face and was subsequently fined the considerable sum of 325 rupees.[30]

Lesser folk might also suffer for derogating the honour of their fellows—we have cases of fines inflicted for false charges of unchastity. Or, to take another charge, Mahadu Mali falsely accused Brahmaji Dhangar of theft and dishonoured him (*be-aab kela*). Both parties were obscure villagers, but the matter duly came before the village administrator, and Mahadu was fined two rupees. In the same village, Appa Sonar spoke in an unwarranted (*gair-sanadi*) manner to Govindpant Kulkarni, and was fined one rupee; and Nava Chambhar had to pay the same sum for an impertinent speech to a [government?] peon.[31]

RIGHTS IN THE HOUSEHOLD

Members of a household, needless to say, had very unequal rights. Those of young children were particularly tenuous, and parents could, and did, sell them into slavery during hard times,[32] give them away in marriage, or hand them over for adoption. Female slaves or concubines might have only a conditional right to life in a royal household; when Janoji Bhosle died in 1772, the chronicler records 'all the dancing girls committed *sati*'—and it seems unlikely that this was of their own volition.[33] On the other hand, a favoured concubine could exercise considerable power on behalf of her master. Thus Kusaji Pant, a village astrologer, had a Rajasthani (Rangdi) slave-woman whom he despatched to collect his *baks* in kind, and she seized whatever she chose from the fields; if the farmers protested then she subjected them to vile abuse.[34]

Regularly married wives would have more definite rights in the household, especially after they had borne children. Although the proverb ran 'the daughter belongs to the father; the land belongs to the monarch',[35] yet examples are not lacking where the mother acted independently on the all-important issue of marriage. Thus, five years after the marriage of her daughter, the wife of Nimba Pathara decided that the groom came from a low-status family, and asked the learned (and, it transpired, avaricious) Brahman Vireshwarbhat to annul the match.[36] In another instance, when a Brahman took a lower-caste mistress and rejected his wife, the latter was able to move the peshwa's government to suspend her husband's land rights until he agreed to live conjugally with her. Characteristically, the mistress was more severely punished: she was imprisoned in a fort, and her three children handed over to the legitimate wife to bring up.[37]

Marital conduct was private to a very limited extent as a case of 1782 makes clear. Kusaji Hazari and his wife were expelled from the village of Vasgad for reasons that remain unclear; he took her to the boundary of Khatav and began beating her. The villagers of Khatav came out and asked, 'What reason do you have to beat your wife in the forest?' They then took the couple back to Vasgad, and the people of Vasgad told him to give them security (*zamin*) that he would not beat his wife before they would allow him to take her away. He went away and lodged a complaint that they were detaining his wife, which led to a record of the facts of this case.[38]

Respectable women or women of status (*garti bayka*) could also expect protection: thus some women who had been lured from home and taken to Pen to be sold in 1780 informed the customs officers and guards there that they were respectable, whereupon the sale was stopped and an enquiry instituted.[39] The meaning of respectability is made clearer by a case from 1754–5. The widow of Devji Parata, a Koli, was charged with sexual misconduct and arrested; thereupon her kinsfolk came and petitioned, saying 'do not enslave our kinswoman'. Therefore, with due regard to her respectable status, she was to be fined fifty rupees and set free.[40] Avowal by the extended kin rather than wealth or status seems to be the proof of respectability here.

Husbands were often able to get their wives restored to them after they had eloped or been abducted; in one case a husband who had abandoned his wife, and gone to another province, returned after many years to find her remarried. A panchayat met and he 'nobly' gave up his rights in favour of the second husband.[41] In another case where the husband did not return for many years, the father remarried his daughter, and undertook to provide another wife for the missing husband if he returned.[42] He had an evident right to have a wife, but not necessarily a specific one. The gift of a bride could also be a part-settlement of a debt; when Dadaji Raghunath's father was owed 1,500 rupees by Bhagvant Uddhavmall at 5 per cent per mensem, it was finally arranged that the ensuing debt would be liquidated by Bhagvant giving his sister in marriage together with gold ornaments weighing a *ser* (worth approximately Rs 1,200 at the time).[43]

Respectable widows had enforceable claims on their sons for maintenance—so in 1768–9, Kali of the Jadhav family was able to secure provision for herself from her sons.[44] Similarly, when a low-caste man, Subhana, unwarrantedly troubled his mother he was fined half a rupee.[45] In many cases in fact, widows controlled large estates as guardians of infant heirs, and the widowed mothers of princely sons could exercise considerable power even after their children reached maturity. But such families would be few: all too often older widows, with no value in the marriage market, would have no effective rights or claims, and be excluded from the household or the kin-fraternity to take their chances among the beggars who thronged the courts and temples.[46]

Female-headed households were only regarded as normal among professional entertainers or prostitutes—the subordinate members in this case would frequently be slaves, and the powers of the head of the household would be considerable. Gajra Naikin told a questioner in c. 1820: 'If I have a girl who is of no use at all, I sell her if I get a good price.'[47] And a half-century earlier, the qazi of Pune had his estate seized (perhaps temporarily) by the government because he presided over the marriage of a dyer with the daughter of a dancing-girl's (*kalavantin*) slave-woman despite being warned not to do so.[48] The professional independence of the dancing girl was recognized by Peshwa Madhavrao. In 1763–4, one Birajkuwar complained that she had joined the entourage of a retainer of Sher Jang and gone with him, leaving her goods in the city. The local Maratha administrator learned of this and (perhaps on account of consorting with the enemy) seized her property and fined her 100 rupees. The peshwa ordered full restitution to be made, adding: 'A professional woman went where she saw an opening; this being so what right have you to take her goods and fine her?'[49]

THE RIGHT TO PRIVATE FORCE

The Powers of the Creditor

The economy that we are discussing was characterized by widespread recourse to credit on the part of both great and small, and the authority of the state could be invoked to recover debts. This was a slow process, however, and furthermore, involved the payment of a fee amounting to a quarter of the property recovered. Many creditors preferred to attempt direct recovery by harassment and cunning; Thomas Coats, who lived for many years in Pune when it was ruled by Peshwa Bajirao II, recorded that debtors 'were seldom submitted to imprisonment, but the modes of annoyance resorted to by the creditor were perhaps more effectual in bringing them to a speedy settlement.'[50] These rights were widely accepted; thus, while reporting a case in which a businessman was punished for pressing a debtor, the peshwa's agent at the court of the Raja of Nagpur added scathingly: 'Such is the political ethic (*rajnit*) here!'[51]

Despite Coats' comment, creditors did sometimes seize their debtors—in the late seventeenth century, one Sambhaji Patil fell into debt to the Gosavi fraternity, and so they confined his family and children. This compelled him to sell his hereditary rights in order to satisfy them.[52] The same powers existed a century later: in 1787 Ganoba Naik Kumadi took two debtors to his house and employed heavy pressure on them; he was ordered by the government to desist, but did not do so, and they both died. He was, therefore, fined 20,000 rupees.[53] Clearly, the right of the creditor extended to coercing the person of the debtor but not to taking his life.

Similar rights to direct enforcement could be claimed over runaway servants. For example, Arjuna Koshti employed a servant who had run away from the employment of one Tulgavkar, and then obstructed the latter's attempt to recover him. Arjuna was fined three rupees.[54] Such rights would obviously depend on there being a sufficient imbalance of force between the opponents and persist as long as such an imbalance existed. It is, therefore, not surprising to find examples of such private redress well into the present century.[55]

Powers within the State

The ability to exercise such rights obviously depended on the political strength of the persons concerned, just as the right to buy an elephant would depend on having the wealth to do so. So the wealthy and powerful had (and have) more rights than the lowly and poor. An act of robbery or private vengeance that might cost a poor man his life, or at any rate, everything that he and his kin possessed, would bring a powerful man (or woman) only a few words of reproof. So, for example, when the eminent lady Daryabai Nimbalkar besieged and plundered a *math* (religious foundation), she and her associates were merely sent reproachful letters from the king (chhatrapati), telling her to restore the looted property.[56] Great families were given much latitude in the way they conducted their internal disputes. Rajasbai Patankar complained, in 1752–3, that Dharrao Patankar had plundered the traders of Sambhapur, looting all their property. The king wrote back: 'You are kinsfolk. It is well if you come to an arrangement among yourselves; the Court cannot be useful in this matter.'[57]

That great men might adopt Dharrao's methods even in relation to the monarch is shown by a letter of the same year, addressed to Rajshri Shivaji Salokhe, who evidently had some money claims on the state. 'You have been disturbing the subdivision of Atpadi and what need or right (*prayojan*) have you to do this? Despatch your accounts with a clerk to the Court. After considering them the appropriate orders will be issued.'[58] The power of the chhatrapati was in decline at this time, as real authority shifted into the hands of his nominal subordinate, the peshwa; but the same methods were adopted by the latter's retainers as well. So, in 1784, the noble Manaji Sinde set off from Shrigonda with 200 soldiers, and (probably) extorted money from, or robbed, some villages. The complaint against him was sent to his superior and kinswoman Sakhubai Sinde, whose report we have. She states that she summoned him, whereupon he said that he had merely gone on a hunting expedition.

> Then I told the noble [*chiranjiv*—an honorific title] that, if after this you go anywhere and cause turmoil, it will not be good for you. There is an order from the government to that effect and I concur. Thereupon he spoke much, saying: 'The expenses of my following are great, my resources do not cover my expenditures … How long can I hold my breath?' [Sakhubai resumes] Let the Peshwa be gracious and make a settlement. I myself have been tangled in [Manaji's] debts for the last twenty-seven months. I have repeatedly petitioned the government, but no settlement has been made to date. Therefore the government should make an arrangement for Manaji's past debt and future needs.[59]

Otherwise he would presumably go on levying tribute at random from the villages.

Liberties stemmed from powers. So, in 1799 Gavhar and other leaders of the Sindhi soldiers employed at Pune went to Sakharam Ghatge and demanded pay—no doubt in a riotous and insolent manner. Ghatge, however, was connected with the powerful ruler Daulatrao Sinde, and the latter had some of the leaders put to death. The remaining soldiers then protested: 'We have served in this realm for forty or fifty years, but nothing like this has ever happened; but now this has occurred. Then let the Saheb consider this, and we shall follow his orders.' Then came the threat: 'If our lord does not do us justice then all the Sindhis will die' (that is, mutiny).[60] The sense of grievance was evidently strong in this case, and it is interesting that the lapse of forty or fifty years was considered sufficient to authenticate a 'traditional' right—this is the period that Clanchy believes to be the limit of non-literate memory.[61]

CONCLUSIONS: RIGHTS AND CUSTOMS

It would be far from original to say that Indian society in the eighteenth century was characterized by a normative inequality. This has been said not only of the past, but of the present, by Louis Dumont[62] and others. However, this inequality certainly seemed to characterize the society whose conceptions of rights we have been trying to fathom through the materials presented above. It would certainly be difficult to find a universal or equal right anywhere in the evidence that we have seen. Men and women, chiefs and servants, peasants and clerks, buffoons and prostitutes—members of these and various other social categories had various rights, but not as partakers of a universal right of man, citizen, or anything else. If their rights had a source, it was the dead past resurrected in the present as custom; and custom, I would venture to say, was largely an epitome of past balances of social power. The customs of the country aligned themselves silently along past lines of force, just as the palaeomagnetism of the Deccan lavas still follows the lines of the earth's magnetic field fifty million years ago. But as those rocks were open to erosion and deposition, so also was custom subject to contest and redefinition. And it may be because of this that

we find that the deep respect for past practice discussed in the opening section of this paper: even if those powerful in the present were
not the lineal descendants of the powerful of the past, they intended
to retain all their privileges, and, if possible, to revive others that (in
their eyes) the corruption of modernity had allowed to decay. The
procedures of authentication were by their nature such as to ensure
that they would have their way, since the eminent and powerful would
gather to scrutinize documents and attest traditions.[63]

Customary rights might all too often be but ancient abuses; indeed
at times none too ancient: how long after the institution of universi-
ties, examinations, and the Bar has it taken for customary rights to
riot, to pay without work, or to obstruct justice, to be established by
privileged groups of students, academics, and lawyers (to mention
only the likely readers of this paper)?[64] I would certainly be prepared
to maintain that, like myself, all my readers also belong to that happy
category of those who are 'customarily' more equal than others.

NOTES

1. G.S. Sardesai (ed.), *Selections from the Peshwa Daftar* (Bombay 1931–4), vol.
39, pp. 141–2; here, and throughout this paper, all citations from Marathi sources
have been translated by me.

2. V.T. Gune, *The Judicial System of the Marathas* (Poona 1953), p. 350.
Four valuable appendices of Marathi documents occupy pp. 139–372 of this
work.

3. G.C. Vad, P.V. Mawjee, and D.B. Parasnis (eds) *Selections from the Satara
Raja's and Peshwa's Diaries* (various parts, Poona 1906–11; henceforth *SSRPD*),
vol. 8, p. 129.

4. A. Manwaring, *Marathi Proverbs* (Oxford 1898), no. 674.

5. *SSRPD*, vol. 1, doc. 309, pp. 183–4.

6. H. Beveridge (trans.), Baini Parshad (rev.), *Maathir-ul-Umara* (reprint,
Patna 1974) p. 77. For a wider consideration of these issues see M. Anderson,
'Islamic Law and the Colonial Encounter in British India' in David Arnold and
Peter Robb (eds), *Institutions and Ideologies* (London 1993), and also Radhika
Singha, 'Criminal Communities' in this volume.

7. A.T. Steele, *The Law and Custom of Hindoo Castes within the Dukhun* (2nd
ed. London 1868), pp. 122–3.

8. The issue of change over the period 1720–1818 from which our evidence
is drawn has also been left in abeyance—in large part because, in my judgement,
neither norms nor processes changed significantly over this period.

9. Sardesai, *Selections*, vol. 43, p. 132.

10. Gune, *The Judicial System of the Marathas*, p. 271.

11. G.C. Vad and P.V. Mawjee (eds), *Decisions from the Shahu and Peshwa Daftar* (Poona 1909), p. 29.

12. Gune, *The Judicial System of the Marathas*, p. 287, emphasis added.

13. A.G. Pawar (ed.), *Tarabaikalina Kagadpatren*, (Kolhapur 1970) vol. I, doc. 62.

14. Pawar (ed.), *Tarabaikalina Kagadpatren*, vol. 2, pp. 301–2.

15. Ibid., pp. 169–70.

16. A government order of 1771–2 puts a younger son in control of his deceased father's office because he was born of a regular marriage, while his older half-brother was born of a secondary union. *SSRPD*, vol. 7, pt. 2, p. 182.

17. S.N. Banhatti (ed.), *Ajnapatra* (Pune and Nagpur 1986), pp. 95–6.

18. Thomas Coats, 'Account of the Present State of the Township of Lony', *Transactions of the Literary Society of Bombay* (1823) vol. 3, p. 183.

19. Sardesai, *Selections*, vol. 31, pp. 80–1.

20. V.G. Khobrekar (ed.), *Records of the Shivaji Period* (Bombay 1974), pp. 92–3.

21. R.V. Oturkar, *Peshvekalin Samajik va Arthik Patravyavahar* (Pune 1950), p. 24.

22. *Watan* is a term difficult to translate—the term was usually applied to an exclusive hereditary claim to render service and receive emoluments,

23. Oturkar, *Peshvekalin Samajik*, p. 67. He responded with abuse, and was fined and punished.

24. Molesworth compiled his dictionary in the 1820s, and it was revised in the middle of the nineteenth century. I have used the Shubdha–Saraswat reprint, Pune 1982.

25. For a full discussion of the village *watandari* system, see H.K. Fukazawa, *The Medieval Deccan—Peasants, Social Systems and States*, chapter 8.

26. Case cited by H.K. Fukazawa, in ibid., pp. 213–5.

27. *Selections from the Baroda State Records* (Baroda 1934), vol. 1, p. 7.

28. Pawar, *Tarabaikalina Kagadpatren*, vol. 1, p. 230.

29. This document was published by V.K. Rajvade in *Bharata Itihasa Samshodhaka Mandala* (henceforth *BISMT*), *Chaturtha Sammelanvritta*, pp. 56–7. It purports to be a copy of a decision made around the time of the legendary famine of 1396–1408, but it is almost certainly a later fabrication. The fact that such documents came to be fabricated is (in my view) significant in itself.

30. Gune, *The Judicial System of the Marathas*, p. 355.

31. N.G. Chapekar, 'Chiplonkar', *BISMT*, vol. 6, nos 1–4, 1925–6, pp. 133–4.

32. A petition to the Gaikwad of Baroda from the peasants of a famine-stricken tract states matter-of-factly, 'we have subsisted up till now by selling our children and cattle …'

33. The phrase is a cryptic one; *Natakshala sati gelya*, literally 'The dancing-hall went to immolation.' The chronicle also records the strenuous (and successful)

effort to prevent the legitimate queen Daryabai from following their example. K.N. Sane (ed.), *Kavyetihasa Sangraha* (1885), no. 16, p. 79.

34. Oturkar, *Peshvekalin Samajik*, pp. 65–6.

35. Manwaring, *Marathi Proverbs*, no. 1424.

36. He tried to extort an extra fee by beating the groom, who complained so the whole matter came on record. Sardesai, *Selections from the Peshwa Daftar*, vol. 43, pp. 3–4.

37. *SSRPD*, vol. 8, pp. 259–60.

38. V.V. Khare, *Aitihasik Lekhasangraha*, part 7 (Miraj 1912), pp. 3680–1.

39. Sardesai, *Selections from the Peshwa Daftar*, vol. 43, p. 52.

40. *SSRPD*, vol. 2, pt. 2, p. 67.

41. Oturkar, *Peshvekalin Samajik*, pp. 92–3.

42. Ibid., p. 96.

43. V.K. Rajvade, *Marathyanchya Itihasanchi Sadhanen*, 24 vols (Pune 1909), MIS, vol. 6, pp. 7–8.

44. *SSRPD*, vol. 7, pt. 2, p. 171.

45. Chapekar, *Chiplonkar*, pp. 133–4.

46. An undated report from an official in charge of distributing charity on behalf of the peshwa states that he had been instructed to bestow alms to the mendicants and holy men accompanying the government cavalry, but they were few. But a great uproar was being created by the throng of women beggars, including many widows. He was instructed not to give alms to the latter unless the distribution to Brahmans, both men and women, was complete, and something was left over. Sardesai, ed., *Selections*, vol. 43, p. 97.

47. Ibid., vol. 42, pp. 56–7.

48. Vad (ed.), *SSRPD*, vol. 8, p. 259.

49. Ibid., vol. 7, pt. 2, p, 244.

50. Thomas Coats, 'Notes Respecting the Trial by Punchiet …'

51. T.S. Shejwalkar (ed.), *Nagpur Affairs* (Poona 1959) vol. 2, p. 312.

52. Vad et al., *Decisions from the Shahu and Peshwa Daftar*, p. 34.

53. Gune, *Judicial System of the Marathas*, p. 353.

54. See Note 32.

55. See D. Symington, *Report on the Condition of Aboriginal Tribes* (Bombay 1938), pp. 12, 41–2.

56. *SSRPD*, vol. 1, p. 111.

57. Ibid., p. 187.

58. Ibid., p. 115.

59. *Historical Papers of the Sindhias of Gwalior 1774–1794*, Satara Historical Society (Satara 1934), vol. I, p. 36.

60. Sardesai, *Selections*, vol. 41, pp. 18–19.

61. M.T. Clanchy, 'Remembering the Past and the Good Old Law', *History* no. 184, 1970.

62. For a telling critique of Dumont, however, see A. Beteille, 'Homo Hierarchies, Homo Aequalis', *Modern Asian Studies*, vol. 13, 1979, pp. 529–48.

63. See the excellent description provided in Gune, *Judicial System*, chapter 4.

64. Scarcely a week passes without the vigorous exercise of such rights some-where. For example, a riot in Calcutta because a professor is caught for travelling without a ticket (*Statesman*, New Delhi, 25 September 1994, p. 6) or the Delhi High Court having to intervene to protect judicial officers at the Shahdara courts from intimidation by lawyers (*Indian Express*, New Delhi, 22 September 1994, p. 4) and seventy persons injured during riots in Bangladesh as the right to cheat in examinations is reaffirmed (*Guardian*, London, 15 July 1995, p. 14).

2

Bandit as King*

Malavika Kasturi

[...]

[A]n analysis of most stories relating to Rajput bandits suggests that blood feuds, enmities, rebellion against the state for confiscation of rights, loss of land, and economic hardship appear to have been the commonest causes for banditry. Many British officials, including the resident of Gwalior, were unable to understand the manifold and complex reasons fuelling 'Rajput banditry',[1] which they assumed was driven by 'pride, laziness and poverty',[2] or was the choice of men addicted to plunder as an 'honourable' pastime. The evidence suggests that the linkages between banditry and the economy, power, and politics were varied and complex, as were the targets and goals of Rajput bandits.

British policy-makers viewed 'Rajput banditry' as a law and order problem and a direct threat to British 'paramountcy' from the beginning of the nineteenth century. Their explanation for banditry was devoid of specifications of time, place, and linkages to politics, society, and the economy. For the lineages under study, brigandage constituted merely one strategy of self-expression in the language of violence,

* This essay was originally published as 'The Bandit as King' in Malavika Kasturi, *Embattled Identities: Rajput Lineages and the Colonial State in Nineteenth-century North India* (New Delhi: Oxford University Press, 2002), pp. 200–28.

rebellion, and lineage identity; its complexity slipped through most colonial records in which bandits were primarily viewed as criminals. Plundering and raiding, part of a specific strategy utilized by lineages to augment resources, negotiate power, and reinforce honour, were practical and culture-specific political responses to pre-existing structures and codes of authority. Its elite nature and its connections with state-building and *bhumeawat* (rebellion) in the pre-colonial and colonial period defined Rajput banditry and determined its modus operandi and success.

The general literature dealing with brigandage has been influenced by the notion of 'social banditry'. In this schema, banditry is perceived as a form of 'primitive rebellion' occurring in pre-capitalist societies in which bandits, as robbers of a special kind, were regarded as outlaws and delinquents by the state and supported and revered by the peasant community as heroes and avengers.[3] However, Rajput *dakaiti* (banditry) does not fit this analytical model even if, at times, it seems to share some of its superficial features. By and large, Rajput *dakait*s had elite origins, preying on the lower classes traditionally protected by bandits fitting into the 'Robin Hood' mould—with whom they shared a relationship based on coercion, co-operation, and ties of allegiance. Peasants, who feared rather than revered the bandits, were the prime targets of attack. Likewise, *mahajan*s (bankers) were both allies as well as victims of the bandits.[4] Rajput brigands were usually perceived as *baghi*s or rebels with a cause by members of their own lineage whose support implicitly legitimized banditry.[5] In return, dakaits, who were usually quite indiscriminate, killing and looting all who came in their way, steered clear of settlements inhabited by their own clansmen and friends.[6] Needless to add, bandits attacked other Rajputs with whom they were involved in feuds.

The theory of social banditry is also predicated on the notion that plunder is largely the resort of communities undergoing economic stress and decline. Economic determinants, I argue, while extremely important, had a varying relationship with *thakur* (Rajput landholder) brigandage, which was rooted in its own cultural dynamic—bhumeawat. Interestingly, the history of Rajput 'outlawry' in the precolonial period indicates that powerful lineages, unlike 'social bandits', took to dakaiti, which overlapped with bhumeawat, in periods of growth and political expansion as well as economic decline. Rajput *biradaris* (brotherhoods) often resorted to depradation to wage war against the centralized authority or to broaden their resource base and power to such an extent that they were able to found independent polities. Subsequently, many of these new kingdoms, which were perched on a precarious agrarian base, depended partly on plunder. The political processes relating to state-building, therefore, mediated the relationship between economic variables and Rajput dakaiti. Economic crises merely aggravated the reasons why élite groups took to plunder.

Bandits were closely linked to the power structures spawning and supporting them. The success of brigands in pre-colonial India depended on the support extended to them by local rajas and zamindars. Evidence suggests that princely rulers often used bandit gangs in power struggles and partook of the proceeds of plunder. [...]
[...]

While its pre-colonial origins are important, the reasons behind Rajput dakaiti in nineteenth-century north India are unique, as they are structured by the colonial context. As part of bhumeawat, such 'outlawry' was part of the multi-layered response by Rajput biradaris at both ends of the economic spectrum to the fundamental transformations taking place in political and social relations in agrarian society under British rule. Thus, dakaiti often had a political and cultural edge in a political and economic environment in which powerful biradaris, rich and poor, attempted to redefine their identity and status and negotiate their authority vis-à-vis each other, the colonial state, and other social groups. Banditry was lent a meaning in a litigious environment generated by changes in land tenures, property rights, and the rise in land sales in and after the 1830s. Dakaiti, then, as previously, did not always constitute the knee-jerk reaction of groups undergoing economic hardship. This is not to suggest that economic decline did not play an important role in fuelling banditry. Indeed, the loss of land and impoverishment due to bad seasons and famines provoked short-term participation by poor Rajput zamindars and cultivators pushed to the edge in grain riots, dakaitis, and other acts of rebellion in north India. The contraction of *naukari* (service) also played a fundamental role in impelling many Rajputs in north India, described variously in records as 'starving men-at-arms' and 'bold freelance soldiers', to take to banditry. Economic, political, and cultural variables, in various permutations and combinations, provided the dynamic for dakaiti.

From the inception of British rule, revolts involving plunder by Rajput magnates against the East India Company occurred in most parts of north India. Dakaiti and bhumeawat interpenetrated in 1842 and then again in 1857, when bandits such as Diwan Despat and Raghunath Singh gathered armies and joined hands with regional rebel leaders to fight the British. These movements were much wider in scope, nature, and impact than any of the earlier stray revolts against British rule. After 1857, the state, which expanded its coercive and administrative machinery, cracked down on threats to 'law and order'. Efforts were made to set severe limits to the expression of the 'wild' and 'primitive' aspects of Rajput martial culture, except in areas at the margins of colonial rule such as Bundelkhand. While accurate figures are not available for the period before 1857, after that year there were so many outbreaks involving thakurs in Bundelkhand that special anti-dakaiti operations were carried out between 1858 and 1875, 1880 and 1885, and 1890 and 1893. This is in complete contrast to the rest of the provinces, where, while 'affrays' continued to occur, the extent of Rajput dakaiti was more or less contained by the 1860s.

In British Bundelkhand, at the height of the anti-dakaiti operations in the late nineteenth century, Rajput dakaiti took on special characteristics. As elsewhere, a combination of economic and political reasons influenced the biradaris of this region to take to plunder. The expansion of Company power in this region, which was slower than in other parts of the North Western Provinces, created a situation ripe for unrest, for memories of conquest were still raw. The upsurge in banditry during this period may also be related to the long-term structural economic crisis, which set in by the 1840s, partly due to the decline in the external demand for cotton as a commercial crop. After this period, the region was gradually transformed into one of the poorest and most ecologically vulnerable parts of the provinces.[7] By this point, there had also been a great decline in Rajput power, position, and status due to the shifts in proprietary rights and the contraction of the resource base. The dwindling of opportunities to participate in the military labour market hit this region particularly

hard, as the Bundelas were bypassed in the recruitment drives for the
Company army. Increasingly, the British did not even pretend to take
any interest in Bundelkhand, which they perceived as a marginalized
zone in more ways than one. Rajput dakaits, many of whom were
from powerful and influential lineages, were leaders of skeletal gangs
that filled out during the cycles of death and distress that plagued the
region. Between 1869 and 1877,[8] and in 1889 and 1892, for example,
a series of extremely bad harvests[9] led to a steep increase in 'heinous
crime' in the Jhansi division.[10] The Bundelkhand 'outbreak' of 1891
was a product of this period. The fear of Rajput banditry during
times of scarcity dictated famine relief in both British territories
and some princely states, particularly Bundelkhand and Gwalior by
the 1890s.[11]

Whether or not the Rajputs of this region survived the fallout of
multiple social and economic stresses depended on a variety of local
circumstances and perceptions of influence and status. Thus, powerful biradaris in straitened circumstances who would not endure the
stigma of undertaking manual labour, were the most likely to take to
banditry. Further, the association of banditry with bhumeawat made
it an 'honourable calling' which the thakurs pursued with 'pride', for
it was an accepted means of asserting their power, identity, and rank,
and adding to their resources.[12] Under trying circumstances, the
response of many Bundela biradaris, observed the superintendent of
Chanderi, was 'either condescend to a lower estate, or plunder, the
first is beneath their dignity, the second is considered an occupation,
and not only profitable, but gentlemanly'.[13] Not surprisingly, then,
the Rajputs of Bundelkhand participated with greater intensity in
bhumeawat in all forms, especially dakaiti.

British attitudes towards dakaits were rooted in a unique set of
imperatives. Unlike its pre-colonial predecessors who had found
bandits useful, the colonial state did not make deals with Rajput bandits. Dakaiti, like *thugi*, was perceived as dangerous to British power
and security from the early nineteenth century, and was presented
by officials as an overwhelming threat, to be speedily eradicated. In
this manner the notion of the 'dacoit menace' was born in official
discourse, to be followed by the creation of the Thugi and Dacoity
Department.[14] The British also sought to contain agrarian violence

and banditry through an aggressive policy of disarmament, demilitarization, the passage of the Arms Act, and police and judicial reforms. In Bundelkhand, however, the weakness of the colonial administration and law, together with the proximity of the princely states strengthened the ties of kinship, patronage, and alliance that sheltered 'outlaws'. British policies towards brigandage were also influenced by the fact that for many dominant biradaris here, dakaiti constituted a form of political rebellion against an alien state that had denuded them of power.

THE COLONIAL STATE AND EARLY ATTITUDES TOWARDS DAKAITI

From the early nineteenth century, the British designated as 'criminal' all mobile groups they saw as vagrant, dangerous, and predatory, lacking the 'attractive, familiar, and desirable virtues of settled peasants'.[15] Changing notions of territoriality and power also contributed to official conceptions of criminality. Therefore, Rajputs, who ignored the boundaries separating 'British' districts from the princely states, aroused great suspicion. Colonial officials, who earmarked mobile Rajput bandit gangs for special attention, argued that the containment of the 'system of depredation' depended on encouraging agricultural expansion and the forcible sedenterization of semi-peripatetic groups.[16] In 1863, the settlement officer of Lalitpur asserted that 'the peace and the prosperity of the district depend on the mass of the agricultural population being content and well-to-do; when food and clothing are plentiful at home, the Boondela will think twice before he takes to the jungle and the Aheers will not be so prone to cattle lifting'.[17]

Otherwise, the British argued, these biradaris would make 'the minds of the quiet and well disposed uneasy',[18] since they disrupted the lives of those engaged in fruitful and productive occupations such as tilling the land. Officials were clear that Rajput bandits were to be curbed, disciplined, and rooted within bounded and defined spaces.

The evolution of British attitudes towards mobile Rajput bandit gangs may be viewed against the backdrop of official attitudes towards both thugi (according to colonial perceptions, the ritual strangling and murder of wayfarers) and dakaiti. Until the 1830s, local magistrates and the police dealt with cases of dakaiti.[19] The Thugi and Dacoity Department, on the other hand, focused exclusively on those called *thugs* (stranglers) in official discourse, who were perceived as the more significant source of danger.[20] In 1839, this policy was defended on the grounds that thugi and dakaiti needed to be tackled separately, for they were different types of offences. In this context the general superintendent of Thugi and Dacoity observed that otherwise these crimes would

> be too much blended one in the other to afford any line of distinction sufficiently clear for our purpose ... and deprive ourselves of the prospect we now have of employing sufficiently the means which providence by a happy combination of circumstances, seems to have placed at our disposal ...[21]

The Company finally turned its attention to dakaiti in the late 1830s, drawing its inspiration from its thugi legislation. Official conspiracy theories about 'hereditary' fraternities of dakaits spread throughout the country in an 'organized system of depredation' mirrored earlier fevered descriptions of structured *phansigar* (strangler) gangs. The recognition of the exact differences between thug and dakaiti, if any, remained unclear in the official imagination. In this period, many supposed hereditary thug communities, such as the Kanjars, Buddhuks, and Sansiyas, began to reappear in departmental records as dakaits as the Company's interest in the thugi campaign waned.[22] In a manner reminiscent of the exercises undertaken against the thugs, registers of famous dakaits and gang members were prepared with details of their parentage, caste, age, and residence.[23] To aid magistrates and the Thugi and Dacoity Department, efforts were made to gather as much information as possible on bandits. Further, by Act XXIV of 1843, all offenders convicted of belonging to a gang of dakaits were liable to transportation for life and/or imprisonment with hard labour. The Act also made receipt of stolen property a punishable crime.[24] By the 1850s, dakaiti was considered of such importance that magistrates in the North Western Provinces were asked, in their half-yearly statements on crime, to give complete details of all 'outrages' taking place in their respective districts and the caste of all bandits.[25]

Most dakaits, in the manner of the thugs before them, were mistakenly considered 'habitual' and 'hereditary' gang robbers. Not surprisingly, attempts to differentiate between 'professional' dakait castes and 'ordinary' bandit gangs was difficult in view of evidence indicating that bandits belonged to a multiplicity of castes and communities.[26] Nevertheless, this mode of classifying bandits was not given up in official records. As regards Rajput biradaris, although officials asserted that many thakurs followed dakaiti as a 'profession', pursued by both fathers and sons,[27] they refused to classify the entire social group as 'hereditary' bandits, in deference to their position as powerful landholding élites. As members of 'non-professional' dakait gangs, Rajputs were arrested only on charges of specific acts of robbery.[28] Moreover, to convict individual Rajput prisoners, accurate information regarding gang membership and participation in dakaitis was deemed necessary.[29] As most bandits usually preyed simultaneously on several districts in north India, evidence to convict them was hard to collect. Matters were complicated as the police and *thanadars* (inspectors) protected dakaits in return for a percentage of their booty. In most cases, magistrates could not secure convictions against whole gangs, while those bandits who gave a guarantee to the state for their good behaviour after the completion of their sentences, often abused the privilege.[30] The colonial state fought many battles with Rajput zamindars, who either belonged to bandit gangs, or harboured dakaits on their estates.

Drawing upon the anti-thugi programme, the evidence of approvers was increasingly used to nail bandits.[31] Men turned state approvers for a number of reasons, including anger at betrayal by old friends.[32] If subordinate members of gangs were important as potential sources of information,[33] greater efforts were made to convince leaders of gangs, who were in the greatest danger of harsh sentences if convicted, to turn approvers.[34] Approvers were useful for solving all cases, even those considered closed.[35] For example, in 1841, Dulloo, son of Sewa Singh Rajput, pointed out the hiding place of four men who murdered a thakur landholder in Rampur in 1834, and who had since been hiding in Moradabad. In return for this information, Dulloo petitioned that the rest of his tenure in jail be shortened.[36] From the 1840s, dakait approvers were exempted from sentences of death and transportation for life if they testified against their associates.[37] After their release, some Rajput approvers such as Aman Singh became *barkandazes* (matchlockmen), stalking their old comrades.[38] Others were at grave risk from their gang mates, especially those they had betrayed.

Dakaities across boundaries, posed specific dilemmas for the colonial state throughout our period. Mainpuri, Etawa, Farrukhabad, Kanpur, Agra, Gorukhpur, Shajahanpur, and large parts of the Jhansi division were prey to bandit visitations from Awadh, Gwalior, and the Bundela states. As bhumeawat occurred near the boundaries between British and 'princely' territories, these areas were always potentially open to 'disturbances'. Often, even after the concerned durbar acceded to the demands of the Rajput magnates involved in uprisings, the latter refused to disband their impromptu armies, which were thereafter maintained by plundering expeditions in British districts.[39] In 1847, the collector of Allahabad noted that banditry had been restricted in all parts of the district, except the areas bordering Awadh. Here, most Rajput dakaits were either residents of Awadh, or inhabitants of Allahabad, who took advantage of the facilities of easy escape across porous boundaries.[40] Until Awadh was annexed in 1856, men such as Bhagwant Singh and Daulat Singh laid siege to the British districts.[41] Further, official records in the 1850s were full of references to cross-border 'criminal confederations' existing between groups such as the Bhadauriyas of Gwalior and their relatives in Etawa, Mainpuri, and Fatehgarh, who participated together in local feuds and expeditions of plunder in British territories.[42] The magistrate of Etawa, for example, received many complaints of 'combinations' of bandit leaders across the frontier and local Bhadauriya landholders, who took revenge on their neighbours, including moneylenders, by destroying bonds and account books.[43] Along most borders, Rajput zamindars protected thakur bandits from a sense of honour and with a view to their own security.[44]

The clashing of jurisdictions and the technicalities of law often set at naught efforts to catch bandits across boundaries. Political agents in all princely states were authorized to put down frontier dakaiti.[45] However, such a policy was problematic for many 'native' states refused to cooperate with British magistrates to trap bandits preying across borders. Further, compact states such as Awadh, which could defray the costs of dakaiti campaigns in a way that was not possible in Gwalior (a princely kingdom whose territorial boundaries overlapped with that of other polities), often refused to acknowledge as their citizens bandits who lived nomadic lives.[46] After the Great Rebellion, to a large extent, Rajput banditry was brought under control within the centralized administrative zones of the North Western Provinces. However, districts bordering 'foreign' states, especially Bundelkhand, remained hotbeds of Rajput banditry.

THE ANTI-DAKAITI CAMPAIGN IN BRITISH BUNDELKHAND AND THE CHAMBAL VALLEY

The interaction of specific political, cultural, and economic variables in Bundelkhand put pressure on pre-existing subsistence patterns so that banditry took centre-stage in the nineteenth century as other options were gradually closed to the biradaris of the region.[47] The issue was further complicated in 1857, when Bundelkhand went into rebellion. At that point, the Rajputs were able to build up a successful revolt against the colonial state. After British counter-insurgency measures weakened the rebel stand, they swelled the bands of 'outlaws' in the ravines.[48] Bandits in this region cooperated in large measure with dakaits in princely states, so that official concern about Rajput 'outlaws' spilt over the boundaries of British territory into the adjoining princely states of Bundelkhand and Gwalior. These areas had a long tradition of banditry centred around the Chambal, Pahuj, and Scinde rivers in Kachwahaghar, Bhandere, and Chanderi, for the social geography of the region was conducive to banditry. The rugged terrain and ravines cut by the Chambal and Pahuj rivers had been for centuries the favourite haunt of 'outlaws' in and around Gwalior.[49] As gangs assembled in the ravines from all over and made periodic forays into other parts of Gwalior as well as nearby British districts, this area was targeted by the Gwalior troops and the Thugi and Dacoity Department.[50] The anti-dakaiti programme in this area peaked between 1880 and 1893. Similar operations were conducted in the Bundela states, where a special agent for the suppression of dakaiti for Bundelkhand was appointed to coordinate all affairs dealing with the 'outbreak' which took place between 1890 and 1893.[51] Now, the British redoubled their efforts to guard the areas bordering the 'native' states. In all vulnerable zones, they watched ghats, strengthened police posts, and established an effective system of patrol, while they gave arms of a superior nature to the border protection forces.[52]

In Gwalior, the British were convinced that a want of efficient control and supervision combined with corruption and laxity on the part of officials had contributed to the lawlessness of Rajput zamindars and their followers. As in the British districts, the thrust of punitive actions here was lost because many local officers and *amils* (district revenue official) were corrupt. In 1839 itself, one of Scindia's amils in Bhilsa was accused of participating in dakaitis and of being allied with bandits he was supposed to apprehend.[53] In 1840, amils, zamindars, and approvers were instructed that their sole duty consisted of hunting for brigands and giving the durbar intimations of their places of abode and their movements.[54] These men were, however, unable to resist the wealth and power of bandit leaders.

Despite the best efforts of the durbar and the Thugi and Dacoity Department, brigandage was not eradicated. This is not to suggest that vigorous action was lacking. By May 1886, the durbar established posts garrisoned by their regular troops in most places under attack by thakurs and put pressure on local *amildar*s (revenue officials) and other government officials. Many gangs scattered all about the country as people increasingly began to give information about their movements.[55] Pitched battles were often fought between the special dakaiti police and outlaws. 'Outlaws' whose grievances were perceived as real were conciliated and granted amnesties. Sometimes, famous fugitives were given back their old possessions in the hope that they would forswear banditry. But offers of amnesties held out to outlaws were not trusted after Mazbut Singh, a prominent dakait, was induced to come in on a promise of pardon and then shot down. This act of 'treachery' incensed the thakurs and neutralized the efforts of the durbar.[56] Further, regions bordering on Bundelkhand remained vulnerable. In the Chanderi pargana in Isagarh, out of seventy-five villages, thirty-six settlements were at the mercy of bandits between 1880 and 1888.[57] This tract had always had a reputation for being infested with bandits, even when it had been under the control of the *subadar* (governor) of Jhansi and the British government in an earlier period.

The stern measures carried out under the aegis of the Thugi and Dacoity Department in central India were neutralized by British policies towards the princely states. In kingdoms such as Gwalior, for example, by supporting the rights of the thakurs to revolt against the durbar, the British encouraged bhumeawat and banditry. The rights of criminal jurisdiction of durbars were severely restricted within their territories and were mediated by British political agents. Consequently, most princely states were not particularly well-equipped to deal with brigandage, given the concomitant decline of their judicial and administrative apparatus.[58] Also, since borders and jurisdictions were intermixed, the British police found it difficult to pursue 'marauders' into the Bundela states. Despite the treaties signed with the rajas and *jagirdar*s (holders of military assignments of land) of Bundelkhand regarding the extradition of 'outlaws', the princes flouted promises violating kinship, community, and political alignments of the region.

The British grappled with brigandage with varying degrees of success in their own territories. Before 1857, the colonial state marched against semi-independent Rajput lineages in British Bundelkhand when they engaged in plunder. Zamindars in this region were induced to help the state hunt for bandits and in return were rewarded in various ways by being given swords, *khilat*s (insignia of honour), and *sanad*s (contract).[59] In 1893, after the 'disarmament' of Bundelkhand, a promulgation declared that 'every person in British India aware of the commission of a dakaiti, or of the intention of any other native Indian subject of Her Majesty to commit such an offence beyond the limits of British India' was liable to persecution under the terms of the Indian Penal Code.[60] However, as laws and regulations regarding 'disarmament' were not rigidly enforced in the Jhansi division, and given that the colonial coercive machinery was weaker here than elsewhere in the North Western Provinces, dakaits found the frontier friendly territory. The impact of the state judicial and coercive machinery was less able to penetrate local society in such zones.

British Bundelkhand, in particular, was used as a base by Rajput bandits from the 'native' states, but fewer incidents of plunder occurred here, as dakaits found it difficult to have enemies on both sides of the border.[61] Between 1889 and 1893, 233 dakaitis took place during the 'Bundelkhand outbreak' in the Bundela states. Colonial officials were horrified to find that ninety-one of the 114 men convicted in the Bundelkhand Agency between 1889 and 1893 were residents of

British territory.[62] Kulpahar, Jaitpur, and Jhijhan in Hamirpur, Padra
and Deori in Jhansi (the latter on the banks of the Dassan) were popular hideouts, often sheltering wanted bandit leaders such as Durgai
Lodhi, Sultan Singh, and Hirdi Sah, all of whom were residents of one
or the other of the princely states. Some gangs were so confident of
protection that they went openly about their business in the villages
in which they sought shelter. After successful ventures, dance and
thanksgiving festivals were held by the *gole* (bandit gangs). Pujas and
sat narain kathas (story of Vishnu) took place, the expenses for which
were defrayed by the charity fund created by keeping aside a certain
amount of the loot for the purpose. On such occasions, Brahmins and
priests were fed, religious texts based on the life of Vishnu were read
out to listeners, and collections of money made. The celebrations were
usually brought to an end with a huge feast. The loot was disposed
of through an accredited medium, usually the local *bania* (moneylender) while the villagers freely gave supplies of arms, ammunition,
and clothes were freely given to the bandits.[63] One of the principal
aims of the agent in charge of the special operations against dakaiti in
1890 was to apprehend the allies of the bandits in the Jhansi division
by stationing special police in settlements harbouring 'outlaws'. At the
height of the anti-dakait movement, an informer came upon Durg
Singh, the nephew of Raghunath Singh (an infamous Bundela bandit
who long eluded capture), collecting *mahuwa* (a local plant) at night,
for it was not possible to get food from villages under surveillance
in the Jhansi Division.[64] These measures went hand in hand with the
stern punishment of those captured, including transportation for life
or even death. Nevertheless, it was soon clear that dakait gangs, supported by a network of kinship and service alliances, were 'not to be
picked up like peafowl around a village'.[65] Such ties put a spoke in the
wheel of the anti-dakaiti measures.

DAKAITI AND KINSHIP

British officials argued that the timeless ties of alliance and kinship
was among the principal reasons that enabled thakur lineages to hold
out against the coercive apparatus of the colonial state. While it is true
that kinship and familial bonds were significant in the articulation of

identity, they had, nevertheless, a dynamic of their own. Further, such ties were reconstituted over time as they interacted with numerous variables. In north India, kinship and lineage networks were constantly negotiating with and defining themselves against state power both prior to and during colonial rule. Amongst Rajput biradaris in Bundelkhand, the hierarchical ties of kinship and dependence probably grew in importance in the nineteenth century as one of the primary mechanisms for the assertion and articulation of rank, power, and domination. These ties shaped the ambivalent attitudes of various social groups towards 'landlord' bandits in agrarian society. The colonial state was soon involved in a tussle with kinship and community bonds while formulating policies to contain Rajput banditry.

Dakaits evaded capture for long periods, not least of the reasons being the loyalty and support of kinsmen. The power exercised by Rajput landowners-turned-bandits within local society was based on the bonds amongst extended kinship networks dispersed over a wide area. As early as 1838 it was observed that there was every reason to believe that 'our dacoit subjects do not exclusively commit dacoities in our territories or that the dacoit subjects of other states confine their illegal depredations to the territories of their states'.[65] During the outbreak of banditry in Lalitpur district in 1890, the general superintendent of Operations for the Suppression of Thugi and Dacoity observed that there was also 'marked excitement' amongst the Bundelas of Orchha. He concluded that as these thakurs were generally 'of the same race and brotherhood', it was hardly surprising that 'the spirit of violence and disorder excited' in one locality should have communicated itself by 'contagion' to the other district.[66]

The Bundelas, Chandelas, and Panwars, who were involved in banditry, intermarried with one another. This worked to their advantage: as Sleeman noted, these biradaris ' ... are linked together by family ties and assist each other on all occasions and in none so readily as in their bhoomeawuts'.[67] Both active and passive support was extended to an outlawed Rajput by his biradari. According to the district superintendent of police of Lalitpur:

At present any Thakoor who falls into debt or who commits a crime for which he is liable to arrest, settles the matter by walking off into the jungle, where collecting a band of followers he lives by plundering, and protected and fed by his nominally faithful brethren defies all our efforts to arrest him.[68]

The entire Bundela biradari in Lalitpur was aware when any member of their community became a bandit, for their sanction was obtained and their support assured.[69] When Jaswant Singh of Dilwara became a dakait before his creditors had him jailed for debt, the biradari closed ranks behind him as it was a matter affecting their local power and standing. At a panchayat it was decided that Jaswant Singh should commit bhumeawat and that the other Rajputs would assist him in any way possible.[70] According to the Deputy Commissioner of Lalitpur, in 1863 although of old standing and influence, Dilwara was 'crumbling to pieces and though these men hold their heads high enough they are poorer than many of their poorer neighbours, with subdivided fields and few resources to share'.[71]

The complicity of the Rajputs with dakaits was so well known that when land belonging to proclaimed outlaws was put up for sale, no outsider bid for the shares concerned.[72] Many brotherhoods furnished their quota of men to various gangs, although they would not necessarily participate in banditry themselves. In return, they were entitled to a share of the loot. In addition, biradaris either turned a blind eye to the activities of the bandits or offered them food and succour. By giving information to the district authorities, they would have deprived themselves of any profit they hoped to reap.[73] Not surprisingly, betrayals largely occurred when unresolved feuds and disputes existed between the parties concerned.

The case of the Toria jagirdars indicates in many ways how Rajput kinship loyalties influenced banditry and provided a support network to dakaits. In the late eighteenth century, Arjun Singh, the grandfather of Despat and Nanneh Diwan (well-known bandits) and the jagirdar of both Jhijhan and Toria near Kulpahar, had his rights guaranteed by the Marathas after a period of initial resistance.[74] When the rights of the peshwa in Bundelkhand were transferred to the East India Company, the latter confirmed the sanads of all chiefs and jagirdars found in possession of proprietary rights. It seems that the Company returned Jhijhan to Arjun Singh in *lambardari* (revenue system), for in the first settlement of Hamirpur in 1833, Nirpat Singh, son of Arjun Singh, was *lambardar* (revenue payer on behalf of small landholders) of Jhijhan.[75]

The participation of subsequent generations of the Toria brotherhood in banditry owed much to economic pressures, the loss of ancestral property, and private feuds. After Jawahar Singh, son of Nirpat Singh and older brother of Despat and Nanneh Diwan, inherited the estate, the family fortunes declined. The jagir was in the least prosperous part of Hamirpur in Panwari pargana. By the 1830s, over half the uninhabited villages in Hamirpur were in this area. The famines of 1833–4 and 1837–8 had devastating effects on landlords and tenants. Since he was in straitened circumstances, Jawahar Singh gave up his lambardari to one Mohan Chaube, who soon appropriated all the ancestral rights of the family and refused the Toria jagirdars the rights to *jalkar, phulkar*, and *bankar* (water, fruit, and jungles).[76] According to local tradition, Chaube persecuted the family to such a degree that in 1847 or 1848 he was murdered by Despat, one of Jawahar Singh's younger brothers. Despat also killed Nanneh and Sardar Ghaube, *pattidar*s (proprietor in co-sharing village) and relatives of Mohan Choube. He subsequently fled and became an outlaw.

In 1857, Despat attracted many Bundelas to his camp and became the leader of a large band. He assisted the armies of Nana Sahib and the widow of Parichat, the late raja of Jaitpur, amongst others. Despat was killed in 1863 by the *purohit* (priest) of Dhoni, in Chattarpur, who was hiding some of the plunder collected by Despat and had every interest in getting him out of the way. After his death, his younger brother Nanneh Diwan and his nephew, Kunjal Shah, took up the feud against Despat's enemies. These two men had been with Despat's band when he was killed. One of their first acts was to murder Mohan Lal, the brother of Mohan Ghaube. Their gole committed no less than sixteen dakaitis until Nanneh Dewan was killed in 1865 and Kunjal Shah in January 1866.[77]

In 1866 the district superintendent of Hamirpur hoped that:

> … no further trouble may now be anticipated from any of the members of this turbulent family which has for so many years now furnished leaders to the factious and discontented amongst the Boondelas in these parganas … it is well understood that under our Government,

bhoomeantee is not the safe and profitable career that it used to be under native rulers; and the Boondelas have fully realised the fact that the British authorities will allow of no compromise, or offer any terms, save those of unconditional surrender and submission.[78]

Nevertheless, the relationship between banditry, feuds, and bhumeawat among the Toria biradari remained a close one after Raghunath Singh, another of Despat's nephews, became a brigand. Raghunath Singh himself was a resident of Jaitpur pargana in Hamirpur. At a meeting of the panchayat, his biradari decided that he should become an outlaw since the government had refused to make any provisions for the widow of Nanneh Dewan.[79] Raghunath Singh's career began in October 1867; he carried on the family feud against the betrayers of Despat when he killed Mehilal, the *pundit* (priest) of Dohni, who had turned informer.[80]

Officials hoped that after the capture of Raghunath Singh in 1868, the spirit of 'turbulence' that had 'excited' the Toria family had been finally curbed. They believed that the example made of Raghunath Singh, who had been transported to the Andamans, would work to good effect on those who had in the past resorted to dakaiti to put pressure on the state to grant them favours. Additionally, to 'purchase peace and immunity', the state settled an annual allowance on the Toria biradari. However, none of these ploys worked.[81] In the 1890s, Durg Singh, a nephew of Raghunath Singh, ventured into the old 'family profession' which the colonial state had hoped the Toria family had forsworn for good.[82] The pattern set by the biradari ensured that resistance to the colonial state was passed from one generation to the next. As the subsequent section indicates, the challenge posed by such lineages was heightened by the local support they generated.

THE UNIVERSE OF DAKAITI

A study of the composition of bandit gangs indicates that while they consisted of men belonging to various communities, Rajputs usually constituted the backbone of these groups.[83] The leaders were invariably Rajputs. Of course, there were exceptions to this rule. Durgai Lodhi rose to be a leader in his own right after serving in two

Rajput goles led by Pahalwan Singh of Bhandere and Parbat Singh of
Lalitpur. After 1890, he formed a gang of his own, chiefly composed of
Bagpura Rajputs from Bijawar.[84] Gangs usually consisted of a core of
trusted companions and periodically contracted or swelled depending
on the numbers willing to join them on marauding expeditions. In
Bundelkhand, the existence of many boundary disputes, and thus of
numerous disgruntled thakurs, meant that dakaits experienced no
difficulties whatsoever in finding new recruits.[85]

Bandits received shares of loot depending on the role they played
in dakaitis[86] and their status[87] within the gang. All members of bandit
gangs were bound together by fictive ties of *bhaibandhi* (brotherhood).
The concept of bhaibandhi enabled the sympathizer and part-time
gang affiliates to define the boundaries of the group, and symbolically
signified brotherhood and a shared heritage among dakaits.[88] The
world of the bandits was divided into that of neutrals, helpers, and
opponents.[89] The followers of dakait leaders supported them in the
resolution of all disputes, past or present, but all this did not imply
that goles were monolithic entities. They were often divided into
factions headed by different leaders and broke up because of feuds
and rivalry.[90] The gang of a notorious Bundela bandit leader called
Bankaji contained five leaders subordinate to the former. While these
men committed robberies on their own account, they accompanied
Bankaji on important forays. After a while, this band broke up into
various parts, all of which had their own headquarters and leaders.[91]
Inter-gang fights were also common.

In most cases men were tied to bandit leaders by bonds of loyalty
and service, while others were forcibly recruited. Mazbut Singh of
Narwar, who was said to have thirty to forty men in his gang, had
about twelve regular members in his employment, who were mostly
Rajputs with firearms. The rest were Chamars who had been coerced
into service.[92] Sometimes, peasants joined gangs seduced by the
lure of plunder and adventure. In Bundelkhand as in other regions,
their participation in such activities depended on the vagaries of the
weather. It was quite common for cultivators to leave their fields in
slack agricultural seasons, between March and the middle of July until
the rains advanced, for the marauding life under one or the other of
the more notorious dakaits of the neighbourhood. Dakaiti increased

in bad seasons, but decreased in years of good harvests. The 'outbreak' of dakaiti between 1890 and 1893, for example, which coincided with a series of famines and droughts, put great pressure on the populace in comparison with earlier years and probably coincided with an increase in the size of gangs. In addition to Rajputs, Khanjars, Lodhis, Kolis, Chamars, Gosains, Mewatis, Gujars, Ahirs, and Gonds were some of the many communities represented in bandit gangs.[93] In addition, Rajput gangs also recruited members of the so-called 'criminal tribes'.[94] In the 1840s, Sleeman expressed his scepticism of any plan ignoring the role of the zamindars in controlling the activities of these robber gangs. The Criminal Tribes Act of 1871 also emphasized the role of landholders in keeping the 'criminal classes' in check. One of the reasons for the limited success of the Act was its inability to break the connection between the zamindars and those living on the fringes of society.

Even those who were not formally inducted into bandit goles offered them support for one reason or the other. The study of the forays of the Toria jagirdars (mentioned earlier) highlights the important role played by alliance and service networks in the world of bandits. Although the area was previously controlled by the Toria biradari and was held by other parties in 1869, the influence of the lineage does not seem to have declined.[95] Many peasant communities, including the Ahirs of the surrounding areas, were connected to the Toria jagirdars through bonds of service and dependence.[96] Local traditions, collected in 1867, which related that Nanneh Diwan's nurse was an Ahirin and all Ahirs were his foster brothers committed to his service, were proof of the continuing links between thakurs and the peasant castes.[97] Important members of Raghunath Singh's gang were Ahirs.[98] Such bonds were of special significance in a period during which the Rajputs sought to reassert their superior social and ritual rank in agrarian society in north India against all comers. In Bundelkhand, peasant communities did not challenge the social relations of domination and subordination to the same extent as their compatriots in other districts of the North Western Provinces.

Despat, Nanneh Diwan, and Raghunath Singh were related by ties of blood or bhaibandhi to almost every one of the ruling families of Bundelkhand. Consequently, they were at once a source of awe and

dread. In 1867, the inhabitants of Jhijhan and Lugasi, near the ancestral village of the Toria jagirdars, were charged a levy of one rupee per
plough to support Raghunath Singh and his band, which they paid
without resistance.[99] According to the magistrate of Hamirpur:

> … the Thakoors [Boondelahs] and Aheers as a general rule willingly
> assist and feed the dacoits, while those of other castes, Brahmins and
> Lodhies do so, usually, out of fear, and whereas in some cases their
> villages are small and situated in a large tract of forest, it is a little
> difficult for them to resist the claims of a band of armed men.[100]

The entire population of the area from Narwar in Gwalior to Jhansi
lived in abject fright. After sunset, all houses were closely fastened and
not one door was opened until sunrise. Every morning the chief men
in vulnerable villages would be seen issuing forth from the houses of
Chamars where they were accustomed to spending nights for fear of
being attacked in their own.[101]

In Bundelkhand, arguments in favour of not informing against a
locally dominant thakur were many, for if detected the lives of the
informer and his family were in danger. The enmity was often passed
down from one generation to the next of the aggrieved family until
revenge had been taken on the informer and those close to him.[102]
The power wielded by important Rajput landholders like the Raos of
Kakerbai was so immense that very few actually came forward to give
direct evidence against them.[103] In most of the Bundelkhand districts,
relations of obedience and respect were deeply structured. The close
ties between the Bundelas and the bandits, and the control exercised
by both parties over jungles in which tenants had rights to collect
wood and grass, added to Rajput influence. In Lalitpur the Rajputs
were especially powerful, for the district was isolated due to poor
communications. Hence, thickly forested areas like Belabehat were
especially difficult to penetrate. The police had little scope for success
in wooded territory far away from roads and footpaths. Supported
by their biradari and feared by other communities, the Bundelas did
pretty much as they pleased.[104]

In adjoining Gwalior, matters were not very different. Before
1857, the durbar had found it difficult to suppress gangs and those
who provided them with support in areas such as Tomargarh and

Kachwahagarh.[105] The situation had not changed much by the 1880s, when Gwalior seemed to be spending money in vain in an effort to capture famous 'outlaws', including Chapra, Maharban Singh, Hiraju, and Nawal Singh. Due to the apparent failure and lax policy of the Gwalior durbar, the strength of these gangs increased until they gradually established a reign of terror in the countryside. Indeed, the policy of the durbar until the 1880s had been to conceal as many dakaitis as possible from the 'paramount power' so as to reduce interference in its internal affairs.[106] In 1887, the *tumadar* (head of irregular corps of soldiers) Mohammad Waris sent by the durbar to split up the existing goles, found armed dakaits roaming about the country in gangs of fifty to a hundred men. While he received insufficient help from the local population, the dakaits were given ample time to abscond. The power exercised by the bandits over the villagers was such as to render all state efforts useless.[107] Popular attitudes towards bandits, however, were not uniform. They were not always viewed as heroes, except by members of their own lineages, while the views of others, tempered by a combination of loyalty, complicity, and fear, came in the way of British policies to put an end to the 'dacoit menace'.

THE 'WILD' FRONTIER

Although it seemed that the intense wave of banditry in Bundelkhand had been brought under control by the end of the nineteenth century, officials were unsure of its complete eradication. In 1893, the gloomy prognosis of at least one school of opinion was that 'the thakur looks upon dakaiti as an honourable calling and on the slightest provocation takes to the dang, and once having gone out although having done nothing for which the law could touch him, he has neither the pluck nor the common-sense to return to his home.'[108]

   While this conclusion may be questioned, it is clear that dakaiti could not be curbed by repressive measures alone, for they were not foolproof. Despite the belated disarmament of Bundelkhand, the populace hoarded arms on a large scale. This trend was impossible to curtail even when anti-dakaiti operations were conducted on a war footing, given the region's proximity to the borders of princely states such as Gwalior.

Rajput banditry was lent its specificity by the complex interplay of changing social, economic, and political forces. Equally important was the cultural tradition of bhumeawat, which shaped the thrust and contours of elite dakaiti in the nineteenth century. Thakur banditry, as a constituent of bhumeawat, often had political underpinnings, and to that extent was a form of cultural resistance to British encroachment into their spheres of influence. The available evidence points to close connections between feuding, rebellion, and elite 'Rajput banditry'. Rajput dakaiti, therefore, was part of a multi-layered response by biradaris to the British attack on their territory, power, honour, means of subsistence, and military masculine culture. Given this, it is not surprising that the Rajputs of the marginalized zone of Bundelkhand embraced banditry with a vigour possibly unequalled in the rest of the provinces. It was not, on the other hand, the product of a primordial instinct or, for that matter, 'social banditry'.

Often, Rajput biradaris perceived dakaits as baghis or rebels. However, the aims of elite Rajput bandits remained extremely limited. Unlike 'social bandits', they fought largely for their own elite interests and to protect the world of the 'little kingdom' from caving in. They were aided in this task by the framework of shifting alliances forged between various brotherhoods and other communities to whom they were linked by ties of fear and obligation. The limited success of the anti-dakaiti operations also highlighted the differences in perceptions of criminality. Colonial and indigenous attitudes were opposed, the latter being structured by a multiplicity of compulsions and loyalties.

The colonial state consistently viewed dakaiti as a threat to its stability, in contrast to the pre-colonial polities, which had maintained an uneasy partnership with bandit gangs. The government attempted to eradicate such 'uncontrollable' group behaviour permanently as part of its drive to separate its 'civilized' from its 'predatory' subjects. The British did not recognize the validity of collective violence by the Rajputs as a form of cultural and political protest or as a means of asserting group identities, honour, and power. In the eyes of officials, it was vital that the coercive state structures domesticate the representatives of such indigenous masculine martial cultures. If not, they argued, the coercive and moral underpinnings of British rule would be undermined. Consequently, policy makers viewed the retreat of widespread 'disorder' represented by the untamed martial masculine culture of 'turbulent' biradaris from all areas except the frontier territories as a triumph.

While bhumeawat and banditry were banished to the peripheries of the North Western Provinces by the 1860s, subsequent anti-dakaiti operations were unsuccessful in their attempts to eradicate banditry from the frontier territories. British judicial machinery was unable to emerge as all-powerful in Bundelkhand, in particular where jungles and poor communications were a barrier in the path of centralization. Gangs continually crossed over from British to 'native' territory with comparative ease, ignoring multiple political boundaries and jurisdictions, thereby complicating matters. While the police of adjoining princely states and the British provinces periodically met at conferences from the end of the nineteenth century onwards to devise means of catching outlaws who fled across borders, extra-territorial cooperation did not wholly solve the problem of dakaiti. Indeed, brigandage intensified during times of political unrest and both world wars,[109] and the bandit reigned as king in Bundelkhand and the Chambal valley well into the twentieth century.

NOTES

1. While bandits belonged to a number of heterogeneous castes and social groups, this chapter focuses specifically on Rajput *dakaits*.

2. Officiating Agent to Governor General (AGG), Central India (CI), to Secy, Government of India (GoI), Foreign Development (FD), 5 June 1888, FIA, August 1888, no. 140 (NAI).

3. E.J. Hobsbawm, *Primitive Rebels, Studies in Archaic Forms of Social Movements in the Nineteenth and Twentieth Centuries* (Manchester 1959), pp. 1–3. Also see E. J. Hobsbawm, *Bandits* (London 1969).

4. M. Kasturi, 'Rajput Lineages, Banditry and the Colonial State in Nineteenth Century British Bundelkhand', *Studies in History* (*SIH*), 1999, vol. 15, no. 1, p. 87.

5. Interview with Mahindra Pratap Singh Bundela and Ram Singh Bundela, Narhat, Lalitpur district, 16 April 1994. Rajput *biradaris* often viewed members of their lineage who took to banditry as individuals who justly defended the moral order by fighting against external threats. They thus perceived themselves as fulfilling their moral duty or dharma by participating in dakaitis. C. Winther, 'Chambel Valley Dacoity: A Study of Banditry in North Central India', PhD dissertation, Cornell University, 1972, pp. 229–30.

6. Officiating Agent, Lieutenant Governor (LG), North-Western Provinces (NWP), to Secy, GOI with Governor General (GG), 6 September 1842, Foreign Political Constitution (FPC), 2 November 1842, no. 235 National Archives of India (NAI).

7. Kasturi, 'Rajput Lineages', *SIH*, pp. 80–7.

8. Deputy Inspector General of Police (IGP), North-Western Provinces & Awadh (NPsA), to IGP, NWP & A, 1 June 1878, NWPPP, 15 August 1878, vol. 69, Index 2, Uttar Pradesh State Archives (UPSA), Lucknow.

9. S. Freemantle on Special Duty in Connection with Revenue Settlements in Bundelkhand, to commissioner, Allahabad Division (AllD), 9 November 1889, Dept. 1, Bundle 25, F/341/ 1899 (JCOERR).

10. Police Administrative Report of 1889 sent by police commissioner, Jhansi Division (JD), to IGP, NWP & A, 10 March 1890, Bundle 319, Dept. 14, F/36/1888–89 Jhansi Commissioner's English Record Room (JCOERR).

11. Kasturi, 'Rajput Lineages', p. 86.

12. Resident, Gwalior, to First AGG, GG, CI, 23 June 1888, FIA, August 1888, no. 140 (NAI).

13. Report on Chanderi district, by superintendent, Chanderi, 1 December 1844, JD/Pre-MR, Basta 17, vol. 86, Uttar Pradesh Regional Archives, Allahabad (UPRAA).

14. Radhika Singha, *A Despotism of Law* (New Delhi 1998), pp. 168–227.

15. S. Nigam, 'Disciplining and Policing the "Criminals by Birth", Part 1: The Making of a Colonial stereotype—The Criminal Tribes and Castes of North India', *Indian Economic and Social History Review* (*IESHR*) 1990, p. 145. There were striking parallels between British attitudes towards Rajput bandits 'criminal tribes', thugs, and other semi-peripatetic communities, all of whom were perceived as 'primordial', dangerous, wild, and untrustworthy; Singha, *Despotism*, pp. 179–86.

16. Sleeman suggested that the extension of cultivation and tillage by small cultivator proprietors who would be jealous of the preservation of their property and resources would result in the suppression of banditry. General Superintendent for Thugi and Dacoity (GSTD), to commissioner, Rohilkhand division, 11 February 1840, Thuggee and Dacoity Department (TDD), Branch G–10, no. 52 (NAI).

17. Settlement officer, Lalitpur, to commissioner, JD, 21 July 1863, Dept. 1, Settlement Basta, Bundle 56, F/138/1869 (JCOERR).

18. Deputy commissioner, JD, to commissioner, JD, 15 January 1863, JD/Post-MR, Box 14, Dept. 22, F/101/1863 (UPRAA).

19. GSTD, to Asst., AGG, Ajmer, 2 August 1833, TDD, Branch G–2 (NAI).

20. Ibid. On the myth of *thugi*, see Singha, *Despotism*, pp. 167–99.

21. Ibid.

22. Singha, *Despotism*, pp. 175–6, 217. For a detailed study of thugi and dakaiti legislation, see ibid., pp. 203–20.

23. GSTD to C.E. Mills, 15 April 1839, TDD, Branch G–9, no. 120 (NAI).

24. Act XXIV/18 passed by GG, 18 November 1843 (An Act for the better prevention of the Act of Dakaiti), TDD, Branch H-1 (NAI).

25. GSTD to magistrate, Azamgarh, 5 March 1850, TDD, Branch G–19, no. 37 (NAI).

26. Members of supposedly 'professional' dakait castes such as the Buddhuks were made up of a number of social groups. GSTD to Secy, GOI, 27 May 1835, no number, TDD, Branch G–5 (NAI). Likewise, thug gangs quickly reformed out of 'the loose and idle characters around who were incited to join them by the valuable booty they were accustomed to bring back with them from their distant expeditions ... in the Doab, Bundelkhand, Gwalior, Malwa and Rajputana'. GSTD to AGG, Jabalpur, 4 July 1835, no number, TDD, Branch G–2 (NAI).

27. Resident, Gwalior, to first assistant AGG, CI, 23 June 1888, FIA, Aug. 1888, nos 139–40 (NAI).

28. GSTD to first assistant resident, Lucknow, 27 June 1839, TDD, Branch G–9, no. 305 (NAI).

29. Such information was especially important when dealing with princely states, which often refused to arrest the accused on the grounds that innocent men were always seized by the British. GSTD to Capt. Birch, 24 May 1839, TDD, Branch G–9, no. 210 (NAI).

30. GSTD to F.C. Maddock, 26 February 1839, TDD, Branch G–8, no. 257 (NAI).

31. GSTD to officiating under Secy, GOI, 25 October 1853, TDD, Branch G–19, no. 30 (NAI).

32. GSTD to Secy, GOI, 28 May 1838, no number, TDD, Branch G–5, (NAI). See the case of Aman Singh, a Rajput bandit from Fatehpur in ibid.

33. GSTD to assistant AGG, Ajmer, 27 July 1833, TDD, Branch G–2 (NAI).

34. GSTD to J. Curie, 27 March 1839, TDD, Branch G–9, no. 75 (NAI) and letter from GSTD, to asst. magistrate, Agra, TDD, Branch G–10, no. 578 (NAI).

35. GSTD to magistrate, Farrukhabad, 6 March 1839, TDD, Branch G–10, no. 40 (NAI).

36. GSTD to registrar, NA, Allahabad, 5 June 1841, TDD, Branch G–13, no. 351 (NAI).

37. GSTD to magistrate, Hamirpur, 27 March 1839, TDD, Branch G–9, no. 74 (NAI). Many approvers, despite the assurances given to them, were still sentenced to life imprisonment without reference to the conditional exemption. No guilt was felt on this score, for it was argued that no bandit who knew that he was going to meet his accomplices and friends would choose to cooperate with the state by tendering information about their activities. GSTD to officiating Secy, Govt., NWP, 4 September 1856, TDD, Branch G–20, no. 69 (NAI).

38. GSTD to magistrate, Etawa, 7 June 1851, TDD, Branch G–19, no. 67 (NAI).

39. GSTD to Colonel A. Spears, 22 April 1839, TDD, Branch G–9, no. 137 (NAI).

40. Extract from a letter from the magistrate and collector, Allahabad, to Secy, GOI with GG, (undated), FPP, 11 December 1847, no. 206 (NAI). After the annexation of Awadh, efforts were made to eradicate banditry using the same system prevalent in the North-Western Provinces. See GSTD to Secy, GOI, 21 March 1856, TDD, Branch G, Serial 19, no. 24 (NAI).

41. Resident, Lucknow, to Pol. Secy, GOI, 19 July 1841, FPP, no. 58 (NAI).

42. GSTD to Secy, GOI, 21 March 1856, TDD, Branch G–19, no. 24 (NAI).

43. GSTD to Secy, Govt., NWP, 23 August 1853, TDD, Branch G–19, no. 23 (NAI).

For similar interactions between the Rajputs of Awadh and Shajahanpur, see letter from magistrate, Shahjahanpur, to officiating commissioner of circuit, Bareli, 18 May 1841, FPC, 19 July 1841, no. 60 (NAI).

44. Resident, Lucknow, to Secy, Govt., NWP, 3 April 1847, FPP, 11 December 1847, no. 152 (NAI).

45. Sleeman suggested that a court made up of political agents of each state and members of all states control inter-border dakaiti. He even mooted a suggestion that the jurisdiction of this court could be extended to cases other than those dealing with frontier banditry. There were however few takers for this plan. GSTD to Colonel Spears, 22 April 1839, TDD, Branch G–9, no. 210, (NAI).

46. Secy, GOI, to resident, Indore, 26 July 1841, enclosed in letter of Secy, GOI, Pol. Dept., to GSTD, 26 July 1841, no. 2064, TDD, Branch H–2 (NAI).

47. For details see Kasturi, 'Rajput Lineages', *SIH*, 80–7.

48. Tapti Roy, *The Politics of a Popular Uprising: Bundelkhand in 1857* (New Delhi 1995), p. 193. On rebels turned bandits such as Barjor Singh, Daulat Singh, and Jawahar Singh, see the letter from Lieutenant Liddell commanding at Jhansi, to GG, CI Field Force, 10 June 1858, JD/Post-MR, Box 12, Dept. 21, F/12/1858 (UPRAA) and letter from deputy commissioner, JD, to commissioner, JD, 18 January 1859, JD/Post-MR, Box 10, Dept. 21, F/51/1859 (UPRAA).

49. AGG, CI, to Secy to GOI, 12 October 1889, FIA, Nov. 1889, no. 141 (NAI).

50. GSTD, to Secy, GOI, Home Dept., 3 August 1871, no. 561, TDD, Branch G–49, July–Dec. 1871 (NAI).

51. Ibid.

52. IGP, NWP & A, to Chief Secy, Govt., NWP & A, 9 March 1888, FIA, March 1888, no. 296 (NAI).

53. Resident, Gwalior, to LG, NWP, 10 December 1836, FPP, 24 April 1837, no. 77 (NAI).

54. Officiating resident, Gwalior, to officiating Secy, GOI, 13 October 1840, TDD, B2, no. 21 (NAI).

55. Note on the Operations Against *Dakaits* in 1885–6 by asst. pol. officer, Indore, enclosed in a letter from AGG, CI, to Secy, GOI, 27 September 1886, FIA, October 1886, no. 268 (NAI).

56. GSTD, to Secy, GOI, FD, 14 December 1887, FIA, March 1888, no. 481 (NAI).

57. Ibid.

58. Kasturi, 'The Social History of the Rajput Clans in Colonial North India, circa 1800–1900', unpublished PhD dissertation, Cambridge 1996, pp. 75–9.

59. Officiating deputy commissioner, Lalitpur, to commissioner, JD, 21 June 1875, JD/Post-MR, Box 15, Dept. 21, F/149/1875–6 (UPRAA).

60. Secy, Govt., NWP & A, to commissioner, AllD, 27 June 1893, JCR Block, Box 30, F/189C/1894 (UPSA).

61. Note by asst. AGG, CI, 17 November 1893, Half Yearly Report on *Dakaiti* in Bundelkhand in 1893–4 (HYR), Dept. 18, F/345/1893–99 Jhansi Collectorate English Record Room (JCERR).

62. The Statement Showing the Number of Persons, Residents of British Territory Convicted For *Dakaiti* in the Bundelkhand Agency Between 1889–93, by Superintendent for the Suppression of *Dakaiti* Operations in Bundelkhand (SDOB), 30 September 1893, HYR (JCOERR).

63. SDO to Political Agent, Bundelkhand, 30 Sept. 1893, HYR (JCERR); *sat narain katha*: a form of religious meeting in which the story of Vishnu is recited in prose form to a number of listeners usually after a puja.

64. Ibid.

65. AGG, CI, to Secy, Govt., NWP, 29 January 1873, JD/Post-MR, Box 16, Dept. 21, F/ 125/1873–4 (UPRAA).

66. Extract of a report in the first and second six months of 1838 for the district of Hoshangabad, enclosed in a letter from AGG, Jabalpur, to GSTD, FPC, 16 March 1840, no. 116 (NAI).

67. GSTD to Secy, GOI, FD, 16 July 1891, *Report of the Working of the Thuggee and Dacoity Department for 1890: Selections from the Records of the Government of India in the Foreign Department* (Calcutta, 1892), p. 6. According to the AGG in CI, the reasons behind the 'outbreak' of dakaiti in 1890 were linked to news that Lalitpur was about to be broken up and that the deputy commissioner would disarm the Rajputs of the district. KW1, AGG, CI, 3 July 1890, FIA, April 1891, nos 196–9 (NAI). It is also likely that bad seasons and economic hardship contributed to the upsurge in banditry during this period.

68. Officiating agent, LG, NWP, to Secy, GOI with GG, 6 September 1842, FPC, 2 November 1842, no. 235 (NAI). In 1871, it was noted of the Rajputs of central India and Bundelkhand that 'there was a strong feeling of clanship among them, which could not be too ... closely watched'. See letter of GSTD to Secy, GOI, Home Dept., 3 August 1871, no. 561, TDD, G–49, July–Dec. 1871, no. 561 (NAI).

69. DSP, Lalitpur, to deputy commissioner, Lalitpur, 29 August 1865, JD/Post-MR, Box 13, Dept. 21, F/109/1866 (UPRAA).

70. Deputy commissioner, Lalitpur, to commissioner, JD, 15 January 1863, JD/Post-MR, Box 14, Dept. 21, F/101/1863–4 (UPRAA).

71. Deputy commissioner, Lalitpur, to commissioner, JD, 1 August 1864, JD/Post-MR, Box 14, Dept. 21, F/101/1863–64 (UPRAA).

72. Ibid.

73. Ibid.

74. Deputy commissioner, Lalitpur, to commissioner, JD, 17 March 1864, JD/Post-MR, Box 13, Dept. 21, F/109/1866 (UPRAA).

75. For details see the letter from district superintendent, Hamirpur, to magistrate, Hamirpur,10 March 1866, NWPPP, 13 November 1869, vol. 50A, Index 59, Progs. 50 (UPSA).

76. Ibid.

77. Ibid.

78. Ibid.

79. Ibid.

80. Note on the Measures Taken for the Repression of the Band of Outlaws Under Raghunath Singh, officiating deputy IGP, NWP, NWPPP, 13 November 1869, vol. 50A, Index 130, Progs. 38, (UPSA).

81. Magistrate, Hamirpur, to commissioner. AllD, 26 November 1867, ibid., Index 9, Progs. 26.

82. Memorandum by commissioner, AllD, 31 May 1869, ibid., Index 222, Progs. 26.

83. SDOB, to PA, Bundelkhand, 30 September 1893, HYR (JCERR).

84. Translation by Inspector Mohammad Waris of a Report Regarding Dakaits Who Commit Depredations in the Districts of Bhandere, Narwar, Bajrangarh, and Isagarh in Gwalior state as well as in Other States, 15 November 1887, enclosed in letter from GSTD, to Secy, GOI, FD, 14 December 1887, TDD, Cons. C, no. 1 (NAI).

85. SDOB, to PA, Bundelkhand, 30 September 1893, HYR (JCERR).

86. PA, Bundelkhand, to first assistant, AGG, CI, 17 November 1893, HYR (JCERR).

87. Translation of statement of Churaman, resident, Pawaiya (Panna), thirty-two years, cultivator, accused number one in the court of magistrate, third class, Mahwa, 6 September 1917, enclosed within free translation of a vernacular report dated 27 July 1917, submitted by Nazim, Ajaigarh State, BA, Jud. B, F/131-B/1918 (NAI). Gangs seldom retained any considerable part of the plunder near their place of residence but distributed it for security among Rajput landholders.

88. Translation of statement of Jhilkwa witness, caste Dhanwa (Ahir), resident, Serona (Panna), twenty-seven years, cultivator, 6 September 1917, enclosed within free translation of a vernacular report dated 27 July 1917, submitted by Nazim, Ajaigarh State, BA, Jud.–B, F/131–B/1918 (NAI).

89. Before being accepted as full-time members of bandit gangs, men had to undergo specific rituals of acceptance. Winther, 'Chambel Valley Dacoity', p. 100.

90. Ibid., p. 95. In addition to their support networks, bandits also depended on folklore and superstitions to guide them. During their plundering expeditions, Rajput gangs were guided by omens, which were variously interpreted in attempts to make sense of life and the supernatural world. See Kasturi, 'Rajput Lineages', p. 96.

91. Winther, 'Chambel Valley Dacoity', pp. 170–94.

92. Note on Operations Against *Dakaits* in 1885–86 by assistant political officer, Indore, enclosed in a letter from AGG, CI, to Secy, GOI, 27 September 1886, FIA, October 1888, no. 268 (NAI).

93. Demi-official Memorandum on Periodical Lawlessness, NWPPP, vol. 68, 4 May 1878, Index 6, Progs. 2 (UPSA).

94. App. 1, List 11 submitted to Chief Secy, Huzur Durbar (Gwalior), enclosed in a letter from San Subah, Pranth Isagarh, to Chief Secy, Huzur Tahsil, Gwalior, 28 March 1899, FIA, June 1899, nos 92–3 (NAI).

95. Nigam, 'Disciplining Criminals by Birth', *IESHR*, pp. 131–64.

96. Secy, Govt., NWP, to Secy, GOI, FD, 2 July 1869, NWPPP, 13 November 1869, vol. 50A, Index 224, Progs. 30 (UPSA).

97. Magistrate, Hamirpur, to commissioner, AllD, 26 November 1867, Ibid., Index 6, Progs. 8.

98. Deputy IGP, NWP, to IGP, JD, 19 September 1864, JD/Post-MR, Box 14, Dept. 21, F/ 107/1864–65 (UPRAA).

99. Magistrate, Hamirpur, to commissioner, AllD, 26 February 1869, NWPPP, 13 November 1869, vol. 50A, Index 203, Progs. 59A, (UPSA).

100. SOP, Hamirpur, to personal asst., IGP, NWP, 16 December 1867, ibid., Index 2, Progs. 35.

101. Magistrate, Hamirpur, to Secy, Govt., NWP, 1 January 1868, ibid., Index 6, Progs., 28.

102. Note on the Operations Against *Dakaits* in 1885–6 by asst. pol. officer, Indore, enclosed in a letter from AGG, CI, to Secy, GOI, 27 September 1886, FIA, October 1886, no. 268 (NAI).

103. Deputy commissioner, Lalitpur, to commissioner, JD, 17 March 1864, JD/Pre-MR, Box 13, Dept. 21, F/109/1866 (UPRAA).

104. Deputy commissioner, Jhansi, to commissioner, JD. 3 September 1869, JD/Post-MR, Box 13, Dept. 21, F/ll/1869 (UPRAA).

105. DSP, Lalitpur, to deputy commissioner, Lalitpur, 29 Aug. 1865, JD/Post-MR, Box 13, Dept. 21, F/109/1866 (UPRAA).

106. Officiating resident, Gwalior, to officiating Secy, GOI, 13 October 1840, TDD, Branch B–2, no. 21 (NAI).

107. Demi-official Letter from Colonel Henderson, GSTD, Indore, to W.J. Cunningham, 19 February 1886, KW/2, FIA, October 1886, nos 267–8 (NAI).

108. Note on Operations Against *Dakaits* in 1885–6 by asst pol. officer, Indore, enclosed in letter from AGG, CI, to Secy, GOI, FD, 27 September 1886, FIA, October 1886, no. 268 (NAI).

109. SDOB, to PA, Bundelkhand, 30 September 1893, HYR (JCERR).

110. Judicial and police officers belonging to princely states and British districts sharing borders, met periodically to work out common strategies to catch bandits and the problems relating to overlapping jurisdictions. See letter from SOP, Ajaigarh, to vakil sahib, Ajaigarh, 20 May 1919, BA, Jud. B, F/131–B/1918 (NAI). See note enclosed in a letter from PA, Bundelkhand, to AGG, CI, 20 January 1919, BA, Jud. B, F/346–B/1918 (NAI).

II

Colonial Concerns

3

Issues of Islamic Jurisprudence*

Scott Alan Kugle

Jurisprudence is the nexus where authoritative texts, cultural assumptions, and political expediency come together during a crisis. It is therefore not so much a thing or a system as it is an experience, an interpretative experience. Yet the practice of jurisprudence is very different from other types of interpretation because it is also an exertion of power. A legal interpretation is a decision which mobilizes coercive forces to immediately solidify the interpretation into a social reality. The administrative structure of courts and the legal rhetoric that flows through them disguise jurisprudence 'as a system' rather than revealing its nature as an interpretative experience; this disguise serves to heighten the authority of these exercises of power and to limit the ability to contest them to specialists.

This theoretical perspective is crucial in analysing the legal 'system' called Anglo-Muhammadan law, through which the British colonial state anchored its authority and asserted its rule in South Asia. Anglo-Muhammadan law disguises itself as a system; however, it should properly be seen as an interpretative experience that regulates and justifies the raw exercise of power. The law embodies the cumulative experience of the British rulers in India, as they both appropriated and rejected the Mughal polity which they conquered.[1] They brought

* Excerpted from 'Framed, Blamed and Renamed: The Recasting of Islamic Jurisprudence', in *Modern Asian Studies*, vol. 35, no. 2, 2001, pp. 257–313.

Islamic legal texts and specialists together with British assumptions, and joined them to the political needs of a modern state. Thus, Anglo-Muhammadan jurisprudence acted as the interface between the East India Company (as an early modern state) and the surrounding society, which it could not comprehend but had to control. Jurisprudence forms a way to index two juxtaposed experiences: first, the experience of the British in a precarious position of power, and second, the experience of south Asian Muslims steadily displaced from their former positions of authority [...]

Until 1862, Anglo-Muhammadan jurisprudence embodied in an uneasy balance two differing conceptions of self, state, and society, which overlap through the medium of law. Muslims and the British had different ideas about what constituted 'law', how the state was involved with it, and how 'law' fit into surrounding social relations. This paper will focus primarily on the formative period of Anglo-Muhammadan jurisprudence, during the sixty-year period from 1771 to 1832. This early period is most interesting and important, for English jurists had not yet legislated into oblivion many of the overtly Islamic facets of the law. Rather, the British in Bengal needed Islamic jurisprudence as a language through which to speak to the Indians they ruled, and to speak of their own needs with each other [...]

[Under the East India company state] the British notion of 'natural law' or 'humanity' replaced Mughal custom as the vehicle through which *shari'ah* was administered. 'Humanity' assumed that people acted principally as individuals, rather than as religious or corporate groups; 'natural law' presupposed the existence of society in an abstract sense, which can be disciplined into efficiency and productivity [...] Resting government on 'natural law' means setting up the channels through which individuals can take their place in such a society. The Anglo-Muhammadan courts were one of the chief channels by which the state enacted this vision of society.

In the courts that administered Anglo-Muhammadan law, the state defined the public realm, while all people who entered its arena came as private citizens. In this framework, crime became a violation of the public order and the state assumed the right and responsibility to prosecute and punish.

> Crime in the eyes of the prevailing Muslim law was, generally, a private offence. Punishment had become a public responsibility, but complaint, even in serious cases such as murder, remained the prerogative of the affected family, a private and corporate body ... In 1792 the British made certain actions, including murder, crimes in the eyes of the state.[2]

The British administered exemplary punishments for the purpose of discouraging other such individuals from the same crime in the future. Magistrates felt that amputation of hands or feet for theft was 'inhuman' because it was cruel to 'the individual' and made the thief a 'burden on society'.

> Mutilation which is too common a sentence of the Mohummudan [sic] courts, though it may deter others, yet renders the criminal a burden to the public, and imposes on him the necessity of persevering in the crimes which it was meant to repress.[3]

They discouraged mutilation in favour of hanging in a public square during business hours, which was painless for 'the individual' and instructive 'for society'. The criminal (and the victims' families) were important only as public symbols of deterrence.[4]

In order to establish this system of 'public justice' the magistrates tried to suppress the practice of 'private justice', found most notably in the victim-centred justice of retaliation and pardon (*qisas* and *diyah*). In Mughal jurisprudence informed by *fiqh* (legal decisions), crime was understood as an affair between two interdependent parties. The Mughal state did not prosecute anyone unless a victim (or their family) came forward with a complaint; at any stage of the trial, the victim could offer a pardon and the parties would be released. If a person murdered their child, this did not constitute two independent parties (for it was intrafamilial) and did not constitute a 'crime' in which the state had any role. It was not the role of the Mughal state to 'repress crime' but rather to see that an aggrieved party has a chance to achieve some retribution.[5]

The British reformed judicial method in order to suppress this conception of 'private' justice, which recognizes the inviolability of extended family, religious identity, or social grouping.[6] If the victim expressed a desire to pardon their aggressor, the magistrate would simply filter the facts as if the victim did not desire pardon,[7] since this was not the legitimate role of a victim. Judges used the same procedure if a child was killed by parents—the family relation was simply not recorded in the 'facts' of the case. The substance of the law was pristinely Islamic, but the court procedure did not let it function in an Islamic way, according to the presuppositions of fiqh as to what constitutes a 'crime' or a 'person'. The qazi never had a chance to declare qisas valid under shari'ah.

In this way, the social background of the victim became irrelevant in criminal proceedings. Mughal criminal proceedings had distinguished different levels of punishment according to the social background of the victim. British courts also erased these distinctions. In British notions of justice, individuals were given equal treatment before the law. In their view, the state was the only institution which was to mediate between an individual and society; therefore, British jurists rid procedural law of qisas and diyah, legal institutions which made criminal prosecution and punishment the imperative of the aggrieved parties. Yet too often 'public' interest remained undifferentiated from state interest.

The British state claimed that its mediation between an abstract society and individuals improved adjudication because it could administer punishments with equality, without being informed by the status of social groups. British magistrates refused to recognize different standards of justice for different social classes. This created a distance between legal authority and the surrounding social context. This distance was a central component of British power in South Asia: it was one of the main rhetorical points used to justify British modification of Mughal criminal court procedure.

The assumption that conflicts in court centred around two individuals disconnected from their social habitation led to the British habit of assigning a winner and loser, one right and the other wrong. In this context, 'good conscience' became a code word for the ability of the judge to determine right from wrong, and assign penalties. Thus British 'public' justice gave priority to decisions that gave clear title to one 'private' person, rather than making decisions for the betterment of the community as a whole. As local arbitrators, qazis had previously approached decision-making with an interest in reconciliation more than punishment. They tended to 'shy away from making awards which satisfied one party by aggravating another. Living in the midst of the disputants, they were inclined to seek first an amicable compromise … [or] deferred judgement, hoping that the contestants would cool off or lose interest'.[8] This aspect of Islamic judicial practice was totally truncated by British procedural changes, in the interest of increased efficiency and public order […] the public/private dichotomy was injected into the substance of Islamic law and […] the British incorporated fiqh into an Anglo-Muhammadan system. In the field of criminal jurisprudence, the procedures of Anglo-Muhammadan law changed the criteria for punishment from questions of situation to questions of intention. In fiqh, argues Forte, theft is seen as 'manifest criminality'. This means that 'theft' is defined by common experience rather than by external legislation about what constitutes 'theft'.[9] Judging whether the situation conforms to a common notion of 'theft' is what constitutes guilt; determining intent was only minimally important. For instance, if stolen goods were returned prior to the trial, the situation was no longer criminal.

Qazis' methodology in a potential case of theft was to separate out an act of crime from the similarity it bore to other legal actions. A series of categories measured the situation, and separated out cases of theft which merited punishment:[10] Such categories included adult responsibility of the thief (*baligh* and *'aqil*), the non-coerced condition of the thief (*niya*), minimum value of the stolen object (*nihab*), type of good stolen (*mal*), relation of the thief to the victim, and the location of the stolen object (*hirz*).

These categories show that qazis were interested in regulating the interaction of interdependent social groups, rather than representing a general public. This is especially evident in the last category of hirz, or safekeeping. In order for theft to have occurred, the property must have been lying in a situation of hirz, in a place which is regarded as protected within the range of a family's ownership.

Islamic law maintains a sense of things being properly in their ordinary place of safekeeping, such as goods in a shop, personal possessions in a house, an animal in a fold … however, household goods and clothes are not secure in a stable, nor are gold and silver coins that safe in a courtyard of a house.[11]

Qazis did not possess an all-embracing authority to define property rights, except in situations outside of specific, family-centred situations. If wealth is left in a public place and removed by another person, the qazis cannot determine that the removal was 'theft' because the original owner did not treat it like wealth and keep it within safekeeping.[12] Qazis clearly delegate a large responsibility for determining property rights, ownership, and protection to families themselves. If families regulate their spheres of safekeeping, then the qazi can punish a thief; however, if there are situational irregularities then he will not generally apply the punishment for theft.[13] The Mughal state represented by qazis was not an all-pervading entity which could define and regulate property from the ground up, regardless of social groupings or community dynamics.

The shift from fiqh to Anglo-Muhammadan jurisprudence left no room in judicial decisions to weigh community interest. The British procedure erased the situational categories previously used to judge theft. Under the colonial state, thieves were guilty because of their intent to steal, which posed a threat to the well-being of society. Property was therefore defined by the courts, and had little in common with social groups and boundaries. From a utilitarian standpoint, that a crime depended on the willingness of the victim to complain was 'a law of barbarous construction, and contrary to the first principle of civil society, by which the state acquires an interest in every member which composes it, and a right in his security'.[14]

Theft was not a 'private' matter just between the affected and affecting parties.[15] On the one hand, it was a matter of state protection of society in general; on the other, punishments for theft were also public, including public hangings and fines levied on entire villages from where a thief hailed [...]

NOTES

1. This study uses the term 'Mughal' broadly, meaning not only the Mughal empire proper, but also those regions like Bengal, which gained autonomy, but whose administration still followed patterns instituted by the Mughal empire.

2. Lloyd I. Rudolph and Susanne Hoeber Rudolph, *The Modernity of Tradition: Political Development in India* (Chicago 1967), pp. 282–3.

3. J. Harrington, *An Elementary Analysis of the Laws and Regulations* (Calcutta 1807), vol. 1, p. 302.

4. The deterrence of highway robbery was so important that Hastings relied on public notoriety, eschewing due process or the need for evidence, to convict a suspected 'dacoit' and transform him or her into a symbol of deterrence.

5. And of course it was in the state's own interest to see that criminals do not obstruct the state administration, military apparatus, or collection of taxes. Yet the Mughal state was not a force in shaping 'shari'ah'. If there was state interference (which there often was) it was in the interest of securing legitimacy from the scholars and jurists (as was the purpose of Emperor Aurangzeb's collecting and compiling *fatawa*), not interfering in the interest of a positive, abstract notion of 'society', in which people need state guidance.

6. This example also provides an excellent example of British manipulation of procedural law to affect covert changes in substantive law.

7. Jorg Fisch, *Cheap Lives and Dear Limbs: The British Transformation of the Bengal Criminal Law* (Wiesbaden 1983), p. 45.

8. Rudolph and Rudolph, *The Modernity of Tradition*, p. 108.

9. David F. Forte, 'Islamic Law and the Crime of Theft', *Cleveland State Law Review*, vols 34–5, 1985–6, p. 49.

10. Forte, 'Islamic Law and the Crime of Theft', p. 54. He claims that situational elements became especially important in cases of theft because of the harsh penalty that applied if the case was shown to be undoubtedly a case of theft. He overstates this case, ignoring the role of extraordinary justice (*ta'zir*) which could be used at the qazi's discretion. Forte's vision is clouded by his obsession with severed hands and feet.

11. Forte, 'Islamic Law and the Crime of Theft', p. 63.

12. Interestingly, if a family allows a guest to enter their house, and the guest takes some goods, this is not 'theft' because the guest has been incorporated into the family and is part of the safekeeping structure of their household. Forte, 'Islamic Law and the Crime of Theft', p. 63.

13. Ibid., p. 55.

14. Harrington, *An Elementary Analysis of the Laws and Regulations*, vol. I, p. 303, as quoted in Fisch, *Cheap Lives and Dear Limbs*, p. 34.

15. A change in the laws of evidence illuminates this fundamental shift. Under Anglo-Muhammadan procedure, one thief was allowed to witness against another thief. In a system where crime is seen as a private matter between two parties, if one of the parties is an unreliable witness (as thieves were presumed to be) then there was no case. But if theft is a crime against the public and a thief is to be tried solely on intention to steal, anyone can serve as a witness regardless of external criteria, like social status or trustworthiness.

4

Criminal Communities*

Radhika Singha

[...]

The Thuggee Act XXX of 1836 ruled that

1. whoever shall be proved to have belonged, either before or after the passing of this act, to any gang of Thugs, either within or without the Territories of the East India Company, shall be punished with imprisonment for life, with hard labour.

2. And ... every person accused of the offence ... may be tried by any court, which would have been competent to try him, if his offence had been committed within the Zillah where that Court sits, any thing to the contrary, in any Regulation contained, notwithstanding.

3. And ... no Court shall, on a trial of any person accused of the offence ... require any Futwa from any Law Officer.

The act had many novel features: it applied with retrospective effect and it extended the jurisdiction of the Company's courts for this offence to territories outside the dominion of the Company. The offence could also be tried in any court of the Company irrespective of where it had been committed, and without reference to the forms of Islamic law.[1] That a cant term like 'thug' was acceptable at a time

* Excerpted from Radhika Singha, *A Despotism of Law* (New Delhi: Oxford University Press, 1998).

when a penal code upholding precision and exactness was on the agenda is an indication of the success of a publicity campaign in official circles. Except for a few pettifogging judges everyone knew what thuggee was.[2]

The conception of communities socialized into criminality, with its members plundering or robbing as a 'profession', did not suddenly emerge in the 1830s.[3] The theme has a history coterminous with the very inauguration of the Company's judicial initiatives. On the one hand Warren Hastings had stressed the need for uniform procedure; on the other he formulated Article 35 of 1772, which extended punishment for dacoity from the individual offender to his family and village.[4] Hastings had also argued that conviction under Article 35 should be allowed on the grounds of public notoriety for dacoity. Professional crime had to be punished by different standards of evidence from those applied to offenders charged for a single crime.[5]

The theme of criminal communities was also used to justify special executive powers or punitive drives of various sorts. The targets of such measures were supposed to have placed themselves outside the pale of society, thereby forfeiting their claim to the protection of regular procedure. In very general terms, such drives can be attributed to the wider process of colonial pacification, to the effort to make the subjects of empire both taxable and 'policeable'. However, one also has to take account of the constant reordering of the hierarchy of objectives within colonial law and order. The form of action, military pacification or judicial prosecution, police surveillance or reclamation, imposed its own constraints for the institutions of colonial order were not infinitely flexible. In addition, such drives may seem to be imposed by state on society, but the interplay between colonial order and social hierarchy could shape the initiative differently at different social levels, and points of resistance could force a reassessment of strategy.

The Thuggee Act, for instance, indicates a degree of conflict between institutional priorities. It was far easier to prosecute a prisoner on a charge of belonging to some ill-defined criminal collectivity than to establish individual responsibility for a specific criminal offence. But how far was this dualism between the professional/hereditary criminal and the casual offender to be pushed?[6] At what point would the formal consistency of rule of law, and the principle of judicial control over executive action, be jeopardized? Arguments for special powers against thugs or 'professional dacoits' had been countered by these hesitations. So what combination of circumstances shaped this manifestation of Providence, the mission to extirpate thuggee in India?[7]

The formulation of the Thuggee Act cannot be attributed only to complaints in judicial correspondence about the inadequacy of existing laws against professional or hereditary criminality. Magisterial and judicial action had been taken in British territory against people suspected of being thugs, or of belonging to a dacoit tribe, well before the acts of 1836 and 1843,[8] but using legal provisions applicable to all offenders. Nor is it clear that special measures were required because the crime of thuggee had reached crisis proportions.[9] Official reports stress the discovery of the ramifications of thuggee rather than its escalation as the reason for sanctioning a campaign.[10] There was no clamour from their Indian subjects for measures against thuggee: the major complaint of officials was the difficulty of working through layers of collusion or concealment to assess the extent of this crime.[11] Thugs did not attack parties which included Europeans, so it was not a crime which directly affected the safety of British travellers.

However, the establishment of a government monopoly in opium in Rajputana and central India after the wars of 1817–18 and the flow of remittances from Bombay and Surat to finance this commodity, had increased the Company's stake in the safety of the traffic in this region.[12] The government was also concerned to protect *sipahi*s of the Bombay and Madras armies, moving through central India on their way home to Hindustan. They represented, after all, a certain outlay in terms of training and political attachment.[13] These factors had prompted British residents and political assistants in the princely states to intervene in the arrest and trial of suspected thugs in the years following the Pindari and the Maratha wars.[14] Yet the Company had been reluctant to take over jurisdiction for this offence from the Indian princes and chiefs.[15] Even within its own territories the Company's government had rejected various suggestions made by its officers for special powers or special laws against notorious thugs or members of dacoit tribes.

I suggest that in its initiation the thuggee campaign was woven into a political elaboration of paramountcy, expounded, not through military, fiscal, or diplomatic arrangements, but through a rhetoric of authoritarian reform.[16] The thuggee campaign appealed to all shades of reform opinion, both Evangelical and Utilitarian. Grafted as it was on to existing agencies—the administration of the non-regulation districts and the Company's political agencies in the princely states— it was not expected to be a very expensive proposition either.[17] The crime was approached with a different sense of mission now. Even before 1830, wrote Meadows Taylor, large gangs of thugs had been apprehended, especially in Bundelkhand and Malwa by Major Borthwick and Captains Wardlow and Henley, 'but without exciting more than a passing share of public attention. No blow was ever aimed at the *system* if indeed its complete and extensive organisation was suspected, or, if suspected, believed'.[18] This systematization imposed on the crime of thuggee mirrored the new role outlined for the para- mount power. The thugs were 'Citizens of India and not of any par- ticular division'.[19] Only an all-India counter-system, in the form of the paramount power, could therefore root out this evil. 'So extensive and long standing a confederacy' needed general and comprehensive mea- sures, argued F.C. Smith, agent to the Governor-General in the Sagar and Narbada territories. It was no longer enough to expel thugs from the Company's domains—such a policy of dispersion was of dubious value. Instead, the paramount power ought to assume responsibility for eradicating this 'scourge'.[20]

The position of the Sagar and Narbada territory was particularly strategic for the launching of operations, surrounded as it was by a varying and decentred topography of Indian states.[21] These districts had been annexed from the Marathas in 1817–18 and were classed as a non-regulation area, administered by an agent to the Governor- General who was responsible only to the Supreme Government.[22] Legal procedure was kept very loose because of the recent acquisition of the area.[23] In 1836 F.J. Shore, criticizing the lack of supervision in the Sagar and Narbada territory, said this had made it 'a theatre for the experiments of incipient legislation'.[24]

The other feature of the campaign was the way in which these officers of the Political Department expounded upon the unique

knowledge they had acquired of thuggee to legitimate the special procedures adopted for its prosecution. Yet it was not in fact the cracking
of some code which had put them in a position to hunt out thugs.[25]
The main source for compiling lists of suspects and accumulating
evidence for their conviction remained, as before, the testimony of
accomplices who had turned approvers.[26] But the extensive recording
of thug beliefs, slang, and superstition seemed to authenticate the difference between the hereditary cult-oriented criminal and the casual
offender; and this won the case for special procedures.

A certain institutional friction developed between the machinery
of the Thuggee Department and the judicial and executive machinery
of the regulation provinces. Sleeman and others presented this conflict as a problem of persuading the judicial establishment to believe
in the reality of thuggee, but it was as much a problem of keeping
executive discretion under judicial control. The effort to restructure
forms of social existence which seemed antithetical to the creation
of orderly productive tax-paying subjects, and to do so through the
regular mechanisms of civil authority, created new areas of executive discretion within the interstices of the rule of law. At one level
the thuggee and dacoity Acts were an effort to clothe crude devices
for securing conviction with the semblance of due process. But they
were also defended by arguments about the peculiar characteristics of
Indian society or the backward state of Indian civilization. At the same
time this discretionary authority had a certain disruptive potential for
stable, bureaucratic procedures of law, so such initiatives were usually
followed by a counter-pull, however weak, to define its boundaries.

The point of retreat from such drives is as significant a feature of
the administrative shifts related to the policing of criminal communities as the point of inauguration. What explains the claim that the
thuggee threat had been extirpated? Anything less than success is
of course an embarrassment for a highly publicized campaign.[27] Yet
when such campaigns proved disruptive of the general goals of law
and order, for instance, by generating resistance on sensitive issues
such as religious mendicancy, then a more flexible strategy might
have to be formulated. A criminal community could be discovered in
another incarnation with its particular 'profession' or 'clan' regrouped
for another initiative in law and policing.

One reason why, from the late 1830s, Sleeman began to assert that thuggee as an organized system had been extirpated may lie in an embarrassing realization of the fact that the charge of systematic murder and robbery of travellers could not be established against the various mendicant bands and peripatetic groups which had begun to be swept up by thuggee assistants. The apprehension that any long-term involvement with projects of reclaiming criminal communities would prove an onerous and expensive task may also have encouraged Sleeman to claim an end to the campaign.

THE CIVIL AND THE PREDATORY

To examine the context for legal innovation. I start by outlining British attempts to understand and categorize criminal communities, with the Company's drives towards paramountcy providing a crucial backdrop. The Sagar and Narbada territories, where the thuggee campaign took shape, bordered the terrain of an earlier initiative against a 'predatory system', in the form of the Pindari campaign of 1817–18.[28] The Marquess of Hastings characterized the Pindaris as predators, even as robbers, to reject any proposal that the Company's government should negotiate with them to avoid the expense of war. The invocation of the criminal metaphor continued in the instructions to military officers before the campaign: that since the Pindaris were public robbers, they were to be tried on capture and if found guilty they were to be summarily executed; but cultivators were to be left undisturbed. [...] But the method used was entirely that of military attack until leaders surrendered or were killed, and followers melted away. On 25 November 1818 Hastings reported that their annihilation could be regarded as complete.[29] And yet the Pindaris, said to have been extirpated, had at times been rumoured to have swollen to huge numbers.
[...]

At the time it was argued that a clear demonstration of overwhelming military supremacy, a ban on 'predatory warfare', and the fixing of state boundaries would force armed bands to dissolve into the peaceable sections of the population. And yet those who had swelled the ranks of various mercenary bands in central India could as well

take to the roads to rob travellers.[30] If there was any unease about
the social flux unleashed by colonial tranquillity, it was reflected in
attempts to set out typologies distinguishing between peaceable and
predatory sections of the population. Malcolm made such an effort
in *A Memoir of Central India,* 1823, but this categorization was not
attended by a call for special laws or for special jurisdiction in the
Indian states. He regarded political anarchy, not some immutable
principles of social organization, as the generator of 'predatory' communities, and paramountcy as the force of stabilization. However, the
interesting point about Malcolm's typology is that the distinctions
between the peaceful and the predatory constantly seem to dissolve.
[...] The fluidity of the line between the civil and the predatory
and between military service and robbery is evident at all levels of
Malcolm's typology.

In Meadows Taylor's novel, *Confessions of a Thug,* the thug hero,
Ameer Khan, takes service with a Pindari chief on the reasoning that,
'I was a soldier by inclination if not by profession, and I thought ...
we might make as good a thing on it as if we went out on expeditions
on our own.'[31] But, as pointed out earlier, the Pindaris and the thugs
tended to be regarded as two distinct groups in official accounts.[32]
I will now examine these overlaps more closely, to suggest a perspective on the thuggee phenomenon. There was a way of life in which a
particular form of predation could form a part, sometimes a regular
part, of a range of subsistence options, but it was not the criminality
by birth and profession projected by the Company's police and legal
drives.

CRIMINAL COMMUNITIES AND 'WAY OF LIFE' CRIMINALITY

I begin with a tentative search within the narratives of those arrested
for thuggee, or for belonging to a dacoit tribe in the 1830s and 1840s
for points of distinction between the prisoners' own interpretation of
their activities and that imposed by the concerns of British examining
officers. The records of the Thuggee Department are promising for
their sheer density. The prisoners' narratives were not just determined
by the department's need to accumulate evidence and to sustain a case
for special police and legal measures; the examining officers also saw

themselves as recording British mastery over an Indian underworld, now sorted out into various communities with their rules, language, and social practices.[33]

The approvers who provided much of this information had to convince the officers of their usefulness by vaunting the range of their expeditions and attacks. But the reliance which the Thuggee Department had to place on the evidence of approvers also gave the latter a certain bargaining power. The certificate given to the approver stated that he would 'serve Government and be treated well; and have all (reasonable?) indulgence...'[34] Band leaders of especial notoriety sometimes entrenched themselves as the favourites of a particular officer who would call upon them to regale European visitors with accounts and demonstrations of their craft. One could argue, therefore, that approvers did have a limited licence for self-expression; their responses to the examining officers certainly display points of dispute and evasion. For instance, when Sleeman sought to impress the fact of 'mastery' on some thug prisoners, arguing that the *iqbal* (good fortune or grace) of the Company had prevailed over that of their female deity, he received ambivalent responses. One prisoner argued that in Calcutta even the Company offered worship to the Goddess Kali.[35] And again, the prisoners would agree that thuggee was their 'business' but they would insist that this business be recorded in certain descriptive terms and not in others—as an activity linked with skill, honour, and adventure, not as theft. Reynolds, who took down the depositions in Hyderabad, reported that 'the denomination of thief is one that is particularly obnoxious to them, and they never refrain from soliciting the erasure of the term, and the substitution of that of T'hag whenever it may appear in a paper regarding them.'[36] Perhaps the term 'thief' was rejected because it suggested they might prey on their neighbours' property, or steal goods entrusted to them, attributes of low social status within their own community.[37] Prisoners arrested for thuggee made a distinction between the norms they would observe within their own village and those which determined their search for legitimate prey.[38]

How does one deal with the admission of many of those swept up for dacoity or thuggee that robbery was indeed their profession and their identification of other groups on similar terms?

Can these statements just be dismissed as the product of colonial stereotyping, or as structured solely by the process of prosecution? Different skills, means, and patronage would mediate access to different sorts of crime. In certain contexts the element of 'predation' could become more marked as other sources of livelihood contracted. The booming military market of eighteenth-century India encouraged a regular outflow of mercenary bands, especially from Hindustan into the Deccan and central India in search of service. Highway robbery was probably always an option for such bands as they moved between one employer and another or to and fro from home. In 1812–13 Thomas Perry, the magistrate of Etawah, made enquiries about a group of mercenaries brought into the district by the Marathas, and subsequently sheltered by zamindars, who loaned them money to be repaid from expeditions into the Deccan.[39] Amaun, the brother of one such patron, Chaudhary Lalljee, chief zamindar of village Sindaus, was asked: 'Whom do they call Thugs?' His response: 'They are generally denominated Sepahees. They travel on towards the Dekhun, many people say that they plunder, rob and murder.' However, other inhabitants of Etawah also termed themselves sipahis and made the occasional foray into the Deccan. This was the case with one Bukht, of the Lodeh caste, whose brother Doorjun was a humble ploughman.[40] The same Doorjun was also questioned about one Ghuseeta: 'Used the world to call Ghuseeta a Seepahee also?' 'Yes, a Seepahee and Thug—he was a jemadar of Thugs.'[41] The victories of the Company brought about a contraction in this market for mercenary employment which probably made this flow between service and banditry more one way and permanent.

Mercenaries who regularly set out after the rains would have a knowledge of the major routes and the confidence to plan and co-ordinate the inveigling and killing of large parties of travellers. Other sources of livelihood gave access to forms of crime not requiring that degree of organization. '"Real" crime,' writes Douglas Hay, 'is shorthand for a large part of the life of the poor.'[42] A pastoralist is in a particularly favourable position to steal cattle and to dispose of them, but putting poison into the food of a traveller to stupefy and rob him can be done by almost anyone. In all cases it would be a mistake to exaggerate the degree of specialization involved.

Interspersed with the prisoners' statements that robbery was their 'business' are others which indicate that this element was interwoven with other patterns of subsistence.[43] The picture which emerges from these accounts is one of a striking diversity of occupation among those arrested as thugs or dacoit bands, though many of these had regular links with agricultural communities.[44]

Members of the bands whom Sleeman classified as Badhaks alias Bagree dacoits sometimes described themselves as spending eight to ten months in the year hunting.[45] Such bands of hunters and fowlers sought the patronage of princes whether in their *shikar* expeditions or as auxiliary contingents in their armies; but they could also organize independent raids. In the official presentation of criminality by profession these other components are ignored or regarded as mere disguise: Thugs took up cultivation or service with Indian chiefs as a 'screen' for their activities, Badhaks (Buddhuks) set out for a dacoity in the 'guise' of bird-catchers.[46]

In the official interpretation of professional/hereditary criminality the elements of dissonance and displacement in the prisoners' accounts, between their status and activity under a former political order and that in the present, or the change wrought by famine or other calamity, were usually ignored. But there is a definite element of band lore too in these depositions, which buttressed the official presentation of criminal cultures. This lore is organized around the search for sources of legitimacy for their *chakri*, their livelihood, which they linked variously to the sanction of antiquity, family tradition, divine power, and political charisma.[47] The existence of band lore, a common slang, and a shared knowledge of major attacks, does suggest long terms of association, as does the ability to co-ordinate action in large gangs. But equally significant is the ease with which identities constituted around a particular form of *naukri-chakri*, could shift among men who sought service. This is strikingly illustrated in the thug prisoner Imamee's description of one 'Hor-mat Khan alias Mungulea, formerly caste Gururea and a thug by trade but now a Mussalman and a Sipahi in a Regiment at Male-gaon …' [48] Malcolm had observed that many Hindus who had joined the Pindaris became Muslims.[49] Campbell noted the connection between service to the court of Lahore and 'being a Sikh'.[50]

This band lore was constituted around the 'profession'; but it did not necessarily establish a strong fraternal link with other members or dominate all other social affiliations. As Stewart Gordon points out in a very perceptive article on thuggee, there was no system of reprisals against those who betrayed the 'fraternity' by turning approver.[51] Sleeman registered the presence of certain caste and religious animosities between the approvers.[52] They would generally show a concern only to shield members of their own family or caste. In fact some of the approvers seemed to regard their assistance to thug-hunting detachments as having put them in service to the Company, and Sleeman encouraged this sentiment.[53] The approver Bukhtawar said they were not apprehensive about informing on former accomplices because they had become servants of the government.[54] Ram Bux, recounting his services to the government in catching thugs exclaimed, 'they are all my enemies now!'[55]

The approvers swept up in the 1830s and 1840s cite the antiquity or long tradition of their 'business' as one among the other factors which established its legitimacy. However, their accounts of actual attacks do not go further back than the early nineteenth century.[56] Even the thug genealogies which Sleeman constructed do not seem to stretch further back than three generations and include the names of adopted children.[57] Official histories of thuggee referred to the immediate political background but also sought to push its origins into the remote past, gleaning chronological points from stray references to predatory gangs in Persian chronicles or in accounts of European travellers to Mughal India.[58] The stress placed by officers on strangling as the distinguishing mark of this 'ancient fraternity' also disassociated the method of murder from issues of convenience and context and gave it cult status. 'The Thugs adopt no other method of killing but strangling,' declared Lieutenant Reynolds.[59] But the prisoners' narratives show that the strategies of gang robbery had been somewhat different in the early nineteenth century, especially in the Indian states. Travellers had associated in large crowds for safety, and bands of armed men in search of service were a common sight. Men who associated to rob travellers could travel with arms and in large numbers without arousing suspicion. They could use a greater measure of open violence and take fewer precautions over the disposal of bodies.

At a continuous but diffuse level the official attitude towards the culture of men on the road—mendicants, peripatetic professions, bands who frequented forest zones or the fringes of cultivation—had always been one of unease. Such groups seemed to elude the reach of taxation and policing; their way of life was considered motley and suspect.[60] Even an ethnographic interest in certain wandering tribes of India, who were believed to resemble the gypsies of Europe, was tinged with a suspicion of criminality or immorality in their lifestyle.[61] The religious mendicant was always an object of official suspicion, but police measures were reined in because of the veneration in which they were held.[62]

Though Sleeman usually avoided any essentialist descriptions of Indian society, he too shared a suspicion of mendicant bands. He considered the 'monastic orders' analogous with the Pindaris, thugs, and dacoits, in being composed 'of persons floating loosely upon society, without property or character, with the object of acquiring the property of others....'[63] He mistrusted the various peripatetic professions, such as the bullock-transported pack trade in raw produce which he regarded as a source of great insecurity to life and property.[64] Such bands seemed particularly inaccessible to the control of the state. The thuggee campaign reinforced this latent suspicion about these wandering professions. In his vocabulary of thug 'language', *Ramaseeana*, Sleeman listed various peripatetic communities as thug-tribes.[65]

There were various patterns, not necessarily those of displacement, which contributed to the phenomenon of men on the road. Seasonal movements of labour, famine migration, and pilgrimage tended to flow into each other. There were communities which provided various goods and services to settled communities—grain transporters,[66] cattle dealers, medicine men, basket weavers, entertainers, and petty pedlars. There were others who subsisted in a forest ecology on the margin of cultivated areas—hunters, woodcutters, pastoralists.[67]

Yet the contribution of paramountcy to the phenomenon of men on the road was scarcely acknowledged in official accounts. The idea that certain patterns of crime on the high road were related to declining opportunities of service with chiefs or rulers is suggested only in Sherwood's 1816 report.[68] Sleeman blamed vagrancy and highway robbery on the fact that Indian rulers disbanded their militias all at once, or discharged the disabled or those with an injured horse without making any provision for them. However, he did not examine the pattern of permanent disbandment itself.[69] The discontent of the dismissed Muslim cavalryman was given some recognition, but there was little acknowledgement of the loss of employment, periodic or regular, which a polity of competing states and dispersed focuses of authority had given to men of humbler rank: those who joined the infantry swelled the ranks of army auxiliaries, or foraged, brought supplies, and cut grass for draught cattle and horses. Instead, the desire to feel in control of this floating population encouraged the putting together of official typologies of criminal cults and criminal tribes.

The other issue in evaluating the 'reality' of criminal communities, whether that of thug gang or dacoit tribe, is of how distinct as a social group they were in the indigenous perception. The beliefs and rituals assembled around a plundering raid were familiar to Indian society in other contexts—so it was not this lore which marked these bands out as startlingly different in Indian eyes.[70] The method was what distinguished various sorts of crime in the indigenous perception, whether thagi, inveigling and deceiving, or *phansigiri*, strangling.[71] In a seventeenth-century autobiography of a Jain businessman, the *Ardha-Kathanak*, when two travellers are charged with being thugs it is because they were suspecting of putting counterfeit coins into circulation, not because they belonged to a murderous band.[72] The word *phansigar* is certainly used in indigenous accounts to refer to a person who regularly strangled and robbed travellers,[73] but not to suggest affiliation to a peculiar sect. It is for this reason that official accounts could be very uncertain about whether Indians knew about thuggee or whether the system was veiled to them too.[74] The case for special measures had rested on the argument that such communities stood outside the pale of society. The Pindaris were the 'dregs' of society, the thugs originated from parties of 'vagrant' Muslims, the Buddhuk were outcaste Hindus and Muslims.[75] The taint of immorality and debauchery was sometimes introduced to accentuate this marginality.[76] Yet again, it was often stated that the thugs could be model family men or respected members of their village. If known thugs were accepted within society, then the justification for special measures was difficult to maintain. Officials who wanted a swifter pace of institutional change, or Evangelicals who stressed the need for social intervention, pressed towards the conclusion that the whole of Indian society stood condemned and urgently in need of reform.[77]

How far was the official suspicion of wandering bands shared by their Indian subjects? The line between life on the road and in sedentary occupations was made porous by diversity in sources of subsistence, ecological reversals, political enterprises, and patterns of trade and pilgrimage. But such a lifestyle was perceived by Indians as different from that of the agriculturist who had to protect his crops and property from wandering bands.[78] Every region seems to have had a catch-all label to characterize wandering communities. One peripatetic band examined by Sleeman as a dacoit tribe said they called themselves Bhats (usually translated as bards) but were called Sansiyas, Kanjars, Mahars, Jats, 'according to the country in which they happen to be, for they have nowhere any fixed habitations, and the people among whom they encamp, call them after the wandering or vagrant tribe, whom they appear most to resemble'.[79]

One also comes across the occasional pejorative inflexion over a lack of discrimination in the social norms of those associated with a peripatetic lifestyle. Most strikingly, the narratives of members of such bands, whether termed thugs or dacoit tribes, often reveal an anxiety to defend themselves against the suspicion of social laxity.[80] For instance, the members of a Buddhuk gang would claim that they refused admittance to Muslims, or to untouchable castes,[81] even though it is clear that such bands absorbed new members from various social strata through marriage, adoption, and the drift of men from other occupations. So a certain terminology of low social status, buttressed by the interaction between British officers and upper-class Indians, could feed into the idiom of criminal communities. Conversely, the defence which some prisoners made on behalf of their status could strengthen the official argument about rule-governed criminal communities.

In conclusion, I would argue that the so-called thug gangs seized in various episodes related to the territorial expansion of the Company from the late eighteenth century, and had taken shape against a background of intense military activity and its aftermath. Men could form a band and set out in search of military service, or dissemble as soldiers to attack other parties of recruits or travellers.[82] However, gang robbery on the roads was not only the preserve of mercenary bands. In the flux of state-building and given the wide dispersal of arms, peripatetic communities providing services of various sorts or bands of mendicants might occasionally take to highway robbery.[83]

NOTES

1. The judicial weight of the *fatwa* on the final sentence had been drastically curtailed by the early nineteenth century but it was still regarded as an essential procedure of the criminal trial.

2. In Anglo-Indian parlance, thugs were believed to constitute a hereditary criminal fraternity, organized around beliefs and rites, which upheld a profession of inveigling and strangling travellers. In contrast to dacoits, thugs were believed to murder by stealth rather than by armed attack. However the defining line between dacoity, thuggee, and highway robbery was never very clear.

3. Cf. Jonathan Duncan, Resident of Benaras (RB), to Governor General (GG) in Council (C), 27 February 1792, Bengal Revenue Judicial consultations (BRJ) P/127/78, 13 April 1792, pp. 526, 535. E. Moor reported that in India robbery was, like begging, a hereditary craft, and not one viewed with great moral turpitude. E. Moor, *Hindu Infanticide: An Account of the Measures Adopted for Suppressing the Practice of the Systematic Murder by Their Parents of Female Infants; with Incidental Remarks on Other Customs Peculiar to the Natives of India* (London 1811), pp. 153–4; R. Jenkins, *Report on Nagpoor,* 1827, p. 294; J. Shakespear, Acting SP, WP, 'Observations Regarding Badheks and Thegs', 30 April 1816, *Asiatick Rresearches,* XXIII, 1820; J. Malcolm, *Memoir,* II, 1823, pp. 182–8.

4. The argument was that the dacoits of India were 'robbers by profession, and even by birth; they are formed into regular communities...' Committee of Circuit to Council at Fort William, 15 August 1772. *Elementary Aanalysis,* I, pp. 300–1.

5 Warren Hastings (WH) to Council, 10 July 1773, and extract from progs of the Governor and Council, 19 April 1774, J.E. Colebrooke, *Supplement,* pp. 114–19, 122.

6. Sandria Freitag argues that arrangements for dealing with collective crime grew up as a covert legal structure forming an alternative to the overt legal structure 'ostensibly geared to individuals' which provided the reassuring appearance of rule of law: 'Crime in the Social Order of Colonial North India', *Modern Asian Studies,* vol. 25, no. 2, 1991, pp. 227–31. In contrast, I argue that both these elements existed in uneasy relationship within the same body of law, and their co-existence explains certain contradictions within it. Even if extraordinary measures to deal with criminal communities took shape in territory outside the Company's regulations, or within the field of executive discretion, they eventually had to be integrated to rule of law.

7 W.H. Sleeman, often referred to the circumstances facilitating the thuggee campaign as 'providential'; *Ramaseeana: A Vocabulary of the Peculiar Language Used by the Thugs* (Calcutta 1836), pp. 46–7. W.H. Sleeman, military officer, who joined the Political Service, and who, as assistant to the Agent to the Governor-General in the Sagar and Narbada territories (SNT), successfully established a reputation for himself as architect of the thuggee operations (henceforth WHS).

8. Act XXIV of 1843 was 'for the conviction of professional dacoits, who belong to certain tribes, systematically carrying on their lawless pursuits in different parts of the country ...'

9. The famines of 1833–4 in Bundelkhand, and subsequently in the Upper Doab, Delhi region, and Rajputana in the later 1830s strengthened the belief that the flow of people on the road ought to be monitored for organized crime. However, the outlines of the campaign had taken clear shape before this conjuncture.

10. In 1830, Sleeman had warned of the increasing magnitude of thuggee, but so had Ochterlony, the British resident in Malwa and Rajputana, some eight years earlier. Cf. Sleeman's letter to the Calcutta Literary Gazette, 3 October 1830, in G. Bruce, *The Stranglers: The Cult of Thuggee and Its Overthrow in British India* (London 1968), pp. 81–3. D. Ochterlony to G. Swinton, Secy., Pol. Dept, 30 April 1822, in N.K. Sinha and A.K. Dasgupta (eds), *Selections from Ochterlony Papers* (Calcutta 1964), p. 244.

11. Cf. W.H. Sleeman, *Rambles and Recollections*, 1844, revised, annotated edition, 1915 (reprint, Karachi 1980), pp. 78–9, n4.

12. Till 1830 the Company maintained a monopoly over the sale of opium from this region. Thereafter it sustained its revenues by issuing passes for the transit of opium through Company territory. The operations against various species of plunderers in central India and Rajputana intertwined with the policing of the opium line and the Company's efforts to increase its own revenues from trade and commerce at the expense of local chiefs. The government was also concerned about the safety of its treasure consignments, still vulnerable to sudden attacks in forest terrain from hunting bands such as Buddhuks or Karawals.

13. F.C. Smith, Agent to Governor General (AGG), SNT, to W.H. Macnaghten, 29 May 1832. Selected records of the Central Provinces Secretariat, 1829–32. Mss Eur Dll, IOL, p. 132.

14. Cf. Extract Bengal Political Consultations, 20 April 1824, no. 43, BC F/4/984, 1828–29.

15. Ochterlony, resident in Malwa and Rajputana, had recommended the same measures in 1822 which were implemented in the 1830s. He suggested that the paramount power set up courts to try robbers and murderers, 'ceasing to enquire to what state the Culprit is a Subject, or in whose dominion the Crime was committed'; but the Company would not commit itself. D. Ochterlony to Secy. Pol. Dept., 30 April 1822 and Secy., Pol. Dept. to Ochterlony, 24 May 1822: Sinha and Dasgupta, *Selections from Ochterlony Papers*, pp. 244, 249.

16. It was during Bentinck's governor-generalship, Lee-Warner remarks, that a new conception of political duties was developed 'which, derived from the law of nature or the requirements of civilisation, affected British relations with every Native state.' Sir William Lee-Warner, *The Native States of India*, 1910 (reprint, New Delhi 1979), p. 100.

17. The Bentinck government, committed to retrenchment, would have discouraged the assumption of major administrative responsibilities in the princely states. Sleeman's proposal that the Company take over the administration of district Bhilsa from the Gwalior regime to protect travellers was rejected on the grounds of expense, and because the Gwalior durbar would object. G.W. Swinton, Chief Secy., to F.C. Smith, AGG, SNT, 4 August 1830, Mss. Eur D1188. H.H. Spry, medical officer at Sagar, recalled that booty recovered from thugs was enough to pay for all incidental charges of the department up to 1834 and for two new prison houses at Sagar. H.H. Spry, *Modern India* (London 1837), pp. 162–3.

18. Meadows Taylor, *Confessions of a Thug* (1839; London 1986), introduction, p. 5 (emphasis added).

19. F.C. Smith to W.H. Macnaghten, Secy., 26 June 1833, Home, Thuggee and Dacoity Department (T&D), Cons B.2, no. 4, p. 295, NAI.

20. F.C. Smith to Chief Secy. to Govt., 20 June 1832, *The Correspondence of Lord William Cavendish Bentinck* (*CLWCB*), vol. II (Oxford 1977), pp. 836–7.

21. On the south lay Hyderabad and Berar; to the north and west, Bhopal, Gwalior, Bundelkhand, and Baghelkhand.

22. The agent was assisted by political officers drawn from both the civil and military services of the Company. The political officers combined the duties of revenue collector, civil judge, and magistrate, and had the same powers to arrest and try offenders as the magistrate. The agent held biennial sessions in his judicial capacity as commissioner.

23. It was supposed to rest on the 'spirit' of the Bengal regulations but with a due regard for local usage.

24. F.J. Shore, officiating commissioner SNT, to Secy. Sadar Board of Revenue, Allahabad, 7 May 1836, Home Misc., vol. 790, p. 422.

25. Reeves, for instance accepts this mythicization of the campaign. 'Once his [i.e., Sleeman's] officers were armed with a systematic account of the signals it was possible to identify thugs and thug operations'. P.D. Reeves, introduction to *Sleeman in Oudh: An Abridgement of W.H. Sleeman's a Journey through the Kingdom of Oudh in 1849–50* (Cambridge 1971), p. 12.

26. That is, prisoners who confessed to their crime and agreed to give evidence against their accomplices in return for pardon or remission of sentence.

27. Governor General Auckland suggested that Sleeman postpone the publication of his report on 'gang robbery by hereditary profession', till more progress had been made in putting it down. W.H. Sleeman, *A Journey through the Kingdom of Oude in 1849–50* (London 1858), vol. 1, p. xxvi.

28. The Pindaris, better described as a phenomenon than as a particular community, emerged in central India as bands of military auxiliaries, who served the various powers in that area, in particular Holkar and Sindhia, and began to

acquire a territorial foothold on the Narbada. Those with a horse had been used by Indian princes to skirmish with the enemy's army and to pursue it into retreat. Among their numbers were also those who would forage for the army, carry grain to it, and dispose of their own booty and that of others in the aftermath of a successful campaign.

29. Political letter to the court, 25 November 1818, para 23, in B.K. Sinha, *The Pindaris* (Calcutta 1971), p. 174. Pindari leaders and their immediate followers were given grants of land to settle them in Bhopal and in Gorakhpur, ibid., pp. 175–83.

30. In fact pacification created easier targets by multiplying smaller parties of travellers, less apprehensive about encountering armed bodies. Cf. J. Stewart, resident, Indore to G. Swinton, Chief Secy., 12 August 1829, 'The very pacification of Malwa has led to the extension of this murderous system to a degree unknown before.' Sleeman, *Ramaseeana*, p. 378, also pp. 411–12.

31. Taylor, *Confessions of a Thug*, p. 336.

32. Sleeman, *Ramaseeana*, pp. 4–5.

33. Yet thuggee with its suggestion of conspiratorial agency could evoke more uneasy visions of India as well. Discussing the symptoms of derangement among Europeans J. Macpherson, MD, said, 'Insane patients very generally dislike natives and, when they suspect conspiracies, notions of Thugs, & c. are very common.' J. Macpherson, MD, 'Report on Insanity among Europeans in Bengal', *The Indian Annals of Medical Science*, April 1854, pp. 704–5.

34. WHS to W.G. Bird, 5 April 1839, Home Dept., Cons G8, July 1838–August 1839, NAI.

35. Sleeman, *Ramaseeana*, pp. 76–7 [...] In general the prisoners tended to blame their own actions, their non-observance of the rules which brought access to supernatural power, rather than the defeat of the source of power itself.

36. Lieutenant Reynolds, 'Notes on the T'hags', *FRAS*, vol. 4, 1836, pp. 200–13.

37. Cf. J. Paton papers, British Museum (BM) Addl Mss 41300, pp. 24–5. However, among humbler orders of society, one does come across admissions about certain forms of theft as interwoven with their livelihood. But here again distinctions were made between the kind of crime they would or wouldn't commit. A Dosadh, a low-caste labourer, interrogated for robbing a British lieutenant, declared, 'I was not a Camp thief that I should rob the *Pultun* (regiment) but only thieved for my own livelihood.' Declaration of Bholah Dosadh, village Pondahpoor, pargana Ballia, 4 March 1788, BRC P/51/25, 3 October 1788, p. 735.

38. Nasir, thug approver, said that those who had committed an ordinary murder would be haunted, but not if the murder was committed during a thug expedition because this was sanctioned by the Devi. Sleeman, *Ramaseeana*, pp. 175–6.

39. T. Perry papers, Add 5380, Cambridge University Library, pp. 38–70.

40. Examination of Doorjun Lodeh, resident of Sindause, 1 January 1813, ibid., p. 70.

41. Ibid. There are many references in the 1830s to thugs being searched out from the regiments of Indian rulers.

42. Douglas Hay, 'War, Death and Theft in the Eighteenth Century', *Past and Present*, (May 1982), vol. 95, pp. 117–60.

43. Cf. deposition of Dhokul Singh, cited above.

44. S. Nigam stresses the peasant origins of thugs and Buddhuks, which he says, were ignored by official discourse. 'Disciplining and Policing the "Criminals by Birth", part 2: The Development of a Disciplinary System, 1871–1900', *IESHR*, July–September 1990, vol. 27, no. 3, pp. 274–5. I stress instead the diversity of occupation among those characterized as thugs and dacoits. Of these, the various peripatetic communities began to be directed into the ranks of agricultural labour, or later into the ranks of quarry, factory, and mine labour. Meena Radhakrishna, 'The Criminal Tribes Act in the Madras Presidency', *IESHR*, (July–September 1989), vol. 26, no. 3, pp. 269–95.

45. W.H. Sleeman, *Report on Budhak Alias Bagree Dacoits* (Calcutta 1849), p. 130. The Raja of Kottar is described as keeping bands of Buddhuks to supply his table with game, ibid., p. 54. Buddhuk was one of the denominations for bands on the margin of forests, who engaged in hunting, trapping, and fowling. They also provided irregular levies for the army of the Nawab of Awadh or swelled the retinues of powerful zamindars. Their skill with bow and spear and their tradition of association with military raiding allowed some of them to organize lightning raids on consignments of treasure, often at a great distance from their own residence.

46. Sleeman, *Report on Budhak Alias Bagree Dacoits*, p. 17.

47. Baz Khan, tried in Jabalpur in 1826 is reported to have stated 'almost vauntingly that his forefathers for seven preceding generations have been Thugs of the *Badshahee Duftur*, or enrolled as thugs in the Royal records at Dehly'. Administration of justice in the SNT, Bengal Judl. letter, 12 July 1827, BC F/4/1159, p. 48. *Chakri, naukari-chakri*: service, employment.

48. Deposition of Imamee, 19 August 1831, forwarded by WHS to Resident, Nagpur, 17 October 1830, in *Selections from the Nagpur Residency Records, Volume 4, 1818–46* (Nagpur 1954), p. 274.

49. Malcolm, *Memoir,* II, p. 177.

50. G. Campbell, *Memoirs of My Indian Career,* (London 1893), vol. 1, p. 66.

51 S.N. Gordon, 'Scarf and Sword', *IESHR*, (December 1969), vol. 6, no. 4, pp. 403–29.

52. Cf. Sleeman to F.C. Smith, 11 March 1831, in G. Bruce, *The Stranglers.*

53. '[W]e require to raise them a little in their own esteem, and make them feel a little exalted as the servants of the state ... The terms *Sarkar ka Naukar* and a decent appearance have a wonderful effect in making them exert themselves.' WHS to resident, Hyderabad, 16 July 1832, Home, T&D, Cons G.l, June 1832–May 1833, pp. 66–7, NAI.

54. Sleeman, *Ramaseeana*, p. 186.

55. J. Paton papers, BM Addl Mss 41300, p. 9. Some approvers suggested that they could help the police to detect other 'classes' of thieves as well. Ibid., pp. 19, 29.

56. The men seized by Reynolds in the Nizam's territory in the early 1830s confessed to having made annual expeditions over the previous twenty-five to thirty years. Reynolds, 'Notes on the T'hags', p. 213. Cf. also deposition of Rambux, thug approver, 15 April 1837, Paton papers, BM Addl Mss 41,300, p. 8; and Sleeman, *Ramaseeana*, Appendix I, pp. 101–10.

57. Sleeman, *Ramaseeana*, Appendix A.

58. Cf. Sleeman's citation of Thievenot's *Travels* (1687) for a reference to robbers who used a noose. Sleeman, *Ramaseeana*, p. 11. Also V.A. Smith's editorial note in Sleeman, *Rambles and Recollections* citing the history of Firoz Shah Tughlaq (1351–1388). The following example illustrates the historicization of lore. Feringea, an approver, had claimed that all the operations of their trade were to be seen in the sculptures at Ellora. This claim was abstracted from his other assertions—that these caves were the work of some unknown supernatural agents, and that everyone's trade, however secret was described there—and given the status of a historical fact by W. Crooke who thereby traced thuggee into early Hindu history. Cf. Francis Tuker, *The Yellow Scarf* (London 1961), Appendix 2, pp. 197–8 for Feringea's account, and ibid., p. 63, for Crooke's rendition in *Things Indian* (London 1906).

59. Reynolds 'Note on the T'hags', p. 201. Sleeman traced the historical roots of thuggee through this feature. The Thugs, he writes, were the descendants of the Sagartii, a pastoral group of Persian descent who put their enemies to death by throwing a leather noose over them. Sleeman, *Ramaseeana*, pp. 4, 11.

60. Cf. Commissioner, Kumaon to SP, Delhi, 23 September 1823 for a reference to 'motley assemblies' of people in the foothills, 'persons of the lower classes engaged in the cutting and transporting of timber and other Jungle products, together with Brinjaras, Herdsmen, shikaris, and ca.' Since the conquest of Kumaon, he reported, these areas were becoming more orderly. COK, Pre-Mutiny, Judl. letters issued, 1822–25, Basta 23, UPSA. Cf. also Sleeman to W.H. Macnaghten, 10 September 1836, on classes 'known' to practice thuggee though none had as yet been convicted; those who roamed with bears and monkeys, *daturias* (poisoners), Bairagis, mendicants, and Multanis, a class of transporters. Home, T&D, Cons G.4, September 1836–March 1838, pp. 23–5, NAI.

61. J.A.R. Stevenson of the Madras Civil Service combined his account of the phansigars, with one of the Shudgarshids, a 'tribe of jugglers and fortune tellers', described as 'notorious for kidnapping children' and for an 'abominable traffic' in the sale of sinews as charms against evil. 'Some Account of the P'hansigars, or Gangrobbers and of the Shudgarshids, or Tribe of Jugglers,' *Journal of the Royal Asiatic Society of Great Britain and Ireland*, vol. 1, 1834, 280–4.

62. Cf. Judge-magistrate, Jaunpur, 15 August 1815, for a complaint about religious vagrants exacting tribute, fakirs giving poison to pilgrims to rob them. *Home Misc.* 775, pp. 620, 628. Shore's suggestions for a 'punitive discipline' of arrest and hard labour for all such 'idle scamps', and the registration and surveillance of stationary fakirs was typical of the official attitude. F.J. Shore, *Notes on Indian Affairs*, (London 1837), vol. 2, pp. 411–12. In the 1820s and 1830s, missionaries attacked the government for countenancing idolatry by collecting pilgrim tax, a theme which mingled with utilitarian arguments against the loss of productive labour

and life which pilgrimage was supposed to entail. J. Statham, *Indian Recollections* (London 1832), pp. 138, 144, 159. J. Peggs, *Pilgrim Tax in India* (second edition, London 1830), p. 47.

63. Sleeman, *Report on Budhuk Alias Bagree Dacoits*, p. 268. However, he also acknowledged that religious mendicancy had been the 'great safety valve through which the unquiet transition spirit has found vent under our strong and settled government.' Sleeman, *Rambles and Recollections*, vol. 1, p. 446.

64. Ibid., p. 83.

65. Cf. Sleeman, *Ramaseeana*, pp. 85, 126, 144 for references to Multani, Lodaha, and Qulundera thugs.

66. Captain J. Briggs, 'Account of the Origin, History and Manners of the Race of Men called Bunjaras.' *Bombay Transactions*, (1819), vol. 1, pp. 159–83. R.G. Varady, 'North India Banjaras', *South Asia*, ns, vol 2, nos 1 and 2 (March–September 1979), pp. 1–18.

67. Cf. E. Balfour, 'On the Migratory Tribes of Natives in Central India', *Journal of the Royal Asiatic Society of Great Britain and Ireland*, vol. 13, no. 1 (1844), pp. 29–47 for a sampling. C.A. Bayly draws attention to the very significant space which tribal and nomadic people occupied on the social map of eighteenth-century India and the importance of their interaction with the arable economy and its more hierarchical landed society: *Indian Society and the Making of the British Empire* (Cambridge 1988), pp. 29–31.

68. 'It may be conjectured that many persons, deprived by the declension of the Mohammedan power of their wonted resources, were tempted to recourse to criminal courses to get their subsistence'. Sherwood, 'Observations Regarding Badheks and Th'egs', p. 271.

69. Sleeman, *Rambles and Recollections*, pp. 443–6.

70. The examining officers of the Thuggee and Dacoity Department were in fact becoming acquainted with popular religion and culture but refracted through the prism of criminality. A characteristic example was the assertion that the Bhawani temple at Mirzapur, a popular site of pilgrimage, was filled with thugs and subsidized by their offerings. W.H. Sleeman's letter to the *Calcutta Literary Gazette*, 30 October 1837, in G. Bruce, *The Stranglers*, pp. 81–2, and Lt. Reynolds, 'Note on T'hags', p. 202.

71. Stewart Gordon points out that thugs did not enter the local folklore of bandits and robbers. 'Scarf and Sword: Thugs, Marauders, and State-formation in 18th Century Malwa', *IESHR*, (1969), vol. 6, pp. 408–9.

72. Cf. R.C. Sharma, 'Aspects of Public Administration in Northern India in the First Half of the Seventeenth Century', *Journal of Indian History*, LIV, part I (April 1976), pp. 107–15.

73. Cf Aurangzeb's farman of 1672, ordering punishment for a strangler who was 'habituated to this misdeed ... or is notorious among people for this misdeed and the Nazim of the Subah knows about it or vestiges of strangulation and property of people are found with him ...' *Mirat*, p. 249.

74. Meadows Taylor, for instance, asserts that the system of thuggee was unsuspected by the people of India, but a couple of pages later says that landholders and

village chiefs had had connections with thugs for generations. Introduction to *Confessions of a Thug*, pp. 1, 3.

75. J. Paton to Caulfield, acting resident, 25 January 1840, Foreign Pol., A, 9 March 1840, no. 122, NAI. Criteria such as dietary habits and a wandering way of life were invoked to lump together diverse groups, but such arbitrary categories could create problems of consistency.

76. Plunder obtained by murder was spent on 'debauchery and indulgence' wrote J.A.R. Stevenson. 'Some Account of the P'hansigars or Gang-robbers', p. 280. Briggs attributed the poverty of the Banjaras to their 'dissolute and wandering habits' and their drinking. 'Account of the ... Bunajaras', p. 181.

77. C.E. Trevelyan, 'The Thugs or Secret Murderers of India', *The Edinburgh Review*, vol. 64, 1837, pp. 357–95. Cf. also J. Paton, BM, Addl Ms 41300, p. 278.

78. Balfour reports that the Bauries who obtained their living from the forest could be fined and even put to death by Indian rulers if they pilfered from fields and stacks of grain. E. Balfour, 'On the Migratory Tribes of Natives in Central India', p. 35.

79. Sleeman, *Report on Budhuk Alias Bagree Dacoits,* 1849, p. 265.

80. Sahib Khan, a thug approver from a Telingana gang, claimed they were high-caste Muslims, vehemently denying that they were Kanjars, low-caste peripatetic grain traders. Sleeman, *Ramaseeana*, p. 162. One band referred to another disparagingly as Handeewuls, suggesting they ate in old and dirty plates. Ibid., p. 95. Captain Ramsay said that though the Sansi dacoits were often styled Kanjars, they rejected the appellation, stating that the Kanjars were all Muslims. Sleeman, *Report on Budhuk Alias Bagree Dacoits*, p. 253.

81. Sleeman, *Report on Budhuk Alias Bagree Dacoits*, pp. 253, 283, 2161.

82. Cf. Sleeman, *Ramaseeana*, Appendix I, pp. 101–10, and Appendix T, pp. 294–5, for a description of this situation in central India in the early nineteenth century.

83. Among these would be communities such as the Buddhuks, accustomed to the use of hunting weapons, and to raiding tactics, who had once formed auxiliary detachments to armies but were being marginalized by the shift to trained infantrymen.

5

Development of Discipline*

Sanjay Nigam

The discourse on criminal tribes was affirmed in the Act of 1871, which both cast a specific 'type' and sought to mould it further by an entire apparatus of surveillance and control. That the knowledge of groups officially designated as criminal by birth, creed, and caste developed an entire apparatus of coercive and disciplinary measures—registration, roll-call, limitation on movement, the pass system, agricultural settlements, reformatory camps, workhouses, the separation of children from their parents—is a clear indication of the operation of power/knowledge, the operation of discursive practices. In other words, in the practices of segregation, exclusion, and resettlement envisaged in the Criminal Tribes Act of 1871, the power of colonial discourse is first confirmed by the creation of a criminal type with which these practices were intended to deal.

Of course, the Criminal Tribes Act was not the earliest of the coercive measures aimed at aggregates of individuals considered hereditary criminals; the Buddhuks, and the thugs before them, were controlled by a combination of military and disciplinary techniques.

* Excerpted from 'Disciplining and Policing the "Criminals by Birth", Part 2: The Development of a Disciplinary System, 1871–1900', *The Indian Economic and Social History Review*, vol 27, no. 3, 1990. Copyright © The Indian Economic and Social History Association, New Delhi, 2008. All rights reserved. Reproduced with the permission of the copyright holders and the publishers, Sage Publications India Pvt. Ltd, New Delhi.

The campaigns of the Thugi and Dacoity Department, the establishment of a school of industry for thug approvers at Jabalpur and an
agricultural colony at Gorakhpur for the Buddhuks were some of the
early attempts to control and reshape these groups into hardworking
subjects.[1] However, the systematic arrangements for the control of
groups proclaimed under the Act of 1871, marks it out from these
earlier measures. The reformative discipline now envisaged was for
the first time clearly set out and put to work under the rules promulgated by the Act. The criminal tribes were thus enclosed within an
extraordinary space: a network of registration, inspection, limitations
on movements, passes and the roll-call had now been elaborated by
the state for this very special purpose [...]
[...]
With the legislation of the Criminal Tribes Act, the procedures of
control and surveillance were systematized. This transition was from
the haphazard methods of 'hounding and pursuing' to instituting a
system of surveillance with a view to changing and controlling every
aspect of the existence of the 'tribes'. The Act can therefore be seen as
combining both punishment and the objective of that punishment.
This section examines the working of the Act between 1871 and 1895
to control the Bawarias, Sanorias, Aherias, and Harburahs: it describes
the expectations of the British government and the role of the landed
classes in the control and resettlement of the criminal tribes.

The vision that the landholders were prepared to reclaim regarding the criminal tribes could not be realized. This delusion had two
sources: first, [...] there was no precise legislated definition of the
police responsibility of the landholders; colonial relations of power
specified that the crimes of the criminal tribes and the illegalities of
the landed classes would be administered differently.[2] Second, this
failure had its origins in the complex relationship between landholders and the criminal tribes.

One point of departure in understanding the relationship is the
peasant origins of the criminal tribes. Yet this is persistently obscured
by the official discourse that represented the criminality of the 'tribes'
as an inherent characteristic sharply distinguishing them from the
rest of the population, be they lords or peasants. However, the peasant background of the groups considered criminal by birth is repeatedly emphasized in official and non-official writings. For instance,

Sleeman's writings on the Buddhuks and the thugs show not only that these groups were drawn from the peasantry, but that they maintained their links with their communities by either cultivating land themselves or by depending on the protection and support of their villages.[3] In some instances, the element of coercion was the dominant feature of the relationship between landholder and criminal tribe; such was the relationship between the Bawarias of Muzaffarnagar and Saharanpur and the landlords of those districts. In other cases the criminal tribes were not manipulated and coerced into crime. With the Sanorias of Tehri, Banpur, and Lalitpur we have an example where the illegalities of the state and peasant groups converged. Thus the groups brought under the Criminal Tribes Act should not be regarded as if they had uniform and regular characteristics or as if some abstract set of rules governed their relations with the rest of society.

Even before the proclamation of the Bawarias of Muzaffarnagar, local officials had advised moving them to an alternative site. They were seen as being 'entirely at the mercy of Mundee Hussan'. The Bawarias had made an effort of settling down in Bidauli; they had brought uncultivated land under the plough and for the first two years they did not leave Bidauli on thieving expeditions. But the landholder, Mehendi Hassan, 'oppress[ed] those who [tried] by culture and care to make their land productive'. As soon as uncultivated tracts were broken up by Bawaria cultivators, Mehendi Hassan would jack up the rents and let out the plots to other tenants.[4] Thus Mehendi Hassan, by having the Bawarias located on his lands, gained in four different ways: first, by having a canal cut through his land—almost entirely by Bawaria labour—he increased the rental value of his lands; second, making the Bawarias break-up uncultivated tracts; third, by letting out these new plots at high rents to 'better' tenants; and fourth, by squeezing the Bawarias on to poor tracts, he forced them to give up agriculture and leave Bidauli on thieving expeditions. He thus reproduced the relations that had existed between the Bawarias and their landlords at their previous site. Commenting on this relationship, the inspector general of police, Carmichael remarked, 'He is shrewdly suspected of making the Bowreeahs give him a share of their plunder whenever they return from their marauding expeditions'.[5]

The recommendation to shift the Bawarias to a different site was not accepted, and the Bawarias were proclaimed in 1873.[6] The objective of the proclamation was 'not to attempt to establish a reformatory, but to compel the tribe by a system of registration and roll-calls not to wander without permission, and to pursue heartily the occupation they nominally follow'.[7] Since their settlement in Bidauli, a large number of Bawarias absconded: of the 1,676 Bawarias that had been settled in Bidauli in 1863, only 846 remained to be registered under the Act in June 1873. During the first year of its operation, the pass regulation had little effect on the Bawarias; seventy-five left Bidauli without passes; 129 returned from earlier desertions and imprisonments; a further twenty-one deaths and forty-six births put the Bawaria population at 905. Even so, 771 Bawarias had deserted the colony since its inception in 1863.[8]

The surveillance of the Bawarias was organized by the establishment of a police *chauki* at Bidauli consisting of one subinspector, two head-constables, seven chaukidars, and three Bawaria informers. Each morning the chaukidars arrived at the Bawaria villages for an informal inspection. These inspections served to remind the Bawarias of the presence of the chaukidars who remained with the Bawarias till noon. In the evening before sunset, after the Bawarias had returned from their fields, they were assembled for a head count. The roll-call was formally taken two or three times a week at irregular intervals by the subinspector or the head-constables. The headman of each family was responsible for his household's presence at the roll-call. Each Bawaria was expected to answer by name at the roll-call, and all absentees were to be reported to the district superintendent. The district superintendent made frequent visits and the magistrate visited Bidauli a few times in the course of the year.[9] Thus the reformative discipline was distributed across various levels of surveillance: first, the individual answering to his name at the roll-call; then the head of the family, the informers, the chaukidars, the village headmen, who watched, counted, reported at periodic intervals; and finally, the district superintendent who maintained the Bawaria register and the magistrate who supervised the whole project.

Despite the abscondings, district officers were optimistic about the Bawarias; they seemed to be actively involved in agriculture; more than 115 Bawarias had returned to the colony, and punishments had been few.[10]

This initial optimism was overshadowed by a sense of frustration with the working of the Act; by 1878, the failure of the Bidauli project was evident. The roll-call and the pass regulation seem to have had little effect on the movements of the Bawarias who 'come and go as they like'.[11] In 1878, 115 Bawarias absconded and the total population shrank to 884.[12]

Two contradictory explanations of this failure can be recovered from the official reports. The first extended the knowledge of the criminal tribes to explain the causes of this failure; thus its essential didactic quality cannot be detached from the rest of its existence. Accordingly, the inspector general of police Tyrwhitt claimed that the 'hard fare of the village ryots, coarse bread and dal [did not suit the Bawarias' taste] for the luxuries of life … [that] they have for centuries obtained by theft …'. It followed that the criminal tribes would abscond to 'obtain by plunder what they would not attempt to do by the sweat of their brow'.[13] But district officials painted a different picture. They argued that the inability of the Bawarias to hold their plots in face of Mehendi Hassan's machinations was the main reason why they gave up agriculture and absconded. In November 1877, Elliot Colvin, the commissioner of Meerut, visited Bidauli. He reported that the Bawarias could not be expected to break up new land and settle down as honest peasants if they knew that at the end of each year they were 'not only liable to ejectment but knew … they would be dispossessed'. Mehendi Hassan had refused to allow the Bawarias any security of tenure whatsoever. He told Colvin that he would give up the canal water rather than allow the Bawarias occupancy rights. Colvin concluded that for Mehendi Hassan the Bawarias 'are to be used as pioneers or rather cat's-paws to break up the jungle lands, they are not to be allowed to attach themselves to the soil and full use is to be made of the power of shifting their holdings'.[14]

By 1878, 730 of the original 1,676 Bawarias remained in Bidauli. Colvin suggested that they should be collected into two villages, Jinjhara and Singhara, in the Bidauli pargana; a tract which the canal cut through. These villages, he recommended, should be acquired for 20,000 rupees from Mehendi Hassan; this would rid the Bawarias of his pernicious influence.[15] The Government of India, however, was not enthusiastic about this proposal as it 'interfered with the principle of competition'. Instead, it suggested that the Bawarias be dispersed to the villages from where they had been brought to Bidauli in 1863.[16]

The refusal of the government to acquire the two villages of Mehendi Hassan Khan should not be taken to mean that the colonial state played the role of a neutral ombudsman; it is suggestive rather of the contradiction in the strategy of reclamation through agricultural resettlement. The choice of Bidauli as a Bawaria settlement was motivated by a host of considerations among which the 'peasantization' of the Bawarias was just one: the Gujars had to be subdued, grazing land brought back under the plough, and the Bawarias had to be induced to settle down as full-fledged *kisans*. However, the introduction of the principle of competition, the coercive and legal backing that the landholders had from the law to increase rent, in order to restrict occupancy tenures, and to eject tenants, meant that in the person of Mehendi Hassan the colonial state confronted its own creation. The state needed the support of the landlords to subsume the criminal type into an honest peasant, a service not always performed to the satisfaction either of the agent or the object of this disciplining. Consequently, while the agricultural settlements languished, the apparatus of surveillance grew to assist in this process of peasantization.

Perhaps the term 'confront' is inappropriate. For, after all, Khan was not disciplined for reneging on his agreements and neither were the water resources restricted as some officers had threatened. Perhaps failure is an equally inappropriate characterization of the Bidauli project. If registration and the restrictions on the movements are taken, together with the government's reluctance to resettle the Bawarias on Mehendi Hassan's lands, it seems that the idea was to draw the disobedient criminal types into accepting obedience, poverty, and industriousness. Such an interpretation seems possible, especially in the light of the remarks of certain officials who blamed the 'failure' on the lack of industriousness of the Bawarias ('they can obtain by plunder what they will not by the sweat of their brow'), on their lack of obedience ('they have for centuries obtained [luxuries] by theft') and on their rejection of poverty ('the criminal tribes are not content to live on the hard fare of the village ryots').

The Sanorias of Lalitpur were brought under the Criminal Tribes Act in March 1874. By this proclamation, 154 male Sanorias were registered in twenty-one villages.[17] No special police force was stationed to oversee the Sanorias. This was mainly because the organization of police surveillance in twenty-one villages involved considerable expense. Even the monthly expense of 258 rupees for maintaining a police force in Bidauli had been considered excessive.[18] The registered Sanorias were required to present themselves every morning at their respective police stations; the women were not allowed to stay away from their villages overnight and some Sanorias were recruited as spies.

However, if fiscal considerations discouraged the establishment of special surveillance-police, this absence involved political costs. For one, the requirement that the Sanorias present themselves for a roll-call each morning at local police stations meant that precious hours were lost and individuals could begin work on their plots only at midday. Also, punishing women for overstaying their leave was a source of harassment.[19] But most galling of all was the system of passes. The absence of a special police force meant that rather than applying for a pass to the deputy superintendent of police and wait for its issue, the Sanorias, who often needed to visit their relations in Tehri, simply absconded. Once they had left their designated village without a proper pass, they dared not return to Lalitpur, fearing arrest and punishment. They usually joined their relations in a thieving expedition from Tehri, preferring to risk an arrest for thieving rather than returning to Lalitpur to be arrested for breach of the pass rules.[20] In the absence of a local apparatus of surveillance, the controls envisaged in the rules remained imperfect. On the one hand, the absence of the chaukidars and local policemen meant that the Sanorias were hardly aware that their activities were under constant inspection. On the other, the roll-call which cost them crucial hours of work, and the pass system that forced them to abscond, went against the very objective of surveillance, which is control of movement and resettlement.

Not surprisingly therefore, the Sanorias began absconding from their villages. In 1877, only 100 of the 154 registered remained. This phenomenon was explained by officials in the same terms as had been used to account for the Bawaria abscondings. The criminal tribes, it was argued, shared a collective 'distaste for the hard and uncertain nature of agricultural toil'; they were 'not content with the poor fare of the village cultivators'; moreover, 'they would always ... find means to leave their homes on plundering expeditions which ... they infinitely prefer to the tame and depressing labour of field tillage'.[21] The inherent criminality of the Sanorias remained an explanation for all phenomena; it was the reason used for the deployment of special measures of surveillance and was equally an explanation of why these measures remained ineffective.

However, the Sanorias presented the officers with a dilemma, for although they were referred to as a caste, the Sanorias came from various castes: 'The Sanorias are not a tribe with whom the practice of thieving is a hereditary occupation but [according to the Government of India] "an organised fraternity of vagrant thieves"'.[22] Consequently, local officers considered it wrong to impose restrictions on the movements of Sanoria women and children.[23] Some attempts were also made to improve the system of passes to prevent the Sanorias from absconding and proposals were made to simplify the procedures of issuing passes.[24]

Behind these readjustments there seems to have been a calculation of balance between repression and leniency. If the restrictions—such as roll-call and passes—appeared too repressive there was always the fear that the Sanorias would disappear into the states of Tehri and Banpur.[25] But if the instruments of surveillance were absent or not visible then there was the risk of surveillance not functioning at all. To be effective surveillance had to be interiorized by the Sanorias and all those brought under the Criminal Tribes Act. And to be interiorized, surveillance had to be visible. Thus local officers stressed the urgency of establishing small police chaukis that could localize the surveillance of the Sanorias and regulate their lives without appearing to repress them.[26]

In the absence of these readjustments, the Sanorias continued to abscond, and in 1880 their number fell to seventy-seven. In 1881 the number increased to ninety on account of twenty-two releases from jail, but nine Sanorias absconded that year.[27] In 1884, thirteen more absconded but four were recaptured. The district police stepped up surveillance measures: roll-calls were taken more often and frequent inspections and house checks were conducted. The effect of these measures was almost immediate and district reports claimed that 'Sanaurias know that they are being watched ... and are more cautious.'[28]

The inspector general of police endorsed the district's suggestion to improve the surveillance over the Sanorias and of taking effective steps to ensure their resettlement in agriculture. He accepted in principle that the presence of a local police force to keep a watch on the activities of the Sanorias, as also the removal of all unnecessary restrictions on Sanoria women and children, was vital to the project of their reclamation. The restrictions on the movements of the members of the Sanoria families, he regarded as 'neither just nor politic'.[29] Further, he outlined a plan of reclamation which would give the Sanorias rent-free land for seven years, followed by seven years of moderate rents, and after this period regular rents would be levied. The plan also made provisions for liberal *takavi* advances. The success of this plan was clearly not calculated in economic terms but by the expectation of converting the Sanorias into hardworking peasants, solely dependent on agriculture for their livelihood or to put it more precisely in the words of the inspector general of police, 'If the scheme is to be a success we must not count the cost of it too closely ... the object we have in view is not to increase government revenue but to reclaim a very troublesome class of criminals.'[30]

It is interesting to note that although it was widely known that the Sanorias were not a caste, that they did not live by thieving alone, and that they were in fact peasant cultivators, yet the image of the Sanorias as a criminal tribe, born to crime and living solely by the proceeds of plunder, died hard. Liston, the deputy commissioner of Lalitpur, following the official discourse on criminal tribes, assumed that the Sanorias lived off plunder alone.[31] Much to his consternation, Liston realized that his opinion was ill-founded:

> In my report [for] 1882, on the working of the Criminal Tribes Act I had allowed it to be a fact that these Sunoria families lived on the proceeds of their gang fellows' plundering expeditions. I did so trusting too much to the police officers' reports. Last year I made enquiries and found reason to doubt the truth of this. Now it turns out that most of these people have means of livelihood ... these people cannot be said to have no means of livelihood.[32]

But even the reports which had allowed Liston to categorize the Sanorias as living off plunder had returned the land held by them for the past five years.

Table 5.1

Sanorias in Lalitpur	1877–78	78–79	79–80	80–81	81–82
Land in bighas		376	386	429	426
No. of families holding land	47	48	49	57	58
No. of families without land	9	22	28	33	31

Source: NWPO Jud. (Cr.) Progs, December 1878, November 1879, August 1880, August 1881, and August 1882

Yet Liston had persisted in the belief that thieving was the Sanorias' only means of livelihood. In Liston's perceptions we have yet another instance of the embeddedness of the discourse on criminal tribes.

The plan, in the event of Liston's discovery, was altered and land was now offered to four families totalling twenty-five persons, who had no land. The grant consisting 300 acres was offered in the Bir village in the Banpur pargana. Also a grant of 727 rupees was made for the Bir colony: 450 rupees as a *takavi* loan for seed, cattle, and agricultural implements; 250 rupees towards a drinking water well; and twenty-eight rupees for building houses. Liston expected that after the four families had settled down others 'will come from the thieving grounds and settle quietly down'.[33] A police chauki consisting of one subinspector, two constables, and two chaukidars from among the Sanorias, was appointed to implement the surveillance rules.

The Aherias and Harburahs were brought under the operation of the Act in 1873: the Aherias were registered in eleven villages in Etah and the Harburahs in four.[34] In 1874, 969 Aherias and 128 Harburahs were brought under the operation of the Criminal Tribes Act.[35] Although the figures returned in the reports were regarded as unreliable, it was evident that the Aherias and Harburahs began absconding as soon as they were brought under the Act. The reasons are plain. First, the local landowners seemed to have been responsible for motivating these abscondings, and the Aherias and Harburahs were involved with the landed classes in a relationship not different

from the Bawarias and their patrons. Evidence is limited, but to cite
one example, in 1873, sixty-three Harburah men entered the district
and were identified and put under police supervision. Almost immediately, a zamindar offered to be responsible for them. On inquiry
the magistrate discovered that he owned only thirteen bíghas of land
and his interest in them was anything but resettlement on his land.[36]
Second, given the fact that the district authorities 'took little interest
in' the surveillance, the abscondings continued almost unchecked.[37]
Third, the 'absolute hardship' suffered by the Aherias and Harburahs
was yet another reason for fleeing the district.[38]

No special police arrangements were made to supervise the Aheria
and Harburahs and neither was a separate agricultural colony envisaged for their resettlement. The magistrate did, however, attempt to
obtain some land from the local landholders but remained suspicious
of their motives.[39] By 1880, the population of Aherias and Harburahs
had shrunk to 523 and eighty-five respectively. In 1880, fifty Aherias
and fourteen Harburahs absconded and in 1881, forty-five Aherias
and three Harburahs; sixty-two Aherias in 1883, and seventy-seven
Aherias in 1884 and 125 Aherias in 1885. Figures of the Harburah
abscondings were not tabulated for the past few years, but abscondings continued nonetheless.

By the end of 1879, the number of Aherias and Harburahs had
shrunk to 523 and eighty-five respectively. Without an apparatus
of surveillance the application of the Act had little effect on the
movements of the Aherias and Harburahs and large numbers continued to leave and return to the district every year. The following
Table shows that until 1882, the abscondings and returns went almost
unchecked.

Table 5.2

Ahirs and Harburahs in Etah	1880	1881	1882	1883	1884	1885
Numbers absconding	48	88,662	17	20	7	64
Absent on pass	57	1,153	77	126	194	93
Numbers returned	119	187	101	179		

Source: NWPO Jud. (Cr.) Progs, August 1880, August 1881, August 1882, January
1884, September 1884, and July 1885.

After 1883, however, local officers in an attempt to curb the abscondings, liberalized the issue of passes, enforced the roll-call, and began to flog those who were captured outside their registered zones. However, this seems to have been an exercise in tidying up the returns, for although the number of abscondings fell sharply, the liberal issue of passes meant that almost any Aheria or Harburah could now 'abscond' on pass.[40]

In the ensuing decade, plans for the resettlement of the Sanorias, the Aherias, and the Harburahs did not materialize, and though various attempts were aimed at tightening the procedures of surveillance, abscondings continued.

The abscondings disappointed W. Kaye, the commissioner of the Agra division, who considered the Act to be a 'dead letter' in Etah, and recommended that the district be withdrawn from its operation.[41] Of the 969 Aherias originally registered in the district, 209 had absconded to Aligarh by 1885. The difficulty in exercising surveillance over the Aherias was twofold: first, the Act was not in operation in Aligarh, and second, the majority of the Aherias in both Aligarh and Etah were ordinary cultivators, and although they maintained relations with those registered, the extension of the Act in Etah or its application in Aligarh could not be considered.

Even so the disciplinary system was not in vain. Etah district officials interpreted the effect of the Act on the proclaimed Aherias differently from Kaye. For M.L. Ferrar, the magistrate of Etah, surveillance had not been a failure despite the abscondings: the 'harassing attention of the police' had had its effect on the Aherias, so much so that he had to personally intervene on several occasions to remove forty-nine 'respectable if poor' Aheria peasants from the operation of the Act.[42] It is likely that a large proportion of the abscondings were a reaction to police harassment. But the measures adopted by the police had another effect: the involvement of the Aherias in dacoities and robberies in Etah declined, and the magistrate was satisfied that most of the registered Aherias and Harburas were taking to agriculture. Although warrants had been issued for the arrest of those who had absconded to Aligarh, no arrests were made as the Aligarh police considered the mere threat of arrest sufficient to keep the runaway Aherias under control. Their confidence was well-founded and the emigrants settled down in Aligarh as peasant cultivators and labourers. Thus when the magistrate of Etah recommended that the district be removed from the operation of the Criminal Tribes Act, his reasons were different from those of the divisional commissioner. For him the Act had run its course, 'and those [Aherias] who [were] inclined to break the law [were] ordinary thieves to be disposed of by ordinary police'.[43]

Thus the abscondings lent themselves to two opposing interpretations of the working of the Criminal Tribes Act. The district authorities did not attach any unfavourable significance to the figures as there was other evidence to suggest that the surveillance had been effective. But to the commissioner of the Agra division and the inspector general of police of the North Western Provinces, the abscondings appeared to be a measure of the failure of the Act and an indication of the inability of the district authorities to exercise surveillance successfully.[44] William Crooke, who succeeded M.L. Ferrar in Etah, corroborated his predecessor's conclusions. The system of passes and the roll-call had had a positive influence in repressing crime and 'there is no evidence', Crooke confirmed, that the 'members of the tribes [Aherias and Harburahs] here have shown any special criminality … during the past three years'.[45] He, however, disagreed with Ferrar on the question of withdrawing the district from the operation of the Act. Surveillance had forced the errant Aherias to seek occupations in agriculture and 'if the Act was withdrawn they would undoubtedly revert to a life of crime'.[36] Instead, Crooke felt that the Act should be extended to the neighbouring districts. On the whole he expressed satisfaction that most Aherias had some 'ostensible means of honest living' even though these means were 'very precarious and uncertain'.[47] Patently, the acceptance by the Aherias of honest poverty was a clear measure of the success of the disciplinary system.

The threat of arrest and the pressure of constant police harassment made the Aherias accept cultivation with all its uncertainties as a desirable option. There is some evidence to suggest that the registered Aherias usually held some land or worked as agricultural labourers in Etah, supplementing their meagre incomes from land with burglaries, robberies, and petty dacoities. Once the system of roll-call and passes was rigorously imposed, the Aherias of Etah eschewed serious crimes and returned to agriculture, and were no longer regarded as 'the turbulent criminal class they were supposed to be'.[48] Settlement in agriculture, therefore, functioned as an equivocation between reformation and repression. Such a calculus was integral to the disciplinary mechanism, and was clearly recognized as such by police officers.[49]

These considerations motivated the vigorous enforcement of the disciplinary rules on the Sanorias of Lalitpur with telling effect: 'the bulk of the people [Sanorias], it was reported in 1888, under surveillance are settling down to a life of industry'.[50]

Although serious crimes among the Aherias and Sanorias declined as the measures of surveillance were strictly enforced, plans to resettle them, particularly the Sanorias, remained ineffectual. During 1890 and 1891, no special measures were taken to assist the Aherias of Etah either. Assistance was considered unnecessary and wasteful especially since they were taking to agriculture on their own. So successful was the surveillance that the magistrate of Etah cancelled the registration of 56 Aherias during 1889–90.[51]

The scenario at Lalitpur was different. While a number of names—thirty-seven in all—were removed from the registered list in consideration of good conduct, yet many Sanorias absconded mainly because of bad harvests and the high prices that prevailed in Lalitpur during 1890 and 1891.[52] An inquiry into the conditions of the Sanorias in the two settlements of Bir and Sanwano in Lalitpur revealed that the Sanorias had good reason to abscond. G.L. Lang, the commissioner of Jhansi, personally visited the settlements in February 1891. He found the Sanorias entirely dependent on rainwater for cultivation. As a consequence, they could cultivate only one crop in the *kharif* season; their fields went uncultivated during the *rabi*. Besides, they had no working capital and no moneylender to advance credit. They raised money for the kharif seed by selling wood and grass 'but none had the means or the energy to raise a winter crop'.[53] These difficulties, together with the fact that plots were scattered over large distances, made rabi cropping impossible. The commissioner regarded the land held by the Sanorias to be 'practically valueless', and recommended an immediate investment of 400 rupees in wells to rescue the colony from imminent collapse and abandonment.[54]

However, the desertions from Bir and Sanwaho did not disturb the
equanimity of the police. For one, the Tehri durbar had agreed to help
keep the activities of the Sanorias in check, and those Sanorias that
did abscond had neither the means nor the support of former patrons
to take to their erstwhile expeditions. Therefore, the inspector general
of police advised against any further investment in the two Sanoria
settlements. The lieutenant-governor of the North Western Provinces
agreed, and instructed the abandonment of the experiment. The
government was not interested in the fate of the Sanorias after their
crimes had ceased to be a threat to law and order.[55] This abandonment was restricted to the withholding of all future investments, but
police surveillance was to continue as before. In 1892, the government
of the North Western Provinces emphasized that the surveillance
of the Sanorias was not to be relaxed; rather it suggested increased
surveillance.[56]

By 1892, the Aherias were no longer considered a law and order
problem either, as a majority of those registered had settled down
in agriculture. The following year Etah was withdrawn from the
operation of the Act, though a special police force was retained.[57] In
Lalitpur, in the absence of any further grants, the population of Bir
and Sanwaho dwindled away. Those who remained, cultivated one
harvest and subsisted as agricultural labourers during the rabi season
on plots and sites that had artificial water resources. In 1895 the *Report
on the Working of the Criminal Tribes Act* commented with regard to
the Sanorias:

> The working of the Act cannot be said to exhibit any advance; at the
> same time ... [as far as the] proclaimed population [of Sanorias] is
> concerned the tribe cannot be charged with having done much
> harm within these Provinces, and the number who evidently visited
> other parts of India on predatory expeditions appears to be very
> small.[58]

The application of the Criminal Tribes Act to the Bawarias, the
Sanorias, the Aherias, and the Harburahs between 1871 and 1895
shows that resettlement of the criminal tribes was envisaged as an
apprenticeship not in successful agriculture but in the virtues of moral
livelihood itself. Thus the procedures of surveillance, the 'failure' of

the Bawaria experiment at Bidauli, and the abandoning of resettlement schemes in Etah, Bir, and Sanwaho reveal a disciplinary system, which was initially linked to a didactic plan of resettlement, as a part of a different strategy. The criminal tribes were not only forced to take up the honest livelihood of peasant cultivators but were made to accept the social and economic insecurities associated with it. In this, the Criminal Tribes Act attempted to divide the space within which poverty and crime existed. In its stead it sought to produce two segregated domains: one of the moral poor and the other of the criminal tribes.

[...]

The category of criminal tribes was stereotypical in the sense that its defining characteristics though seen to be rooted in Indian society and its past were brought together in an ahistorical and decontextualized form. The criminal tribes were at once a metaphor for Indian society and a set of 'abnormal' native people who had to be disciplined and controlled by the colonial state. Thus the language that had been developed to explain the criminality of the criminal tribes also spelt out the terms of their reclamation. Disciplinary power was exercised to control and convert them into settled peasants—the moral subjects of the Raj. Hence agricultural resettlement along with surveillance was regarded as the appropriate path to the 'normalization' of the criminal types. However, the strategy of agricultural reclamation presented a contradiction, and in the long run surveillance and punishment took precedence over resettlement. This was because the inability of the criminal tribes to take to agricultural cultivation was rarely seen in the light of landlord power, usurious dealings, or crop failures. Rather, this was mostly regarded as an indication of their unwillingness to accept the hard life of a peasant, an attitude that tended to reinforce the stereotype of innate criminality.

NOTES

1. North Western Provinces, Police Proceedings (hereafter NWP, Police Progs.), 22 September 1866, no. 15.

2. See Part 1 of this essay: 'The Making of a Colonial Stereotype—The Criminal Tribes and Castes of North India', *Indian Economic and Social History Review* (*IESHR*), vol. 2, 1990.

3. For a detailed discussion, see Sanjay Nigam, 'A Social History of a Colonial Stereotype. The Criminal Tribes and Castes of Uttar Pradesh, 1871–1947', unpublished PhD thesis, University of London, 1987.

4. Government of India, Legislative Proceedings (GoI, Leg. Progs.), July 1872, no. 117.

5. North-Western Provinces and Oudh, Judicial [Criminal] Proceedings (NWPO, Jud. [Cr.]) Progs, May 1873, North Western Provinces, and Oudh Judicial (Criminal) Proceedings.

6. North-Western Provinces (NWP) Jud. (Cr.) Progs., June 1873.

7. GoI, Leg. Progs, July 1872, no. 116.

8. NWP Jud. (Cr.) Progs, July 1876.

9. GoI, Leg. Progs., July 1872, no. 118.

10. No. 641C, 1 July 1875, NWPO, Jud. (Cr.) Progs., July 1876.

11. No. 2133A, 27 September 1878, NWPO, Jud. (Cr.) Progs., December 1878.

12. Statement Showing the Criminal Tribes Proclaimed under Act XXVII of 1871, 31 March, as returned by District Officers, NWP, Jud. (Cr.) Progs., December 1878.

13. No. 2133A, see Note 11.

14. No. 19, 31 January 1878, NWPO, Jud. (Cr.) Progs, April 1879.

15. From W.C. Plowden, Comm., Meerut Div. to the Sec. to Govt. NWPO, Jud. (Cr.) Progs, April 1879.

16. From C. Brenard, Offg. Sec. to the Govt. of India, Home Dept. (Judicial), to Sec. to Govt. NWPO, no. 597, 22 May 1879; from Sec. to Govt. NWPO, to Comm. Meerut Div., no. 796, 5 June 1879, NWPO, Jud. (Cr.) Progs, June 1879.

17. Notification no. 488A, Judicial (Cr.) Dept., 19 March 1874, NWPO, Jud. (Cr.) Progs, June 1873.

18. From Offg. Sec. to Govt. NWP, to Inspector General of Police (IGP), no. 499A, 17 July 1876, NWPO, Jud. (Cr.) Progs, July 1876.

19. From DIGP (deputy inspector general of police), NWPO to IGP (inspector general of police), no. 641C, NWPO, Jud. (Cr.) Progs, July 1876.

20. From Major J. Liston, Dy. Comm., Jhansi Division, NWPO, Jud. (Cr.) Progs., May 1879.

21. No. 2133A, 27 September 1878; no. 1702A, NWPO, Jud. (Cr.) Progs., December 1878.

22. From J.W. Quinton, Offg. Comm. Jhansi Div. to IGP, NWPO, no. 339, Jhansi, 27 February 1879, Jud. (Cr.) Progs., March 1879.

23. No. 373, 21 December 1878, NWPO, Jud. (Cr.) Progs, May 1879.

24. Ibid.

25. No. 641C, 1 July 1875, NWPO, Jud. (Cr.) Progs, July 1876.

26. Ibid.

27. No. 1314, 23 June 1881, NWPO, Jud. (Cr.) Progs, August 1881.

28. No. 1659A, 20 June 1883, NWPO, Jud. (Cr.) Progs, Jan, 1884.

29. No. 835A, 12 January 1883; no. 25, 6 December 1882, NWPO, Jud. (Cr.) Progs, January 1884.

30. No. 835A, 12 January 1883.

31. No. 25, 6 December1882, NWPO, Jud. (Cr.) Progs, January 1884.

32. No. 220, 20–21 October 1883, NWPO, Jud. (Cr.) Progs, January 1884.

33. Ibid.

34. Notification no. 1752A of 1873, Jud. (Cr.) Dept, 22 October 1873, NWPO, Jud. (Cr.) Progs., October 1873.

35. Statement showing the state of several criminal tribes proclaimed under Act XXVII, 1871 on 31 December 1874, NWPO, Jud. (Cr.) Progs., July 1876.

36. No. 67, 4 June 1873, NWPO, Jud. (Cr.) Progs, 1873.

37. No. 2133A, 27 September 1878, NWPO, Jud. (Cr.) Progs, 1878.

38. No. 430C-A, 22 July 1879, NWPO, Jud. (Cr.) Progs, November 1879.

39. No. 614C, 1 July 1875, NWPO, Jud. (Cr.) Progs, July 1876.

40. No. 149, 30 April 1883, NWPO, Jud. (Cr.) Progs, January 1884.

41. No. 3977/XV-40, NWPO, Police Progs, July 1888.

42. No. 91, 20 February 1868, North-Western Provinces and Oudh, Police Proceedings (NWPO, Police Progs), July 1866.

43. Ibid.

44. No. 233/VIII-325, 21 June 1886, NWPO, Police Progs, July 1888.

45. No. 409, File 325, 26 Aug. 1887, NWPO, Police Progs, July 1888.

46. Ibid.

47. Ibid.

48. No. 3046A, 3 November 1888, NWPO, Police Progs, January 1889.

49. No. 1471A, 12 June 1886, NWPO, Police Progs, July 1886.

50. No. 3046A, see Note 48.

51. No. 1929A, 29 July 1889, NWPO, Police Progs, September 1889.

52. No. 1190A, NWPO, Police Progs, August 1890.

53. 2011/1V-A-11, 21 February 1891. NWPO, Police Progs, May 1891.

54. Ibid.

55. Police Department Resolution no. 550/VIII-819-4 of 1891, dated 26 May 1891, NWPO, Police Progs, May 1891.

56. No. 1516/VII-528A-12 of 1892, NWPO, Police Progs, November 1892.

57. No. 4648A, 2 October 1893, NWPO, Police Progs, January 1894.

58. NWPO, Police Progs, December 1895, no. 1.

III

Surveillance and Subversion

6

Police and Public Order*

Rajnarayan Chandavarkar

British rule in India was characteristically autocratic and repressive. It could at times be brutal and violent. The rhetoric of civil liberties and individual freedoms decorated its claims to legitimacy but, in practice, these considerations occupied a lowly place in its order of priorities. In a history characterized by annexation and conquest and by the maintenance of dominion by force, it is not surprising that the organization and activities of the police should be taken to reflect the authoritarian nature of colonial rule. For some, it has appeared to be 'expressive of the very nature of colonial rule in India'[1]

By focusing upon the administration and organization of the police, historians have often tended to foster the supposition that it constituted a monolithic force.[2] However, this organizational perspective has made it difficult to resolve apparent contradictions in the nature of colonial policing and sometimes served to proliferate confusion. Thus, in one account, the police appeared to constitute the most effective and powerful instrument of colonial repression, but they were also found to be 'often inadequate to meet the major crises of rural control'. On the one hand, 'the coercive strength and disposition of

* Excerpted from Rajnarayan Chandavarkar, *Imperial Power and Popular Politics: Class, Resistance and State in India, 1850–1950* (Cambridge: Cambridge University Press, 1998).

the colonial police' was said to be nourished by colonial and racist ideology; on the other hand, we are told that 'India's colonial regime fell short of being a police state' or a 'society ruled through fear' because of 'Britain's own political culture' whose innate liberalism served as a check upon unbridled despotism. Colonial and racist attitudes, presumably not drawn from 'Britain's own political culture', underlay the violence of the state, yet, largely, 'the police alignment was with the propertied classes and not merely the ruling race'. Thus, the police have been portrayed as the main force of a colonial state which was both hegemonic and vulnerable; characterized as coercive yet found to be ineffectual; motivated by racism yet restrained by an inherent metropolitan liberalism; allied closely with Indian propertied elites and yet the bludgeon of the ruling race.[3]

This chapter will suggest that generalizations about the nature of policing should rest most securely upon the investigation of its daily operations rather than its administrative design or its organizational form. Accordingly, it will focus upon what might be described as 'everyday policing'. Its aim is to place police methods of operation in relation to the social organization of the neighbourhoods in Bombay city in the late-nineteenth and early-twentieth centuries. The daily operations of the police were determined by the financial and political constraints within which they developed. At this quotidian level, the police were integral to the processes by which power relations were negotiated in the street and the neighbourhood, and thus constituted an important element in the formation and consolidation of local power. Their actions influenced, as, indeed, they came to be moulded by, patterns of local dominance. Furthermore, at lesser levels, albeit less systematically, the working classes, too, could draw upon, appropriate' and deploy their personal and social caste and kinship connections with the police. As the police became embedded within the social and political networks of the neighbourhood, they operated less as simply an instrument of social control, but proved more responsive to influences which were relatively autonomous of their own internal structure of command. In this light, and viewed through the prism of their daily operations, the police, far from being monolithic, appear to have been responsive to varied and often conflicting sets of social pressures.

It is not intended to suggest that we should replace the notion that the police were indiscriminately repressive with the notion that they were uniformly benign. In Bombay, as elsewhere, the police lacked the political and financial resources to control and discipline the working classes as a whole. The conventional and pragmatic response of the police has been to proceed selectively. Some elements among the poor and the working classes, singled out for particular attention, must have experienced the police as a particularly brutal and violent force. But if the police were open to recruitment by diverse groups within the urban neighbourhoods, they could not fulfil their disciplinary, even coercive, function systematically. On the contrary, their selective interventions were probably often experienced as somewhat arbitrary, but they would have seemed no less oppressive and no more limited for being less systematic. If the police lacked the political and financial resources to set out to control and discipline the working classes as a whole, they also found it difficult to proceed more selectively by identifying particular social groups as the targets of their actions. For the task of establishing a general and uniformly applicable consensus about the particular social groups to be discriminatingly identified as the proper objects of policing often proved beyond the capacity of the colonial state in India. From the perspective of everyday policing, it would seem implausible to portray the police as simply and unproblematically the enforcers of social control designed by the colonial state and its collaborators or to suppose that they were able consistently to give practical effect to the intentions of the official mind. Indeed, frequently, their methods of operation undermined and contradicted the most carefully devised blueprints of the colonial state.

Two further considerations embedded the police more deeply within the social organization of the neighbourhood. First, in India the police force had military origins. Its primary concern was to police those who had been subjugated, to facilitate the collection of revenue, and to ensure the free movement of goods. After the 1860s, when a uniform police system was put in place, the police understanding of its own role, and its perception of crime and the social order were coloured by its military antecedents. The police were liable, therefore, to understand crime primarily in terms of rebellion and disorder, public and political security, rather than simply in terms of law-breaking and the security of property and the person. Of course, no police force could set itself the task of rooting out crime wherever it was to be found, with any realistic expectation of accomplishing it. On the contrary, police activity, and the operation of the criminal justice system as a whole, often served to define and indeed, therefore, to create crime. The more conscientiously the police set out to abolish crime, the more likely it was to both become aware of it, generate fresh categories of offences, and criminalize old patterns of behaviour. The operations of the police imparted to the notion of public security an explicitly, and narrowly, political meaning. For this reason, it neither sought to intervene energetically nor to disturb too greatly the practices by which offences against person and property were handled within informal social networks or local power structures. Of course, the police everywhere have relied to varying degrees upon the collaboration of local residents. Its consequence in India was that propertied elites, merchants and industrialists, and local magnates, created their own private arrangements for protection and policing. For this reason, too, the scope and the daily practices of the police, and their apparent ambiguities and contradictions, need to be situated within the context of the social relations of the neighbourhood.

Second, although the colonial state increasingly assumed that the maintenance of public order was ordinarily the duty of the police, troops were frequently summoned to deal with 'local disturbances'. Significantly, public order policing in India, even after the 1860s, was largely conducted by the army. When the police were called upon to deal with 'local disturbances', their strategies were largely shaped by their own relationship to the social organization of the neighbourhood. It was at this quotidian level that the parameters within which the police approached larger and more dramatic problems of public order were defined. Senior police officers recognized the value of establishing close connections with the informal social networks of the neighbourhood, both to detect crime and to protect the public order. But such connections only served to heighten their anxieties about the quality of the discipline of their rank and file.

Frequently, faced with 'a local disturbance', the police felt they were unable to cope and that they were in danger of being overrun by the 'mob'. They required the army to stand by and strengthen their nerve and sometimes to intervene and restore order. The armed force which the colonial state could command was formidable and when it perceived a serious threat to its security, it unleashed it with a ruthless, sometimes murderous, brutality. Its sanction and its power were essential to the maintenance and perpetuation of British rule. Yet the British sometimes appeared unable to deploy it to repress their opponents. The British in India did not—they could not—constitute an army of occupation. Had they attempted to so style themselves, the armed force at their disposal would have seemed woefully inadequate.[4] In any case, they did not rule India for its own sake; their purposes were global and imperial and extended beyond the limits of political dominion. For the historian, therefore, the central problem in the policing of colonial India is how to match the repressive power of the state to the fragility of its control. It was primarily because the police established these connections within the neighbourhood, remained open, however unwittingly, to its influences, and sought to maintain public order through these alliances, that they were able to postpone for a time having to bear the ultimate cost of their most brutal repressive efforts. Thus, the supposedly 'coercive disposition' of the police force and its repressive practices were inextricably connected to the nature of its daily operations in the street and the neighbourhood [...]

NOTES

1. David Arnold, *Police Power and Colonial Rule: Madras, 1859–1947* (New Delhi 1986), p. 235.

2. Percival Griffiths, *To Guard My People: The History of the Indian Police* (London 1971); Anandswarup Gupta, *The Police in British India, 1861–1947* (New Delhi 1979); Arnold, *Police Power and Colonial Rule*; Peter Robb, 'The Ordering of Rural India. British Control in 19th-century Bengal and Bihar', in David Anderson and David Killingray (eds), *Policing the Empire, Government, Authority and Control, 1830–1940* (Manchester, New York 1991), pp. 126–150.

3. Arnold, *Police Power and Colonial Rule*, pp. 147, 230, 233, 235.

4. Thus, in 1938, there was one British soldier to every 88 square miles of the territory and for every 20,000 inhabitants of the subcontinent. 'The British Element in Internal Security Troops', Appendix E to Annex 2, CID 198-D, CAB 6/6, PRO, cited by D. Ornissi, *The Sepoy and the Raj: The Indian Army, 1860–1940* (London 1994), p. 212.

7

Disciplining 'Natives'

Prisons and Prisoners in Early Nineteenth-century India*

Anand A. Yang

> The general features of the system of Prison Discipline recommended
> by the Committee are these: viz. that a Penitentiary for all prisoners
> sentenced to more than one year's imprisonment shall be established
> in the centre of every 6 or 8 districts, and that a better system for the
> classification of prisoners shall be adopted: that each prisoner shall
> have a separate sleeping place: that solitary confinement shall be much
> resorted to: that monotonous, uninteresting labour within doors shall
> be enforced upon all prisoners sentenced to labour: that prisoners shall
> be deprived of every indulgence not absolutely necessary to health, and
> that the management of each penitentiary shall be committed to an
> able trustworthy Superintendent, either European or Native.[1]

These recommendations, proposing a new system of punishment for
the emerging British empire in India, formed the blueprint for penal
reform in the nineteenth century. Grounded in the fresh conceptions
of punishment that had been sweeping across Europe and the United

* This essay was originally published in *South Asia*, vol. X, no. 2, December 1987,
pp. 29–45 and is reproduced here with permission. An earlier version of this
paper was presented at the Tenth Conference of the International Association of
Historians of Asia, Singapore, 17–31 October 1986.

States since 1780—and that would continue to reshape systems of punishments in many parts of the world till 1850—the ideas of the 1838 Committee on Prison Discipline were also crafted to fit the imperatives of the growing colonial system.[2]

The lead in penal reform in India was taken by the 1835 Law Commission that was charged with the task of revamping the judicial system. According to Thomas Babington Macaulay, the head of this Commission, the development of a new penal code had to be accompanied by prison reform. In his words, 'the best Criminal Code can be of very little use to the community unless there be a good machinery for the infliction of punishment'.[3] And for Macaulay, who also became the chief architect of prison system, 'a good system of prison discipline' was one:

> where the criminal, without being subject to any cruel severities, is strictly restrained, regularly employed in labour not of an attractive kind, and *deprived* of every indulgence not necessary to his health, [and] a year's confinement for two years in a gaol where the superintendence is lax, where the work exacted is light, and where the convicts find means of enjoying as many luxuries as if they were at liberty.[4]

For the 1838 Committee the prison with its new regimen of diet, work, and solitary confinement was to be the centerpiece of the new 'science' of punishment. Transportation was another technology in which the Committee placed its faith. By stiffening the conditions of incarceration and by transporting offenders overseas, the Committee sought to construct a system of punishment which provided the right calculus of terror and deterrence. Both elements were considered necessary because the British system of punishment had eliminated some of the more sanguinary punishments prescribed by indigenous law, such as mutilation, and had reduced the number of cases in which capital punishment was applicable. Thus, imprisonment, the chief form of punishment, had to be made a 'terror to wrong-doers', an objective which transportation was also seen as realizing.[5]

This paper examines the effects of the extension of the new system of discipline and punishment to India by looking at its workings in the prisons of Bihar.[6] It focuses specifically on the effects of the introduction of the ration and messing system, a system aimed at stiffening the conditions of incarceration by removing the 'indulgences' allowed prisoners for purchasing their foodstuffs and preparing their own meals. How the new system of punishment fitted in with the imperatives of colonial rule is also of interest, although not pursued at length here.[7]

The rise of British authority and power in India coincided with the emergence of new philosophical ideas of punishment in late eighteenth- and early nineteenth-century England, ideas which made it 'just, reasonable, and humane to immure prisoners in solitary cells, clothe them in uniforms, regiment their day to the cadence of the clock, and "improve" their minds with dosages of scripture and hard labour'. Between 1770 and 1840 this form of carceral discipline 'directed at the mind' replaced a cluster of punishments 'directed at the body'—whipping, branding, the stocks, and public hanging.'[8] Transplanted to India—although in a highly selective way because the idea of inflicting pain to the body continued to be an important operating principle—these conceptions of punishment were incorporated into a larger structure of colonial administration and rule. That is, the new science of punishment constituted part of a larger package of changes introducing penal and criminal codes, and establishing more effective mechanisms of control, particularly the formation of an organized and professional police force. These changes were designed not only to enhance and consolidate the rising power of the colonial state by creating a more complete infrastructure of control but also to augment the authority of the Raj by appropriating for the state the power and influence necessary to become the 'ultimate source for norms, and definer of what was appropriate [behaviour].'[9] Thus, the recommendations of the 1838 Committee—although reflecting the 'whole Benthamite cast of mind' and the 'voice of the new Poor Law', intellectual wellsprings from which contemporary penological theory in England emanated—ultimately diverged from the new theories of punishment current in the European setting. And thus little in the report speaks in the voice of 'humanitarianism'. Nor is there much about reformation or rehabilitation, a notable contrast to the intense and heated disputations dividing English prison reforms from Bentham onwards over the 'twin aims of deterrence and reformation'.

Such differences originated in the fact that discipline and punishment under the British Raj were inextricably linked to that regime's strategies of power and rule.[10]

Designed to attack the mind, the new forms of discipline and punishment in India, at least in one important respect, also assaulted the body. This clash surfaced principally over the innovation of messing. In stripping prisoners of their money allowances and substituting a system of rations in its place, Indian authorities recognized that they were militating 'against the prisoners' comfort and inclinations'. They also seemed to be aware that they were incurring other 'risks' in enforcing the new regimen:

> … through the frauds of contractors and jail servants, the food supplied for prisoners may not be of wholesome quality: that the average ration cannot in each particular instance be a sufficient allowance of food; and that particular prisoners may suffer in health from the want of those condiments or narcotics to which they have been accustomed'.[11]

Much consideration was also given to matters relating to the appropriateness of the kind of rations distributed, from the standpoint of both their fit with local dietary customs and their suitability for keeping prisoners healthy. Far less attention was paid to the cultural, religious, and social consequences of this change, consequences which were the inevitable result of imposing messing on a society where status was closely linked to ritual purity, and rules of purity expressed specifically in matters relating to the ingestion of food. Largely ignored therefore was the fact that *both* the preparation and consumption of food constitutes a ritual and social act in Indian society, an act in which who a person accepts food from and with whom he eats manifests his caste status vis-a-vis the others. Although the rules regulating it are stricter for higher than lower castes, as Louis Dumont notes,

> The fact remains that one can scarcely ever eat side by side with any but one's equals, … meals are not those pleasant conversational gatherings with which we are acquainted: they are technical operations which leave room for only a limited margin of freedom.[12]

What effects the new philosophy of punishment had on the lives of the prisoners themselves forms another interest of this study. By looking at the confrontation over messing, my intention is not only to show generally the ways in which inmates reacted to and resisted the new regimen but also to sketch a portrait of the people behind the walls since the issue was likely to affect different castes differently. Any study of prisons that includes prisoners in its focus also aims at correcting much of the contemporary literature on prisons in which, to use Michell Perrot's words, 'prisoners ... have disappeared from their own history'.[13]

Even before the Committee's report on prison discipline was published, its deliberations had set changes into motion. At its prompting, in 1837, the Bengal authorities began to push for the abolition of money allowances and the introduction of the ration system. By April 1838, the new system was already in place in many districts; in a few, rations were distributed through messes. In the Bihar districts, except for 'some discontent', said to stem from prisoners disenchanted with the loss of their money allowances, the switch to the ration system was effected smoothly.[14]

The practice of providing prisoners 'with a daily money allowance' came under critical fire because it 'permitted [them] to purchase their own food from one or more shop-keepers who are allowed access to the prison'.[15] Under the ration system, however, 'no convicted prisoner [was to] be hereafter allowed to cook his own victuals but that a Brahmin and Mussulman cook be provided for each Gaol'.[16] Although the Committee couched its argument in altruistic terms by claiming that the ration system was designed to 'ensure a proper variety of foods, and a sufficient quantity of stimulating condiments to assist digestion',[17] its primary reasons for recommending the shift pointed to a different set of circumstances. Its real target was the practice of giving money allowances, which it said enabled prisoners in Bengal to 'fare better, and more fully, than the agricultural labourers'.[18] In the North-Western Provinces, it noted, in an equally disapproving tone, that 'prisoners, in almost every case, live upon the best wheaten flour: whilst it is well known that the laboring population there lives upon food of a very inferior quality'. As a result, it estimated that 'a prisoner there, instead of living like the mass of his class out of Gaol, enjoys the food of a sepoy, or a well-fed domestic servant'.[19]

Since the customary allowance hitherto allotted prisoners offered them a 'more dainty and generous diet than nine out of ten of the population of the country', the Committee proposed restricting their diet in any locality to the 'coarsest grain on which the mass of the people of that district lives'.[20]

In seeking these strictures, the Committee obviously drew on the Benthamite 'rule of severity', a rule also underlying the Poor Law Report of 1834, which stated that 'no prisoner should enjoy a better lifestyle than that of the poorest of free persons'.[21] As in the manner of the Royal Commission on the Poor Laws whose report shaped the basic doctrines of the New Poor Law in England, the report of the Prison Discipline Committee adjudged the diet of Indian prisoners as unnecessarily abundant. And as in the case of the indigent for whom the New Poor Laws proposed a uniform system of relief defined by the principle of 'less eligibility', that is, conditions were to be 'less eligible' or less attractive for people seeking relief than those existing for 'honest labourers', the diet of Indian prisoners was to be regulated along similar lines.[22]

The Committee also inveighed against money allowances, singling them out as the currency of corruption among prisoners and guards alike. In its view, moreover, the allowances, varying from five pie to one anna and a quarter, were excessive because they enabled prisoners to accumulate savings.[23]

The money allowance system especially drew the stern disapproval of the Committee because it provided indulgences, which had to be removed if imprisonment was to constitute a term of severe punishment. This same logic also informed the Committee's recommendation to prohibit prisoners from engaging in the 'daily enjoyment of marketing', a practice said to constitute 'a great alleviation of the punishment of confinement to any class of men, but which we believe to be peculiarly agreeable to the Indian character'.[24] Nor was a convicted prisoner to be permitted to cook his own meals because that activity was 'one of the greatest enjoyments of every individual amongst the lower orders in India, even when at liberty, and consequently this long operation must be the chief alleviation of the tedium of a prisoner's life...' Therefore, the Committee concluded that by stripping prisoners of the two pleasures of marketing and cooking would add materially to the severity of the punishment of imprisonment, and so make it possible to reduce proportionally the term of imprisonment, without taking away from the efficacy of the punishment'.[25]

Once rations were in place, the Bengal authorities turned their attention to the matter of messes. At first their directive merely encouraged the formation of messes and, even then, only wherever and whenever possible.[26] By 1840, the call for the introduction of messes assumed a more insistent tone, and by July 1841, government plans were well under way to extend the messing system to all the jails of Bihar.[27]

In almost every Bihar jail, prisoners greeted the new measures with open hostility. Typical of their response was that reported for the Behar (Gaya) Jail where 'all sorts of threats were uttered by the convicts against their guards etc. and they declared that they would rather die than submit to what would deprive them of their castes'.[28] In Saran district's Chapra jail the order provoked a 'serious disturbance' in 1842 among the seven hundred inmates: serious not only because the prisoners were united in their protest, but also because it threatened to erupt into a 'popular outbreak' when a 'mob' of 3,000 to 4,000 townspeople assembled at the prison gates.[29] Although such resistance compelled the local authorities to suspend the experiment in Chapra and in only the Tirhut and Champaran jails were messing arrangements even partially implemented, it also prompted them to seek additional information regarding caste and religious rules regarding food. As a result, the Saran magistrate produced a report identifying prisoners by caste as well as by subcaste. He also informed his superiors that

> … the subdivisions of caste are endless; and I feel convinced not only that their [prisoners'] feelings are for the most part sincere and genuine but that nothing—no force, restraint or punishment however severe and cogent—will induce *all* of them to act against them. With the assistance of two or three companies of regular sepoys I could doubtless keep the people at large from interfering with, or coercing me in the execution of my duty as manager of the jail; but I am convinced that even then they would still—at least several of them—only do what they thought would be no detriment to their caste and social position, *and to that of their families.*[30]

The Chapra experience also led the Bengal authorities to urge local administrators to proceed more cautiously: not to establish messing by relying on 'undistinguishing forces', not to drive prisoners 'to extremity on a subject like this', not to coerce them into forming messes but to

> consult them as to the number of constitution of the messes ... listen to all not very unreasonable objections, bear with many frivolous-seeming scruples, insist only where they can surely and safely enforce their views, and with a good grace give up, at least for a time, points which they see before hand, it may be extremely difficult to carry.[31]

The 1842 'mutiny' and 'general revolt' of the entire prison population of the Saran jail, and the loud murmuring in other Bihar jails, slowed down the efforts of the authorities but did not dissuade them from giving up the objective of making messing the standard practice in all jails. On the contrary, wherever it could be enforced—in the jails of Bengal proper—it was, although with varying degrees of success and firmness.[32] Furthermore, instead of shaking the government's faith, resistance to the new regimen reinforced its conviction regarding the appropriateness of extending messing to all jails. The growing attachment to messing was sustained by a faith in its value as a mechanism for inducing 'discipline and orderly behaviour' and a 'powerful aid' in stiffening the conditions of punishment. As one local administrator informed his superiors, the best recommendation for enforcing messing was the prisoner's

> unmitigated dislike [of it] ... (I)t would be a poor instrument of jail discipline were it otherwise. The feelings with which the people at large look upon it are those of indefinite dread. Formerly the jail was hardly regarded as a place of punishment ... Now the very mention of the jail inspires terror.[33]

Messing, in short, held out the promise of making imprisonment a 'terror to wrong-doers'.

Thus, the government returned to the subject of messing in 1845, when it renewed its efforts to extend it to the jails of Bihar. Although proceeding with greater caution than before, and although seemingly chastened by the 1842 fiasco, which the authorities now attributed to the overzealous and coercive methods employed by local officials, the government refused to consider the possibility that the very practice of messing was the issue of contention.

Indeed, the intense and widespread prisoner resistance to messing in 1845 suggests that the very system was the issue and not the care and caution with which messing was being introduced. The Patna authorities gauged the depth of this sentiment when they admitted that the system could not be introduced without a threat of coercion, if not coercion itself. Magistrate J.E. Little, therefore, requested that a detachment of twenty sepoys be stationed within the Digha penitentiary walls during meal times. 'I do not mean,' he wrote, 'that the prisoners should be compelled to eat at the point of a bayonet but I think the sepoys should be sent as a precaution to overawe them in order to prevent violence ... By these means. I have every hope that the system will be introduced without any disturbance ... I feel convinced that if they think we are determined to carry out the measure they will submit to it without any further opposition.'[34]

In prison after prison, however, inmates refused to comply with official orders mandating that they 'engage in messes'. Even before such directives could be implemented, prisoners appeared to have received advance notice of government plans and geared up for action. Their resistance assumed a variety of forms: in some instances protest was articulated verbally; in other cases it was manifested through outright confrontations.

Prisoners in the Saran jail initially responded by refusing to partake of their meals under the new system. Although otherwise continuing to 'work as usual', over 600 prisoners—the entire population of the jail—refused their food for two days in a row. They also submitted a petition demonstrating against the orders.[35] In Patna, the magistrate was compelled to relax the rules because prisoners were on the verge of starvation after not having taken their meals from Monday morning to Friday.[36]

Prisoners also let their jailers know directly of their grievances. When the Shahabad *darogha* (Indian local head of police), at the behest of his superiors, rounded up thirteen of the most influential prisoners under his charge to tell them that they should organize themselves into messes and appoint cooks, they 'impertinently submitted "that they would eat no victuals but those prepared by their own hands and accordingly could not join in any messes".[37] The following day the magistrate, E. Radcliffe, himself sought to reason with the prisoners. Upon arrival—to continue the saga of 'insubordination' in the magistrate's own words—he encountered 'a prisoner who had been always exceedingly respectful, and the best paper manufacturer in the Jail' and about whom he 'was confident from his former good character that he would accede to the Government wishes. He however displayed the same insolent behaviours and was accordingly confined in the same ward as the thirteen above mentioned'.[38]

Insubordination, moreover, verged on violence. The Shahabad magistrate was provided a preview of this during his tour of the district jail. When he convened the influential prisoners to find out why objections to messing existed, 'Peryaj Pandee [Pandey] stood up and cried out in a most insolent tone of voice "that he was a Brahmin and that he would never eat in company with others, or his life should be the penalty" or words to that effect.' And when Radcliffe ordered his arrest, all the other prisoners jumped up, ready to rescue him. After securing Pandey, he returned home and had been there only ten minutes before he received word that the other inmates had rescued the fifteen prisoners he had especially confined, beaten up several guards, destroying jail machinery in the process. Although the prison was secured, the inmates were persuaded to lay down their weapons, and Pandey and three other ring-leaders of the 'riot … summarily punished', when Radcliffe returned there with other officers and guards, the prisoners continued to resist the messing order. In the aftermath of this incident he once again assembled several influential prisoners—five on this occasion—but 'their unanimous answer was "that any order that I would issue besides this about the messing system they would be willing to carry out" but that as this militated against their castes, life would be of no value afterwards'.[39]

Protest against the messing system, vigorously and boldly manifested through open confrontations, also erupted in other jails. Indeed, to read the accounts of these prison disturbances is to encounter gestures and actions which highlight the intensity of the opposition as well as the lengths to which prisoners were willing to resist before they were suppressed.

Consider the case of the Patna penitentiary whose wards were set up on an experimental basis at Digha, four to five miles outside the city.[40] Despite his worst fears because of the vociferous objections of prisoners to the messing system, it was here that Magistrate Lillie sought to carry out the government order. Backed by a force of *barkandazes* (armed guards) recruited from the city and from the Mithapur jail of the city, he had the prisoners locked up in their respective cells on 11 August, had dinner prepared for them, and placed before their cells. Only twenty out of the 120 prisoners agreed to eat their meals, the rest refusing on grounds that they could not vouch for the 'purity' of the food since it had been cooked on the outside and, therefore, could have been tampered within transit. The following morning, Lillie personally supervised preparations of their morning meal and, as a result, persuaded about 100 convicts to eat; the rest were confined to their cells. Confident of success, he returned to Digha later that afternoon in the hope of having all the prisoners messing together. While overseeing the dinner arrangements, however, he was confronted by four Ahir prisoners who demanded that they be allowed to eat with their caste-men interned in another ward for having earlier refused to mess. While being led off by three barkandazes, the four prisoners broke away from their escort and rushed towards the adjacent ward to free their mates. Led by the four Ahirs, the other prisoners then turned on the guards, some arming themselves with swords seized from the guards, others finding bamboos and brickbats to launch an attack. The magistrate's party retreated in the face of this assault. A relief force had to be sent from half a mile away before a counter-attack could be mounted. But prisoners continued to resist, even showering the British officers leading the relief party with bamboos and bricks. In response the sepoys were directed to open fire, killing one prisoner and wounding several. Only then were the prisoners forced back into their cells.[41]

The same scenario, with a few variations, was repeated in the jail of Saran and Behar districts. In Saran, Magistrate H.W. Russell first sought to introduce messing among the Muslim prisoners (fifty-two out of a total of 662) because he thought they were few in number and least likely to raise objections. Not only did they refuse to comply, but when Russell was personally supervising their organization into messes, prisoners of the Chapra jail en masse rushed the magistrate's party. While some of the guards accompanying Russell took refuge in one of the inner quarters of the jail, many of the prisoners, now carrying implements liberated from the tool shed, forced the magistrate to evacuate the inner area of the prison. With Captain Elwall and his *najibs* (militia) guarding the outer gates—this force had been called in—the magistrate ordered 100 barkandazes armed with *lathis* (clubs) to march in to disperse the prisoners but they were driven back by brickbats. The prisoners then rushed the outer gates but were met by a volley of fire that killed or seriously injured five of them.[42]

On 11 September, 'a serious insurrection' occurred in the Behar jail at Gaya, housing over 1,400 inmates, after the local authorities had seemingly succeeded in separating upper-caste prisoners— Brahmans, Bhumihars, Rajputs, and Kayasths—not only into a ward of their own but also into a distinct mess of their own caste men. However, when T.C. Trotter, the magistrate, approached the Dusadhs and the 'lower classes' who numbered in the 'hundreds', they attacked and wounded his darogha, and disarmed his police constables. Armed with whatever implements they could lay their hands on—shovels, sticks, and *lotas* (brass pots for cooking and drinking)—they also sought to assault the magistrate but were met by a hail of bullets which momentarily halted their advance and instantly killed five 'prisoners… The insurgents were not however checked, and another volley was rendered necessary to compel the great body of them to return to their wards'.[43]

Although driven back to their wards, the inmates of the Behar jail remained defiant. Unless the gates of the jail were opened from the outside, they refused to turn over their casualties who they claimed numbered one dead and eighteen or twenty wounded. Fearful that this was merely a ploy on the part of the prisoners, the judge and the magistrate—concerned about their ability to control the enormous prison population—chose not to take action but to await reinforcements. Not until the arrival of two companies of troops six days later, on 17 September, did the local authorities finally decide to enter the jail, where they found both dead bodies as well as wounded prisoners.[44]

At least one prisoner also sought to publicize his plight through other channels. Two days after the Digha penitentiary outbreak, on 14 August, a Patna resident lodged a complaint about the 'oppression' committed there. In his petition, Akul Mehto, father of Gungoo, one of the prisoners wounded in the Digha firing, also offered an alternative account of the events that led to the outbreak. In his recounting, his son along with the other Ahirs were preparing to sit down to eat the rice they had cooked when Magistrate Lillie came up and touched their food. Only then did the prisoners refuse to partake of their meal. Subsequently, Lillie returned with Captain Boileau and several sepoys and ordered the firing. Akul Mehto also reported that the next day, 13 August, his son and some thirty or forty other prisoners were manacled, given thirty blows each with a rattan and then locked up in their cells without food or water. From this sequence of events, the petition concluded that the magistrate's intention was 'to take the caste of us poor people, besides and in addition to this, what power had Captain Boileau to shoot us poor prisoners'.[45]

For local authorities the intensity of the violent outbreaks in their jails was further heightened by the very real threat of the disturbances spilling over into the wider community. A familiar sight at the scene of the disturbances were townspeople, apparently ready to enter the fray on the side of the prisoners. At Chapra jail, a crowd of some 6,000 people equipped with lumps of *kunkur* (gravel) were said to have gathered to assist in a jail-break.[46] Concern regarding the possibility of an outbreak uniting prisoners and their friends in town prompted the Shahabad magistrate to seek military assistance to control the Arrah jail.[47]

Only in the Gaya jail in Behar was the situation different. According to Magistrate Trotter, he had little to fear from the townspeople of Gaya because 'there is no apparent sympathy on the part of the People with the Prisoners, and indeed we have had every reason to think, that they would have acted against them'.[48] Nevertheless, he, too, requested for troops, which he stationed in town during the trial of the insurrection ringleaders and until their transfer out of the locality. His concern, no doubt, was also prompted by the fact that an attempt had been made to set the Gaya courthouse on fire, purportedly to burn the evidence that had been lodged there on the 'late outbreak in Jail'.[49]

That popular support ranged on the side of the prisoners and against the British authorities over the issue of messing is also apparent from the kinds of rumours that circulated in the wider population.[50] Particularly in Patna city, where the administrative antenna was perhaps most closely tuned into the sentiments of the local population, popular reaction to messing was clearly discernible. According to the Patna magistrate, who claimed to have his finger on the pulse of that city:

> great excitement has arisen in this City, from false reports industriously spread and generally believed, that persons had arrived with the intention of kidnapping children; a number of strangers have suffered ill treatment in consequence and among them, a poor half caste Christian named William Law, who was robbed, severely beaten and was with difficulty rescued by the Police; the most absurd reports have gained credence one of them is, that Government have caused the erection of a large Tank in the Mauritius, and that water will not be obtained in it until 500 children have been sacrificed, and their blood sprinkled over the bottom of it.[51]

And two weeks after the Digha disturbance, Patna's session judge, A. Smelt, reported that people in the city were in 'a very excited state ... Influential natives have spread the most absurd stories, regarding the object of Government, these have gained credence among the ignorant and the prejudiced ...'[52]

Nor did the government note with any less apprehension the careful attention their Indian army recruits paid to news regarding messing. A letter—intercepted by the authorities—addressed by sepoys of the 29th Regiment at Berhampore to those Shahabad prisoners banished to the Purnea jail explains why official concern was warranted:

> We continually desire to hear of your welfare ... On no account make yourself uneasy ... The duty of man is to wield the sword and the Bludgeon. Jails were built for the reception of men. Again on no account make yourself uneasy. I heard that the Magistrate persisted in ordering that you would all eat in one place and that from this circumstance arose the disturbances, no one would consent to eat, and therefore a riot took place. We are much delighted that you should have done so good a deed, without exception all the troops serving under the English, were

delighted on hearing this. The day on which the English shall attempt
to destroy our religion, every Regiment will revolt, and whenever such
revolt takes place, in one day they will depart to their own country. The
times are the times of Ram Luchman Bhurrut and Sutrogun the four
brothers. These days are like unto their days but their domain ceased
what rule can stand.[53]

Since the Bihar districts were a major area of military recruitment, jail
outbreaks there were naturally of interest to those serving in the army.
That letters from home conveyed such information is apparent in the
case of a Shahabad sepoy posted to the 6th Regiment Gwalior contingent. His source told him specifically about an incident involving
a group of prisoners who had had their food stirred by a magistrate
(that is, the Digha incident) who then insisted that they eat it.[54]

That the issue of messing spilled over prison walls and into the wider community is also evident from the 'Patna Conspiracy'. Organized
by a handful of Patna city residents, the conspiracy aimed at uniting
local inhabitants—Hindu and Muslim—with sepoys stationed at the
nearby military outpost of Danapur to foment a rebellion against the
British authorities. The conspirators also sought to rally the influential
landholders of the region, including Kunwar Singh who spearheaded
the 1857 rebellion in Bihar, and the King of Nepal to their cause. One
of its leaders apparently had ties to the Mughal emperor.[55]

At his trial, one of the conspirators, Sheikh Pir Bux (Peer Buksh),
munshi (writer) of the 1st Regiment of Infantry at Danapur, confessed
that he had been initially recruited by Rahat Ali (Rahut Ally) who
complained to him about 'the indignities which the prisoners had been
made to suffer. He (Ali) said that all the zamindars and *omlah* (amla,
Indian office staff) and people were interested in the matter, he then
showed me a long paper, in which all the *omlah* of the courts, zamindars and others had signed and bound themselves by an oath to act
in concert when required'.[56] Ali also informed the munshi that he had
seen a government gazette declaring that Hindu and Muslim women
would be compelled to appear in public, that all people would be forced
to dine together, and that the practice of circumcision—a Muslim
custom—would be hereafter abolished.[57] Indeed, such accounts were
so widely circulated in the area that 'native officers' stationed at nearby Danapur brought up the matter with their commanding officer.

Major H. Rowcroft later recalled that his subordinates spoke to him 'strongly ... [regarding] the intention of the Government to destroy their castes and make all Christians, and that the messing system in the Jails was only the commencement of the arrangements, and mentioned that, the people in the District and at the men's homes were excited and alarmed'.[58] Some sepoy also informed Major Rowcroft that 'when on leave of absence at their villages, their relations told them if they would not make a stand for their religion, they would have to fight against their brothers and relations'.[59]

The issue of messing, no doubt, aroused an audience far beyond the walls of the prisons because it touched on a religious and social matter of fundamental concern to the entire Indian population. And it raised the ire of many because it followed on the heels of other British innovations that generated equally disquieting fears about possible government interference in local beliefs and customs.[60]

Conditions and confrontations in the jails of Bihar also attracted a wider constituency because most inmates were local inhabitants. And certainly in the eyes of many in local society, some prisoners—those implicated in illegal affrays and riots originating in land disputes— were not to be counted among the criminals they had been adjudged to be by British law.[61] In Patna this distinction formed

> the chief cause of the Sympathy of the inhabitants of the city and District with the prisoners ... [as] the higher castes, who have no more repugnance to being indirectly or directly in land disputes resulting in homicides, affrays, assaults etc. having relations, friends of dependants, in the Jails besides being themselves liable to be sent there on account of their own acts.[62]

Similarly, the Arrah jail outbreak in Shahabad generated public interest and concern because many people differentiated between the ordinary criminals and those incarcerated for their involvement in land disputes. The imposition of messing on the latter, regarded as 'the more respectable and influential class' and 'not considered by the people to be guilty of the moral turpitude that attaches to a felon', was viewed as an unduly harsh punishment. Far fewer eyebrows would have been raised had the measure been applied only to the ordinary criminals.[63]

That people made such distinctions is also apparent from the responses to messing noticed among Biharis serving in the British army. According to Major H. Troup, the commander of the 66th Regiment stationed in Danapur, not only did men of all ranks take a keen interest in messing when it was introduced in the nearby jails, but 'many members of the Regt. … [asked] what were the motives of the Govt. … for the first time after so many years passing an order, that to use their own words, made every man an outcast who passed through the Jails, for you know Sir said they that many respectable men go there from one cause or another'.[64]

To what extent people on the outside made such distinctions can also be gauged by assessing the varying degrees of community support lent to the different jail outbreaks. Thus, prisoners who fought in the jails of Patna, Shahabad, and Saran drew crowds threatening to intervene on their behalf, while a similar occurrence in the Gaya jail, in contrast, was attended by only a few interested onlookers. The critical difference lay in the fact that the first three jails housed a large number of people of 'respectable class, confined for offences originating in disputes about land'.[65] In Gaya, on the other hand, the bulk of the prisoners and, certainly, 'the ringleaders in the late outbreak … were men of the lowest caste and most desperate characters who had before been sentenced by either the Sessions Court or Nizamut Adawlat'.[66]

The different social and economic backgrounds of prisoners in the different jails provoked varying responses in the jail guards. In the three district jails where community support was overtly manifested, prisoners were tacitly, if not openly, aided by their guards. At the Chapra jail, where collusion was most clearly in evidence, prison guards, although armed with lathis, not only refused to charge the rebellious inmates who were chained by leg irons, but fled when prisoners let loose with rocks and brickbats. The district judge, an eyewitness to this scene, testified that the guards failed in performing their duty because of 'their having Friends amongst the Prisoners'. To continue with his observations, many of the guards were 'friends and relatives of the prisoners themselves … [who] frequently offer themselves for service, for the express purpose of communicating freely with the prisoners, or in order to supply them with liquors, connive at their idleness or facilitate their escape'.[67] Only at Gaya did the guards carry out their duties effectively.[68]

Nevertheless, in all four incidents the prisoners who rushed to man the barricades were the ordinary prisoners. Notwithstanding the fears of the local authorities that the 'respectable class' would naturally assume charge of the resistance, the principal actors were invariably drawn from the general prison population. At the Behar jail outbreak, for instance, the lead was taken by Ahir prisoners, their primary roles in the insurrection showing up clearly in the subsequent prosecution of rioters. Singled out at this trial were thirty-six prisoners, including Belwa Gwalla and a number of other Ahirs; the rest were predominantly of other low castes—Dusadhs, Rajwars, and Kurmis.[69] At the Patna jail, the resistance was also headed by Ahirs described by the magistrate as 'felons of the Gwalah caste'.[70]

In part, the primary role assumed by low-caste prisoners, especially Ahirs, reflect their large representation in the prison population. Of the 662 prisoners in the Chapra jail, for instance, the single largest group were the Ahirs with 175 (26.5 per cent of the total); the other castes with appreciable numbers were Koiris and Brahmans (each with 102 or 15.4 per cent), Rajputs (101 or 12.8 per cent), and Dusadhs (85 or 7.8 per cent).[71]

Prison authorities were surprised by the active lead taken by low-caste prisoners because they assumed that they would be the most passive and, certainly, the least likely to command leadership roles. From the British perspective, high-caste status was not only to be equated with superior social and economic standing but also positions of authority in local society. Thus, in imposing messing on the prison population, the local authorities treated the 'respectable class' with greater consideration than they did the so-called ordinary criminals of lesser castes. Months after the Gaya jail riot had become history, at least one local official realized that such assumptions had fuelled the fires of resistance in the prison outbreaks. In his words, messing had been 'introduced in too off hand a manner, and ... the ignorant and low caste prisoners, were not informed'.[72]

Thus, jail discipline was introduced to Bihar prisons in the form of messing. Although inmates invariably took to the barricades to resist it, their protests were met with, and subdued by, firepower. Military force, used to put down the uprisings, resulted in the shooting of five prisoners in Saran; in Patna one was mortally wounded. In the Behar jail, inmates, although denied food for three days, sustained an 'open insurrection' for four days, yielding only after eighteen of their number had been killed and twenty wounded.[73] No casualties were reported in the quelling of the Shahabad jail uprising but, as the details of its suppression indicate, resistance was broken down at the point of the bayonet. Called in to enforce messing in Shahabad, a company of the 66th Regiment began its task by first isolating those inmates 'most violently opposed to the new order of things'; the rest were ordered to organize themselves, by their respective castes, into messes. But the fires of protest continued to burn: prisoners persisted in voicing their objections, and much to the surprise of the magistrate, even the lowest castes, the Dusadhs and Chamars, joined the chorus of dissenters. The next step was to round up 'all those who absolutely refused and seemed equally to disregard force or persuasion' and send them away to other prisons. Nor did that put an end to protests; one or two 'decided recusants' had to be flogged before messes could be organized in a manner not to injure their caste or wound their prejudices. Nevertheless, as the Shahabad magistrate reported, obviously with a sense of triumph: 'We have thus accomplished in two days, a measure opposed to the prejudices and opinion of the people throughout the Behar District ... and it must be deemed a subject of the highest congratulations, that the introductions of a system which threatened in the first instance to be attended with the most serious consequences, has terminated so satisfactorily to all concerned'.[74]

Once the military regained control of the prison, local authorities quickly stepped in to break down inmate solidarity by removing the so-called ringleaders to jails in other areas. For instance, Belwa Gwalla, identified as one of the principal instigators of the 'riot and ... insurrection' in Gaya, was sent off to the Alipur jail in Calcutta to complete the remaining three years of his original sentence. At the expiration of this term in 1849, he was to be transported overseas for the rest of his life.[75] His fellow-inmate, Kehree Gwalla, was within a few days of completing his sentence when he was implicated in the riot, an involvement which resulted in another fourteen years of imprisonment, with labour and in irons, and banishment to the Bankura jail in

Bengal. Also sent to Bengal, to the Burdwan jail, was Bhowani Singh, charged with playing an active role in the Chapra jail uprising.[76] Many of the 'more influential and active prisoners' from the Saran jail were dispatched to the jails of Monghyr, Purnea, and Tirhut.[77] Purnea also received inmates from Shahabad, and as its district magistrate found out, his new charges were not about to give in easily. For two days the rebellious convicts from Saran and Shahabad—all of them to a man— refused to eat their meals. Only 'after a great deal of persuasion and no inconsiderable threats', and beatings of several prisoners with a rattan, was he successful in enforcing the messing system.[78]

In the aftermath of the uprisings, the government sought to build up its coercive machinery. In place of the existing prison guard force (barkandaz), largely locally and apparently indiscriminately recruited, a new force of station guards, the *najib*s (militia), was established. Modelled along lines of, and even incorporating some members of, the special militia organized to combat thugi, the new guards were to be a 'well selected', and 'well armed and well disciplined, force' trained in the use of firearms. In addition, each prison was to be headed by a jailor, either a non-commissioned European officer or a 'respectable' Anglo-Indian.[79]

Thus, resistance to messing was crushed by the overwhelming coercive power of the colonial state. As in 1842, the new round of protests in 1845 only served to make local authorities even more determined to press on with the new system of discipline and punishment. Indicative of the official stance was the resolution made in the aftermath of the Arrah and Chapra jail outbreaks condemning the 'open and audacious violence' and threatening to prosecute 'as offenders against Jail discipline such convicts as may resist by violence the introduction of the system. Convicts who oppose passive resistance to the measure by merely refusing food may be left to the effects of their obstinancy'.[80]

Because the government regarded its insistent position on messing as based on a new 'science' of punishment grounded in sound moral and health principles, and because messing was regarded as stiffening the conditions of incarceration, 'native' resistance to it was largely discounted, and its most violent manifestations countered with deadly force. Indeed, resistance was deemed as threatening not only the new disciplinary regimen but also challenging the very foundations of colonial power and authority. Thus, opposition by prisoners could not be allowed to turn back the development of a new system of discipline and punishment.

NOTES

1. Legislative Despatch to India, 30 October 1839 (no. 19), India and Bengal Despatches, 7 August to 27 November 1839.

2. For a 'reading' of the report of the 1838 Committee, a text that constituted the first systematic exposition of a penological theory for colonial India, see my 'Disciplining Colonial India: The Technology of Punishment in the Early Nineteenth Century', paper presented at the Association for Asian Studies, Boston, 10–12 April 1987.

3. Macaulay, 'Minute', 14 December 1835, in C.D. Dharker, *Lord Macaulay's Legislative Minutes* (Madras 1946), p. 278. On Macaulay and the intellectual currents of his milieu, see John Clive, *Macaulay: The Shaping of the Historian* (New York 1975); Eric Stokes, *The English Utilitarians and India* (Oxford 1959), p. 217.

4. T.B. Macaulay, *The Complete Works of Lord Macaulay* (London 1889), vol. 2, p. 26. Also Clive, *Macaulay*, p. 449.

5. Transportation was considered to be a particularly severe sentence because of indigenous social and religious attitudes regarding the crossing of 'black waters'. Macaulay, Minute of 14 December 1835; *Report of the Committee on Prison Discipline* (Calcutta 1838) (hereafter cited as P-D Reports), p. 81. See also Jorg Fisch, Cheap *Lives and Dear Limbs: The British Transformation of the Bengal Criminal Law 1769–1817* (Wiesbaden 1983), for an insightful analysis of the stiffening of punishments under the British system of criminal justice.

6. Until 1912, Bihar was under the jurisdiction of the Bengal Presidency. In the early nineteenth century, it included the districts of Behar (later divided into Patna and Behar districts, Tirhut (later Mazaffarpur and Darbhanga), Saran (later Saran and Champaran), and Shahabad.

7. For additional details, see my 'Disciplining Colonial India'.

8. Michael Ignatieff, *A Just Measure of Pain: The Penitentiary in the Industrial Revolution, 1750–1850* (New York 1978), p. xiii.

9. Sandria B. Freitag, 'Collective Crime and Authority in North India', in Anand A. Yang (ed.) *Crime and Criminality in British India* (Tucson 1985), p. 141. See also my 'Disciplining Colonial India' for a discussion relating the new 'science' of punishment to the emerging colonial state.

10. See my 'Disciplining Colonial India'; Michael Foucault, *Discipline and Punish: The Birth of the Prison*, trans. Alan Sheridan (Middlesex 1977). See also E.T. Stokes, *The English Utilitarians and India*, pp. 217–8; Christopher Harding, Bill Hines, Richard Ireland, Philip Rawlings, *Imprisonment in England and Wales: A Concise History* (London 1985), p. 127.

11. Judical Dept. 766, 14 December (no. 16) 1842, India and Bengal Despatches, 13 July to 28 September 1842.

12. Louis Dumont, *Homo Hierarchicus: The Caste System and Its Implications*, Mark Sainsbury (trans.) (Chicago 1970), p. 130. Cooked food, which is especially vulnerable to impurity, requires the most elaborate precautions when involved in transactions between different castes.

13. Michell Perrot, 'Delinquency and the Penitentiary System in Nineteenth-Century France', in Robert Forster and Orest Ranum (eds), *Deviants and the Abandoned in French Society* (Baltimore 1978), p. 215.

14. See responses to circular of 20 December 1836, Bengal Criminal Judicial Consultations (BCJC), 9 to 30 April 1839, 9 April, esp. no. 43.

15. See *P-D Report*, p. 30.

16. Ibid., p. 34

17. Ibid.

18. Ibid., p. 30.

19. Ibid.

20. Ibid., p. 31.

21. Harding, *Imprisonment in England*, p. 127.

22. Valerie J. Johnston, *Diet in Workhouses and Prisons, 1835–1895* (New York 1985), p. 14.

23. *P-D Report*, pp. 30–1. The rate was higher in the North Western Provinces, from three-quarters of an anna (nine pie) to one anna and a quarter a day.

24. Ibid., p. 31.

25. Ibid., p. 34.

26. Circular, J. Hawkins, registrar, Nizamat Adawlat (NA) to session judges, magistrates, and joint magistrates, n.d., BCJC, 25 July to 22 August 1839, 15 August, no. 22.

27. Registrar to J.H. Young, deputy secy., Government of Bengal (GoB), no. 757, 27 April 1841, BCJC, 27 April to 8 June 1841, 27 May, no. 49.

28. E. Drummond, magistrate [Mgte.], Behar, to C. Garstin, sessions judge of Behar, 15 July 1842, BCJC 1 to 22 August 1842, 8 August, no. 41.

29. G.D. Wilkins, mgte., Saran to G. Gough, sessions judge, Saran, 12 June 1842, BCJC, 23 May to 27 June 1842, 27 June, no.15.

30. Ibid.

31. F.J. Halliday, Secy., to Hawkins, registrar, no. 787, 27 June 1842, ibid., no. 16.

32. Hawkins, registrar, to Secy. Halliday, no. 3736, 28 October 1842, ibid., 27 February to 27 March 1843, 20 March, no. 9. Messing was also extended to the North Western Provinces where it provoked a considerable 'emeute' in the Allahabad jail. See J. Thornton, Secy., Govt., NWP, to Secy. Halliday, 1 July 1846, BCJC 2 to 9 December 1846, 2 December, no. 53.

33. E.A. Samuells, Mgte., Tirhut, to Alexander Grant, sessions judge, Tirhut, no. 185,18 July 42, BCJC, 20 March 1843, no. 22. Because messing was regarded negatively by the prisoners, local administrators such as Samuells considered it

an especially appropriate punishment. Therefore, they tended to downplay the importance of heeding religious objections to messing.

34. J.E. Lillie, officiating mgte, Patna. to Turnbull, no. 408, 23 July 1845, BCJC, 30 July, no. 65.

35. R.H. Russell, officiating mgte., to H.V. Hathorn, sessions judge, 28 June 1845, BCJC, 9 to 23 July 1845, 23 July, no. .

36. Lillie to sessions judge, no. 508, BCJC, 1 to 29 October 1845, 17 October, no. 42, enclosure.

37. E. Radcliffe, mtge., Shahabad, to under secy., 8 July 1845, BCJC, 9 to 23 July 1845, 8 July, no. 51.

38. Ibid.

39. Ibid.

40. Turnbull, under secy, to Secy., GOI, no. 1949, 29 October 1845, BCJC, 5 November to 10 December 1845, 3 December, no. 28. The original plan had been to build a central penitentiary there for all the *Bihar* districts.

41. Lillie to under secy, no. 445, 7 August 1845, BCJC, 20 August to 3 September 1845, 27 August, no. 40.

42. Russell, officiating mgte, Saran, to superintendent (suptd.) W. Dampier, 18 July 1845, ibid., 3 Sept., no. 112.

43. T.C. Trotter, mgte, to R. Forbes, sessions judge, Behar, no. 480, 12 September 1845, BCJC. 10 to 24 September 1845, 17 September, no. 62A. Altogether ten were killed and five wounded.

44. Forbes, sessions judge, to Secy. Halliday, no. 170, 17 September 1845, ibid., 1 to 29 October 1845. 17 October, no. 50. The final tally of deaths in the Behar jail was eighteen. See Trotter to Forbes, 25 September 1845, BCJC, 5 November to 10 December 1845, 5 November, no. 34.

45. 'True translation of a Petition of Akul Mehto, a Gwalah in caste ... d. 14 Aug. 1845', and Lillie to under secy., no. 460,16 August 1845, BCJC, 20 August to 3 September 1845, 27 August, no. 43A, 43. Lillie's letter claimed that he was 'too alive to the feelings of the caste of the natives ever to do anything which hurt their prejudices...'

46. Dampier, suptd., to Secy. Halliday, no.1589, 23 July 1845, BCJC, 20 August to 3 September 1845, 3 September, no. 112.

47. Radcliffe to under secy., 29 July 1845, BCJC, 23 July to 13 August 1845, 13 August, no. 35.

48. Trotter to Forbes, 25 September 1845, BCJC, 5 November to 10 December 1845, 5 November, no. 34.

49. Forbes to Secy. Halliday, no. 186, 10 October 1845, and Trotter to Forbes, 25 September 1845, ibid., 5 November, no. 34.

50. For a study of rumours as the undercurrents of popular mentalities, see my 'A Conversation of Rumours: The Language of Popular *Mentalities* in Late Nineteenth Century Colonial India', *Journal of Social History*, vol. 20, no. 3, 1987, pp. 485–505.

51. Lillie to suptd., Dampier, no. 356, BCJC, 10 to 24 September 1845, 17 September, no. 67.

52. Smelt to Lillie, 29 August 1845, BCJC, 10 to 24 September 1845, 10 September, no. 34.

53. 'Translation of a letter addressed by several sepoys of the 29th Regt at Behampore to Seopertab Sing and other convicts in the Jail of Purneah', BCJC, 1 to 29 October 1845, 17 October, no. 55A. This letter concluded by saluting 'all those Brahmins and Rajpoots who are with you. It is necessary that you should lose no time in replying to this, relate minutely all that is occurring ...' The four brothers are the heros of the popular Hindu epic of the Ramayana. The advent of the rule of Rama, the eldest brother, is equated with the return to a golden age of Hindu rule.

54. E.F. Lantour, mgte., Behar, to suptd of police, 12 April 1845, BCJC, 2 to 9 December 1846, 2 December, no. l.

55. A brief and inadequate sketch of these events is in K.K. Datta, *Anti-British Plots and Movements before* 1857 (Meerut 1970), pp. 21–34. On Kunwar Singh's role in this conspiracy, see K.K. Datta, *Biography of Kunwar Singh and Amar Singh* (Patna 1957), pp. 61–9.

56. 'The statement of Shaikh Peer Buksh Moonshee ... taken before J.E.S. Lillie, officiating mgte. of Patna', BCJC, 28 January to 11 February 1846, 28 January, no. 43C.

57. Deposition of Pir Bux Munshi, 7 March 1846, BCJC, 4 to 25 November 1846, 18 November, no. 28.

58. Rowcroft, Comdg. 1st Regt., N.I., to Dampier, suptd., police, 14 April 1846, BCJC, 2 to 9 December 1846, 2 December, no. 47.

59. Cited in Datta, *Biography of Kunwar Singh*, p. 63.

60. See testimony of defendents in the Patna conspiracy, in India, Board's Collections, 1845–46, vol. 2147, 'Patna Conspiracy'.

61. For an analysis of criminal riots as land disputes—confrontations which were endemic in rural society—see my 'The Agrarian Origins of Crime: A Study of Riots in Saran District, India, 1866–1920', *Journal of Social History*, vol. 13, 1979, pp. 189–206.

62. Lillie to suptd. Dampier, 14 April 1846, BCJC, 2 to 9 December 1846, 2 December, no. 12.

63. Radcliffe to Dampier, 11 April 1846, ibid.

64. Troup to Dampier, 15 April 1846, ibid.

65. Dampier to Halliday, Secy., GOB, no. 825, 20 April 1846, BCJC, 2 to 9 December 1846, 2 December, no. 11.

66. Lantour to suptd, 12 April 1846, ibid., no. 12.

67. Hathom to Secy, Halliday, no. 129, 31 July 1845, BCJC, 20 August to 3 September 1845, 3 September, no. 111.

68. Lantour to suptd, no. 1, 12 April 1846, BCJC, 2 to 9 December 1846, 2 December, no. 12.

69. B.J. Colvin, officiating registrar, N.A., to Secy., Halliday, no. 13, 9 January 1846, BCJC, 28 January to 11 February 1846, 11 February, no. 54.

70. Lillie to suptd Dampier, no. 215, 14 April 1846, BCJC, 2 to 9 December 1846, 2 December, no. 12.

71. Officiating mgte Russell to Secy., Halliday, 24 July 1845, BCJC, 23 July to 13 August 1845, 30 July, no. 54. Ahirs were also the single largest caste group in the general population.

72. Lantour, mgte, to suptd. of police, no. 1, 12 April 1846, BCJC, 2 to 9 December 1846, 2 December, no. 12.

73. Judicial Despatches, 15 July (no. 7) 1846, India and Bengal Despatches, 5 August to 30 September 1846,12 August (P.C. 5273).

74. Radcliffe to under secy., no. 301, 6 August 1845, BCJC, 20 August to 3 September 1845, 20 August, no. 33.

75. Colvin to Halliday, no. 13, 9 January 1846, BCJC, 28 January to 11 February 1846, 11 February, no. 54; and Tumbull, under secy., to officiating mgte, Behar, no. 424, 18 February 1846, BCJC, 18 February to 4 March 1846,18 February, nos 96/97.

76. Forbes, sessions judge, Behar, to Lantour, officiating mgte, Behar, n.d.; and Minute by Lieutenant-Governor of Bengal, 29 March 1855, BCJC, 31 May to 7 June 1855, 31 May, nos 256 and 257.

77. 'Note by the Secty. re: the disturbance ... in the Sarun Jail', 23 July 1845, BCJC, 9 to 23 July 1845, 23 July, no. 46.

78. G. Martin, mgte, Purnea, to Secy., GOB, no. 365,1 September 1845, BCJC, 10 to 24 September 1845, 10 September,no.69.

79. Many of the ranks of the barkandaz were said to be relatives and retainers of the better-off prisoners. Hathom, sessions judge, Saran, to Secy, Halliday, no. 129, 31 July 1845; G.A. Bushby, Secy., GOI, to Secy Tumbull, GOB, no. 1576, BCJC 20 August to 3 September 1845, 3 September, nos 111 and 20. See also India, Board's Collections, Bengal, Judicial, 1846, PC 5273, no. 102786, 'Nujeeb Guards'.

80. 'Note by the Secty. re: the disturbance ...', 23 July 1845, BCJC, 9 to 23 July, 23 July, no. 46. The authorities in London were far less sanguine about the appropriateness of messing, especially in the wake of the uprisings, but recognized that its abrogation might be construed as 'giving way to insubordination'. See Despatches to India, 12 August (no. 7), of 1846, India and Bengal Despatches, 12 August 1846 (PC 5273).

8

The Self and the Cell
Indian Prison Narratives as Life Histories*

David Arnold

The prison figured prominently in the Indian middle-class imagination and experience between the 1890s and 1940s. This arose in part from the centrality of jail-going in the civil disobedience movements led by M.K. Gandhi, but it also reflected the extensive British recourse to imprisonment to combat opposition of all kinds, and even before the 1920s the prison had widely come to symbolize the oppressive nature of colonial rule in India. The purpose of this essay is not to try to provide an objective account of prisoners' lives and the conditions in which they were confined, but to examine the self-perceptions of middle-class prisoners and to present the narratives they produced as a significant sub-genre of modern South Asian writing about the self, and as an important contribution to the production of Indian life histories.

Although a large number of what can broadly be described as prison writings were produced during the freedom struggle and in its immediate aftermath, there was no standard format by which authors' diverse impressions and experiences were transformed

* Excerpted from David Arnold and Stuart Blackburn (eds), *Telling Lives in India: Biography, Autobiography and Life History* (Delhi and Ranikhet: Permanent Black, 2004).

into written texts. They range from 'jail diaries' kept during imprisonment (and not always intended for a wider audience) to polemical
narratives of prison life written up for publication, sometimes as
newspaper articles, shortly after the event, and autobiographies in
which a large part of the author's account is devoted to jail experiences or in which the time spent in prison is represented as being of
particular personal or political significance. The prison also found its
way into many novels and plays, though no attempt will be made to
examine them here.

It might be argued that any connection between the prison and
autobiography was largely fortuitous: certainly, the taste for autobiographical writing was well established in India, in English and in the
vernaculars, long before Indians began to write about their prison
experiences in the 1890s and 1900s. But, while prison may not in itself
have generated the Indian urge to autobiography, it surely gave it a significant impetus. The prison was the birthplace of some of India's most
celebrated autobiographies, notably Jawaharlal Nehru's *Autobiography*,
first published in 1936 and originally to have been entitled *In and Out
of the Prison*. Gandhi also began *The Story of My Experiments with
Truth* at Yeravda Jail near Pune in the early 1920s, and a number of
other nationalist autobiographies were written largely or entirely in
jail, though they do not necessarily thereby give prominence to prison
experiences.[1] It became as much a nationalist convention for political
prisoners to write their prison memoirs as it was a patriotic duty for
newspaper editors and book publishers to put them into print. It is
indicative of the popularity of the genre, the breadth of its intended
readership as well as its diverse authorship, that prison memoirs
were written not just in English (like Nehru's) but in virtually every
major Indian language from Gujarati and Marathi to Hindi, Bengali,
and Malayalam. Some of these vernacular works, like Upendranath
Bandyopadhyay's *Nirbaster Atmakatha* ('The Autobiography of an
Exile'), recounting his experiences of imprisonment in the Andaman
Islands, enjoyed considerable popularity and had passed through several editions by the 1970s. Prison narratives were written to inspire
as well as inform. Prison elicited many life histories that would not
otherwise have been written. It could provide the time as well as the

incentive for autobiographical writing, though it should be noted that conditions in jail were not always so conducive for middle-class prisoners, some of whom (like M.N. Roy) were deliberately denied ink, pen, and paper as well as access to books and newspapers. For others, it was only following their release that writing became emotionally as well as physically possible. After a long and gruelling period of confinement, writing about jail experiences might be a kind of necessary self-purging, answering a therapeutic need to 'imprison' the ordeal of incarceration on paper and so to come to terms with the humiliation and suffering involved.[2]

It is one of the arguments of this essay that prison constituted more than just the occasion for autobiographical writing. Despite the often deadening routine and isolation, for many political activists–authors the months and years spent in prison were among the most meaningful periods of their lives, and they left it very different from when they entered. For others the experience, while certainly testing, was less transforming, and their memoirs tend more to political polemic than psychological self-analysis. Even so, incarceration forced many writers to strengthen or redefine their sense of identity and purpose, particularly in relation to the prison's other inmates, the officials, warders, and convicts who differed so markedly from the jailed but who, nonetheless, appeared illustrative of the nature of state and society under colonial rule. The writers of prison narratives were almost invariably middle class, though not, after 1930, exclusively male.[3] They therefore represented only a minority of prisoners, even during the civil disobedience campaigns, and even in the Andamans—the penal colony whose brutal practices they helped publicize through their own struggles.[4] Despite their authors' middle-class origins, these narratives turn the prison into a significant site for the observation and representation of the subaltern classes. In an institutional arena where the individual identity of the majority of inmates was almost lost in a sea of regulations and statistics, subsumed within colonial categories of race, caste, and religion, and the only 'life history' was that manufactured by the state for its own administrative needs, political prisoners often authored life stories for those 'common criminals' who left no written record of their own.

'AN UNKNOWN PLACE'

'Prison,' wrote Nehru of his first term of incarceration in 1921–2,
'was still an unknown place, the idea of going there still a novelty.'[5]
However, as Nehru acknowledged later in his autobiography, imprisonment for political offences was not in fact so new. Since the 1890s,
the Maharashtrian Bal Gangadhar Tilak and a number of Bengali
revolutionaries had been imprisoned, and Gandhi had been jailed
several times between 1908 and 1914 in the course of his satyagraha
(civil disobedience) campaign in South Africa. But what was different
for Nehru in 1921 was that middle-class Indians had begun systematically to court imprisonment in support of the nationalist cause.[6] Even
so, the jail was not such an 'unknown place' in 1921. The prison had
been a site of contention in India for more than fifty years, going back
to the protests against common messing in the jails of Bengal and the
North Western Provinces in the 1840s, the liberation of prisoners during the 1857 rebellion, and periodic controversy from the 1870s over
the treatment of both male and female prisoners. Prison issues gained
fresh intensity with the imprisonment of Surendranath Banerjee in
1883, followed by Tilak in 1897 and again in 1908, and reports of the
systematic abuse of prisoners at Port Blair in the Andamans from
1906 onward.

In nineteenth-century India the prison was one of the most visible
manifestations and menacing symbols of colonial rule, and part of the
contentious history of the prison and the array of penological practices that surrounded it was authored not by the middle classes but
by popular rumour and report. A site of pollution as well as physical
pain, a place where caste was reputedly broken and religious taboos
violated, where men and women from all castes and classes were
subject to cruelty and deprivation, the prison held a deep and troubling significance for Indian society. The number of prison inmates
might be small relative to the size of the total population, but from
debt or disloyalty, from alleged infanticide or conspiracy to murder,
few even of the higher castes and most privileged classes could feel
safe from its clutches. If the prison was a common target for peasant
insurrection and tribal revolt, it was also from the 1870s a subject for
numerous tracts and plays, especially those produced by the Bengali

intelligentsia.[7] As Nehru put it from the perspective of the early 1920s, the middle classes viewed prison with 'repugnance'. 'In our minds the place was associated with isolation, humiliation, and suffering, and, above all, the fear of the unknown.'[8]

One of the first impulses of the middle classes was to seek to expose the secretive life of the prison and open it up to public account-ability, to transform it from a 'hell on earth' to a place of humane detention and rehabilitation. In the late 1890s the editor of the Bengali weekly *Hitavadi* wrote a series of articles based on his recent prison experiences, calling for the reform of jail conditions while simultane-ously revealing some of the more sensational aspects of convict sub-culture.[9] Commenting on these articles, another Bengali paper, *Samay*, described British rule as resting on two instruments of coercion—the police and the jails. The police were bad enough, with their repeated acts of 'cruelty, barbarity and injustice', but what went on in the jails was 'a thousand times more dreadful, more cruel and more fiendish'. It was not only the lower classes who suffered:

> Educated people belonging to the higher classes are not infrequently imprisoned with or without reason. But none of them ever care to write a book or a pamphlet describing what goes on in the Indian jail … Englishmen have written books on jail life in England, and have thereby improved the condition of the inmates of English jails. The condition of Indian jails is miserable, because no one has written anything about it.[10]

GANDHI'S 'JAIL EXPERIENCES'

Although it was to be another twenty years before conditions in India's jails were extensively publicized, Gandhi's first experiences of imprisonment in South Africa effectively initiated a new phase in the middle-class discovery of the prison. Between January 1908 and December 1913 Gandhi was imprisoned four times, totalling nearly seven months in all: his longest period of confinement was in Pretoria jail, from February to May 1909. Imprisonment for Gandhi was a necessary part of the struggle to defend Indian rights against racist laws and discrimination in South Africa. As he told an audience in Johannesburg in May 1909, 'If you go to gaol, you will be assured of victory.[11] But the experience of imprisonment contributed—to an extent Gandhi did not anticipate and historians have seldom recognized—to his personal and political evolution in these years. Although his metamorphosis from anglicized lawyer to incipient mahatma had begun several months earlier, the impact of the 'education' he received in prison supports the view that Gandhi's emerging political identity owed at least as much to his South African experiences as to his Kathiawari upbringing or his student days in London.

Curiously perhaps, Gandhi made only passing reference to his South African jail experiences in *The Story of My Experiments with Truth*, written in the mid-1920s and begun in jail, but he had already given a more extensive account of them in *Satyagraha in South Africa*, much of which was also written during his imprisonment at Yeravda in 1923–4. He also wrote about his initial jail experiences at the time and at considerable length, in both Gujarati and English. His articles in *Indian Opinion* were intended to be 'useful to others'[12] by accurately informing the Indian community about prison conditions and so, by overcoming their nightmares, encouraging them to participate in civil disobedience. They also chart Gandhi's personal transformation. His experience of jail proved to be extremely traumatic and as such can be taken as indicative of the wider capacity of the colonial prison to transform the lives of its inmates, and even to force them to radically rethink their identity.

Despite the prior determination to endure prison hardships as part of the self-sacrifice demanded by satyagraha, Gandhi's first experience of jail in 1908 threw him back on many of the antipathies of class and religion that made prison such a place of fear and loathing for the Indian middle class. Moreover, in South Africa there was the additional factor of racial repugnance at being confined with those whom Gandhi habitually called 'Kaffirs'. To be treated, in terms of food, dress, and accommodation as no better than black Africans, when one of the primary motives behind the struggle in South Africa was precisely to establish equality with whites, was deeply galling to Gandhi. This, he reflected in March 1908, was an 'experience for which we were perhaps all unprepared',[13] and yet being 'classed with Natives' was bitter confirmation of the 'degradation' Indians were subjected to in South Africa:

We could understand not being classed with the whites, but to be placed on the same level with the Natives seemed too much to put up with. I then felt that Indians had not launched on passive resistance too soon. Here was further proof that the obnoxious law [the Asiatic Registration Act] was intended to emasculate the Indians.[14]

Being threatened, taunted, and abused by 'Kaffir' prisoners and warders further convinced Gandhi that the 'separation' of Indians and Africans was a 'physical necessity'. Indian prisoners, he declared, had nothing in common with Africans and everything to fear from them. 'Kaffirs,' he wrote, 'are as a rule uncivilized—the convicts even more so. They are troublesome, very dirty and live almost like animals … The reader can easily imagine the plight of the poor Indian thrown into such company!'[15] Deep offence was felt, too, at being denied European or Indian food and being obliged to eat 'Kaffir' food— maize meal. African and European prisoners received food 'suited to their tastes', Gandhi protested, while Indian needs were ignored. The prescribed diet was 'totally unsuitable' for Indians, who were 'either in the habit of taking European food or mostly so.'[16] He protested, too, at the inclusion of animal fat in food served to Indian prisoners, as being unacceptable alike to Hindus and Muslims, and demanded rice, pulses, and ghee instead. Though Gandhi was apparently unaware of it, his struggle in South Africa re-enacted many of the scenes of dietary confrontation that had been staged in India's own prisons over the previous sixty years.

Gandhi saw himself as leading a largely successful struggle against such injustices and winning a number of important concessions from the jail authorities.[17] But the prison changed Gandhi more than Gandhi changed the prison. The experience of incarceration profoundly affected his evolving political ideas and overturned many of the conventional beliefs and assumptions he had hitherto shared with other middle-class, high-caste Indians. In this sense Gandhi's 'jail experiences' have something of the flavour of a conversion narrative. While at times comparing his ordeal to that of Daniel in the lion's den, Gandhi could declare with all the zeal of a recent convert that prison was also a place of instruction, conducive to self-purification and moral regeneration. He described the hardships of jail life as 'mostly imaginary' and encouraged Indians to think of prison as 'a holy and happy place', a 'palace', even a 'paradise'.[18] Citing Bunyan and Tilak as examples, he presented prison as a place where 'conscientious men' had 'achieved great things'.[19] At a more mundane level, prison food, so loathed at the outset, came to signify a duty to curb indulgence. The sparseness of jail diets was a reminder that back in India there were millions of people who had far less to eat. Even 'mealie pap', judged inedible in January 1908, had within a year become 'a sweet and strength-giving food', which 'with some adjustments' could be made a 'perfect diet'.[20] And while remaining staunchly opposed to mixing with 'Kaffirs', the prison, which confronted Gandhi with the many troubling divisions in Indian society—between Hindus and Muslims, high castes and low—encouraged him to see the camaraderie of prison life as helpful in countering such 'false distinctions'.[21]

Despite his growing disillusionment with modern civilization (proclaimed in *Hind Swaraj* in 1909), Gandhi identified the prison as a model of sanitation and hygiene from which Indians might profitably learn. Stung by allegations that Indians were 'uncivilized' and 'dirty', and that their insanitary practices spread plague and other epidemics, Gandhi approved of the 'excellent' sanitary regime he found in jail. While doubting that the ventilation in the cells quite met 'modern requirements', he invoked the authority of 'medical science' in support of hard beds and the liberal use of disinfectant and whitewash. He even asked, for health's sake, to have his hair cropped and moustache shaved off, though prison regulations did not require it.[22] Prison labour, for all the undoubted hardship and humiliation involved, caused Gandhi to reflect positively on 'the great Ruskin' and his revelation that the life of labour was the 'life worth living'.[23] Even cleaning out latrines and carrying buckets of urine—in caste terms extremely offensive and a repeated cause of protest among political prisoners in India in the 1920s—was ascribed moral as well as sanitary value and set Gandhi thinking about the inequities of untouchability. It was wrong, he wrote, 'to think of any work as humiliating or degrading'.[24]

For Gandhi, who had begun his experiments in *brahmacharya* (celibacy) less than two years before his incarceration, the constraints of prison life and control of his 'animal desires' became closely linked. Twenty years later, in one of the few direct references to jail experiences in his autobiography, he observed: 'I saw that some of the regulations that the prisoners had to observe were such as should be voluntarily observed by a brahmachari, that is, one desiring to practise self-restraint.'[25] Prison was free from sexual temptation (though not, to judge from his encounters with African and Chinese prisoners, from sexual menace), just as it denied other indulgences, like rich food and idleness. In prison 'all of one's bad habits fall away. The mind enjoys a sense of freedom ... The body is held in bondage, but the soul grows more free.'[26]

Gandhi undoubtedly found prison life in South Africa harsh, brutal, and inhumane, especially when he was kept in virtual isolation in Pretoria jail in 1909. Even from the vantage point of 1932 he recalled his time in South African jails as his 'real imprisonment', harsher than anything he had experienced subsequently in India.[27] And yet, for all the hardships, the experience paradoxically provided Gandhi with a model of how Indian society might be purged of some of its most undesirable and harmful practices. Prison life in South Africa taught him to think and feel differently not only about society, but also, crucially, about his own body. Through the ordeal of imprisonment he came to regard his body with a peculiar detachment, as an object to be disciplined not indulged, ordered not obeyed. This process had begun earlier (during his days with the Indian ambulance corps during the Zulu Rebellion of 1906) but was accelerated and intensified by the prison experience. Still in many ways shy and acutely conscious of his physical frailty, Gandhi sought to compensate for this through strict physical as well as mental self-control. Jail-going required 'a well-disciplined body': 'a physical wreck' would 'not be able to bear gaol life'. A satyagrahi, he added, 'knows that his body is lent to him on hire. He should prove a worthy tenant by keeping it clean and glowing with health.'[28]

In coming to terms with prison's hardships and humiliation, Gandhi came to see his body as a potent symbol, a vehicle by which to convey, even without words, what he suffered, believed in, or aspired to. While being transferred from Johannesburg to Volksrust jail in November 1908, Gandhi was seen at the railway station in his prison clothes by some Indian passengers (who, aptly, happened to be tailors). 'Of course, talking was not allowed,' but seeing his prison clothes 'some of them were filled with tears. Since I was not free even to tell them that

I did not mind my dress or anything else, I merely remained a silent spectator'—an onlooker, as it were, to the spectacle of his own body.[29] Gandhi learned through such episodes that the body, even that of the prisoner, dishevelled and clad in convict clothes, could be extremely eloquent, without needing any verbal appeal for sympathy or solidarity. Aided by his jail experiences, he learned to use his clothing, his body, and the marks of physical suffering as symbols of great potency and communicative power.[30]

Gandhi's prison experiences were further reflected in other aspects of his personal and political metamorphosis. Some writers have sought the origins for the Phoenix Settlement, begun in 1904, and Tolstoy Farm six years later, in a creative reworking of Indian tradition or in the influence of Ruskin or Christian monasticism. All these doubtless played a part, but Gandhi himself acknowledged the importance of prison to the evolution of his ashrams. In particular, Tolstoy Farm, set up to support satyagrahis and their families, was intended to harden them for civil disobedience and imprisonment. Life on the farm borrowed the prison's strict disciplinary regime and time-regulated working day, its common messing, and the minimizing of personal needs and privacy. As in prison, the food was basic but wholesome, and 'served in a single dish ... a kind of a bowl such as is supplied to prisoners in jail.' 'We had all become labourers and therefore put on labourers' dress but in the European style, viz., working men's trousers and shirts, which were imitated from prisoners' uniform.' Work at Tolstoy Farm, Gandhi recalled, 'was certainly harder than that in jail.' The 'inmates' ate, dressed, even shaved their heads like prisoners, and a well-known picture of Gandhi as a satyagrahi in 1913 shows him with his hair cropped and clothed like a convict.[31]

After leaving South Africa in 1914 Gandhi partly abandoned the prison model, identifying more strongly with peasant life instead, but the experience of prison was not entirely forgotten. Indeed, it was reinforced by the collective experience of nationalist jail-going in India over the next thirty years. Significantly, in 1915 his new commune was located close to Ahmedabad's Sabarmati jail, which he dubbed 'our other ashram',[32] and in 1931, during his meetings with the Viceroy, Lord Irwin, he insisted on eating with the utensils he had saved from Yeravda jail.[33] That Gandhi continued to regard his 'jail experiences' as critically important to himself and others is also evident from his efforts to maintain a jail diary in 1922–3, and the subsequent publication of a second series of articles about prison, and from Mahadev Desai's detailed account of his 1932 imprisonment. When Desai died in detention in August 1942, Gandhi insisted that his physician, Sushila Nayar, take over responsibility for keeping an 'authentic' record of his daily prison life.[34] But if his prison experiences were so crucial to Gandhi, why was so little said about them in his autobiography? One reason is that *The Story of My Experiments with Truth* is a highly selective account of Gandhi's life, which, rather than attempting to give a complete account of his life, uses certain personal episodes to illustrate moral 'truths' and weaknesses. Further, Gandhi probably felt no need to discuss his early prison experiences in the autobiography, having only recently described them in *Satyagraha in South Africa*. The autobiography ends in 1920, and by the time he wrote it his positive perception of his jail life had been overshadowed by the very different experience of his two years of 'solitude and introspection' at Yeravda.[35] Although Gandhi liked to regard himself as 'a seasoned jail-bird',[36] this had ended in February 1924 with his release following an operation for appendicitis, but also in his virtual mental and physical collapse. His first taste of prison in India left Gandhi appalled at the intransigence of the authorities and their determination to starve him of the 'oxygen of publicity', but also at the conduct of his fellow Indians—convicts and officials alike. Prison was no longer 'paradise', or even a convenient model for how Indian society might reform itself. On the contrary, he now saw prisons as 'hot-beds of vice and degradation', full of violence, corruption, and a depth of moral depravity he had not expected to find among Indians.[37] Yet, deeply troubling though the Yeravda experience undoubtedly was for Gandhi, none of this anger and disgust was allowed to infiltrate the uplifting story of his 'experiments with truth'.

INDIA: 'A VAST PRISON'

It was a common convention among middle-class nationalists in the 1920s and 1930s to assert that under colonial rule India was itself a prison. Thus, the Congress leader C.R. Das declared in 1921 that, while

technically free, he felt 'the handcuffs on my wrists and the weight of
iron chains on my body ... The whole of India is a vast prison'.[38] It was
further claimed, in the manner of Henry David Thoreau more than
half a century earlier, that under an unjust government 'the true place
for a just man is also a prison'.[39] Thus Gandhi, who only read Thoreau
in South Africa after developing his own theory of civil disobedience,
declared at his trial in 1922, that '[u]nder tyrannical rule, the jail
will always remain a gateway to freedom', and, following his release
from Yeravda two years later: '[a]s long as the entire country remains
imprisoned, we can take no rest or peace'.[40] In similar fashion Nehru
remarked in 1933 that 'the whole country seems a vast prison',[41] and
in his autobiography he quoted (or rather paraphrased) Thoreau as
saying that '[a]t a time when men and women are unjustly imprisoned
the place for just men and women is also in prison'.[42]

The view that colonial India was in effect a prison, and hence that
being in a real prison could be no worse and even a more honest
place to be, was loyally repeated by many nationalists of the period.
C. Rajagopalachari, the Tamil Congress leader, imprisoned in Vellore
jail from December 1921 to March 1922, confided in his diary after
only a few hours' confinement, that prison was 'a delightful place'. The
next day he mused: 'Have I really become so free that Government
have [sic] to lock me up if they wish to keep me? For the first time in
my life I felt I was free, and had thrown off the foreign yoke'.[43] A few
days later, the experience of being locked up every evening led him to
comment: 'Why do not people realize the fact that the nation is locked
[up] and imprisoned like this, not at 6 p.m., but every hour day in and
day out, so that it is one long night of slavery. Realizing this, one feels
free when one has actually to be shut up like this by the tyrant's arm
that holds the country'.[44]

Rajagopalachari was far too guarded about himself and too wily
a political campaigner to reveal much in his (published) diary about
his inner self, but he did reveal for the benefit of his middle-class
readers some of the hardships of jail life—the physical discomfort, the
unwholesome food, the crude sanitation, the bug-infested hospital,
the constant lack of privacy, and the resentment at being treated like
a 'common criminal'. 'Our food is the same as that of the ordinary
criminals,' he wrote in December; 'we are locked in and let out at the

same hours, we have to eat on the filthy ground, standing, or sitting on our toes, and hurrying it off the plate, like beggars being fed.' But, as a loyal Gandhian, this merely confirmed in him the need to suffer stoically for freedom's sake. Nationalist prisoners were not going to be broken by such treatment. 'Government does not know that this merely enhances our sacrifice, and strengthens our determination. Special comforts would undermine our strength in a subtle manner.'[45] If he 'hungered' it was not for better food, but for more nationalists to join those already in jail.[46] 'Nothing,' he wrote, 'has so strengthened the nation as the cheerful manner in which numbers of the most cultured classes have undertaken to suffer, and are undergoing the rigours of the worst forms of jail life.'[47] As his term came to a close, he declared that his three months in jail had been 'one of the happiest periods' of his life. Almost uninterrupted communication with other Congress prisoners had made it like 'a college hostel', so reminding him 'of the happy days of youth' that he 'hardly felt that it was a prison' at all.[48] Even toward the warders and officers, whose conduct he had railed against during his first weeks of imprisonment, Rajagopalachari now felt more mellow, if only from the belief that Gandhian humility and the satyagraha spirit had won them over and generated a new respect for political prisoners. That he had ever felt bitterly toward them was presented as evidence of the authenticity of his 'jail experiences'.[49]

It was also one of the conventions of prison writing to claim that in many respects political prisoners were freer than those set to guard over them. As Rajagopalachari remarked in his diary: 'The life of the warder is little better than that of his fellow inmate, the convict … His life is on the whole a miserable one, though he takes unconscious vengeance for it by brutality toward the … convicts.'[50] Similar observations surface in a number of other prison narratives, as in V.D. Savarkar's account of his imprisonment in the Andamans, first published in Marathi in 1927. Sentenced to life imprisonment for involvement in terrorist activities, Savarkar served thirteen years in prison (from 1911 to 1924), almost all of it in the notorious Cellular Jail at Port Blair. In a narrative of more than five hundred pages, Savarkar is almost entirely silent about his earlier life: the jail experience seems to encompass his entire existence. Like Rajagopalachari, he is hardly concerned with his inner self, concentrating instead on the brutal experience of imprisonment and his politically inspired observations of fellow convicts and warders. The prison becomes the nation, or rather the nation in the making, populated by heroes as well as plagued by demons. Prison exemplifies the callous brutality of the colonial regime as well as the defiant suffering of India's imprisoned youth, but it is also a place of ambiguity, in which the dividing line between the prisoner and the jailor is not always as absolute as might at first appear.

In Savarkar's narrative, one of the principal antagonists is an Irish jailor called David Barrie, whose abusive banter and violent conduct mark him out as a renegade who has betrayed the cause of the freedom struggle in his native Ireland by becoming a jailor for the British in India.[51] As the story unfolds, Barrie is revealed as being almost as much a prisoner as the Indians he torments. Savarkar tells Barrie, 'the whole of India is a vast prison-house, as much as Ireland.'[52] But the barely literate Irishman is worn out by more than twenty years at Port Blair and the unremitting struggle to control his prisoners, while Savarkar increasingly strives to educate and lead them: he is ready, on his release, to return to India and fulfill the mission to advance Hindu nationalism that prison life has served only to intensify.

Given the extensive reliance within the Indian prison system on convict warders—convicts given some measure of responsibility as warders and rewarded with certain privileges and improved status—it is not surprising that they figure prominently in most jail narratives. They are often represented as being particularly cruel and rapacious and responsible for much of the corruption and brutality, including sexual violence occurring inside the prison. But in some narratives the warders are given an even more hated role than that of the British themselves, and thus serve to typify the problems that beset the aspiring nation. Apart from Barrie, Savarkar's other main antagonists at Port Blair are the Muslim warders, especially the Pathans, whom he describes as 'bigoted Mohomedans' with a 'fanatical hatred of the Hindus', led by Mirza Khan, the 'Chota Barrie'.[53] The Muslims serve to reinforce Savarkar's identity as a Hindu nationalist in opposition to the followers of a rival faith, who latch on to the power of the British by seeking to convert Hindu prisoners and who want to turn the prison into a 'jail-masjid'.[54] There are perhaps parallels here with Gandhi's antithetical 'Kaffirs', for both sets of adversaries serve to represent the uncivilized but threatening Other against which the Hindu prisoner sharpens his own threatened sense of identity.

But, like Irish jailors, convict warders have a liminal quality that makes them both part of the tyrannical regime of the prison and part of the nation envisioned through the prison. While Gandhi clearly loathed much of his time in Yeravda in the early 1920s, and implicated convict warders in many of its brutal torments, he also wrote series of sketches—in effect potted life histories—of the convict warders assigned to watch over him. As if deliberately to remind him of his South African ordeal, or perhaps simply to minimize communication and empathy, Gandhi was assigned a Somali Muslim, named Adan, jailed for being an army deserter. Although Adan knew no English, nor any Indian language apart from a smattering of Urdu, Gandhi apparently won over this 'devout Mussalman' by his kindness (including, by one account, sucking out the poison when he was stung by a scorpion). Having developed a 'deep personal attachment' for Gandhi, there was 'a sad parting' when Adan was transferred to another part of the prison.[55] The almost mythic quality of this encounter is echoed in the succession of convict warders who attend Gandhi—a Punjabi Hindu, a Muslim, a Mahar, a caste Hindu from Maharashtra, a Gurkha, and a Kanarese—who seem almost deliberately to have been chosen to illustrate the inclusiveness of the Indian nation and the Mahatma's universal appeal. No wonder Gandhi remarks that 'Yeravda was to us a whole world, or better still, the whole world.'[56]

In the course of his imprisonment in 1923, Gandhi declared that satyagraha required a prisoner to 'obey all reasonable prison regulations, and certainly to do the work given. Like a prisoner of war, resistance ceased once he was in prison.'[57] Rajagopalachari similarly maintained that it was the duty of prisoners to obey jail regulations: non-cooperation was to cease on entering prison.[58] 'It is to suffer unjust punishments without protest or complaint that we have come here, and we would be destroying our own foundations if we attempt, when inside jail, to agitate, protest or offer Satyagraha against the hardships imposed on us here.'[59] In theory, then, Gandhians rejected any idea of trying to reform the prison from within, whether for their own benefit or on behalf of the rest of the prison population. It would do 'great injury to the movement and impede its progress,' Rajagopalachari remarked, if nationalists did anything to make the world believe that prison life was hard. 'We have gone in for a great cause on which we should concentrate our thoughts and efforts and not fritter them away in the reform of Jail administration and the purification of subordinate officials.'[60]

In practice, however, as with Gandhi's own tussles in South African and Indian jails, political prisoners of all persuasions engaged in sustained and often bitter struggles with the prison authorities over such matters as diet, work regimes, the nature of punishments, access to newspapers and books, and the receipt of letters and visitors. In part, this was because they were so outraged by what they experienced, or by what they saw and heard, that (whatever their principles) they felt compelled to protest and try to effect change. But it was more than that. Prison narratives are paradoxically replete with a powerful sense of individual agency. Believing in their ability to confront colonial oppression and injustice even in prison was vital to middle-class prisoners' sense of their own ability to survive the prison ordeal and to their belief that even in jail they were neither powerless nor irrelevant to the political struggle outside. One reason for Gandhi's near collapse in 1923–4 was his frustrating sense of powerlessness in trying to influence the prison authorities or control the conduct and maltreatment of other political prisoners, despite threatening to fast to achieve his goals. Some of the most protracted and hard-fought episodes of defiance were, in fact, carried out not by Gandhians but by other political prisoners, like the Bengali revolutionary Jogesh Chandra Chatterji, who spent twenty-four of the thirty years from 1916 to 1946 in jail. His prison struggles, which included lengthy hunger strikes countered by brutal and painful forced feeding, were vital to the self-representation of his life as one of unremitting revolutionary struggle.[61] As with Savarkar's Andamans 'story', such accounts were also intended to show the major contribution revolutionaries had made to India's freedom struggle and the extent to which their and their comrades' suffering in prison (encompassing exhaustion, torture, madness, and death) gave them as great a claim to national leadership and political authority as the more widely publicized but much milder jail experiences of Gandhi and his followers.

Despite such efforts at resistance and reform, in general the experience of prison, as represented in the narratives, seems to have accentuated social difference, in particular highlighting the gulf between 'ordinary convicts' and political prisoners. The entry of middle-class prisoners after 1890, and more especially from 1920 onward, forced major changes in India's prison regime. Against their inclination, and only as a result of repeated prison protests and outside pressure, the authorities were forced to recognize political prisoners as a separate entity, deserving better treatment than that meted out to ordinary convicts. They were placed in separate cells or barracks (sometimes in parts of the prison formerly reserved for Europeans), given better food and lighter work regimes (or no labour at all), allowed access to books, newspapers, and visitors, and even permitted forms of dress and recreation unthinkable for most prison inmates. Political prisoners were often themselves acutely aware how their own sanity and sense of self were saved through the award of such hard-won privileges. As Gandhi remarked of his testing time in Pretoria jail, 'My books saved me',[62] or as Nehru put it in similar circumstances in the 1930s, 'books, books—what would we do without them to escape from ennui and depression?'[63] But, by the same token, being able to read and write, to remain effectively part of their middle-class world and its accomplishments, accentuated the distance between political prisoners and ordinary convicts.

It was often hard for men like Rajagopalachari not to adopt a superior attitude to prisoners who were 'felons and degraded characters'.[64] For the socialist Nehru, writing in the mid-1930s, the ordinary convicts, especially the 'lifers', occupied a more positive place and he could write about learning from them and their far harsher experience of life, inside and outside the jail.[65] Their entry into his prison narrative parallels his introduction to the peasants earlier in the *Autobiography*. Both bring him closer to the 'real India', the India of the masses that he is slowly discovering under Gandhi's tutorship and which he wants to identify with and understand. Like many other middle-class prisoners of the time, Nehru seeks to refute the crude colonial sociology of 'criminal types' and 'criminal classes' that has become so powerfully entrenched in colonial policing and in juridical and penological practice. These, he insists, are human beings with individual identities of their own. They are, besides, not 'really guilty' men and women at all, but have been driven to crime by material need or by fits of anger and despair. 'A more sensible economic policy, more employment, more education would soon empty out our prisons,' he concludes. But under colonialism, 'Not the least effort is made to consider the prisoner as an individual, a human being, and to improve or look after the mind.' Yet, while empathizing with convicts as the victims of colonialism and capitalism, Nehru can never lose his class distance from them or his hegemonic desire to educate and lead them. He cannot avoid pitying them for not being more like himself. It seems particularly oppressive that such prisoners are cut off from the outside world by their illiteracy and their difficulty in maintaining contacts through letters and interviews, precisely the kinds of links that keep Nehru alert and alive in prison.[66]

Nehru goes only so far in his sociological and sentimental investigation of non-political prisoners. M.N. Roy, jailed in 1931, went further along the path of representing the prison as a meaningful site for social observation and analysis. For Roy, so long an exile, the prison almost becomes India. After five years spent continuously in jail, he can see a central prison as 'a fairly representative replica of the entire country' and hence a suitable basis for generalizing about India as a whole.[67] What fascinates and yet perturbs Roy is that, although many crimes are committed either under the pressure of economic necessity or as a result of the constraints imposed by Hindu society, many prisoners accept their fate rather than strive to resist it. In this way, 'the law of karma reinforces the laws of the Imperialist State.'[68] Intent on making the subalterns speak, and to give them a kind of agency by authoring brief life histories on their behalf, Roy recounts six 'typically Indian' life stories of prisoners he has encountered and the 'crimes' that have led them to jail and to the gallows—the incestuous brother who kills his widowed sister; the peasant widow who strangles her illegitimate baby at birth; the old man who murders his erring young wife; the family who slay the village moneylender; the 'madman' who kills his 'witch' wife; the young man who bludgeons to death the religious mendicant who has sexually exploited him. In each of these sociological vignettes, gender, sex, and psychology reinforce the central message that 'crimes are symptoms of social malady'.[69] That prisoners should nonetheless meet their fate with 'supine resignation' is seen by Roy as evidence of India's 'moral degeneration' and the 'shameful psychological state of the Indian masses'.[70]

There is little direct testimony about the prison experiences of the subaltern classes themselves: what we do have is tantalizing but fragmentary.[71] To a large extent the only record of their lives is to be found in the institutional record—in the crude statistics of prison numbers or in accounts of trials, transportation, and executions.[72] As far as the prison bureaucracy was concerned, the essential information was that recorded on the wooden tags prisoners wore, though even these 'histories' could be singularly inaccurate.[73] Paradoxically, then, the life histories of many ordinary prisoners survive only in the second-hand narratives compiled by middle-class prisoners like Gandhi, Nehru, and Roy, and their observations are often too infused with their own social and political concerns to constitute an impartial record.

PRISON AND THE PSYCHE

During his second term of imprisonment, in Lucknow District Jail in 1922–3, Nehru found himself confined in a barrack with nearly fifty other prisoners. Most he already knew, some he counted as friends, but Nehru was dismayed by 'the utter want of privacy', day and night, which became 'more and more difficult to endure'. There was 'no escape … We bathed in public and washed our clothes in public … and talked and argued till we had largely exhausted each other's capacity for intelligent conversation.' It was, he remarked, 'the dull side of family life, magnified a hundred-fold, with few of its graces and compensations.' The 'great nervous strain' of being imprisoned so intimately with others left him yearning for solitude.[74]

By contrast, at Naini Central Jail in 1930 Nehru encountered the 'novel experience of being kept by myself'.[75] His months of solitary confinement, which continued intermittently for the next five years, told heavily on Nehru, but at least he had access to books and could devote his time to voraciously reading and writing. In many ways he preferred this self-absorbed solitude to the crowded life of the prison barrack. Free to pursue his own thoughts, he felt far removed from political infighting in the Congress and the troubles and responsibilities of his home life in Allahabad. He was still very conscious of his isolation and subject to 'prison humours', but without a regime of physical labour to grind him down, Nehru (as revealed in his prison diary, even more than in his autobiography, polished for publication) showed an intense preoccupation with a 'care of the self', which included physical exercise, keeping a careful record of his weight and temperature, and making notes on his mental and emotional state. At one level Nehru wondered why he bothered to keep a diary at all, as there was little worth recording in the dull routine of prison life,[76] but at another he saw its value in keeping himself alert and preventing him from going 'to pieces'.[77] Michel Foucault unwittingly described Nehru's prison life when, in describing the time spent in 'application to oneself', he wrote:

> This time is not empty; it is filled with exercises, practical tasks, various activities. Taking care of oneself is not a rest cure. There is the care of the body to consider, health regimens, physical exercises without overexertion, the carefully measured satisfaction of needs. There are the meditations, the readings, the notes that one takes on books or on the conversations one has heard, notes that one reads again later, the recollection of truths that one knows already but that need to be more fully adapted to one's own life ... [I]t is a sustained effort in which general principles are reactivated and arguments are adduced that persuade one not to let oneself become angry at others, at providence, or at things.[78]

It was in part to counter loneliness and incipient depression that Nehru began his autobiography in 1934. His extensive reading and writing during this and subsequent periods of incarceration did as much as Gandhi's initiation into prison life in South Africa to shape the man Nehru became. Through his intensive bouts of reading and writing in prison Nehru developed his distinctive 'facility with words':[79] this was to form an important element not only in his growing political stature as a speech-maker and writer in India but also his standing as one of India's leading (and most intelligible) spokesmen in the West. Nehru was fortunate to be imprisoned in relative comfort. At times

the colonial authorities seemed remarkably willing to accommodate
the personal needs of middle-class political prisoners, allowing them
reading and writing materials, and even, on occasion, entertainments.
In 1920 J.C. Chatterji and his fellow inmates in Rajshahi were allowed
to play badminton and successfully petitioned the authorities to allow
them to celebrate the Durga Puja festival, during which they were
shown films, albeit war documentaries.[80] But at other times isolation
and the withholding of books, newspapers, and writing materials were
deliberately used to augment punishment and crush prisoners' spirit.
In his five years in jail between 1931 and 1936, Roy was often held in
solitary confinement and for a time (in 1934) was denied access to
pen and ink. He nonetheless contrived to write political tracts and
smuggle them out of jail through his 'secret allies'—fellow prisoners
and sympathetic warders. He also managed to write letters about his
prison experiences, and these, despite the censors, reached the outside
world and testified to the ordeal of his prison years.

In 1934, at a time of extreme physical and mental exhaustion, Roy
began to write the *Memoirs of a Cat*. This was possibly a literary device
borrowed from Bankimchandra Chattopadhyay's *Kamalakanta*,[81] but,
like Nehru and Gandhi, Roy was fascinated by the liminality of prison
cats, creatures able to observe human behaviour intimately while
remaining in the world of animals, critically detached from it, living
within the confines of the human jail but free to slip at will through
the prison bars. Perhaps for Roy, still a dedicated Marxist, to write
directly about himself (in the grand Nehruvian manner) would have
been too bourgeois an indulgence. Seeing the world through a cat's
eyes allowed him to stand outside himself, yet still see Indian society
with feline insightfulness: 'Unfortunately, I have not lived in a human
home [the cat observes]; but prison is also an interesting place. Here ...
the beast in man creeps out of his human skin; and one, with a keen
power of cynical observation, possessed by my species, encounters all
sorts of amusing and illuminating mental phenomena.'[82]

By the time Nehru and Roy came to write and reflect on their prison
thoughts and experiences they had access to a new language of the self,
informed by psychology and psychoanalysis. That the discourse of
psychoanalysis should surface in prison narratives was in part simply
a reflection of wider intellectual trends and fashions, but for Nehru

in particular there was a sense in which the 'unknown' of the prison, with all its torments and terrors, summoned up a need to explore the 'unknown' within himself and those about him. Nehru, who claimed to have been 'saved' by his habit of 'introspection' in prison,[83] presented the whole of his autobiography as a piece of extended self-analysis, an exploration of his conscious and unconscious self and hence a means to understand (and thereby free himself from) his inner turmoil. For him its 'primary test' was its ability to give 'a certain psychological insight into the mind and soul of our national movement'.[84]

In keeping with this psychoanalytical vein, Nehru's autobiography is also about his struggle with the two dominant personalities in his life (by contrast, and not unlike the reticence observed in other life histories in this volume, his wife, Kamala, makes only a shadowy appearance and, apart from the book's dedication, is not even named until more than halfway through the work). These commanding figures are his father Motilal, branded an 'extrovert', and Gandhi, labelled an 'introvert'. Motilal, who died a few years earlier, in 1931, he seems to have the measure of, but the younger Nehru repeatedly invokes the language of psychoanalysis to try to pin down the 'paradox' that is Gandhi (and thus India's and his own). He deploys psychoanalysis as a science that can dispel superstition and help establish his own claim to modernity, while decrying Gandhi's utter denial of the modern world, and to explain his own feelings of both repulsion and attraction towards the Mahatma. In a critical passage reviewing Gandhi's attitudes to sex, Nehru confesses to finding his views on celibacy 'unnatural and shocking', adding that 'if he is right, then I am a criminal on the verge of imbecility and nervous prostration'. He continues:

In these days of the Oedipus complex and Freud and the spread of psychoanalysis this emphatic statement of belief [by Gandhi about the necessity of sexual abstinence] sounds strange and distant.... I think Gandhiji is absolutely wrong in this matter. His advice may fit in with some cases, but as a general policy it can only lead to frustration, inhibition, neurosis, and all manner of physical and nervous ills .... I presume I am a normal individual and sex has played its part in my life, but it has not obsessed me or diverted me from my other activities.... Essentially, his attitude is that of the ascetic who has turned his back to the world and its ways, who denies life and considers it evil.[85]

These ideas are echoed in Roy's prison writings, where they serve even more cogently (but perhaps paradoxically in a Marxist) to stress the importance of understanding the inner self rather than accepting socially determined norms of caste and religion. Speaking through his cat persona, Roy observes that man has not 'lived down his animal self'. 'Modern psychology,' he adds, 'has scant respect for the vanity of man. Psychoanalysis ... demonstrates that human behaviour, base as well as noble, is determined by purely animal motives.' This provides her (the cat is a female as well as a feline alter ego) with an opportunity for a scathing attack on Gandhi's brahmacharya: 'Modern psychology has discovered that active suppression or subconscious inhibition of the sex impulse is the cause of grave mental derangements.' The cat then launches into a textbook discussion of how a human being is dominated mentally as well as physically by his (or her) unconscious,

> which is the accumulated store of natural impulses. The heritage of the whole animal ancestry is deposited in that store. The mental or spiritual aspect of a human being is like an iceberg: only a small part appears above the level of consciousness, the rest remaining submerged in the Unconscious ... What is called conscience acts as the censor, and would not permit civilized human beings to act according to the impulses inherent in their very existence, unless they are dressed up in the glittering garb of hypocrisy and falsehood.[86]

Although for Roy, as for Nehru, the prison necessarily represents backwardness, repression, and a denial of progress, it does at least allow the middle-class author the freedom to explore his prison-based observations of self and society through a modernity of the mind. This is all very different from Gandhi's own approach to autobiography a decade earlier. Although Gandhi had seen aspects of the prison regime in South Africa in 1908–9 as modern, scientific, and even sanitary, by the time he wrote his autobiography in the mid-1920s his attitudes to both prison and modernity had changed. In the Introduction to *The Story of My Experiments with Truth*, he relates a conversation with a friend who observes that '[w]riting an autobiography is a practice peculiar to the West. I know of nobody in the east having written one, except amongst those who have come under Western influence.' To this Gandhi replies that he is not writing a *real* autobiography:

'I simply want to tell the story of my numerous experiments with truth, and as my life consists of nothing but those experiments, it is true that the story will take the shape of an autobiography.' He then adds: 'What I want to achieve—what I have been striving and pining to achieve—is self-realization, to see God face to face, to attain *Moksha* [salvation].'[87] Although Gandhi refers to having gone through 'deep self-introspection' and having 'searched myself through and through, and examined and analysed every psychological situation',[88] this exercise is clearly far removed from the kind of quasi-Freudian self-analysis indulged in by Nehru or Roy's feline alter ego. Gandhi's primary concern is with the pursuit of spiritual salvation, and the moral instruction his life may provide for others, not with unlocking his unconscious.

CONCLUSION

Among the many books Nehru read in the mid 1930s was *Letters from Prison* by the German socialist Ernst Toller. After Toller had praised Nehru's autobiography, the latter replied that

> those who have been in prison and have not finally broken down under the ordeal, develop some kind of common outlook and a bond which unites them invisibly. When I read your beautiful *Letters from Prison* again and again they brought pictures of my own moods and thoughts in prison to me and your book occasionally became a mirror of myself.[89]

It might be argued that all political prisoners share similar experiences and learn to cope with—even to write about—them in not dissimilar ways. In other words, the genre of the prison narrative, far from being specific to India or anywhere else in the modern world, has a universal signification and appeal. But, while this may be largely the case, it is important not to lose sight of what may have been Indian and/or colonial about the narratives discussed here and the circumstances of their production. The nature as well as the number of Indian prison narratives testify not only to the exceptional role of jail-going in the Gandhi-led movements in South Africa and India from the 1900s to the 1940s but also to the extensive recourse to imprisonment to counter political movements of all kinds in British India. The exact nature and conditions of that imprisonment varied very widely (as between, say, Chatterji and Nehru or Gandhi and Savarkar), but intense political activism over a period of roughly fifty years from the mid-1890s to the mid-1940s brought a relatively large number of educated and articulate middle-class men and women into the jails of British India. It gave them exceptional opportunities to observe state and society through the prism of the prison and even, in many cases, the freedom to read and to write about their jail experiences from within the walls of the prison itself. The highly influential precedents of Gandhi and Nehru's prison writings cannot be ignored as factors in stimulating the rise and dissemination of this particular form of life history in India. To argue further that colonial prison, with its sys-tematic assault upon social convention and cultural taboo, was a site of particular revulsion to Indians, more especially to Hindus, would be harder to demonstrate, except perhaps through a lengthy exercise in comparative penology, but it might be that in this lies an additional reason why so many middle-class Indians felt impelled to record their jail experiences, whether for themselves or for posterity.

NOTES

1. For example, R. Prasad, *Autobiography* (Bombay 1957).

2. Cf. B. Keenan, *An Evil Cradling* (London 1992), p. xiv.

3. For example, Mirabehn (Madeleine Slade), *The Spirit's Pilgrimage* (London 1960), pp. 156–71; V. Pandit, *The Scope of Happiness: A Personal Memoir* (London 1979), pp. 101–14.

4. Satadru Sen, *Disciplining Punishment: Colonialism and Convict Society in the Andaman Islands* (New Delhi 2000); Cathy Scott-Clark and Ardian Levy, 'Survivors of Our Hell', *Guardian Weekend*, 23 June 2001.

5. J. Nehru, *An Autobiography* (London 1936), p. 79.

6. Ibid., p. 90.

7. A. Mukhopadhyay, 'Legal and Penal Institutions from a Middle-Class Perspective in Colonial Bengal, 1854–1910' (PhD thesis, University of London, 1996), pp. 265–81.

8. Nehru, *An Autobiography*, p. 90.

9. *Bengal Native Newspaper Reports*, Oriental and India Office Collections, British Library, London, January 1898.

10. Ibid.

11. M.K. Gandhi, *Collected Works of Mahatma Gandhi* (hereafter *CWMG*), 90 vols (Delhi 1958–84), 9: 219.

12. Ibid., 8: 134.

13. Ibid., 8: 120.

14. Ibid., 8: 135.

15. Ibid.

16. Ibid., 8: 39.

17. Ibid., 24: 56.

18. Ibid., 8: 160; 9: 93, 96, 182.

19. Ibid., 8: 160.

20. Ibid., 9: 123.

21. Ibid., 9: 180–1.

22. Ibid., 8:138–41.

23. Ibid., 9:140–1, 181.

24. Ibid., 9: 146.

25. M.K. Gandhi, *An Autobiography or the Story of My Experiments with Truth* (Ahmedabad 1940), p. 245.

26. *CWMG*, 9: 182.

27. M. Desai, *The Diary of Mahadev Desai, Volume I* (Ahmedabad 1953), pp. 12–13.

28. *CWMG*, 9: 236–7.

29. Ibid., 9: 164.

30. E. Tarlo, *Clothing Matters: Dress and Identity in India* (London 1996), pp. 67–77.

31. *CWMG*, 29: 222–4.

32. Pyarelal and Sushila Nayar, *In Gandhiji's Mirror* (Delhi 1991), p. 17.

33. Mirabehn, *The Spirit's Pilgrimage*, p. 122.

34. S. Nayar, *Mahatma Gandhi's Last Imprisonment: The Inside Story* (New Delhi 1996), pp. 75, 176.

35. *CWMG* 23: 196.

36. *CWMG* 23: 130.

37. *CWMG* 23: 507.

38. Nehru, *An Autobiography*, p. 76.

39. H.D. Thoreau, *Walden, and On the Duty of Civil Disobedience* (New York 1962), p. 245.

40. *CWMG*, 23: 6, 383.

41. *Selected Works of Jawaharlal Nehru* (hereafter *SWJN*) (New Delhi 1973–5), 5: 494.

42. Nehru, *An Autobiography*, p. 394.

43. C. Rajagopalachari, *Rajaji's 1920 Jail Life* (Madras 1941), p. 5.

44. Ibid., p. 7.

45. Ibid., pp. 5–6.

46. Ibid., p. 55.

47. Ibid., p. 129.

48. Ibid., p. 139.

49. Ibid., pp. 139–40.

50. Ibid., p. 47.

51. V.D. Savarkar, *The Story of My Transportation for Life* (Bombay 1950), p. 380.

52. Ibid., p. 330.

53. Ibid., pp. 90–1, 200.

54. Ibid., pp. 277–8.

55. *CWMG*, 24: 366–7; K. Kalelkar, *Stray Glimpses of Bapu*, 2nd edition (Ahmedabad 1960), pp. 101–2.

56. *CWMG* 24: 368.

57. *CWMG* 23: 156.

58. Rajagopalachari, *Rajaji's 1920 Jail Life*, p. 90.

59. Ibid., p. 94.

60. Ibid., p. 78.

61. J.C. Chatterji, *In Search of Freedom* (Calcutta 1967).

62. *CWMG* 9: 241.

63. *SWJN* 5: 402; cf. Chatterji, *In Search of Freedom*, pp. 87–8.

64. Rajagopalachari, *Rajaji's 1920 Jail Life*, p. 33.

65. Nehru, *An Autobiography*, p. 96.

66. Ibid., pp. 219–23.

67. Sibnarayan Ray (ed.), *Selected Works of M.N. Roy, Volume IV, 1932–1936* (Delhi 1997), p. 517.

68. Ibid., p. 516.

69. Ibid., p. 531.

70. Ibid., p. 537.

71. D. Arnold, 'The Colonial Prison: Power, Knowledge and Penology in Nineteenth-Century India', in D. Arnold and D. Hardiman (eds), *Subaltern Studies VIII: Essays in Honour of Ranajit Guha* (New Delhi 1994), pp. 148–87.

72. C. Anderson, *Convicts in the Indian Ocean: Transportation from South Asia to Mauritius*, 1815–53 (Basingstoke 2000).

73. Rajagopalachari, *Rajaji's 1920 Jail Life*, p. 8.

74. Nehru, *An Autobiography*, p. 93.

75. Ibid., p. 219.

76. *SWJN* 5: 381.

77. Nehru, *An Autobiography*, p. 348.

78. M. Foucault, *The Care of the Self* (Harmondsworth 1990), p. 51.

79. R.D. King, *Nehru and the Language Politics of India* (New Delhi 1997), p. 153.

80. Chatterji, *In Search of Freedom*, p. 119.

81. S. Kaviraj, *The Unhappy Consciousness: Bankimchandra Chattopadhyay and the Formation of Nationalist Discourse in India.* (New Delhi 1995), pp. 27–71.

82. Ray, *Selected Works of M.N Roy*, p. 464.

83. Nehru, *An Autobiography*, p. 204.

84. *SWJN* 7: 140.
85. Nehru, *An Autobiography*, pp. 512–13.
86. Ray, *Selected Works of M.N Roy*, pp. 469, 478–9.
87. Gandhi, *An Autobiography*, pp. ix–x.
88. Ibid., p. x.
89. *SWJN* 7: 153.

IV
Legalities and Illegalities

9

Distress and Defiance*

Ranajit Guha

> Tam kim maññasi, Assalāyana? Sutan te: *Yona-* Kambojesu aññesu ca
> paccantimesu janapadesu dveva vannā, ayyo c'eva dāso ca; ayyo hutvā
> dāso hoti, dāso hutvā ayyo hotiti?[1]
> —*Majjhima-Nikaya*: Assalayanasuttam (93)

Banjara Singh was a shepherd boy who grew up to be the leader of a
formidable band of dacoits in the Chambal region. His father was a
poor peasant turned poorer when he pawned half of his small plot of
land, sold his flock of sheep, and took a loan from the *sahukar*—all
in order to pay for his daughter's wedding. Then he died. And as we
learn from the testimony of his adversary and biographer:

> The turning point in Banjara Singh's life was the death of his father. He
> disposed of the field to fulfil his duties as a devoted son in connection
> with the last rites of the dead. The sahukar turned up to press his
> demand for the payment of loan. Banjara Singh had no money to
> give. The sahukar remonstrated with abuses. The young man at first
> kept quiet but later retaliated by uttering abuses in reply. At this, the
> sahukar hit Banjara Singh with his stick. At the first touch of the stick,
> Banjara was wild and assaulted him with his lathi. The sahukar fled.
> That night Banjara Singh decided to leave his dilapidated house and his
> semi-deserted village.

* Excerpted from Ranajit Guha, *Elementary Aspects of Peasant Insurgency in
Colonial India* (Delhi: Oxford University Press, 1983).

Many an outlaw's career begins in almost identical circumstances all over rural India. There are regions of chronic poverty like Banjara Singh's own district where for hundreds of years peasant youths have been slipping out of desolate villages and starvation and bonded labour in order to take to dacoity as a profession. There are demographic masses branded by colonial legislation as 'criminal tribes' (a stigma nominally removed since 1952 but still intact in social practice) for whom the very fact of having been thus classified has made crime the only means left for livelihood. The Lodhas are one such group of the rural poor in western Bengal. A forest people they used to earn their living, traditionally, as hunters, trappers and gatherers of food and fuel from the jungle. But the jungle, their provider, was taken away from them by the zamindar and the sarkar as land hunger and rising birth rates combined to turn more and more of the woodlands of Midnapur into paddy fields and villages. Cut off thus from their principal source of subsistence the Lodhas had, by the turn of the century, adopted robbery and theft as almost a second profession. And then, in 1916, the law stepped in to fasten on them a new identity by naming them officially as a 'criminal tribe'.

The Lodhas had taken to crime rather than agriculture because there was nothing for them in agriculture to take to. They had very little land of their own. A study of landholding by a hundred families in five Midnapur villages showed that an average Lodha family of 4.8. members owned 0.65 acre of land, that is, 0.134 acre per head. Of the families surveyed 57 per cent were landless, 20 per cent owned less than one acre, and 17 per cent more than one acre but less than four. No wonder that the Lodha peasant starves most of the time. 'A few families were found in the course of the enquiry … to have no grain of rice for 7 or 8 days at a stretch, and they depended wholly on … wild tubers for their food.' Again, in one of the villages 'a good number of families … were found to starve or remain without any food for the whole day. This is a common phenomenon in the life of a Lodha here. Even the children are kept starving. Sometimes they are found to collect some edible small or big fruits and leaves to tide over the period of starvation. One woman was found by the writer to swallow a morsel of soil in crushing hunger.' What crime, if any, this particular woman was eventually driven to, we shall never know. But the author of the melancholy monograph from which these facts have been taken does tell us of another woman who was arrested and convicted. She was a widow with four children and the only way she could feed them was by stealing food or articles sold or exchanged, for food. Children too had to provide for themselves by similar means. A ten-year-old girl was arrested by the police for theft: she had been 'starving for two days and was tempted to lift [a] brass cup with a view to selling it in the market for a little cash by which she could procure some food to eat.'

Hobsbawm has noticed the distinction made by the English rural labourer of 1830 between two classes of crime committed as an escape from poverty. The labourer 'could seek a relief from poverty in crime—in the simple theft of potatoes or turnips which constituted the bulk of the offences which he would himself regard as criminal, and in poaching or smuggling, which he would not.' Hunger has forced the Lodhas of Midnapur to do away with such fine moral distinctions. Parents have to feed their families, and if crime is the only means of access to articles of common consumption, the morality lies with the criminal. Far from being censured for offences against the law, a Lodha punished by the court would often be regarded by his kin as above reproach. 'In a few cases,' to quote again from the account mentioned above, 'the wives of the criminals defended their husbands as innocent and spotless in character. They strongly asserted that they knew nothing wrong about their husbands.' Impoverished bread-winners do indeed figure prominently in Lodha crime statistics. In a sample of 180 of them listed as criminals it was found out that 82.2 per cent had no land at all, 12.2 per cent owned one acre or less and 5.6 per cent two acres or more, while 9.4 per cent of the same population belonged to small families of one to three members each, 46.7 per cent to medium-sized, families of four to six members each, 31.1 per cent to large families, of seven to nine members and 12.8 per cent to very large families of more than ten members each. Thus the great majority of Lodha criminals are those who have the largest number of mouths to feed and the least resources. What makes the connection between hunger and crime quite explicit is that it is the practice of Lodha dacoits to carry off from the houses they raid everything they can lay their hands on and exchange it as quickly as possible for food;

any foodstuff that can be readily consumed, they consume on the spot during a raid.

Offences of this nature committed in a desperate search for food are not limited to the Lodhas of Midnapur alone. There is nothing in this that is specific to their culture or the region where they belong. Such defiance of the law arises from a common and ubiquitous tradition of resistance to poverty, which, at least during the colonial period, received an acknowledgement from the authorities themselves. This was typically expressed in the words of the Police Report of 1852 for the Lower Provinces stating how the number of dacoities in Birbhum district had suddenly increased by about 100 per cent since the previous year as the direct result of distress following a severe drought:

> There appears a considerable increase in the offence of Dacoitee; but bearing in mind that this is one of the districts in which the people suffered most from the want of rain in 1851 and that the nature of the country affords great facility for the perpetration of this offence and the escape of the offenders, such a result might have been expected.

For the south, too, David Arnold has demonstrated in his excellent study of this subject how drought, dearth, and high prices constituted the most readily identifiable factor in the incidence of dacoity in the Madras Presidency in the late nineteenth and early twentieth centuries. The correlation was indeed so clear that the authorities came to rely on it as 'a true index to the state of distress'—a sort of local barometer of the prevailing degree of deprivation—and 'the Inspector-General of Police invariably prefaced his annual report on crime with a summary of the year's rainfall and grain prices.' Again, in the west, hunger often turned peasant into dacoit as witnessed thus by a young Indian civilian in charge of relief operations in Gujarat devastated by a famine at the turn of the century:

> I had set up camp for a few days on the outskirts of a small village some miles away from the nearest railway. Provisions used to be sent up for me by train from the district headquarters. One day it so happened that the entire supply (amounting in fact to eight loaves of bread) was looted on its way to my camp ... The police blew up the incident out of all proportions. After three days, five Kolis, all skin and bone, were sent

up on charges of dacoity for trial at my own court! 'We had nothing to eat for three days in a row,' they said without any show of repentance whatsoever. 'Our bellies were burning with hunger. Should we have come across all that food and not eaten it?' Indeed, how were they to let all that food go? But how could I let them go without punishment either? So I worked a bit on the evidence provided by the police and defined the offence as a case of theft rather than dacoity. Then I sentenced them to imprisonment for a day and a fine of half a rupee per head. This was the verdict which I entered in the court records, but felt so embarrassed about the whole business that I said to them, 'Now go away. You are free. Don't steal again.' The fine I paid out of my own pocket.

There is more to this anecdote than a parallelism between the various instances of starvation crime discussed above. It helps to define the ambivalence of the deed on which the young and evidently sympathetic officer was asked to sit in judgement. Was it an offence to be interpreted and punished according to the Indian Penal Code or was it to be justified by a code of social morality that provides for a minimum subsistence as an overriding right? A form of violence against property was obviously switching codes when it was brought before the court and obliged the young officer to produce half an answer to that question in terms of one code and half in another.

NOTE

1. (Buddha to Assalayana) 'What do you think about this, Assalayana? Have you heard that in Yona and Kamboja and other neighbouring *janapadas* there are only two varnas, the master and the slave? And that having been a master one becomes a slave; having been a slave one becomes a master?' This is a slightly modified version of the translation of the passage as given in *The Middle-Length Sayings*, vol. II (London 1957), pp. 341–2.

10

The Infanticidal Woman

The Emergence of the Female Criminal in Colonial India*

Padma Anagol

[...]

In 1876, Dinbai, a Parsi widow reputed to be from a 'respectable family' in Bombay, was charged with infanticide when the death of her newborn child was brought to the attention of the police. The High Court sentenced both Dinbai and the midwife who carried out the act to death. In April 1881, Vijayalakshmi, a Brahman widow aged twenty-four, was convicted of killing her newborn illegitimate infant and was also sentenced to death.[1] Both instances generated a massive amount of public debate after Indian-language newspapers published the growing number of convictions for the crime of infanticide. In 1872, statistics revealed that 406 women were tried for the offence in the North West Provinces, while in the Bengal, Madras, and Bombay Presidencies, the corresponding figures were 197, 77, and fifteen convictions respectively;[2] ten years later in 1886, the corresponding figures for these provinces were 227, 309, 373, and 203 respectively. The

* Excerpted from Padma Anagol, 'The Emergence of the Female Criminal in India: Infanticide and Survival under the Raj', *History Workshop Journal*, vol. 53, no. 1, pp. 73–93.

figures for the Bombay Presidency were comparatively lower but still saw a dramatic increase from fifteen to 203 cases in the same period. [...]

The infanticidal woman was a creation of colonialism, emerging clearly after the passing of the Infanticide Act in 1870. Whereas in cases of female infanticide, the practice of killing newborn females in certain communities, responsibility was assigned to the leaders of the groups involved, in cases of infanticide, the blame was exclusively assigned to the woman. It was not that infanticide itself was new, but rather the innovation lay in culpability—the blame had been shifted from the collective, male-led community to the female individual. The rendering of what was a complex situation into one of simple apportioning of blame was what distinguished colonial law from customary practice. Furthermore, Indian men not only condoned this shift, they helped to reinforce it.

Whether infanticide was considered a serious crime in precolonial Indian society with penalties commensurate with those of the British is doubtful. Nor was blame focused exclusively on the woman. Male offenders in infanticide cases were sometimes readmitted into the caste after a ritual purification ceremony that was accompanied by a small monetary fine. The scope and legitimacy of the courts under peshwa rule (pre-British rulers in western India) was always limited in such matters. Adulterous wives were punished and under the peshwas, Brahman women were especially singled out for their 'unchaste' behaviour. Even then, one finds that the punishment tended to be a fine based on the financial circumstances of the woman, although Brahman women who were made pregnant by low-caste men were irrevocably excommunicated from the caste. But even here, the worst fate that the offender faced was being driven off the precincts of the village or town. However, there are no recorded instances of women who aborted foetuses or committed infanticide being punished severely.[3] Local communities through their involvement in caste and village councils more usually dealt with infanticide, and this was the situation which the British encountered when they first began to display an interest in the issue. A case involving exclusion that occurred in 1868 was narrated by Savitribai Phule, who appeased the enraged Mahar (untouchable) community of her village by taking away a young Mahar girl who had an illegitimate child by a Brahman priest to Poona.[4] The flexibility of customary law, based as it was on a consideration of the facts and circumstances of every case, with due regard to local usages and scriptures (texts), only sought as a residual source legal guidance, and has been the subject of comment by a great number of legal scholars.[5] Legal scholarship in this area seems to agree that the Anglo-Indian laws, 'a conglomerate of precedents built on nebulous textual authority' and embodied in the Code of Criminal Law represented by the Indian Penal Code (1860), were received with 'silent non-acceptance', if not downright hostility, by the general population.[6] Legal historians endorse that, in the nineteenth century, official law and customary practice continued to jostle alongside each other, often coming into direct conflict as the former unsuccessfully tried to outlaw the latter.

However, the best guide to contemporary notions on how crimes of infanticide were treated is the Indian public response to the British convictions of infanticidal women. Although they were anxious to point out that the *shastras* considered infanticide a terrible sin visiting the sinner with severe punishment, in practice, popular Hindu opinion, as expressed in articles in the Indian-language press and men's petitions, revealed a more tolerant approach to the crime. Even though Hindu religion and morality mores placed powerful restraints on widows' conduct, lapses had tended to be tolerated by society as long as the widow concealed the fact of her unchastity. Following on from this, contemporary Hindu opinion seemed to have a pragmatic view of the subject, as this statement, made by the residents of Sholapur in a petition to the government on the subject of Vijayalakshmi's prosecution, demonstrates:

> The Criminal Law of the Country so far as it affects the crime of Infanticide by Hindu widows is opposed to the national sense of justice and the prevalent Public opinion is unanimous that so long as widow marriage is forbidden by the caste rules amongst Hindus, it is positively cruel to visit such occasional lapses from moral rectitude as that by Vijayalaksmi with severe penalty.[7]

Moreover, as the case of Bai Rupli demonstrates, customary practice offered the potential for flexibility. When Bai Rupli fell pregnant with the baby of her late husband's eldest brother, the caste *panch* (court) gave them permission to marry. It was only when he subsequently abandoned her and fled the village before they could be married, that another one of her brothers-in-law, Asha Dwarka, killed her to prevent her from bringing shame on her late husband's family.[8] Had she continued to live, she not only would have put the whole family's social relations with the rest of the community at risk, as such liaisons were regarded with ridicule, but could have left them facing a wide range of social sanctions, including excommunication, termed as 'social death' by many petitioners. Even wealthy, powerful, and high-caste Indian families were at risk of losing their social status within the community if one of them fell pregnant out of wedlock. Caste councils were aware of the fact that often families participated actively and perhaps ordered the killing of illegitimate children but the local knowledge and practices of local communities were not accessible to English judges, placed as they were hundreds or thousands of miles away from the far-flung scene of the crime.

Even if a family could have borne the social stigma, there were also economic reasons why Hindu joint families generally refused to rear an illegitimate child, even when the child was born from a blood-tie within the family. If a Brahman widow already had children from her marriage, the question of inheritance rights would surface, as illegitimate children were known to contest for property.[9] In a largely agricultural economy where large joint families depended on land for a living, this was seen as a serious economic threat. To prevent such an occurrence, the joint family often took it upon itself to kill the newborn infant, more often than not without the consent of the mother.[10] Infanticide was, therefore, not necessarily always a singular act by the mother but a collective act by her joint family; a fact disregarded by the British legal system when it defined infanticide as the 'case of a woman killing her illegitimate child directly after birth'.

Certain gender-based inequalities were built into the laws governing punishment with an inherent assumption that the mother was the main murderer in this act. Male participants in the deed could only be charged, under Section 303, as an abettor to the secret disposal of the body. The mother, on the other hand, could be charged separately under three sections: Section 301—culpable homicide amounting to murder; Section 302—exposure and/or abandonment of the child; and Section 303—secret disposal of the body. Despite the fact that Section 302 does make reference to the 'parent', it was only used against the father in a very small number of cases where they were actually charged. Furthermore, when, in 1883, a problem arose over the disposal of a body by a third party with or without the mother's tacit consent, the court ruled that the mother was to be held responsible in all such cases.[11] The essential principle governing the law appears to have been that only the mother had a motive for committing child murder; there was no enactment that recognized that the father of the child would have had a motive in assisting or committing the deed himself in order to escape detection. This meant that even the system of detecting such acts was weighted against the mother; while village police officials were trained to keep a close check on the movements of pregnant women and women who had recently given birth, with midwives made responsible for reporting the births and deaths of newborn female infants, their men folk escaped such scrutiny.[12] The information-gathering service itself shows a bias towards letting off men from any kind of culpability.

This was despite the fact that, as women's petitions from the time demonstrate, it was not always the mother who committed the crime; the petitioners in these instances implicate fathers-in-law, brothers-in-law, their lovers, village *patils* (heads), and even stepsons. Indeed, if the woman could get witnesses, she could successfully reveal the true criminal. This happened in the case of Tukki kom Siddappa, a prostitute, who was successful in implicating the village headman, despite the fact that he was shielded by the village sepoy and the head constable, by getting the midwife and her assistant who attended Tukki's delivery to testify on her behalf, resulting in Tukki's sentence being reduced from transportation to five years' rigorous imprisonment.[13] The way that the penal code was framed forced the mother on the defensive, which meant that, if she implicated someone else, she had to provide the evidence for it. This clause that demanded evidence of proof made it difficult for women to implicate male offenders, as it was very unlikely that a woman who had recently delivered a child would have had the opportunity to observe anything happening around her. This is demonstrated by the fact that, except for one case of a stepson transported for life, there were only five cases of men being arrested for abetting the crime in sixteen years of the Bombay Presidency. Even in these cases, all five men were acquitted and discharged on the grounds of insufficient evidence.

[...]

Indigenous male elites and the colonial authorities argued that Hindu widows were killing their newborn illegitimate infants because of the shame and loss of honour that this involved. However, when we examine the motives of the women themselves, we see motivations more complex than a simple fear of social opinion. Indeed, for most infanticidal women it appears to have been a question of survival. For a Brahman widow, living in a large joint family, raising an illegitimate child was impossible; such an act would have been abhorrent to Hindu custom. Abortion and infanticide alone offered escape from such a situation. Although begging and prostitution appeared to be further options for a woman in such circumstance if she chose to rear the child, they were impossible choices for wealthy Maratha and Brahman widows who, having led a protected and sheltered life with minimal dealings with the outside world, were like orphans themselves when thrown out on to the streets. The only option that they had was to choose between their own life and that of the illegitimate child. The decision, when it happened to be the woman's, was thus always reduced to a question of survival. At the other end of the social scale, the most important motive for women was their ability to feed themselves and the child. Many cases of infanticide were reported during years of famine and plague. Sometimes a whole household disappeared in a plague-ridden town, leaving behind women who, reduced to stark poverty, were forced into terrible decisions. Moreover, as the petitions demonstrate, these decisions were usually made in a traumatized state of mind, with the women debilitated by lack of food or sickness or both.[14] Many women under such intolerable strain took their own lives as well; many reports of infanticide that had occurred in these instances are also accompanied by reports of the mother's suicide. Reporting on the 'New Arrangements in Regard to the Relief Works of the Current Famine', in 1877, the *Bombay Samachar* commented:

> Particularly women with one or more children cannot maintain themselves and their young ones. If the mothers try to feed their

children, half-starving themselves, the children soon become orphans;
if they neglect them, the latter fall victims to starvation.[15]

However, despite the fact that the women in such circumstances, who
were brought to trial, explained the nature of their quest for survival
in their petitions at great length, their views and experiences were
dismissed and no clemency was shown towards them.

The two vital support systems for a woman were her natal home
when unmarried and, after marriage, the family of her husband.
Withdrawal of such protection was a catastrophe for a woman, both
economically and psychologically. Section 302 of the Indian Penal
Code describes infanticide as 'Exposure of child by parent with intention of wholly abandoning it'. However, in all cases of abandonment
by mothers of newly born infants or of children, the mothers themselves had also been abandoned. Infanticidal women had often been
abandoned by parents, brothers or sisters, husbands, or, in the case
of widows, by lovers and relatives. Even if they had not been abandoned, many were terrified that their families would find out and
abandon them or punish them in even worse ways. Petawwa, an eigh-
teen-year-old girl, delivered a child out of wedlock at her sister's house
and admitted that she had killed it as she was afraid that her mother
and brother, with whom she normally lived, would beat her to death if
they found out about her pregnancy and also because she feared 'the
dishonour to herself if the matter became known to the public'.[16]

Desertion of wives seems to have been a common practice, especially among the lower castes in Maharashtra and sometimes among
the Marathas. It was usually a consequence of a new marriage or
favours shown to mistresses and rarely due to economic reasons such
as droughts or famines. Desertion of wives by husbands or of widows
by their lovers was also accompanied by factors such as abandonment
by the family, ill treatment, and violent behaviour towards women by
kin, acute poverty, and a failure to secure gainful employment. Gunga,
a twenty-year-old Mahar, stated in her petition:

> I was a widow but was kept by Dirya Mahar in his house, who had
> promised to marry me. I had intercourse with him and was big with
> child. Subsequently he turned me out of his house. I told him that I had
> the child by him and asked him where I was to go.[17]

She was eventually forced to seek shelter in her sister's house, where she was made to feel unwelcome since she had borne an illegitimate child, which was referred to as a 'scandal'.[18]

A crucial test for the survival of the infant was the ability of the deserted wife or abandoned widow to find employment. Lower-caste women could find employment in the construction industry, but employers often discriminated against mothers with suckling infants and pregnant women. Many cases of such discrimination come to light in the criminal records by female petitioners as well as in newspaper reports. It is therefore not surprising that the women who eventually threw their children into wells or tanks, and sometimes went on to kill themselves, did not do this immediately after the birth of their infants but after a fortnight, a month, or even a year or two, depending on when they reached their nadir. Chandra kom Kundoo stated that she had been abandoned by her second husband before being dismissed by her employer as she was in an advanced state of pregnancy, and then turned out of the house of her sister, with whom she had sought refuge, by her brother-in-law.[19] In Gungi kom Krishna's case, the child died of neglect as her mother-in-law and brother-in-law sent her back to the relief works the fifth day after her delivery. Ill and undernourished, she told the court she did not have enough milk to suckle the child.[20] There are, therefore, instances of deserted women who, in spite of their poverty, illness, and unemployment, would have been willing to look after their children if their natal home had offered some support.[21]

Scholarly works on infanticide often cite status as a determining factor in the commission of the act.[22] A great number of the Brahman widows quoted status as an important motive for committing the act, although it was only one among a range of considerations. Women such as Vijayalakshmi claimed that being a Brahman had been an obstacle to finding employment elsewhere.[23] Brahman widows could only be employed in the houses of Brahmans and only then in the capacity of menial outhouse work in order not to violate notions of pollution, so integral to the caste system. It was a formidable choice for a Brahman widow who had led a sheltered life, and it would have meant a great lowering in the standard of living. More significantly, it meant a precarious existence. Material conditions were ultimately crucial factors because, even those who said it was fear of social opinion knew that, if their unchastity was made public, they would be denied the shelter of the home, whether natal or marital, and would invite the wrath of the caste or village. Status was, therefore, in direct correlation with the economic prospects for a Brahman widow. In the case of lower-caste women, desertion and poverty, abandonment by the husband, sickness and impoverishment, or famine and unemployment, or a combination of several factors led them to make painful decisions such as infanticide, sometimes combined with suicide. Both the Brahman and lower-caste widows had only sexual value to their lovers. Once it turned into reproductive value, women of both classes were rejected and denied any form of shelter or privileges. Infanticidal women in the nineteenth century, whether elite (Brahman) or subordinate (Mang or Mahar), in caste terms, were undeniably the lowest in the gender hierarchy.

Not even if an infanticidal woman had conceived her baby as a result of rape, was any mercy shown, despite the fact that petitions reveal that Indian women, especially widows, were vulnerable to this form of violence, with many instances of widows being raped by a member of a vast network of relations within the joint family; in some cases, the kinship tie was as close as a father-in-law or brother-in-law. When Sangowa, widow of Gursidapa of Kaladgi, conceived after being raped by one of the joint-family members of her husband's family, her father-in-law forced her to commit infanticide by threatening to throw her out of the house if she failed to carry out the act. He was convicted merely of burying the body of the child and sentenced to three months; Sangowa was transported for seven years.[24] Moreover, without the symbolic and real protection of the husband, lower-class widows were as vulnerable as widows of higher castes. Rakhuma, a day labourer, confessed that she had been waylaid while working in a paddy field by a man belonging to her caste a few months after the death of her husband, and that, as a result of this 'forcible intercourse', she had borne a child. She also stated that she had not aborted the foetus because she had one surviving child by her deceased husband whom she loved and wanted to take care of, as the child had no one aside from her. The death of her child borne of rape, she insisted, had been due to malarial fever.[25]

Petitions reveal the pitiful dilemmas of widows who had been raped by very close members of the husband's family, such as a brother-in-law. The notion of pollution attached to widows was exacerbated if they were found to have conceived due to rape. Unwilling to incur the wrath of the family by naming the person involved, the widow usually murdered the newly born infant in the hope that, by getting rid of the evidence of the rape, she would be retained in the family, although, in many cases, they did not even have a say in the matter. In 1885, Rakhuma kom Bala was transported for ten years in spite of her claims that she had been forced to commit the crime under the pressure from her husband's family. Raped by her brother-in-law after the death of her husband, she was told by her father-in-law that the reputation of the family would be in jeopardy if the town came to know of the rape and was thus persuaded to commit the act. Sentencing her to ten years' transportation, the governor commented:

> the case is a bad one of its kind—for the woman's only excuse for killing the child was that she was afraid of being turned out of caste.[26]

The legal interpretations did not consider the circumstances of Rakhuma's conception or the instigators behind the act, but only her role in the commission of the act.

It seems clear that women alone understood the crucial links between infanticide and the survival of the mother concerned. A shared sense of a subordinate status and experience is seen in many cases of infanticide that came in front of the colonial courts. Very often, midwives, grandmothers, aunts, friendly neighbours' wives, or female friends rallied around women who were pregnant with an illegitimate child; their involvement is demonstrated by the number of elderly women, including grandmothers, who were arrested for administering medicines to daughters with a view to causing a miscarriage,[27] or charged with murder, abetting murder, or of disposing of the child's body. Despite the fact that the grandmother was often a relatively elderly lady of fifty or sixty years, and they were usually acting out of a desire to prevent their daughter being humiliated and excommunicated by the caste and village panchayat (councils) for conceiving as a result of coercion by a close relation, the law treated them as harshly as the mothers themselves.[28] Nevertheless, some women continued to act to protect the daughter from the wrath of the family or caste, revealing the solidarity that existed between some Indian women and, it could be argued, even displaying a rudimentary feminist consciousness. A similar trend of assisting female relatives had been noted by Judith Tucker in her study of nineteenth-century Egyptian women; by carrying out what Tucker refers to as acts of resistance within the home, women often attempted to assist those female members most in need.[29]

[...]

We can, therefore, see that, both in terms of assigning responsibility for the killing of an infant and with regard to the circumstances that drove infanticidal women to act in the way that they did, the phenomenon of infanticide was a complex one. However, the intricate web of factors that contributed to the crime was largely lost when deciding on punishment because Section 109 of the Indian Penal Code presented peculiar problems of interpretation to the judiciary in the Bombay Presidency. It was often taken to also include crimes that were not necessarily straightforward infanticide, meaning that women who should have been tried under different laws were instead subject to its strictures. It failed, for instance, to make any provision for married women, especially *savatis* (second wives) who killed legitimate children; a failure that led to further confusion about its inability to distinguish infanticide from infanticide accompanied by suicide. In times of desperation, for instance, some housewives seem to have been driven to throwing themselves and their children into rivers, tanks, and wells. Wife battering, neglect, and ill treatment were the main motives behind such desperate acts of suicide and infanticide, as this petition by Basawa kom Basapa shows:

> I lived happily with my husband Basapa until he married Chanawa by Pat ceremony [customary ritual for a second marriage among lower castes]. Chanawa always quarrelled with me on some pretext or other. My husband treated me very cruelly ... and turned me out of his house. I returned home again but they kept me starving. Having lived in this way for fifteen days I requested him to make some arrangement for my maintenance. He and my co-wife, however, began to beat me and drove me out of the house. They struck me with an iron

ladle and the mark left by it is still visible on my chest. I could not live any longer without food and being disgusted with my existence in this world my head turned and I could not see what to do ... Being unable to bear it any longer. I took my child and went to a well and threw myself into it with the child, not knowing the consequences of what I was going to do.[30]

When a co-wife was involved, women were often driven to commit infanticide along with suicide, as they were convinced that their children would not get a fair chance.[31] Such cases were dealt with by the Governor-in-Council under the category of 'derangement of senses' compounded by ill treatment. Sentences were commuted from transportation for life to ten or seven years' hard labour but never less than five years. The lack of distinction between the various kinds of situations giving rise to this offence led to infanticidal and suicidal women being harshly treated by the criminal justice system.

Neither did the law consider the material circumstances of women arrested for infanticide. As we have seen, Indian elites petitioned strongly in cases of Brahman widows. For women belonging to lower castes and classes such as the Kunbis, Mahars, or Mangs convicted for this act, however, the chances of escaping transportation were slim, and they had to fight hard to have their sentences remitted. Kesar, a widow and a victim of a famine-stricken area, for instance, was convicted of the murder of her eighteen-month-old child. In her petition, she stated that she had been reduced to great distress after the death of her husband, as she had to maintain her mother-in-law as well as the child and herself and could earn little or nothing by her labour. Moreover, her husband's relatives could give no assistance as they themselves were in a similar financial situation. She pleaded that she committed the act under great provocation and in order to relieve the distress she felt at her inability to feed the child and relieve its suffering. Her petition was rejected on the grounds that

it is usual to commute a sentence for a widow who had killed her child in the agony and excitement of childbirth but not for a widow who kills her legitimate child one and a half years after its birth. Her only excuse offered is poverty. Dangerous to commute as lower classes are tempted to free them from responsibility.[32]

It is clearly evident from the case of Kesar that the judiciary was informed by Victorian stereotypes of classism and elitism. Equally, many of the infanticide cases were fraught with ambiguity and the courts dealt arbitrarily with them. Furthermore, none of the legal guidelines made allowances for natural infant mortality caused by sickness and the undernourishment of the mother and child. When, for instance, Durgi, a twenty-year-old Mang offender, pleaded, 'Not Guilty' to the charge, she stated:

> I took care of the child for three months, supporting myself all the while by begging. Then I became ill with fever and the child also became ill, suffering from itches that produced large blotches on its body ... When I became ill, we suffered much for want of food and shelter and the child being very young and ill died as a consequence.[33]

Despite her testimony and the fact that the postmortem report recorded no signs of violence against the child, the High Court disbelieved her as the child was born out of wedlock—proof, in the judge's idea, that she had killed it out of shame. As a Mang, Durgi had no such constraints placed on her by her caste and kin but the law of infanticide was governed so strictly by ideas of 'licit' and 'illicit' intercourse and 'legitimate' and 'illegitimate' children that such assumptions were made even when they didn't apply.

[...]

NOTES

1. All the correspondence between the governor-in-council and the judges, petitions by Vijayalakshmi and extracts from newspapers are to be found in Judicial Department (hereafter, JD), 1881, vol. 46, comp. no. 1036, Maharashtra State Archives (hereafter, MSA).

2. These figures are taken from a table showing the statistics for convictions of infanticide in five provinces from 1870–84, in *Mahratta*, 25 June 1887.

3. See V.S. Kadam, 'The Institution of Marriage and Position of Women in Eighteenth-century Maharashtra', *Indian Economic and Social History Review*, 1988, vo. 25, no. 3, p. 362.

4. See the Marathi work, M.G. Mali, *Krantijyoti Savitribai Jotirao Phule* [The Revolutionary Savitribai Jotirao Phule] (Kolhapur 1980), p. 87.

5. J.D.M. Derrett, *Religion, Law and the State in India* (London 1968); A.C. Banerjee, *English Law in India* (New Delhi 1984).

6. Werner Menski, 'Indian Legal Systems Past and Present' (University of London: SOAS Law Department, Occasional Paper, no. 3, 1997), p. 37; also Vasudha Dhagamwar, *Law, Power and Justice: The Protection of Personal Rights in the Indian Penal Code* (New Delhi 1992), pp. 9–10.

7. Daji Dhalchand Gujar et al. to the Chief Secretary to Government, 25 July 1881, JD, 1881, vol. 46, comp. no. 1036, MSA.

8. JD, 1880, vol. 50, comp. no. 917, MSA.

9. Sudha Desai, *Social Life in Maharashtra under the Peshwas* (Bombay 1980), p. 88; see also Raymond West and Johann Georg Buhler (eds), *A Digest of Hindu Law*, Book I (Bombay 1867), especially Introduction and chapter 6.

10. The head of the household, usually the father-in-law and sometimes older relatives like great-uncles, took such decisions. See the proceedings in the case of Sangowa kom Gursidapa, JD, 1881, vol. 46, comp. no. 996, pp. 115–31; also the proceedings in the case of Thaku, JD, 1882, vol. 52, comp. 1525, pp. 414–15, MSA.

11. From 'Want of Provision in the Law for Punishing Such Crimes as the Prevention of the Crime of Exposing and Abandoning Infants', in JD, 1883, vol. 56, comp. no. 720, MSA.

12. The enrolment of the midwife as an informer was a legacy from the Company's regulations to suppress female infanticide. Lalita Panigrahi notes that a system of rewarding alert midwives was instituted in some extreme cases: *British Social Policy and Female Infanticide in India* (Delhi 1972), chapter 4.

13. JD, 1882, vol. 44, comp. no. 950, MSA.

14. See the proceedings in the case of Mamti in JD, 1880, vol. 45, comp. no. 942, MSA.

15. Reported on 10 March 1877, Native Newspaper Reports (NNR).

16. JD, 1887, vol. 76, comp. no. 298, MSA.

17. JD, 1887, vol. 40, comp. no. 1179, MSA.

18. Ibid., MSA.

19. JD, 1882, vol. 52, comp. no. 1419, MSA.

20. JD, 1890, vol. 107, comp. no. 138, MSA.

21. For example, in the case of Baya who stated that she would not have abandoned her child if her mother had given her shelter: JD, 1881, vol. 47, comp. no. 1301, MSA.

22. For a study of notions of 'shame' and 'honour' as determinants in the act of infanticide in rural Mediterranean society, see Stephen Wilson, 'Infanticide, Child Abandonment, and Female Honour in Nineteenth-century Corsica', *Comparative Studies in Society and History*, vol. 30, 1988, pp. 762–83.

23. Vijayalakshmi's petition, 21 June 1881, JD, 1881, vol. 47, comp. no. 726, MSA.

24. JD, 1881, vol. 46, comp. no. 998, MSA.

25. JD, 1885, vol. 33, comp. no. 1282, MSA.

26. JD, 1885, vol. 53, comp. no. 601, MSA.

27. See the proceedings in the case of Saipi Kome Sonda, sentenced to ten years' rigorous imprisonment for procuring medicines in order to induce

abortions, JD, 1882, vol. 60, comp. no. 865; see also the case of Bhima who inserted a 'medicated twig in the private parts of Ganga' in order to help the latter abort,
JD, 1885, vol. 99, comp. no. 532, MSA.

28. For instance, Madivalowa's appeal was rejected by the governor who stated
that, 'Only mothers killing infants directly after birth are considered by the government'; JD, 1890, vol. 104, comp. no. 238, MSA.

29. Judith Tucker, *Women in Nineteenth-Century Egypt* (Cambridge 1985),
p. 135.

30. JD, 1890, vol. 70, comp. no. 279, MSA.

31. See proceedings in the case of Sakrowa kora Bhimapa, J.D, 1882, vol. 52,
comp. no. 1069, MSA.

32. JD, 1887, vol. 76, comp. no. 298, MSA.

33. JD, 1880, vol. 100, comp. no. 23, MSA.

11

Telling Tales*

Saurabh Dube

Stories of the remotest of pasts have their beginnings in recent tales. Not so long ago, during a dull and dusty summer in central India, I was an optimistic youth, hopelessly haunting the local judicial record office in the city of Raipur. My search was for records that detailed the working out of conflicts between lower-caste tenants and upper-caste landlords in the Chhattisgarh region in the late nineteenth century. It was a characteristically naive thing to do. Almost a hundred years ago, the colonial government had destroyed these records.

LOST AND FOUND

As all prospects appeared lost, I met Sattar. A Muslim from Maharashtra, who had settled in Raipur, he worked in the record office as a peon. Now, Sattar was a lush. By eleven in the morning, he was pleasantly high; by one in the afternoon reasonably—and some-times unreasonably—drunk; and three hours later, he was lost to the world. I had seen him earlier. When I had first walked into the records office, then when I was pleading in vain to be allowed one look at the countless yellow-grey files lying in endless unhappy piles, and, finally,

* Excepted from Saurabh Dube, *Stitches on Time: Colonial Textures and Postcolonial Tangles* (Durham: Duke University Press and New Delhi: Oxford University Press, 2004).

when my face had fallen, completely, totally, and (as it had seemed then) irrevocably. On each occasion, poised strategically on a landing close by, Sattar had uttered the same sequence of sardonic sounds, a sigh followed by silence and then the laconic lament, '*Aur ka karees* (What else to do)?'

An earnest researcher, I had paid little attention to this funny but sad man, an anonymous alcoholic. All this was to change that hot Friday afternoon when I stood near the records office waiting for a bus, or a rickshaw, or a tempo, anything that would carry me away from the dashed desires turned to rubble, scattered at my feet and everywhere I looked. Sattar walked up staggering a little, leaned over, and whispered confidentially, 'There are records, records, records inside about murder, rape, murder.'[1] The moment of high drama ended. Sattar retreated into himself, then sighed, fell silent, and inevitably announced, '*Aur ka karees* (What else to do)?' Yet my chase had begun. The many complicated dealings with Bade Babu—the somewhat cynical Brahman high priest of the records office—that gained me access and then permission to photocopy the records over several months is a tale within the tale, best reserved for another time.

Sattar had led me to an ethnographic historian's gold mine. Thousands upon thousands of pages of material on conflicts and the disputing process, often involving mayhem and murder, between members of families and clans, castes and communities, in twentieth-century colonial Chhattisgarh. Routinely, the records should have met their end several decades ago. Saved because of administrative bungling, they have suggested a large project, studying the interplay and interpenetration of 'official-state' conceptions and 'community-popular' contentions of crime and criminality, legality and property, authority and morality, including rival constructions of the person. The records contain village stories—tales of transgressions and enmities, kinship and neighbourhood, gender and age, authority and honour, caste and boundaries, and witchcraft and infanticide. On offer is an archive of the complex interchange and mutual constitution of everyday norms, familiar desires, and alien legalities: the reciprocal determinations of imperial law and village life, modernity and subalternity on the ground.

Sattar, I believe, has retired. Put differently, as it is sometimes said in Chhattisgarh, '*Ab woh tire ho gaya hai* (He has [re]tired now).' Yet, I continue to work with a boon, the knowledge of a secret, which Sattar granted me. Let me then dedicate this chapter, to Sattar, my comrade and co-conspirator. Is this dedication theatrical? Is this dedication perverse? I am quite certain what Sattar would have said, '*Aur ka karees?*'

READING RECORDS

Out of the large corpus of legal materials, there emerge several tales of intimate disputes in different villages of Bilaspur district in the Chhattisgarh region of middle India. These disputes from the 1920s through the 1940s were located in the domain of the familiar and the quotidian in village life, seized and fashioned into cases in the realm of colonial district judiciary. They traversed and brought together the two arenas. Logics of kinship and neighbourhood, involving a series of transgressions of the norms of the Satnami community, informed the dispute that is discussed in this chapter.

The body of the dispute materials is contained in what Simon Schama has condescendingly deemed as 'records of incrimination'.[2] The Bilaspur district sessions trial cases are large documents. Each case consists of the charge sending the accused for trial to the Court of Sessions, the earlier examination of the accused before the committing magistrate, a descriptive list of exhibits, the documentary exhibits used, the depositions of witnesses for the prosecution and the defence, the examination of the accused, and, finally, the judgement in the Court of Session.

It is from this evidence that I reconstruct several stories of everyday life.[3] The exercise is fraught with difficulties. The cases dealt with the events and the features of a dispute by designating it as a 'crime'.[4] A dispute was fashioned into a 'case' within the colonial judicial system through the privileging of an act—or a set of actions—with serious consequences; for example, a blow struck with an axe that led to a death. The act/actions appeared constructed as the key affairs that defined the crime and occupied the centre of the stage, while the other episodes and elements of the drama constituted the backdrop to this critical event.

The process turned on the discursive strategies of the law. The ordering of depositions of witnesses for the prosecution diverged from the actual sequence of events, arranged instead in a sequence that highlighted the central event of the crime. The depositions of witnesses began with descriptions of acts of murder, injury, or theft, and then retraced their steps to earlier events and to prior patterns in order to fill in the background of the crime. The questions posed during the examinations of the accused attempted to explicate the crime itself. The final, authoritative narrative of the judge drew upon the different accounts rehearsed during the proceedings to present first a summary statement of the pre-history of the crime. Then, it seized upon the final act—its immediate circumstances, the intention underlying it, and the manner of its conduct—in order to determine, through the manifold requirements of judicial proof and legal evidence, the nature of the crime. There was much at work in the constitution of guilt and innocence.

However, it is also possible to pry open the cases, in order to recover what the disputes tell us about the play of relationships—including with the state—within village life.[5] Such a task requires a displacement. Rather than according the decisive act of the crime in question a position of privilege, this final moment now comes to be located alongside the diverse elements and the distinct events of a dispute as only one part of a complex story. The sources allow us to effect such a displacement. We have noted that during their depositions the witnesses retraced their steps to fill in the background of the crime, particularly in the course of their cross-examination. Here the witnesses often constructed a rich and vivid picture of the social relationships, the patterns of solidarity and of enmity, and the occurrences within the village that went into the making of disputes.

There was a gap between the limited range of facts required by the judgement and the abundance of information rehearsed during the depositions. It is important to mind this gap, and work within it. By extracting the fine detail and by seizing upon the repetitions within the narratives of the witnesses, it is possible to trace the interplay between the concerns of the normative order of the law and the processes of signification within village relationships.[6] Through a curious logic, the examinations of the accused also come to our aid here. The accused sought to establish enmity as the reason for their framing by the prosecution. They often narrated the history of the dispute as both cause and proof of this enmity. This once again makes possible a rehearsal of the narratives about the quotidian in village life. Taken together, such readings of the evidence reveal the larger story of the interplay between 'official-state' law and 'popular-community' legalities.[7]

PROLOGUE TO A TALE OF AUTHORITY AND CONFLICT

Soon before the advent of the spring of 1940, a Satnami woman eloped with her young nephew from the village of Darri in the Janjgir Tahsil of Bilaspur district.[8] The matter precipitated a dispute in the village. In the dispute, motifs of kinship and community appeared interwoven with designs of inter-caste relations and entitlements to property. The opposed stands on the issue of the elopement in the village panchayat led to the formation of two 'parties' in Darri. There was a link with earlier tensions over rival claims to ownership of land, also entailing prior alliances of Satnamis with other castes within the village. Two groups of Satnamis clashed in Darri, and other members of the village joined the fray. On the night of 7 May 1940, a group consisting of one Brahman, five Telis, two Bhainas, one Rawat, and six Satnamis (see Table 11.1 and Figure 11.1) beat up ten Satnamis belonging to the rival 'party' in the village (see Figure 11.2).[9] One of these Satnamis died, and the dispute was on its way to being fashioned into a case.

Darri was a small, mixed-caste village, its *malguzari* (village proprietorship) divided into equal parts among the four families of Balaram Lamabardar Teli, Bisahu Teli, Hiralal Brahman, and Balaram Brahman (see Table 11.1). Among the fifty-six tenant–cultivator families listed as owning land in the village, the breakdown according to caste was as follows: eight Satnamis, ten Telis, nine Rawats, eight Bhainas, fourteen Marars, three Dhobis, three Brahmans, and one Bairagi. Brahmans and Telis dominated Darri village. Thus, of the four families of village proprietors, Hiralal Brahman with a total

landholding of 100.60 acres, Balaram Brahman with 27 acres, Balaram
Teli with 30.29 acres, and Bisahu Teli with 25.40 acres owned much of
the land in the village.[10] As we shall see, this pattern of landholdings—
together with the designs of politics and conflicts it engendered—
has significance for the unfolding of the drama of this dispute in
Darri.

Table 11.1: The 'Accused'

Caste	Name	Father's Name	Age
Brahman	Kunjbeharilal	Balakram Malguzar	22 Years
Teli	Balaram	Jhagru Lambardar	42 Years
Teli	Ramtyaloo	Sadasheo	40 Years
Teli	Paltoo	Bhikari	55 Years
Teli	Kanhaiya	Paltoo	20 Years
Bhaina	Balli	Bahorak	45 Years
Bhaina	Balmukund	Jaharoo	45 Years
Rawat	Budga	Bhagat Rawat	55 Years
Satnami	Pila	Kashiram	30 Years
Satnami	Sahas	Kashiram	42 Years
Satnami	Karman	Sahas	22 Years
Satnami	Sukaloo	Gangaram	22 Years
Satnami	Johan	Sangan	30 Years
Satnami	Dasaram	Sangan	25 Years

KINSHIP AND CONFLICT

About three months before the fight on 7 May 1940, Dasaram's wife
Bahartin had run away from Darri with Chait, her distant nephew by
marriage (see Figure 11.1). In a brief elopement, Bahartin and Chait
had stayed away from the village for two or three weeks. On their
return, Dasaram had admitted Bahartin back into his house, and
Chaits's actions stood similarly condoned by the elders in his family. To
some Satnamis, the events of the elopement and after were 'scandalous'
matters, and a group led by Gajaraj had put Bahartin and Chait out of
caste.[11] Significantly, kinship bound Gajaraj's group—through Ratan,
a cousin of Lala on one side and of Sangan on the other (see Figures
11.1 and 11.2)—to the other main section of Satnamis in the village.
This section, together with several non-Satnami members of Darri,
felt that the excommunication of Chait and Bahartin was unneces-

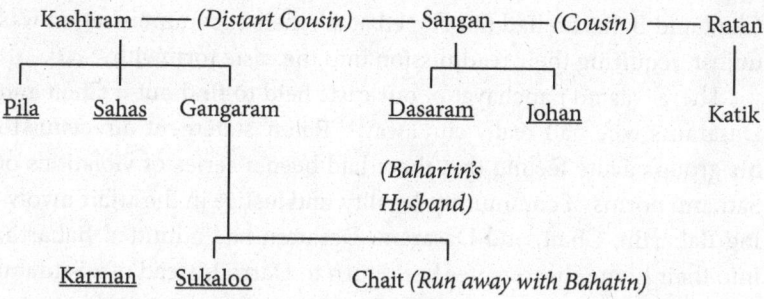

Figure 11.1: Relationships of Sahas Satnami's group

sary, particularly after Dasaram had re-established conjugal ties with Bahartin, apparently ignoring her indiscretion. All sides in the village agreed upon the necessity of resolving questions of the readmission of Bahartin and Chait into the caste after their excommunication by Gajaraj Satnami and his group.

A village panchayat consisting of Satnamis and six members of the other castes met at Johan Satnami's house to decide the issue.[12] The defence of Bahartin and Chait—and, thereby, of Dasaram's conduct in re-establishing conjugal ties with Bahartin—lay in the hands of Dasaram himself and his brother Johan, Sahas (a *pancha*), and his brother Pila. To represent the other Satnami group, summoned were Ratan, Gajaraj, and Baldeo. When the three reached the panchayat they were informed by the panchas that no wrong had been done by Chait and Bahartin. Apparently, the non-Satnami panchas colluded with Dasaram's group, telling members of Gajaraj's group that since

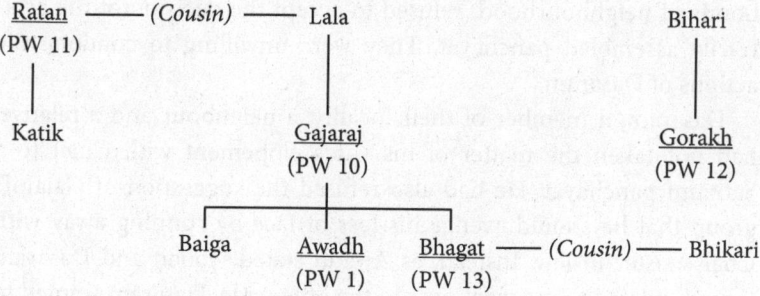

Figure 11.2: Relationships of Gajraj Satnami's Group

Chait and Bahartin had not eloped at all, their excommunication was unjust, requiring their readmission into the caste forthwith.

'There was no panchayat of our caste held to find out if Chait and Dasaram's wife had really run away.'[13] Ratan' statement directs us to his group's acute feeling that there had been a series of violations of Satnami norms of community, legality, and justice in the affair involving Bahartin, Chait, and Dasaram. Dasaram had admitted Bahartin into their home shortly after her return to Darri. Instead of a Satnami caste panchayat looking into this matter, a panchayat consisting mainly of members of other castes deliberated the issue. These panchas ostensibly colluded with Dasaram's group. As Awadh stated, 'persons eloping are required to give a caste dinner' before they are readmitted into the caste.[14] However, in this case, there were attempts to readmit Chait and Bahartin because the very fact of their having eloped stood denied. There was, then, no question of following the norm of a feast to the caste to signify their (re)incorporation into the group. Ratan, Gajaraj, and Baldeo were unwilling to accept this decision.

Ratan, Baldeo, and Gajaraj, in fact, belonged to the five Satnami families who stayed in a separate neighbourhood, apart from the other Satnami families of the village. Gajaraj made this clear:

> There are five localities in the village. They are Bahman para, Bhaina para, Raut para, Patel para, Chamar para, and Gajaraj para. Gajaraj para is the locality where families of us five persons myself, Gorakh, Ratan, Malikram and Katik have got houses. Dasaram also lives in my para and the other accused lived in Chamar para.[15]

Members of these five closely knit families, tied through blood and bonds of neighbourhood, refused to accept the decision of the arbitrarily assembled panchayat. They were unwilling to condone the actions of Dasaram.

Dasaram, a member of their locality, a neighbour and a relative, had not taken the matter of his wife's elopement with Chait to a Satnami panchayat. He had also refused the suggestion of Gajaraj's group that he should avenge his loss of face by running away with Chait's sister-in-law. Instead, as Awadh stated, 'Johan and Dasaram though related to me went over to the other side. Dasaram wanted to readmit his wife and in fact had admitted her in his house.'[16] Lastly, the five families disputed the authority of Gangaram and Sahas, the leaders of the other Satnami section, as the caste leaders of all Satnamis in Darri. 'Gangaram and Sahas are not the headmen of my caste. They are not the headmen of the whole caste but they are the headmen in our village.'[17] Taken together, the five Satanami families of Gajaraj *para* had excommunicated Dasaram, also severing relations with the other Satnamis of Darri unwilling to follow this measure. At the same time, in refusing to abide by the decision of the panchayat to readmit Chait, Bahartin, and Dasaram into the caste, Gajaraj's group had challenged the opinion of dominant members of the village community, who partially excommunicated the five families of the Gajaraj para.[18] An elopement crystallized into two 'parties' in Darri.

There were other tensions in the village because of *chekbandi* (consolidation of landholdings) carried out in 1939. Like many other villages in Chhattisgarh, the landholdings in Darri were extremely fragmented.[19] The consolidation of landholdings had been effected in the *falgun* (February–March) of 1939, and the relevant *parcha*s (papers) were distributed a little later in *aghan* (November–December) and *pus* (December–January) that year.[20] Balaram Teli was the *sarpanch* in the chekbandi proceedings. The other panchas were Budga Raut, Balmukund Bhaina, Bali Bhaina, Ramsai Marar, and Gajaraj Satnami.

Rival, conflicting claims to land followed the consolidation of holdings, pitting the five Satnami families of the Gajaraj para against the 'party' of Satnamis and other castes in Darri. These five families felt that, despite the presence of Gajaraj in the land-consolidation proceedings, the panchas had not been fair to them during chekbandi. Here it is significant that the panchas in these proceedings were themselves the arbiters (or closely connected to the key members) of the panchayat that had deliberated the elopement of Chait and Bahartin. The five Satnami families of the Gajaraj para had formally raised doubts about the authority of these leading lights of Darri, not once but twice.

AN ALTERCATION AND AFTER

It was against this background that there was a minor altercation on the morning of 7 May 1940 in the village. Darri lies next to the river

Son. In summer, the water would dry up and stagnant pools would form where the river ran. One of these pools supplied water to the villagers. The Satnamis used the southern end, while members of the other castes used the northern side. On the morning of 7 May, Malikram and Awadhram, both belonging to the five Satnami families of the Gajaraj para (see Figure 11.2), had gone to the pool.[21] After the two reached there, Awadh took his buffaloes into the water, while Malikram sat on the bank washing his mouth. Once he finished washing the cattle, Awadh drove them out and started moving through the water towards the bank where Malikram sat. Malikram then got up and entered the water. The two began to bathe. At that moment, Paltoo Teli (see Table 11.1) who sat not too far, towards the northern side of the pool, washing his mouth, reprimanded the two Satnamis. 'He said to us as to why we were making the water dirty.' Yet this was not all. 'Paltoo then used abusive language towards us.'[22]

When Awadh and Malikram protested, Paltoo became even more aggressive. He said that had it been any other village, the two Satnamis would have received five shoe-blows each. Awadh and Malikram replied that other people fished in the river and washed their buffaloes, so why was it that they had to face insults for getting the water dirty? On hearing this, Paltoo turned furious. He picked up a stone to hit them, but then changed his mind. Dropping the stone, he gathered his *lathi* (stick), got into the water, and moved towards the two Satnamis. Once Paltoo got close, Awadh snatched his stick and threw it away toward the riverbank. By that time, other villagers had reached the river, and they intervened to stop the fight. Paltoo was about to go home, when his son, Rupcharan, reached the scene. Now Rupcharan tried to snatch the lathi from Paltoo, declaring that since Awadh and Malikram had used foul language against his father he would beat up the bastard Chamars.[23] Once more, other villagers prevented the quarrel from escalating any further. Soon the denizens of Darri returned to the village.

At noon that day, the *malguzar* Kunjbiharilal (see Table 11.1) went to Gajaraj para, meeting all the adult male members of Gajaraj's group at Gorakh's house. Kunjbiharilal said that he had heard of the quarrel near the river that morning, and it was advisable to put an end to such dissensions in the village. All the villagers were gathering in the evening, and there they would effect a settlement. The Satnamis of Gajaraj para agreed to join these deliberations. Later that day, the village *kotwar* (watchman) announced in Darri that a panchayat would meet at the *guddi* (village meeting point), which all villagers were expected to attend. A second 'proclamation' to this effect was also made somewhat later in the evening. Finally, in a third announcement around dusk, the time of the evening meal, the kotwar enjoined all the villagers of Darri to proceed to the panchayat forthwith, declaring that those who would keep away from the meeting will have their 'mothers go wrong with sweepers'. Gajaraj and his group reached the panchayat soon after finishing their evening meal. About fifty or sixty other people, including the Satnamis of the rival group, were already sitting there.

ADJUDICATING MATTERS

The guddi was dark. There was no lantern. The panchayat sat on the bank of a tank. Gajaraj and his group squatted together, facing the other villagers. Balmukund Bhaina asked about the reason for the villagers meeting at the guddi. The malguzar Kunjbiharilal referred to the quarrel in the river that morning, adding that he had called the meeting, also asking Gajaraj and his group to move closer to the other villagers. They moved nearer where Kunjbihari sat with his supporters. Kunjbihari then said that he would select the panchas. Gajaraj's group agreed. Balmukund Bhaina, Balli Rawat, Budga Ganda, Kachhi, and Pila Satnami were named the panchas, and Kunjbihari was selected the sarpanch. There were no objections voiced to this choice of panchas.

Kunjbihari asked Paltoo about the quarrel near the river that morning. Paltoo replied that Bhola and Ramtyaloo were there as well. Bhola and Ramtyaloo then described the altercation, Paltoo providing further details. Next, Awadh and Malikram recounted their version. After this, Kunjbihari asked the panchas and Balaram Teli for their opinion. The panchas merely asked Kunjbihari to give his decision in his capacity as the sarpanch.

The panchas were not consulted and I do not know if they had consulted each other, but Kunjbihari gave out that we were fined. The

panchas had not gone aside to consult each other. It was Kunjbihari
who gave out of his own accord the decision.[24]

Awadhram and Malikram were both fined five rupees each, a large
sum for a minor matter.

As the leader of his group, Gajaraj pleaded before the panchayat
that the two boys, Awadhram and Malikram, had not committed
an offence. He also stated that he was a poor man, arguing further
that the fine was much too harsh. However, these entreaties failed to
move Kunjbihari. The malguzar announced that if the fine was not
paid, Gajaraj and his 'party' would face further sanctions: complete
excommunication from the village would replace their partial excommunication.

Once the malguzar Kunjbihari finished making this statement, the
panchas turned to him and asked, '*Tabhin ki bat kaisan* (what about
the previous talk/decision)?' The records do not tell us of the actual
details of this conversation or of the decision taken earlier, but the
moment he was asked the question, Kunjbihari announced that those
who would not beat the 'Chamars'—Gajaraj and his group—would go
'wrong with their mothers'. The panchayat seemed to have been waiting for this signal. Now the villagers of Darri, gathered at the guddi,
attacked Gajaraj and his group.

In this attack, designated an 'assault' within the sessions trial,
all the members of Gajaraj's 'party' were beaten to the cries of '*maro
maro* (hit them, hit them).' Caught in the midst of a small crowd,
Malikram stood savagely hit with sticks, people bearing down on
him with further blows and kicks to the body. The attack on Gajaraj
was also severe, but his son pulled him out. As Gajaraj's 'party' retreated, Gorakh and Bhagatram, the only members of this group who
had carried sticks, defended themselves, warding off the aggressors'
blows. Members of Gajaraj's group ran to Ratan's house in the Gajaraj
para. Their opponents followed them there, began and throwing
stones on Ratan's house, and abusing Gajaraj and his group.

> After we returned home stones were thrown on my house. I did not
> see the persons throwing the stones but I recognized the voices of five
> persons who were giving abuses 'Chamar saleman ko maro [Hit the

bloody Chamars].' … after this we drank water and we heard the crying of Bunkuwar.[25]

Malikram had not been able to make it by himself to the Gajaraj para.

Here is the testimony of Bunkuwar, the bereaved mother of Malikram, who had also gone to the panchayat.

> Kunjbihari gave the oath to all … for assaulting. All this while I was sitting on the platform under the pipal tree. I left my place on the platform when I heard the voice of my son calling oh mother and ran towards him. He was being assaulted near Dena's house near the lemon tree… My son was lying on the ground face upwards. They were giving fist blows and lathi thrusts. They were repeatedly giving blows like pounding. They gave fist blows at times and stick blows also. All of them beat like that. I did not that time notice blood on my son but I noticed it when I found him lying near my house. Later on I alone went home. At that lane … I brought out light and saw the bleeding of my son. Myself and my daughter-in-law removed my son from the ground near the door inside the house. Later the people from the five families came up there.[26]

Malikram was dead.

Later in the night, Bunkuwar, Gajaraj, Awadh, and Katik started off for the police station house at Champa, about nine miles from the village, reaching there in the morning. Awadh started filing a report of the quarrel and the death of Malikram, when Chinta Kotwar and Paltoo Teli from Darri reached the station house. According to their version, there had been a quarrel in the village, but Malikram, reported to have died, was actually alive and could be seen sitting in his house. Another line of argument informed the defence of the aggressors of Darri before the district and sessions judge. They admitted that there were two 'parties' among the Satnamis of the village, and some agreed that other castes had supported the Sahas' group against Gajaraj's 'party'. Further, they did not deny that there was an altercation on the morning of 7 May 1940. At the same time, all the 'accused' refused to admit that there was a panchayat that night, also denying thereby that Gajaraj's group had been attacked after the meeting. A number of them claimed alibis, established through witnesses for the defence.

The defence argued that the fight in the morning led to injuries to Awadh, Gajaraj, Gorakh, Bhagat, and Bhikari, while Malikram had died because of an accidental fall. That morning the young man had been standing at some distance from others on the riverbank. When the quarrel began, he started to run away, but soon fell, fatally injuring himself. Gajaraj's group had deliberately implicated the 'accused' in the trial because of previous enmity on account of the matters of Bahartin's elopement or/and the proceedings of the consolidation of landholdings. The additional sessions judge did not buy this story and found that 'all the fourteen accused had formed an unnatural assembly with the common object of assaulting Malikram, Gajaraj and the latter's followers who were called at the panchayat ...'[27]

UNRAVELLING STORIES

It would be unfortunate, indeed, if our histories were to end with mere judgements. For long after this dispute within Darri was fashioned into a case in the colonial courts, and the judgement delivered, processes involving the restitution of enmities, the recasting of transgressions, the reworking of legalities would have been a part of the fabric of everyday life in the village. Indeed, one day I hope to develop this tale along such lines. Here, let me only move back and forth among the events and episodes of the narrative to tie up the different strands of this story.

Once upon a time, many fables stood spun out of that simple but overarching opposition between (unchanging) traditional-folk-popular disputing processes and (dynamic) colonial-modern-state legal systems. There are, of course, newer stories being told now of different legal mechanisms and matrices.[28] Yet, in the South Asian context, accounts elaborating the mutual imbrications and implications of these arenas—of modern law and popular legalities—as critical attributes of colonial and postcolonial modernities remain a rarity.[29] What compounds this problem is the assumption of a rather hermetical division between the colonial state (and modernity) and indigenous communities (and traditions) that shores up even the more imaginative writings on these subjects.[30] It is important to think through such received dispositions.

'Gangaram and Sahas are not the headmen of my caste. They are not the headmen of the whole caste but they are the headmen in the village.' With a small Satnami population, Darri did not have a Satnami panchayat in the village; rather, it formed one among a cluster of villages under the authority of a single caste panchayat. Now, during the inter-war years, the 'traditional' organization of the Satnami panchayat appeared elaborated in novel ways, entailing the interplay between state and community.[31] Significantly, in the late 1920s and 1930s, an organization called the Satnami Mahasabha drew upon symbols and metaphors of colonial governance, situating them alongside key signs within the Satnampanth, in order to constitute a new legality, at once religious and political. This was an effort to reform, regulate, and recast the Satnamis, idioms of law, order, and command closely bound to relationships of authority within the community. For example, there was the restructuring of the organizational hierarchy of Satnampanth, its new ranks based primarily on colonial administrative categories, reworking ritual control and adjudicatory mechanisms among the Satnamis. Here the tightening of the organization of the Satnami panchayat afforded an effective mode of intervention in the affairs of the community. The group of villages that had earlier deliberated matters arising in villages without their own Satnami panchayat now received a firm institutional basis, constituted as the *athagawana* (committee of eight villages).[32] Therefore, it is not surprising that Gajaraj's group did not accept Gangaram and Sahas as leaders of the caste. They considered that the real caste authority of the Satnami panchayat lay elsewhere, in the newly constituted athgawana of which Darri was a part.

'Gangaram and Sahas are not the headmen of my caste. They are not the headmen of the whole caste but they are the headmen in the village.' Generally, all the members of a caste stay within one locale, a single para, in a village, but the five Satnami families of Gajaraj's group did not live in the Satnamipara—also known as Chamrapara—of Darri. Instead, the five households formed a separate Gajaraj para, named after Gajaraj, the leader of their group. Members of Gajaraj's group were among the substantial cultivators of Darri. Conversely, Sahas's group consisted of the poorer cultivators and landless labourers who had ties with the dominant members of the village, ties that possibly placed Gangaram and Sahas as the headmen of the Satnamis within Darri. Yet, this was not how Gajaraj and his group thought about the matter. Indeed, the questioning of the authority of Gangaram and Sahas as 'the headmen of the whole caste' by Gajaraj's group emerged linked to the division among the Satnamis in the village. Arguably, this division stood tied to the endorsement of the authority of the ath-gawana—and of the Satnami Mahasabha—by Gajaraj's group, while the position of Gangaram and Sahas as leaders of the Satnamis within Darri rested on their ties with the dominant castes in the village. The elopement of Chait and Bahartin crystallized the division among the Satnamis of Darri.

Bahartin was married to Dasaram, and they lived in the Gajaraj para. Kinship and neighbourhood linked Dasaram and his wife to Gajaraj's group, while Chait was the nephew of Sahas, the leader of the other group of Satnamis. At stake was a double-edged dynamic of kinship and neighbourhood. In keeping with this logic, the elopement of Chait and Bahartin confirmed a threat inherent in the nature of the relationship between the groups of Gajaraj and Sahas, also con-stituting a challenge to solidarity rooted in kinship and neighbour-hood. Moreover, the elopement was a violation of norms of kinship since Bahartin was Chait's aunt. Finally, Dasaram had not followed the suggestion of Gajaraj's group and avenged his loss of face by running away with Sukul's wife. He had accepted Bahartin into his house. Consequently, Dasaram had joined the other group. Prior bonds meant that the division between the rival Satnami 'parties' was the sharper.

We find two simultaneous movements here. On the one hand, there was a challenge to, followed by a severance of, ties of kinship and neighbourhood between the groups of Dasaram and Gajaraj. Awadh made this clear, 'Johan and Dasaram though related to me went over to the other side. Dasaram wanted to readmit his wife and in fact had admitted her in his house.' On the other hand, there were a series of transgressions of norms of caste and kinship. There was no customary feast for the caste after Chait and Bahartin returned to the village. A violation of kinship norms went without an expiation of the offence, and a woman who had eloped and done 'wrong' with her nephew (re)appeared and was easily readmitted into her husband's house. Indeed, in the eyes of Gajaraj and his group, the most flagrant transgression derived from Dasaram's admitting Bahartin into his house without expiating the misdemeanour, premised upon a denial of the elopement.

This was also the argument of the village panchayat that sought to settle the matter. Here the panchas decided that since there was no elopement, all was to go on as before. By closing its eyes to the elopement, this panchayat denied a set of transgressions. It also poached into the arena—and itself transgressed the authority—of the Satnami panchayat that should have adjudicated this matter. 'There was no panchayat of our caste held to find out if Chait and Dasaram's wife had really run away.' Clearly, Gajaraj's group was unwilling to accept the decision of the village panchayat.

There was a link here with earlier tensions in the village over chekbandi, the consolidation of landholdings. The statements of the witnesses and the accused underscore rival and disputed claims to ownership of land between Gajaraj's group and other members of the village, following the chekbandi proceedings. The continued tensions over land alongside the suspicions harboured by Gajaraj's group about the fairness of chekbandi amounted to their questioning the authority of the non-Satnami panchas in charge of the consolidation of holdings. When Gajaraj's group did not accept the decision of the village panchayat over the issue of Chait and Bahartin's elopement, it was once more questioning the authority of the dominant members of Darri. Now, Gajaraj was an important member of the village, the leader of his group who had a para named after him, and the families of Gajaraj and Itwari were among the handful of substantial cultivators, with over ten acres of land, in Darri.[33] To the dominant members of the village, the threat of insubordination from Gajaraj's group could not be any clearer.

There was a partial excommunication of Gajaraj's group, denying them services of the village grazier, and entailing other restrictions.[34] At the same time, there was a feeling among the villagers that these measures were not enough, since the indiscretions of Gajaraj's group were going unchecked. Paltoo Teli voiced this feeling when in the

course of the fight on the morning of 7 May he said that had it been
any other village, the 'Chamars', Malikram and Awadhram, would have
received five shoe-blows each. After the fight, during the day, it was
resolved that members of Gajaraj's group would be fined, and if they
refused to accept the decision of the panchayat they should be beaten.[35]
The dominant members of Darri were worried that Gajaraj's group
may not attend the panchayat, given that they wanted the Satnami
athgawana to settle the issue of the elopement. Unsurprisingly, the
village watchman made three proclamations about the panchayat in
the village; the last announcement incorporating an 'oath'—'those
who do not come will have their mothers go wrong with sweepers'—
was made solely in the Gajaraja para.

At the panchayat, Gajaraj and his group felt that the decision
announced by the malguzar Kunjbiharilal was far too severe. Yet the
pleas of Gajaraj only ended by questioning the authority of the village
panchas for the third time. '*Tabhin ki baat kaisan*? (What about the
earlier decision?)' The question invoked the decision that the villagers
had taken earlier in the day. Kunjbiharilal made it clear that those
who did not beat the 'Chamars' (Gajaraj's group) would go wrong
with their mothers. The honour and authority of the sarpanch and
the panchas, of the village proprietor Kunjbiharilal and his influential allies in Darri were at stake. In order to punish and deter the
repeated questioning of this authority and honour by the Satnamis of
Gajaraj's group, the 'Chamars' had to be beaten up.

At the end, consider the many mix-ups, the critical contradictions,
as the protagonists of this drama elaborated and extended the varied
rules and processes of popular legalities and colonial law. Gajaraj's
group wanted a Satnami panchayat, in this case the athgawana, to
deliberate the matter of Bahartin and Chait's elopement, in order to
reaffirm Satnami norms. Yet, they also wanted Dasaram to avenge his
loss of face by running away with Sukul's wife, an act that would have
drawn upon itself the censure of the novel religious legalities fashioned in the inter-war years, which often fuelled the deliberations and
decisions of the athgawanas.

As for Dasaram, his act of readmitting Bahartin to his home and
hearth after she had returned to Darri was also part of a wider pattern where Satnami men often chose to condone the sexual indiscre-

tions of their wives, arriving at a settlement with fellow caste people by negotiating a minor expiation of the misdemeanour. Of course, it would have been difficult for Dasaram to settle the matter easily. First, there was the new emphasis upon rigid norms governing conjugality, sexuality, and domesticity within the Satnami household—from the late 1920s, fixity of form replacing fluidity of the past, enforced through freshly constituted athgawanas and recently refurbished Satnami panchayats. Second, there lay the desire of Gajaraj's group to seek revenge from their rival Satnamis within Darri, a response touched by a raw, wounded morality of kinship since Chait (an enemy) was Bahartin's nephew. This said, Dasaram's arriving at a settlement with Gajaraj's group may have involved protracted negotiation, but it was also much the viable option. Indeed, disappointed as Gajaraj's group was that Dasaram had not run away with Sukul's wife, they actively desired an expiation of the offence. They felt that Dasaram should give a feast—symbolizing the re-incorporation of Bahartin into home, hearth, and community—and possibly pay a *dand* or punitive fine, a portion kept for the Satnami guru at Bhandar, the rest used for community activity within Darri.

Yet this is not what happened. In the wider context of the division among the Satnamis of Darri, Dasaram chose to break with Gajaraj's group and to take the matter to the village panchayat. Dasaram's act of condoning Bahartin's brief elopement, upon her return to Darri, was altogether not out of tune with Satnami 'tradition'. Dasaram's refusal to expiate the offence was out of tenor with Satnami norms. Dasaram's taking a matter internal to the community before the village panchayat was a transgression of Satnami moral legalities. What, then, of the malguzar Kunjbiharilal and his influential allies in Darri? These men had beaten up Gajaraj's group to punish and deter the repeated questioning of their authority in everyday life within Darri. Yet in the colonial court they received deterrent punishment for 'misusing their authority' in the village.[36]

CONCLUSION: THE SILENCE OF WOMEN AND THE GENDER OF THE LAW

There is something missing in this story. The dispute that we have discussed hinged on an elopement. Yet, Bahartin, the woman protagonist of the story, has been virtually absent from the detailed dramas and the dramatic details of this conflict. Now, there is much more than quick-fix invocations of 'voice' and 'agency' at stake here. Several years ago, Gayatri Spivak reminded us of the structure of interests and the chain of complicities that attend the difficult business of representing the subaltern.[37] This warning in mind, the near absence of Bahartin in my account raises distinct, salient issues.

Of course, commonsense dictates that Bahartin would have exercised her own choice in the matter of her elopement with Chait. At the same time, questions of the volition and the action of this woman warrant understanding as part of the wider arrangements of gender and kinship in Chhattisgarh, especially among the Satnamis. I have shown elsewhere that women of the Satnami community have had a degree of autonomy and a measure of space to negotiate marriage(s), men, and motherhood within the larger constraints of patrilineal kinship. Over time, this relative autonomy emerges tied to the pattern of secondary marriages among the Satnamis, and related to the nature of the Satnampanth as premised upon the principles of a caste and a sect.[38] Bahartin's brief elopement with Chait was in tenor with this broader dynamic of caste and gender. Yet Bahartin barely features in the legal archive.

Should this be surprising? In a pioneering essay, 'Chandra's Death', Ranajit Guha discusses the aftermath of the affair of a lower-caste Bagdi widow and her *nondoi* (husband's sister's husband) as engendering diverse responses from their kin.[39] Here, significant for our purposes are Guha's readings of colonial law and indigenous patriarchy, both critical for his reconstruction of the fear, solidarity, and empathy surrounding the death of the Bagdi widow Chandra. On the one hand, the colonial judicial system dealt with all infractions of law and order by reducing their range of signification to a set of narrowly defined legalities, so that 'crime' was the negativity of the 'law'. On the other, a complex interplay of fear and solidarity marked the transgressions of gender, kinship, and caste within indigenous patriarchy, defining the crushing subordination of women, leaving them with very few critical choices. In an innovative move, Guha rescues the collective crises of the Bagdi family from the impersonal determinations of colonial law. In a provocative manoeuvre, he

recuperates from the dead hand of indigenous patriarchy the alternative solidarity, based upon empathy, between the Bagdi women kin.
To recover the traces of gendered subaltern life in its passage through
time is to read against the grain of these closures, but the twin structures of colonial law and indigenous patriarchy also impose their
own schemes of silence. The dead woman, the gendered subaltern,
Chandra cannot speak.

For all the elegance of these formulations, there is a disturbing
edge to their implications. Once again, much more than the lack of
recovery of the gendered subaltern Chandra's 'voice' and 'agency', it is
Guha's reading of colonial law and indigenous patriarchy that bothers
me here. This is particularly the case as we confront the mystery of the
missing woman, Bahartin, from the legal archive. Having learnt much
from Guha's readings of judicial discourse, I nonetheless suggest that
there are limits to envisioning colonial law as solely possessed of a
relentless desire to establish crime as negativity, which ever detached
critical events of quotidian dramas from their contexts. Such appre-
hensions of colonial justice tend to under-enunciate the wide-ranging
patriarchy of modern law.

I submit, then, that the negative determinations of the law require
reading alongside its overwhelming patriarchy. In the dispute at hand,
while establishing kinship connections, indispensable to determining the context of a 'crime', the law traced the relationships of the
'victim' and the 'accused' through bonds of blood and ties of marriage
among the male protagonists and players. As we have seen, this is
was also true of other events defining the immediate background
and the main drama that went into the making of a 'crime'. Women
such as Bahartin appeared in the judicial archive only when their
implications in dramas of illegalities assumed such density that for
the law to ignore their presence would have been to compromise
the basic plot of its own story. Yet, these women remained in the
shadow of the men, even in such situations. Indeed, leaving aside
'cases' where women decisively stole the stage from men, the patriarchy and the negativity of the law operated through unstated assumptions that it was the actions, relationships, and choices of men that
mattered, placing women on the margins of colonial justice and
social order.

In doing this, the technologies of state law and the economies of modern justice—articulated by the judge and the police, advocates and assessors, lawyers, and clerks—drew in the participation and the energies of the village folk, as victim, accused, and witness. Facing the law as a theatre of power, at once at an alien justice and legality *and* a procedure of settlement and revenge, the participation of colonial subjects could be reluctant and instrumental, their energies could be ambivalent and ancillary. Significantly, the patriarchy and the negativity of the law often set the terms for this participation and these energies, entailing efforts to make the latter correspond to the former, at least within the space of colonial justice. There were several consequences, particularly for the issues under discussion, primarily raised as questions here.

Let us begin by thinking of gender relationships embedded within the structures of kinship in Chhattisgarh less as an unrelenting and seamless indigenous patriarchy, and more as part of inherently varied connections between patriliny and gender, across South Asia and further beyond.[40] Out of these varied binds, there follow different implications for the actions and practices of women within distinct arrangements of patrilineal kinship. Returning to the cases at hand, it was in keeping with its patriarchal and negative determinations that the law understood the constitutive events of these dramas through rigid grids of patriarchal logic. This rode roughshod over the more fluid interplay between gender and kinship in everyday arenas in Chhattisgarh, further ruling out the volition of women here. It followed that women such as Bahartin became mere vectors of a patriarchal logic understood as governing the social order.

Yet, it will be hasty to consider these performances of modern law as sharply separated from the worlds of colonial subjects. If colonial judicial discourse worked thoroughly over the narrative of the crime, the subjects of empire equally participated in processes of the law. On the one hand, through the mediation of lawyers and advocates, the victim, the accused, and the witness learnt to frame their utterances in the syntax of modern law, distinct from the grammar of practical kinship. Along with the discursive operations of colonial justice, this led the colonial subjects to accede to the terms of the negative and patriarchal determinations of state law, especially in the domain of imperial courts. On the other hand, it is critical that we also consider the consequences of such participation and these energies in newer articulations of order and gender, in the transformations of practical kinship, within arenas of popular legalities and quotidian illegalities through their work upon state law. There were novel verities that lay beyond older truths.

At the end, acknowledging the complexity and intractability of subject retrieval, and admitting the absences and fractures within dominant discourses, I raise a final question concerning the absent-presence of Bahartin. Will it be too much to suggest that the dispute discussed in this chapter suggests an excess of meaning and power surrounding the actions of women and the articulations of gender, an excess hardly contained by the judicial archive, colonial law, patrilineal models, and academic discourse? It is barely surprising that there is much of significance in the mutual constitution of colonial law, popular legalities, and quotidian illegalities, articulating empire and modernity.

NOTES

1. By 'rape' Sattar had meant illicit sexual relationships between men and women.

2. Simon Schama, *The Embarrassment of Riches: An Interpretation of Dutch Culture in the Golden Age* (New York 1988), p. 4.

3. For a wider discussion see Saurabh Dube, *Stitches on Time: Colonial Textures and Postcolonial Tangles* (Durham and London 2004).

4. Ranajit Guha, 'Chandra's Death', in Guha (ed.) *Subaltern Studies V: Writings on South Asian History and Society* (New Delhi 1987), p. 140.

5. Here I am drawing upon Ranajit Guha's emphasis upon 'pick[ing] up the traces of subaltern life in its passage through time', but equally combining it with a conceptual salience of the 'everyday' as a critical analytical perspective. Ibid., p. 138. David Warren Sabean, *Property, Production, and Family in Neckarhausen, 1700–1870* (Cambridge 1990); David Warren Sabean, *Kinship in Neckarhausen, 1700–1870* (Cambridge 1998); Michel de Certeau, *Practice of Everyday Life* (Berkeley 1984); and Alf Ludtke (ed.) *The History of Everyday Life: Reconstructing Historical Experiences and Ways of Life* (Princeton 1995).

6. Carlo Ginzburg has drawn our attention to the significance of historical reconstruction for a gap between a dominant, convicting, official voice, on the one hand, and wide-ranging subaltern responses and utterances, on the other. However, it should be clear that the gaps and discrepancies in my sources are different from those elaborated by Ginzburg. Carlo Ginzburg, *The Cheese and*

the Worms: The Cosmos of a Sixteenth Century Miller (Baltimore 1980); and
Carlo Ginzburg, *The Night Battles: Witchcraft and Agrarian Cults in the Sixteenth
and Seventeenth Centuries* (New York 1983). See also, David Sabean, *Power
and the Blood: Popular Culture and Village Discourse in Early Modern Germany*
(Cambridge 1984).

7. Yet it is only after presenting my account of village disputes that I will offer
tentative observations about the exercise of power through the judicial discourse
and practices of the colonial state. My main concern is to tell the larger story
from a perspective that foregrounds the players and the protagonists in the village
dramas.

8. The reconstruction of this dispute is based on *King Emperor vs Balli and 13
others*, ST 34 of 1940, DSC RR.

9. Table 11.1 contains the caste, the name, the father's name and the approx-
imate age of the 'accused' within the trial. Figure 11.1 shows the relationships
among the 'accused' Satnamis, and Figure 11.2 represents the relationships among
the Satnamis who were 'assaulted'. In Figure 11.1, the names of the accused and in
Figure 11.3 the names of prosecution witnesses are underlined, while the names
of the other people who feature in these Figures often crop up in the narrative. I
was unable to trace the names of the women of the two groups of Satnamis from
the depositions of witnesses and the judgement, and, therefore, only the relationships among the men appear in the two Figures. Here, did not the exclusion of
women from the colonial judicial narrative stand in the way of its comprehending
the relationships among the people it was subjecting to 'law and order?' I return
to this question later.

10. Details culled from Bandobast no. 334, Patwari Halka no. 230, Darri
(Sarhar), Group Jaijaipur, 1929–30, BDVSR, BCRR.

11. DPW no. 11, Ratan, ST 34 of 1940, DSC RR.

12. In the panchayat, Sahas Satnami, Balaram Teli, Kunjram Nai, Budga Raut,
Balli Bhaina, and Balmukund Bhaina acted as the panchas. Ibid.

13. Ibid.

14. DPW no. 1, Awadh, ST 34 of 1940, DSC RR.

15. DPW no. 10, Gajaraj, ST 34 of 1940, DSC RR.

16. DPW no. 1, Awadh, ST 34 of 1940, DSC RR.

17. Ibid.

18. 'In the panchayat held over the elopement I was informed by my father,
Malikram, that in all ten of us were excommunicated. We considered that we were
excommunicated without any fault.' Ibid.

19. Two examples: the 10.93 acres of land owned by Gajaraj Satnami stood
distributed over forty-three holdings, only three of these over an acre; likewise,
Balaram Brahmin's 19.03 acres comprised sixty-four holdings. Bandobast no. 334,
Patwari Halka no. 230, Darri (Sarhar), Group Jaijaipur, 1929–30. BDVSR, BCRR.
For a discussion of issues of the fragmentation of landholdings in Chhattisgarh,
see Saurabh Dube, *Untouchable Pasts: Religion, Identity, and Power among a
Central Indian Community, 1780–1950* (New York 1998), pp. 31, 82–4.

20. DPW no. 11, Ratan, ST 34 of 1940, DSC RR.

21. DPW no. 1, Awadh, ST 34 of 1940, DSC RR.

22. Ibid.

23. DPW no. 12, Gorakh, ST 34 of 1940, DSC RR: DPW no. 1, Awadh, ST 34 of 1940, DSC RR.

24. DPW no. 1, Awadh, ST 34 of 1940, DSC RR.

25. DPW no. 11, Ratan, ST 34 of 1940, DSC RR.

26. DPW no. 9, Bunkuwar, ST 34 of 1940, DSC RR.

27. J, ST 34 of 1940, DSC RR.

28. See, for instance, Erin P. Moore, 'Gender, Power, and Legal Pluralism', *American Ethnologist*, vol. 20, 1993, pp. 522–42; Leela Dube, 'Conflict and Compromise: Devolution and Disposal of Property in a Matrilineal Muslim Society', *Economic and Political Weekly*, vol. 29, no. 21, 1994, pp. 1273–84.

29. See, for example, Veena Das, *Critical Events: An Anthropological Perspective on Contemporary India* (New Delhi 1995); Saurabh Dube, 'Idioms of Authority and Engendered Agendas: The Satnami Mahasabha, Chhattisgarh, 1925–50', *The Indian Economic and Social History Review*, vol. 30, 1993, pp. 383–411; Saurabh Dube, *Untouchable Pasts*; Ishita Banerjee Dube, 'Taming Traditions: Legalities and Histories in Twentieth Century Orissa', in Gautam Bhadra, Gyan Prakash, and Susie Tharu (eds), *Subaltern Studies X: Writings on South Asian History and Society* (New Delhi 1999), pp. 98–125. See also, Upendra Baxi, '"The State's Emissary": The Place of Law in Subaltern Studies', in Partha Chatterjee and Gyan Pandey (eds) *Subaltern Studies VII: Writings on South Asian History and Society* (New Delhi 1992), pp. 257–64; and Veena Das, 'Subaltern as Perspective', in Ranajit Guha (ed.) *Subaltern Studies VI: Writings on South Asian History and Society* (New Delhi 1989), pp. 310–24.

30. I discuss the crucial place of metaphors of colonial governance and symbols of state in the structuring of caste dominance, the constitution of community, and the making of alternative legalities and moralities in Dube, *Untouchable Pasts*.

31. Dube, 'Idioms of Authority'.

32. Dube, *Untouchable Pasts*.

33. Bandobast no. 334, Patwari Halka no. 230, Darri (Sarhar), Group Jaijaipur, 1929–30. BDVSR, BCRR.

34. The fight on the morning of 7 May 1940, for example, had brought up the issues of fishing and washing of buffaloes by Malikram and Awadhram in the pond. Now, while there was no ban on fishing in the pond near Darri through a proclamation by the malguzar, and other families did fish there, members of Gajaraj's group had not fished in Darri that year. This could have been one of the restrictions imposed on Gajaraj's group.

35. At the panchayat, 'the panchas were not consulted and I do not know if they had consulted each other but Kunjbehari gave out that we were fined. The panchas had not gone aside to consult each other.' DPW no. 1, Awadh, ST 34 of 1940, DSC RR.

36. J, ST 34 of 1940, DSC RR.

37. Gayatri Chakravorty Spivak, 'Can the Subaltern Speak?', in Cary Nelson and Lawrence Grossberg (eds) *Marxism and the Interpretation of Culture* (Urbana 1988), pp. 271–313. See also Kamala Viswesaran, 'Small Speeches, Subaltern Gender: Nationalist ideology and its Historiography", in Shahid Amin and Dipesh Chakrabarty (eds) *Subaltern Studies IX: Writings on South Asian History and Society* (New Delhi 1996), pp. 83–125.

38. Dube, *Untouchable Pasts*.

39. Guha, 'Chandra's Death'.

40. Leela Dube, 'On the Construction of Gender: Hindu Girls in Patrilineal India', *Economic and Political Weekly*, vol. 23, no. 18, 1988, (ws), pp. 11–19; Joyce B. Flueckiger, *Gender and Genre in the Folklore of Middle India* (Ithaca 1996); Gloria G. Raheja and Ann Gold, *Listen to the Heron's Words: Reimagining Gender and Kinship in North India* (Berkeley 1994); William Sax, *Mountain Goddess: Gender and Politics in a Himalyan Pilgrimage* (New York 1991); Dube, *Untouchable Pasts*; and Erin P. Moore, *Gender, Law, and Resistance in India* (Tuscon 1998).

V

Postcolonial Predilections

12

Outlaw Woman
The Politics of Phoolan Devi's Surrender, 1983*

Rajeswari Sunder Rajan

There is a strikingly iconic scene embedded in the imaginary of modern India: the figure of a woman, her arms upraised, rifle held aloft, facing a vast crowd. This is a scene from the drama of Phoolan Devi's surrender to the Indian government. It was disseminated by the media, as such images are in our time, and made memorable in cinematic recreation. How may we read the meaning and significance of the surrender—in terms not only of this spectacle but also as historical event? As explanation the image tends to be self-sufficient in its own terms, the representation, in the form of the freeze-scene, overwhelming the narrative that precedes or follows it. I want to examine the intriguing force of the image, while also working it into the narrative of Phoolan Devi, centring my discussion on the period immediately leading up to and following her surrender to the police in February 1983.

As I was developing the larger concern of this book, the relationship between women and the postcolonial Indian state, the figure of the female outlaw began to obtrude—first as a theoretical puzzle and then, increasingly, as a 'supplement'. Her figure is not quite contained

* Excerpted from Rajeswari Sunder Rajan, *The Scandal of the State: Women, Law, and Citizenship in Postcolonial India*, (Durban: Duke University Press 2003).

within this relationship, but it has nevertheless come to be central to my understanding of it. The female outlaw, directly confronting and confronted by the executive and judicial authority of the state, stands outside the usual transactions between women and the state. [...] Such exemption, which constitutes her also as exception, indeed contributes to the definition of the outlaw. [...] Phoolan Devi's dealings with the Indian government raise questions for both post-Independence Indian nation-statehood and gendered agency that alter the terms of this relationship. This negotiated relationship will be the matter of this chapter. I suggest that at the very least this is an intriguing crisis of citizenship, but I am inclined to think that it is also a significant one—that it uncovers certain usually repressed aspects of both that are revelatory.

The *surrender* resonates in this argument for two reasons. One, it was a direct, face-to-face, and (precariously) symmetrical encounter between the singular citizen-subject and the officials and representatives of the state, uncommon in the dealings of citizenship (here both 'encounter' and 'singular' are deliberately double-coded words), which forces us to ask: what are the conditions productive of such a crisis? And two, it is a point that marked, as it were, a baptism, Phoolan's entry into a novel territory of citizen-identity, the conditions of which also made visible the contracts that are otherwise naturalized in citizenship. If Phoolan promised to be law-abiding (in/law) as a condition of the state's pardon, the state's pardon too signalled the suspension of its dubious use of force as an instrument of law. This engineered event thus brought to crisis both citizenship and law as aspects of the state, as I hope to show.

I draw my account of Phoolan Devi's surrender from an authorized biography by Mala Sen, *India's Bandit Queen: The True Story of Phoolan Devi* (1991/1993).[1] Phoolan Devi's life story has been made familiar to an international audience through Shekhar Kapur's film *Bandit Queen* (1994), which is largely based on Sen's book. I have also drawn on reports and feature articles about Phoolan Devi in the Indian media.

This is a brief recapitulation of the events of her life as we know it from these sources. Phoolan was born the second of five children into a poor family in rural Uttar Pradesh (UP) and was married off as a child to a much older man. She then escaped to or was abducted by a dacoit gang (the Chambal valley has long been notorious as the home of dacoity). Her evolution into an outlaw is usually explained as her rebellion against her exploitation as a poor lower-caste woman. She quickly attained legendary status as leader of her own dacoit gang. But after the death of Vikram Mallah, her lover and co-leader of the gang, and following the notorious massacre at Behmai village, which she was accused of leading, she was on the run. Eventually, early in 1983, she voluntarily surrendered to the police when assured of fair terms of trial and rehabilitation by the government; and after eleven years in jail awaiting trial, she was conditionally released. Since her release her life has been an escalating sequence of media fame, bourgeois respectability, and political influence. She was elected to Parliament as a Samajwadi Party candidate from UP in 1996, lost the seat in the general elections of 1998, and was re-elected in 1999. A significant aspect of this time was the making and release of the film *Bandit Queen* and the controversy surrounding it.

The reliability of these accounts of her life as 'facts' is admittedly controversial, especially since what have been regarded as the relevant, even crucial, events of her outlaw career—her stripping in the village square, followed by her revenge on her enemies in Behmai— are contested by the issues that Phoolan raised about the film version of her life, namely, her right to privacy and her right to control her version of events, especially about her alleged crimes, which are still pending court trial. This chapter is bounded by these constraints and by the ethical and political considerations involved in any discussion relating to the life of a contemporary figure. The surrender, however, was a public event in an incontrovertible sense, though its political meanings are admittedly open to differences of interpretation. As an event in her life (as much as in the nation's), it appears to me to be legitimately available to the kinds of inquiry to which I open it. It is important, also, not to mystify the reversals in Phoolan's biographical trajectory. There is an inevitability, even inexorability, in the sequence that turns the dispossessed toward dacoity in a particular conjuncture of postcolonial underdevelopment and caste-and-politics nexus and subsequently propels the reformed outlaw (like, for example, the film star) towards electoral politics in a populist democracy. Our understanding of the politics of the surrender must be informed, then, by both the exceptionalism and the paradoxical representativeness of Phoolan Devi's career.

By way of clarifying the position from which I speak, I pause briefly here to explain where Indian feminism stands, first in relation to the state, and then to Phoolan Devi.

First, let me quickly recapitulate the exposition of the introductory chapter of this book. The state has been an important issue for Indian feminism and its 'most constitutive site of contestation', as Mary John has described it.[2] The postcolonial Indian state has been a strong, centralized, and initially socialist state that assumed powers and responsibilities that the autonomous women's movement sought to call to account. In the early post-Independence years, women's organizations displayed conspicuous liberal faith in the constitutional guarantees for gender equality and in legal measures for instituting reform, as well as in the executive machinery of the state—law enforcement, development programmes, implementation of quotas, and so on. But inevitably and in time Indian feminism has developed a critical relation to the state, without, however, relinquishing that relation. The failures of the Indian state in these fifty years of independence are not only those of the gaps between promises and delivery, progressive laws and their failed implementation, but a betrayal at a deeper level: the 'neutral' state has been exposed as a myth as successive governments' support of patriarchal and upper-caste and majoritarian religious interests has become impossible to ignore. Following the Emergency, increasing numbers of anti-state movements have sought to question the powers of the state, its human rights violations, its control of resources, and its monopoly of the television medium. Lately, feminists have insisted that the movement's focus on legal reform activism has limited potential in the absence of the state's commitment to implementation of laws, and that the state's intervention through increased and more stringent legislation only further strengthens its powers; that the struggle for social transformation by democratic processes requires equal attention to other sites, family, religious communities, caste relations, and, increasingly, the market, and to their connections to the state. At the same time, the Indian women's movement, never monolithic in any case, has begun to develop differences even among its broadly left-secular-democratic sections, which I will not address here. [...] The phenomenon of women's mobilization in Hindu right-wing organizations, along with the growing communalization of politics, has also led to a great deal of introspection.

How may we locate the figure of Phoolan Devi within the scenario of feminist politics? The contrast between, on the one hand, a certain low-keyed and ambivalent attitude toward Phoolan on the part of Indian feminism, and on the other, the widespread popular recuperation of her as the type of female heroism cannot have escaped anyone's notice. The recuperation has utilized the idiom of the female goddess, a myth widely spread locally, as well as the image of a commodified underclass/third world/female heroism established internationally by a certain kind of populist feminism. If, by contrast, Indian feminists have been noticeably reticent about Phoolan Devi, the reasons are not hard to seek: Phoolan is not a feminist figure or a figure for feminism. This, needless to say, is not a criticism of the historical Phoolan, for there is of course no reason why she should be either; nor does it indicate a dismissal of her life's vicissitudes as irrelevant to feminism's concerns. Indian feminism has in general been unenthusiastic about embracing militant feminist models, and scepticism about the value routinely attributed to female 'agency' and 'empowerment', as such, has tended to increase in the context of militant Hindutva women leaders. Also, as I have argued elsewhere, feminist theory has found the singular figure, the biographical subject, problematic as the subject of feminism, especially when, as in the case of Indira Gandhi, she exemplifies a unique or exceptional achievement or power.[3]

This, on the one hand. On the other, there is a more complex feminist unease about engaging with the historical 'actual' Phoolan Devi. Mala Sen was quick to point to the failure of the urban, middle-class Indian women's movement to connect to Phoolan's oppression: 'the women at the heart of the events on which they campaigned [in the 1970s] remained faceless, if not nameless ... Nothing they did or said made any difference to the course Phoolan Devi's life was to take'. The unfair and illogical expectation that the women's movement must serve and save all women, everywhere, is one commonly held and is quite often advanced to score points against it. At the other extreme is the criticism that the women's movement espouses only a victim feminism, and hence women who display initiative and individualism are of no interest to it. Thus, if the 'victim' Phoolan (lower-caste poor rural woman, raped and humiliated by upper-caste landlords) escaped its attention as a cause, then the Phoolan who became a dacoit and subsequently a political figure on her own initiative was irrelevant to its concerns as a personality. Unlike Shahbano or Ameena, proper names around which causes were mobilized, Phoolan Devi became a personality whose cause was quickly appropriated by other interests.

I share the caution about recuperating the exceptional woman for feminist meaning. But Phoolan's destiny and the destinations she sought at various points of her life (the surrender marking one crucial turning point) tell us much that is of interest about social and political processes, and it is in pursuit of such an understanding that I undertake this exploration of Phoolan Devi's surrender as an episode in the life of the nation.

The dacoits, locally known as *baghi*s (rebels), of central India (mainly the states of Uttar Pradesh and Madhya Pradesh) are men (and, rarely, women) who leave their villages to join gangs of varying sizes (numbering from seven or eight to as many as fifty or sixty). They camp in the jungles and ravines of the Chambal valley, moving frequently from place to place, periodically entering and raiding a village and quickly departing from it. They are known to slip back into their villages to visit their families and to come and go freely, sometimes even to return to their former lives; but for the most part they live as outlaws. Because many of them deliberately cultivate a code of honourable and even altruistic behaviour—robbing only the rich, giving to the poor, settling local disputes, following devout religious practices, instituting summary justice by punishing landlords and priests, protecting and honouring women, taking care of their own—they gain considerable support from poor villagers and can rely on harbourers and informers among them, as well as on caste- and kin-networks, to protect them from capture. In the popular imagination they are also dreaded and admired figures of heroism. For these reasons dacoits have powerful enemies among upper-caste landlords and rival caste groups and are susceptible to betrayal for money or revenge; hence their lives are precarious. Men join dacoit gangs either because they have already committed a crime in their village—arising from a quarrel, a property dispute, an assault on a woman's 'honour'—and wish to escape or because the gang life supports them in the absence of other means of livelihood. This is a region known for its harsh living conditions, rife with caste conflict and corruption.

This is not the place to explore in any depth the divergent interpretations of dacoity in a criminal framework, but a quick rehearsal of the most influential explanations will be helpful for an understanding of the context of Phoolan's surrender. Historians of the British eighteenth century have been the first to emphatically shift the study of crime from its 'conservative orientation' in viewing it as a problem of policing, to the 'broader framework' of social history.[5] The category of 'social crime' was made distinct, though not in any very clear-cut terms, from ordinary crime.[6] More radically, crime's 'challenge to law' shifted the historian's focus from state power to the 'views and actions' of working-class criminals.[7] This shift was greatly influenced by Eric Hobsbawm's *Primitive Rebels*.[8] 'All kinds of rioters, smugglers, poachers, primitive rebels in industry' were regarded as 'good' criminals, in fact 'premature revolutionaries or reformers, forerunners of popular movements', who often gained the support of 'the community and its culture'.[9]

This is clearly a useful way to understand dacoity, and by now a widely accepted one. While the mythical stature and heroism of dacoits may have suffered considerable diminution in post-Independence India, there is little doubt that they wield considerable regional clout (though whether as benefactors or as terrorists would be a contested point), and police and politicians act in acknowledgement of this reality. Their influence is also borne out by the fact that many 'criminal elements' enter electoral politics successfully.

Hobsbawm holds that instances of banditry in later times are only 'odd survivals' from a pre-capitalist period, and that they are provoked by the uneven development of capitalism or by other sudden disruptions of the social order. 'En masse, they [social bandits] are little more than symptoms of crisis and tension in their society—of famine, pestilence, war or anything else that disrupts it.'[10] Despite its persistence in South Asia and Latin America, 'on the whole,' he writes, 'social banditry is a phenomenon of the past, though often of the very recent past. The modern world has killed it...'[11] If we accept this, we must regard, as many do, its occurrence in modern India solely as a survival.

For the modern Indian state dacoity is a severe embarrassment, not least because it is viewed as an anachronism in this sense. In most explanations dacoity figures as a custom with a long tradition, changed but with a persistence of 'memory and habit of mind' that keeps the tradition alive (Jayaprakash Narayan, cited by Sen),[12] a remnant of a feudal past, in a part of India that has been overlooked in the development process. Geographical heart of darkness (inaccessible, hostile territory, harsh climate, drought); economic failure (industrial backwardness, lack of employment); social marginalization (feudalism, rigid caste-structures, local community justice): these are the plausible reasons offered for the continuation of dacoity into the modern present. All analysts of dacoity in contemporary India—including politicians—are willing to lay the blame for the phenomenon on the conditions of underdevelopment, and hence a problem of administration rather than merely policing.

It is an article of faith of the postcolonial Indian state (as of its predecessor colonial government) that the pre-modern aspects of the nation must be brought into the fold of modernity by administration—through development, education, rule of law. But these aspects (whether dowry, sati, or dacoity), while appearing to be survivals, are instead considerably altered phenomena produced by and feeding into the circumstances of modern social and political realities. In the states of the Hindi belt the nexus of party, caste politics, and criminals is well known, as is also the fact that dacoits illegally acquire high-powered weaponry from police, military, and government arms factories. The notorious sandalwood smuggler Veerappan, who operated in the southern states of Karnataka and Tamil Nadu, skilfully used the media to publicize his exploits and demands. This adaptability, and the pressures of contemporary Indian realpolitik, complicate the paradigms of both primitive rebellion and feudal survival, calling for a more radical revision of our understanding of dacoity in modern India.

One link in pursuit of such an understanding is with the colonial discourses and practices around the abolition and reform of *thugi*, dacoity, and criminal tribes. The continuities between police practices in post-Independence India and their colonial nineteenth-century past was attested by Ayodhya Nath Pathak, the deputy inspector general (DIG) of police in Gwalior, when he suggested that Mala Sen read Francis Tuker's book on Henry Sleeman, the colonial police officer responsible for wiping out thugs in central India, because 'We still use it as part of our syllabus in the Police academy, you know.'[13] Here, as elsewhere, colonial bureaucracy provides the systematized knowledge and understanding that the modern postcolonial state draws on for its own rules and strategies of government. Sleeman's exploits constituted a subculture of police lore that, as much as the official protocols of law, informed the operations of the force in their work. At the same time, while the Indian police forces may demand 'special legislation' to increase their powers, of the kind Henry Sleeman sought—such as the Prevention of Dacoity Act (which was in fact promulgated at the height of Phoolan's activities)—the postcolonial state can no longer draw on the reformist legitimation that empowered Sleeman's campaign against thugi. The tension between the police approach in apprehending dacoits and the political compulsions that recommend either coexistence (wilfully turning a blind eye to their activities) or negotiation with them is a visible manifestation of the problem of the adoption of a simple law-and-order approach to their 'abolition' by the modern state.

Developing the analogies with insurgency—or, broadly, political crime—is another productive or at least suggestive move. In post-Independence India, there have been and continue to be many kinds of insurgencies, secessionist movements, or movements for regional autonomy; Marxist–Leninist people's 'war' groups; and other militant and revolutionary peasant groups, which use violence, mainly in guerrilla warfare and terrorism, to fight the state. Dacoity is not identical with these since its action is not directed at the state, for one thing, but at upper-caste men of property, and it is pursued as a way of life and a livelihood rather than followed as a political programme. All the same it constitutes a challenge to the modern state as it invariably shades into, or is taken over by, political demands. The composition of dacoit gangs in recent times—predominantly men belonging to the lower castes, especially significant in Phoolan's and Vikram Mallah's gang—

has given dacoit activity a distinct political aspect as underclass and caste resistance.

It is often the case that it is *how* the state actually contends with the problem of civil strife that confers the status of 'criminal' or 'insurgent' on its adversaries rather than accordance with some pre-given definition of these types. In the case of terrorism, for instance, Paul Gilbert points out that 'despite their constant insistence that terrorists are simply common criminals, states seldom consistently treat them as such': thus, for example, there are Prevention of Terrorism provisions, special extradition policies, refusal to prosecute for treason, and so forth, that implicitly place (even as they resist placing) terrorists in a special political category.[14] The legal understanding of dacoity as a criminal phenomenon is contradicted by the state's invocation of such special procedures in dealing with it—among them both the Anti-Dacoity Act and the engineering or acceptance of surrenders—based on the acknowledgement of the local realities of its status and practices in a different category, or at least a different register from that of 'ordinary' crime.

In a complex argument, Upendra Baxi has avowed that in the postcolonial state the discourses of 'development' and 'criminality' are interlinked, the latter regarded as a concomitant of the former. While 'progressive criminality' (as instanced by the Bhopal gas leak) is condoned as an aspect of development, 'regressive criminality' (which refers to both economic crimes and certain 'traditional' practices in need of reform or abolition: dacoity falls into both categories) is seen 'to foil or frustrate the objectives of planned development'. 'Criminality', therefore, is a 'notion contingent on the very nature of class and formative practices through legislation and legal administration (enforcement, adjudication).'[15]

The state's power of naming 'dacoity', or 'terrorism', serves important functions for its institutional image. Naming the 'terrorist' is a scapegoating technique, as William Connolly has argued, for covering the deficiencies of the advanced industrial state in the West.[16] In postcolonial India, the dacoit is a less unambiguous scapegoat for a state that, given the uneven development of constitutional rule—its use of force in counter-insurgency or anti-crime crackdowns has always to contend with the problem of legitimacy—seeks to disavow both the phenomenon itself and the use of force, as I will shortly elaborate.

Dacoity is thus suspended between crime and social crime, as well as social crime of the pre-political kind and a more up-to-date model of terrorism/political insurgency/civil strife, and between developmental issues and electoral politics, placing it in a unique position for police and administrative agencies. The different contradictions it thereby poses for the state, both as a matter of naming and constructing it as a 'problem' and in framing strategies for countering it, shed light on the specific politics of Phoolan Devi's surrender.

This brings us to the state's resolution of the conflict by negotiating a surrender. Was Phoolan's surrender a defeat or a victory, and whose?

Mala Sen's book gives a closely detailed account of the political background of the event. The government of Uttar Pradesh had escalated its attempts to put down dacoity in the state during the years of Phoolan Devi's activities, by promulgating an Anti-Dacoity Ordinance in 1981 that gave the police unlimited powers to arrest individuals on suspicion, while simultaneously intensifying operations to hunt dacoits down (there were schemes to flood the ravines, to train leopards to track them, to use aircraft to strafe them in hiding, and so forth, according to reports cited by Sen).[17] These measures led instead to police corruption and to the killing of innocent people in staged 'encounters', against which protests were mounted. The chief minister of the state, then V.P. Singh, having staked his reputation on eliminating the most notorious gangs—he was considered to have a personal stake since he was a Thakur himself and had lost his brother and his family to a dacoit attack—had no choice but to resign following the Behmai massacre and the killings in Dastampur. There was considerable friction between the police forces of Uttar Pradesh and neighbouring Madhya Pradesh, and their morale was low. Malkhan Singh's surrender had been successfully arranged by the Madhya Pradesh police, and many dacoits began to consider giving themselves up. The Phoolan–Man Singh gang was running low on men and supplies and finding it hard to commit dacoities under such intense police surveillance. At the same time, the police felt that it would be impossible to catch Phoolan, given the vastness of the territory in which she could hide. Phoolan was tracked down by the superintendent of police of Madhya Pradesh, Rajendra Chaturvedi, a man trusted by the gangs operating in the region for having successfully arranged Malkhan Singh's surrender the previous year. After meeting with her several times over a long period—nearly a year—he persuaded her to accept the state's offer of amnesty ('The choice is between dying like a dog in the ravines or being hanged by a court'). Phoolan's surrender therefore came out of both parties' sense of impending defeat, but both could turn it to strategic account.

In the 1960s and the 1970s, Sen reminds us, the Gandhian leaders Vinoba Bhave and Jayaprakash Narayan had persuaded large numbers of dacoits to surrender voluntarily in response to their call. These had been greatly admired moral conversions, coded in the language of reform and redemption and masterminded by respected national figures who were not themselves politicians. The climate of the 1980s was a vastly different one. Jayaprakash espoused a Gandhian view of human nature and social transformation. But Gandhian interventions had become awkward for an independent Indian state that had set course on a different—modern statist—trajectory. (Jayaprakash himself was anxious to defend the surrenders' philosophical basis for 'change of heart' as an axiom of 'modern penology'.)[18] In addition, there is a requirement of uniformity and predictability in the conduct of public affairs, especially in the rituals of the state, which makes cultural difference in itself a matter of embarrassment, even without the added imputation in this case of the government's inefficiency and failed toughness in matters of law and order. There was consequently no attempt—as how could there be?—to represent the surrenders of the 1980s as similar to the emotionally charged mass conversions of the earlier years, or as motivated by benevolence on the part of the government; they were an entirely pragmatic negotiation. The moral aura that had given the government its authoritative high ground as well as legitimized the surrenders by representing the dacoits as 'converts' to the right way of life had by now entirely dissipated, rendering much more dubious the profit–loss calculus of this transaction.

However, a closer look at the events surrounding the surrenders to the Sarvodaya leader, Jayaprakash Narayan, in the early 1970s, reveals them to have been a controversial development even then. There was at the time considerable resistance from the police force to promising amnesty to the dacoits as a condition of their surrender. But the main opposition came from the Congress party's chief minister of Madhya Pradesh, P.C. Sethi, to what he regarded as Jayaprakash's upstaging of the state government's initiatives. Jayaprakash was an opposition figure in politics and was soon to become a critic of Indira Gandhi's regime. Sethi complained frequently about the politics of the surrenders: the dacoits were being glamourized, Jayaprakash had 'smuggled in' BBC and news agency personnel to film the events, the dividends paid by the show of force of his government's police was not given due credit, and so on. Jayaprakash went to the press to defend his intervention while also offering to withdraw from further participation. Though such third-party intervention was absent in the negotiations in 1981 (it was the Madhya Pradesh police who took the initiative in contacting the dacoits and arranging their surrender, with the active backing of the state's Congress chief minister, who in turn was authorized by Prime Minister Indira Gandhi herself), there was still a different kind of murky politics around the event—notably caste politics in Uttar Pradesh, and the personality politics of the chief ministers of the two states and their relationship to the centre. The government of Madhya Pradesh scored political points for securing Phoolan Devi and put on a show of the surrender to highlight its success. Chief Minister Arjun Singh's prestige was never higher, and he continued to retain the loyalty of the dacoit constituency. Given such a high degree of politicking around the issue, Phoolan appeared to be a puppet who was manipulated by various parties to their own ends. Kamini Jaiswal, Phoolan's lawyer during her jail term, was emphatic in her view that the surrender was no more than a 'political gimmick' (personal communication).

Framed within such a perspective, one that would grant little initiative to Phoolan's leadership or at best would make her secondary in significance to her gang as an adversary of the state, how far would we be justified in viewing the female outlaw's career and its culminating surrender as a unique transaction between the individual historical woman and the impersonal state having implications for the question of postcolonial citizenship for women? Was she an agential subject in any meaningful way? Is the politics of her identity best understood in terms of her gender or her caste?

Let me address the last question first by way of a preliminary clarification. To separate Phoolan Devi's identity as lower-caste woman into its component parts, even for analytical purposes, is an unproductive exercise, since they are so constitutively interlinked. There is no doubt, however, that one or the other element could be played up by the different parties involved in projecting her persona and the problem she represented, not least by Phoolan herself. Thus caste certainly predominated in the internal politics of the hostility of the state government and the regional elite against her, and it consequently also provided the strength of her own mobilization of a following against her opponents (both as a gang leader and later as a political party candidate).

Her gendered identity was one that demanded negotiation in several contexts. That traditionally male bastion, the dacoit gang, accepted Phoolan's presence and her leadership in large part because she was their leader's mistress and also because an available cultural rationalization of women's vigilante violence is sexual vendetta. In a brief appendix on 'Women and Banditry', Hobsbawm observed that 'the most usual role of women in banditry is as lovers',[19] though women who are bandits themselves are celebrated in the myths and legends of many regions. The woman bandit, like the *serrena* (mountain woman) of Andalusia, 'turns to outlawry in general and revenge on men in particular, because she has been "dishonoured", i.e. deflowered'.[20] Phoolan's career follows this general pattern, her dishonour being both (her) motive and (their, the community's) acceptable reason for her turn to lawlessness. In practice, her presence and role within Vikram Mallah's gang, and within the larger dacoit community and the villages of their operation, seems to have been naturalized by the quick and relatively easy acceptance of her resemblance to the legendary Putlibai or the goddess Durga (just as, at the other extreme, denigration of her was expressed by equally facile sexist abuse, for example, 'Mallah whore'). Both Phoolan and Vikram played up her identification with the militant, fearful, avenging, righteous female figures that were available within the repertoire of the culture, and there is no reason to think that it was not also deeply internalized.

In the discourse of the impersonal modern state, however, this face-saving idiom was not permitted.

What was significantly absent in the official discourse, as well as in the media discourse at the time of her surrender and later of her release from jail, is any recognition of the events in Phoolan's life as *gender* issues of any significance, other than the routine acceptance that her actions were to be understood as 'revenge' for the sexual violence she had been subjected to by upper-caste men in her village. It was Mala Sen's book and, however problematically, the film *Bandit Queen* that first projected a 'feminist' interpretation of Phoolan's story, foregrounding the humiliations she suffered—child marriage, police harassment, threats, rape, public stripping—as typical of lower-caste rural women's oppression. The media typically sought a feminized image of the female dacoit and was not slow in expressing disappointment in sexist terms: for example, 'Phoolan means flower but the bandit queen who surrendered is neither delicate nor meek. She is a short and tough woman.'[21] The politics of the image is, however, a separate issue. What is relevant at this point is to note the active process of demythicization that her surrender initiated in the media, which seemed to involve mainly the offer of a 'realistic' representation of her (lower-caste female) speech and appearance. Following her surrender she was represented by activist women lawyers, first Kamini Jaiswal, who successfully petitioned the Supreme Court for her release in 1994, and then Indira Jaising, who represented her in the *Bandit Queen* controversy.

More crucially, for the state there was the *symbolic* significance of Phoolan's gender to contend with. The genderedness of the state as masculine and its role in gendering and sexualizing its citizens has been extensively argued, among others by Suzanne Franzway, Dianne Court, and R.W. Connell. At the most general descriptive level, the state, they hold, is a patriarchal state, implicated in the 'overall social advantaging of men and subordination of women', in part because 'men have greater access to power in and through the state'.[22] Further, the state is constituted within a 'specialised "public" realm marked out by sexual ideology and the sexual division of labour'.[23] It is constituted in a realm 'culturally marked as masculine': for example, the personnel of the state are predominantly male, especially at the higher levels, a fact that will have significance when I turn to the details of Phoolan's surrender negotiations.

But the state is not only 'gender-structured', as Franzway et al. call it; a great deal of what it *does* is also gendered, especially in the legal system, police, courts, and prisons since the 'process of criminalizing people is markedly gendered'. The majority of criminals are men (just as the majority of welfare clientele are women).[24] (Women in prostitution are an interesting exception—they 'meet' the state as criminals, but of an anomalous kind.) The genderedness of crime as male, and the actual fact that the great majority of criminals are men, is a necessary counterpart to the phallocentrism of the state, given that they are viewed in a structure of antagonism. For the masculinity of the state must always be in evidence (however discreetly) for its authority to stick. It figures not only in the state's militaristic displays and in the rituals and paraphernalia of national symbols and ceremonies but also in the paternalism of its justice and welfare functions, in the professed objectivity and neutrality of its functioning, in the institutional supremacy and authority it represents: signs and claims everywhere simultaneously displayed and disavowed.

Therefore the embarrassment created by the successful *female* outlaw for the state (and for society) can be readily imagined. Phoolan's exploits threatened the state not only as a problem of law and as regional caste conflict but also as one of image. The failure of the Indian state—its government, political leaders, police—to capture her did not make it *look* good. Pressure for her capture was mounted most insistently, of course, by the Thakur community, powerful in Uttar Pradesh politics in the early 1980s. But the interest of the national media (with the international media never far away) was clearly in the sex war. That this encounter was widely perceived as one between a female outlaw and the male personnel of the state is evident in a detail from a newspaper report that Mala Sen quotes to highlight the popular disaffection about the government's amnesty to Phoolan: 'boys from the local students' union threw broken bangles towards the dais'.[25] (Bangles are a symbol of womanhood, and they are offered to men as an insult to their manhood.) In her encounters with the police, Phoolan herself appears not to have been reticent about taunting them about their masculinity—this was an available script for defying the state's armed force, especially given Phoolan's own acceptance of traditional ways of conceptualizing male and female sexualities and gender roles.

If we are to follow citizen–state transactions in the realm of politics and the everyday, the state must be viewed in terms of the actual contradictions of its institutions—interstate rivalries, political parties' conflicts, centre–state relations, the relations between police, government, Parliament, judiciary—and in terms of its functionaries' status, provenance, attitudes, and attributes (which include to a significant extent their class, caste, and gender identities), as of its abstractions and symbolic centres. In this instance, the figure of Rajendra Chaturvedi, superintendent of police of Madhya Pradesh, was a crucial agent in the procedures. Chaturvedi inspired trust because he was a middle-aged Brahman man from Kashmir—his age, sex, official seniority, and distance from regional affiliations gave him prestige in Phoolan's eyes and provided the assurance of his neutrality. Chaturvedi's approach to Phoolan in persuading her to surrender was one of paternalistic condescension, familiarity, and even affection. The terms in which he most often referred to her while speaking to Mala Sen are those of hysterical woman, infant, or untamed animal. We move here from a politics of identity to a discourse of behaviour, specifically gendered female, as Phoolan is reduced from outlaw woman at large to the more familiar figure of unruly female.

Phoolan was also responsive to calls of sisterhood. When Chaturvedi brought his wife to meet her, carrying food, he struck a chord; Kiran Bedi, at the time inspector-general of Tihar jail, was her supporter; most interesting of all were her feelings for Indira Gandhi, a combination of respect, identification, and the conviction that the prime minister as a woman herself had great sympathy for oppressed women. It was true that Gandhi had played a major role in Phoolan's surrender (both Arjun Singh and Chaturvedi himself had consulted her), and while this had primarily to do with wooing votes in the rural Uttar Pradesh–Madhya Pradesh belt, the prime minister's intervention did give Phoolan considerable clout while she was in jail.

There is little question therefore that Phoolan's sex had *relevance* in a variety of contexts and registers: for the myth of the Bandit Queen, for 'politics' as such, for the representations of her in the media, for the image bestowed on the government that sought her capture, for providing a strategic psychological understanding of her for the surrender negotiations, for feminist politics. But the *significance* of Phoolan's identity as lower-caste woman who negotiated with the state following, and as a consequence of, a successful outlaw career requires some further exploration of the politics of her surrender. I do not mean by this to aggrandize her career and her role, or to offer the surrender as a romanticized confrontation between a female David and a Goliath state. On the contrary, granting all the ambiguity of 'surrender' itself (how) does it nevertheless provide a space for viewing the transactions of the not-quite-not-citizen (woman/outlaw) with the state?

> He [Chaturvedi] said … 'Phoolan, we will make a human being out of you!' I asked, 'Will you convert the UP police and make human beings out of them too?'[26]

Phoolan set out the terms of her surrender, and once these were accepted the public event took place in Bhind, Madhya Pradesh, in the presence of the state's chief minister and other officials. Phoolan was then taken away to be lodged in Gwalior jail where she remained for most of the next eleven years until released by the orders of the Supreme Court. I want to explore here some aspects of the agreement.

The terms for the surrender were based on what Phoolan knew of earlier surrender agreements. They included: no death penalty; no trial in the Uttar Pradesh courts; settlement of her family with land and house in Madhya Pradesh; employment in the police force for her brother and brother-in-law; a prison term of no longer than eight years; rehabilitation in Madhya Pradesh after the jail term.[27] She also stipulated that the police would not be armed at the time of the surrender (to guard against the possibility of being shot 'while trying to escape').

A negotiated surrender usually offers the edge to the dacoit over the state. The option to surrender at the culmination of a career in dacoity is one that is always on the cards for the dacoit as an attractive option to capture, while for the state it is a last resort. For the duration of the negotiations, Phoolan became not only the equal but the equivalent of the state, an external adversary rather than a local criminal. This was a moment of power, but also, let us note, only a moment. Once Phoolan gave herself up she had no further bargaining point, leaving all the power in the hands of the authorities. She had, therefore, to do her utmost to get the best possible terms for herself before surrendering. Where the surrender was a unique and final act for Phoolan, for the state it was only one in a series of possible moves. Thus, in these negotiations, the outlaw had the upper hand at the beginning but at the end lost the advantage to the state.

Various terms are loosely used to describe the negotiations: surrender, amnesty, treaty, all military in nature. The actual agreement appears to have been much more informal—it has been described as a 'deal'—despite Phoolan's faith in the binding force of the written word. The state most often negotiates with individuals precisely in the context of their criminality—when it seeks the approver's testimony, offers a plea bargain, or negotiates with terrorists over hostages or ransoms. These are always fraught, contradictory, and contingent situations, though not lacking established procedural guidelines. The state's detractors would argue that (a) ideally it should not be 'negotiating' with criminals in the first place, and (b) arguably it is not bound by its agreement with them once it has done so. The state (when not operating in secrecy) counters these objections by offering arguments about clemency, strategy, expediency, or 'public interest' (as it may do under Section 321 of the Criminal Procedure Code). As a matter of expediency it is called on to honour such agreements in order to establish trust, though clearly it has some license in their observance. Phoolan was granted most of her demands; but her stay in jail extended well beyond the eight years she had stipulated, her family's fortunes were precarious, and she had to resort frequently to the services of her lawyer, the media, and her 'contacts' and to staging scenes and riots in prison to get her demands accommodated.

The actual nature of Phoolan's judicial status continued to be that of a parolee on bail. The validity of the government's 'deal' with her was constantly in doubt, as a matter of legality, expediency, and public opinion. Though it was reported that the Uttar Pradesh government had 'dropped charges' against her at the behest of the Samajwadi party chief minister Mulayam Singh, she still had fifty-five cases pending against her (for some of which, like the possession of arms, she had been tried, convicted, and had already served out a term while awaiting trial). In 1997 a warrant was issued against her in connection with the Behmai massacre (in which she was charged with twenty-two killings), and she went into hiding to avoid arrest. Mulayam Singh, by then the Union defence minister, intervened to ask the Uttar Pradesh government to move a Special Leave Petition before the Supreme Court challenging the Allahabad High Court order that had issued the warrant for her arrest. Legally, no 'amnesty' may be offered to a person charged with criminal offences: she would have to stand trial, unless the government chose to withdraw charges. Or, following a trial and sentencing, there could be a presidential pardon. The validity and duration of Phoolan's freedom was a suspended question during her lifetime.

Both legal and political issues were at stake in this complicated matter. Legally, the government did not have a free hand in dropping charges: it had to seek the court's permission to do so, and this might not always be forthcoming as a matter of course. Politically, it had to balance the claims of the victims' rights (whose cause might be picked up by opposition political parties) and also judge the overall popular climate of feeling for or against the accused. This meant that Phoolan's 'freedom' was conditional, subject to the concerns—and whims—of a government in power (a situation that is contingent in a particularly acute way, given that she was a figure in opposition politics).

The issues that emerged from this encounter were both large and small. The larger issue was that of the politics of civil violence, including dacoity, on which I have based the argument of this chapter. All forms of people's violent opposition—whether as organized crime, rioting, or insurgency—place the state in crisis. While among conservative sections it provokes questions about the state's responsibility for creating situations of lawlessness or for failing to restore the law, it also radically reopens the issue of the state's rights as the sole repository of the legitimate use of force to preserve law and order or punish. Even as crises authorize and consolidate such force, they question an authority that is grounded in it. If the state's 'legitimate' use of force is open to question, its widespread *illegitimate* uses of it—through recourse to counterinsurgency tactics, 'encounter' killings, police brutality, torture, other human rights abuses, corruption, the deployment of informers and spies, propaganda—make its constitutionality even more suspect, so that the state that seeks to preserve its liberal democratic credentials resorts to strenuous denial of such excesses. At other times it seeks constitutional means to legitimize its excesses by declaring states of 'emergency', suspending civil rights and laws of evidence and habeas corpus in order to contain opposition. Phoolan emerged at and created precisely such a point of crisis, challenging both the constitutional 'pretension' of the Indian state and its force monopoly. Upendra Baxi, activist lawyer and legal theorist, holds that Phoolan's exploits demonstrated the citizen's self-enforcement of constitutional rights and values 'in ways that even the best genres of Euro-American theorizing barely glimpse' (personal communication).

The matter of the surrender brings us closer to the heart of the problem of the constitutionality of the state. What does it mean that the state is not constitutively, that is, constantly and at all times and equally, 'legal' but is given to responding to contingent and imperative circumstances within a framework of legality—by taking on board 'exceptional' considerations in securing outcomes? When rules of functioning are kept in abeyance the tension between the possible loss of discipline, authority, and principle on the one hand and the envisaged gains of flexibility and conflict resolution on the other, provides insights into the pragmatics of rule. More crucially, it is when a government offers to suspend hostilities that we become aware of the hostilities it unremittingly pursues through a continuing state of civil war with/within society. Phoolan's surrender brought to visibility this normative Hobbesian nature of the state as a state of nature, as well as the conventions (not necessarily the laws) that regulate 'lawful' citizenship.

The state intended the surrender to look like a way of bringing the outlaw in from the cold. It would reclaim *her* from the state of nature and re-enter her into 'society' by bestowing on her new (appropriately gendered) social identity, citizenship, livelihood, social function. The surrender had to be scripted as a public event in order that Phoolan could be *produced* to the public eye, brought out of the hiding that was the condition of her outlaw existence, and made visible as a citizen 'like anyone else'. (Momentarily only, for she had to be immediately

consigned to hiding again in jail—where, however, the regime of surveillance would take over to maintain her as 'visible' subject.) The
politics of Phoolan as embodied (female) figure for the state was a
matter of recasting her as newly minted subject, with all the appropriate social attributes of the lawful citizen. Her disempowerment had to
be ritually enacted through the laying down of arms, the gestures of
abjection, and her very *appearance*—in both senses of the word.

The rule-of-law state had to produce a *spectacular* surrender also as
a public relations exercise (the 'political gimmick'): it had to overcome
criticism and gain points for ending the career of Phoolan and her
gang by producing the 'reformed' subject of its endeavours to capture
and convert her. For the actual event the script had to be improvised
to some extent (since surrenders are not everyday events). As happens in many such state-sponsored events, chaos reigned, there was
confusion and unruly crowd behaviour, and the police were anxious
not only about protocol but about the safety of all the participants, the
members of the gang and the VIPs present.

Phoolan was groomed for her role, provided crisp khakis to
wear, coached in protocol, and the props were provided (pictures
of Gandhi and the goddess Durga to whom she would give up her
arms). Surrender had to be coded as a performative 'I surrender.' But
Phoolan also turned it into a performance. She, too, resorted to the
public forum as an opportunity to (re-)present herself, undoubtedly
helped in this by the event's confused, improvised script. Both parties
sought to upstage the other, but there was no doubt that the crowd of
some seven thousand, including the media, was there to see Phoolan.
Sen reports Phoolan's 'theatrical humility' before the chief minister,
garlanding him, bowing to him, and laying her arms at his feet.[28]
This was also—not incidentally—the first and the last time Phoolan
would be publicly seen in the khaki police uniform and red bandanna
she wore as an outlaw (afterward she appeared only in the sari). A
journalistic description of her at the surrender typically remarked on
her 'short, snub-nosed figure in a dirty, ill-fitting khaki uniform', a
'boyish figure in a headband who looked more like a youthful *pahari
chowkidar* than the Anarkali of legend.'[29] This androgynous cross-
dressed figure was subversive in the performative sense that Judith
Butler describes:

The structure of impersonation reveals one of the key fabricating mechanisms through which the social construction of gender takes place ... drag fully subverts the distinction between inner and outer psychic space and effectively mocks both the expressive model of gender and the notion of a true gender identity.[30]

Though her appearance in outlaw guise was sanctioned, indeed required, by the surrender script, Phoolan's enactment of the cameo role of the female outlaw as an androgynous armed figure has remained as the indelible image of her myth. To her disappointment she was given no speaking role, but she faced the crowd momentarily, arms upraised with her rifle held aloft. This was the image that came to represent her.

I end this chapter about Phoolan Devi's surrender with a moral—actually two (different) morals—in lieu of a conclusion.

One: Phoolan sought out the nation-space—its structures of state, police, judiciary, public figures, and the media—to negotiate freedom and justice for herself. This observation does not undermine the indictment of constitutional democracy in India that has been the thrust of this chapter—the indictment of vote politics, police criminality and terrorism, the dubious legalism of 'negotiations', and the state's 'production' of the outlaw. (I use 'production' in all the senses of the word: responsibility for the conditions of civil unrest, the governmental construction of the name and category of criminality, and the public display of Phoolan at the surrender.) But it was nevertheless the state's resources that offered the route to Phoolan's escape from her village and community, from her local reputation, the local feuds, her immutable social status there—to the abstract entitlements of nation-state citizenship as guarantor of justice, and to larger and different opportunities. Law and the rights of citizenship, deeply even constitutively, flawed though they may be as structures of egalitarianism and justice, are nevertheless an *option* available to those who have been traditionally denied them under conditions of longstanding oppression. It is an option that may be and has been exercised under varied circumstances, and not one that we would want to do without. Gayatri Spivak concedes that 'citizenship' is 'indeed the symbolic circuit of the mobilizing of subalternity into hegemony'.[31] The perspective of the subaltern reminds us that the critique of the 'nation-state', as such, must also be located in the context of specific histories and viewed in relation to alternative (local, community) structures of regulation and rule. Pranab Bardhan has pointed out that, as community structures and local justice collapse, and local overlords' traditional patronage functions shrink in the modern postcolonial state, the people make appeals to 'supra-local authorities for conflict resolution, arbitration and protection'.[32] Phoolan's career describes one such trajectory, circuitously, via outlawry.

Two: Phoolan ensured her own and her family's safety, secured employment for her brother and brother-in-law, and some assurance for her livelihood through her negotiations. But it is not her exceptional 'luck' that I wish to convey so much as the ironic moral of her story. For what she secured was survival, that is, escape from the death penalty, and the means of livelihood. We must see this not as something she managed to get despite being an outlaw but rather as something *to get for which* she had to become an outlaw. As a reflection on citizenship and the inequalities of access to its privileges for the poor Dalit woman in India, hers is a powerful and ironic parable.

POSTSCRIPT

Phoolan Devi was murdered on 25 July 2001, shot by unknown assailants outside her official New Delhi residence. I have not recast any part of this chapter, written and sent to press before this date, in light of her death in this manner. It does not significantly alter the chapter's argument, which is based on accounts of an earlier period of her life. All the same this fact does, of course, add to the powerful irony of her life story. I would particularly not wish any simplistic 'moral' about 'justice' to usurp the morals with which I concluded. The nature of her violent death is a commentary as much on the lax security maintained by the Indian police as on the piety of truisms such as 'those who live by the sword die by the sword'.

NOTES

1. Mala Sen, *India's Bandit Queen: The True Story of Phoolan Devi* (New Delhi 1991).

2. Mary E. John, 'Gender, Development, and the Women's Movement: Problems for a History of the Present', in Rajeswari Sunder Rajan (ed.), *Signposts: Gender Issues in Post-Independence India* (New Delhi 1999), p. 108.

3. Rajeswari Sunder Rajan, *Real and Imagined Women: Gender, Culture, and Postcolonialism* (London 1993).

4. Sen, *India's Bandit Queen*, p. 54.

5. Peter Linebaugh, *The London Hanged: Crime and Civil Society in the Eighteenth Century* (Cambridge 1992), pp. xviii–xix.

6. Douglas Hay, 'Preface', in Hay, Peter Linebaugh, and Edward Thompson (eds), *Albion's Fatal Tree: Crime and Society in Eighteenth Century England* (New York 1975), p. 14

7. Linebaugh, *The London Hanged*, pp. xxii–xxiii.

8. Eric Hobsbawm, *Primitive Rebels: Studies in Archaic Forms of Social Movements in the Nineteenth and Twentieth Centuries* (New York 1965; first published 1959).

9. Hay, 'Preface', p. 14.

10. Eric Hobsbawm, *Bandits* (New York 1981), p. 24.

11. Ibid.

12. Sen, *India's Bandit Queen*, p. 196.

13. Ibid., p. 25.

14. Paul Gilbert, *Terrorism, Security, and Nationality: An Introductory Study in Applied Political Philosophy* (New York 1994), p. 47.

15. Ibid., pp. 55–7.

16. William Connolly, *Identity/Difference: Democratic Negotiations of Political Paradox* (Ithaca 1991), p. 207.

17. Sen, *India's Bandit Queen*, p. 176.

18. Tarun Coomar Bhaduri, *Chambal: The Valley of Terror* (Delhi 1972), p. 190.

19. Hobsbawm, *Bandits*, p. 135.

20. Ibid.

21. *Times of India*, 13 February 1983.

22. Suzanne Franzway, Dianne Court, and R.W. Connell, *Staking a Claim: Feminism, Bureaucracy, and the State* (Sydney 1989), p. 10.

23. Ibid., pp. 6, 7.

24. Ibid., p. 9.

25. Sen, *India's Bandit Queen*, p. 216.

26. Ibid.

27. Ibid., pp. 212–13.

28. Ibid., p. 215.

29. Punam Thakur, 'Bandit Screen', *Sunday*, 26 March–1 April 1995, p. 69.

30. Judith Butler, *Gender Trouble: Feminism and Subversion of Identity* (New York 1990), pp. 136–7.

31. Gayatri Spivak, *A Critique of Postcolonial Reason: Toward a History of the Vanishing Present* (Cambridge 1999), p. 309.

32. Pranab Bardhan, 'The State against Society: The Great Divide in Indian Social Science Discourse' in Sugata Bose and Ayesha Jalal (eds), *Nationalism, Democracy, and Development: State and Politics in India* (New Delhi 1997), p. 190.

13

Death of a Kotwal

The Injurious Politics of Recognition*

Anupama Rao

On 17 August 1991, Ambadas Sawane, a kotwal in the village of Pimpri-Deshmukh in Parbhani district, Maharashtra, was bludgeoned to death on the steps of a Hanuman temple. Police, party and state government functionaries, and village locals produced contentious and often conflicting interpretations of the murder. All had one point in common: everyone agreed Sawane was killed because he was a Dalit. The brutality of the murder and its symbolic resonance with earlier instances of *mandir pravesh* (temple-entry) generated a great deal of publicity. Sawane's murder was also the first case in Maharashtra to be judged under the Prevention of Atrocities Against Scheduled Castes and Scheduled Tribes Act of 1989 (hereafter POA Act), which prescribes stringent punishment for caste violence.

In his judgement, delivered at the Parbhani sessions court, Justice Adharkar held that Sawane was the victim of a caste crime, but he attributed the cause not to Sawane's 'desecration' of the Hanuman temple, but to his efforts to install an Ambedkar statue in the village.[1]

* This is a shortened version of the essay, 'Death of a Kotwal: The Injurious Politics of Recognition', in Shail Mayaram, M.S.S. Pandian, and Ajay Skaria (eds), *Subaltern Studies XII: Muslims, Dalits and the Fabrications of History* (Delhi: Permanent Black and Ravi Dayal Publisher, 2005), pp. 140–87.

However, of ten accused, Adharkar only found five individuals guilty of bludgeoning Sawane to death, and even they were let off lightly due to absence of 'intent' in committing the crime. Two of the accused were state functionaries: the police *patil* (village police), Kishore Marathe, was accused of inciting the violence, while the village *sarpanch* (village head), was accused of being negligent in his duties.

My analysis of caste atrocity encompasses two interlinked arguments. First, the failure of justice is not merely a problem of implementation, but derives from the production (and protection) of Dalit vulnerability through practices of legal exception.[2] Second, the atrocity-event does not place violence outside sociality and politics, but provides occasion for further politicization: the labour of law lies in objectifying social forms and categories that ground further acts of recognition. This essay examines how juridical assumptions about Dalit vulnerability are impacted by ongoing Dalit politicization as well as by perceptions regarding the Dalit body, which together unsettle the bureaucratization of caste civility.[3]

PUBLICITY, POLICE, AND POLITICAL VIOLENCE

From the start, Sawane's murder was folded into a milieu of increasingly confident Dalit political presence, on the one hand, and emergent protocols for managing caste crime, on the other. The contradictory assumptions of anti-atrocity legislation—to recognize anti-Dalit violence as the result of a prejudice so deep it structures everyday social relations, but to disarticulate embedded violence by simply redefining some acts of caste sociality as crime—formed an additional layer of complexity. Under these conditions, police wireless records, because they operate under conditions of ostensible 'secrecy'—communication within the chain of command, response to government functionaries in Mumbai, and negotiations with political activists and the media—provide an important entry point for understanding the atrocity-event as a complexly ramified, *mediated* event.

The atrocity-event began with the discovery of Sawane lying in a pool of blood outside the Hanuman temple on the night of 16 August 1991. His brother, Kachru, took Ambadas to the police outpost at Tadkalas by bullock cart. From here, he was taken to the primary health centre, and then to Parbhani's Civil Hospital, where he expired.

Sub-Divisional Police Officer (SDPO) Gopalshetty, and Police Sub-Inspector (PSI) Kolhapurkar began the investigation after Sawane's brother, Kachru, filed a first information report.[4] Sawane's death was recorded by the PSI under Section 302 (attempt to murder), and linked with Section 3(x) of the Protection of Civil Rights Act (PCRA) of 1976. Mention of PCRA Section 3(x) signalled that the case merited attention as caste crime. However, the case was not registered under the POA Act, which defines (caste) atrocity and provides extraordinary protection to Dalit victims, including by requiring the accused to prove their innocence.

Gopalshetty and Kolhapurkar also sabotaged the investigation by withholding crucial local knowledge. In a public statement to the press, Gopalshetty had purposefully downplayed the over-determined symbology of Dalit homicide on the temple steps. A police wireless of 19 August noted:

> 7. SDPO from Sailu, S.B. Gopalshetty visited the offence. After visit Gopalshetty saw me, and told me that the incident was not an outcome of casteism but it took place all of a sudden. *Gopalshetty also issued a press release which states that he met the witnesses, majority of whom were from Hindu community and that according to them, the incident took place all of a sudden and there is no communal past history to the village.* [author's emphasis] …
>
> 8. I feel that … [the SDPO] did hurry in issuing the press note which was contrary to the very contents of the FIR and also to the facts subsequently revealed during investigation. It was because of this press note that the Department and also the Govt. of Maharashtra were put in embarrassing position. Not only this, but it resulted in unnecessary criticism by press and various political leaders that the police was partial and hiding the truth.[5]

From a bare read of the press note, it would be seen that the contents of paragraph one indicate that the incident of assault/murder took place due to temple-entry by a Mahar, that is, Dalit, whereas paragraph 2 of the note speaks out an altogether different story that the incident took place all of a sudden due to misunderstanding …

Gopalshetty justified his behaviour to his superior, the superintendent of police (SP) in Aurangabad by arguing that he was interested in maintaining fragile social relations. Ironically, it is this problematic public statement that drew unwelcome attention to the police cover-up of caste crime. The news-reading public would have neither missed Sawane's Dalit identity, nor the bizarre circumstances of his death. Added to this was revelation of complicity between the police and a key accused, the police patil, Kishore Marathe, which emerged in the course of the investigation.

Witnesses told SDPO Parab, who replaced Gopalshetty at the end of August, that the police patil, Kishore Marathe, had incited the villagers to kill Ambadas. According to witnesses, Marathe remained near Ambadas and refused to send for help once he was badly wounded. Sawane's father said that when he asked the patil for help, Marathe had sneered, 'Why don't *you* take him home?' Sawane's father also gave evidence that Sawane had told him, 'They have killed me, Bapu,' and revealed the names of his killers, including the police patil.[6] Interestingly, Sawane himself had been a low-level village functionary. In Maharashtra, kotwals have been drawn from the Mahar community, adding to their ritual function as *veskar*s, who protect village boundaries, by reporting to the police patil and sarpanch. The fact that the police patil was implicated in Sawane's murder, and that he had used his position to protect himself from prosecution raised some questions.[7] Why did the patil have such animus against him? More significantly, how did such deeply consequential lapses by the local police come to light at all?

As we shall see, Sawane's murder was framed by internal conflict between government officers and an external battle of publicity. The local police stationed at the police outpost, Tadkalas, reported to the SP, Aurangabad. However, caste and gender crimes were also monitored by the Protection of Civil Rights (PCR) Cell formed in 1988, headed by the Deputy Inspector General of Police (DIGP) who sits at the Maharashtra State Police Headquarters, in Mumbai. Sawane's homicide was monitored by the PCR in Bombay as the local investigation proceeded. On 28 August, the DIGP sent a wireless to the SP, Aurangabad, noting:

One Kachru Sahebarao Sawane, brother of the deceased, was brought by Vivek Pandit [an activist] who says that the Police Patil of the village is the main accused in this case but is not shown as the accused. Similarly the harijans were not allowed to enter the said temple.[8]

The DIGP–PCR's note indicated a diverse and diffuse field of publicity adjacent to the police chain of command.[9] There was a complex circuitry of debate, exchange, and compromise among different departments of the state and national government, and contingent responses to external political pressures. Mumbai headquarters was under surveillance by the Maharashtra State Government's Home Department, media, political activists, party leaders, government functionaries such as those from the National Commission of SC/ST, and the state and central government's social welfare ministry, by members of the legislative assembly, and NGOs. Local police might have reacted to conditions on the ground, including their own social locations within local economies of caste. But they were compromised by the work of activists and local political leaders who could unsettle this enclosed world of police investigation. Differentiated responses by the Mumbai and local police illuminate the multiple investments which organized the police hierarchy, beginning with the contentious characterization of Sawane's murder.

Central to bureaucratic debate amongst state functionaries and their response to external political pressure was the field of publicity. Police wireless reports were a crucial conduit. Their status as confidential communication offers us entry into the conflictual workings of the state apparatus and access to the politicized nature of bureaucratic knowledge. Together and separately, directives from police superiors and communication from the local police illuminate 'new' demands on the police to make caste crime visible. These transactions show how procedural discussions either foregrounded or avoided caste, depending on political pressures upon the police. Insofar as wireless reports negotiated this wider socius, they make it apparent that the outcomes of state intervention were contingent products of debate and negotiation between the apparatus of the state with divergent, often contradictory, interests.

Even though the police wireless was constituted as a form of secret communication internal to the police, the information transmitted through these channels was susceptible to journalistic publicity, rumour, and political activism. Indeed such alternative practices of localization enabled police to frame their explanation of Sawane's murder around sexual enmity,[10] his political activism, and the fact of temple entry. For example, SDPO Parab noted:

> 4. [...] Dalits in the village even now do not enter the temple. If they want to worship or to take 'Darshan' they offer it from the footsteps of the temple from the outside. It was raining in the village on the fatal night. Kotwal Ambadas according to the F.I.R lodged by his brother Kachru Sahebrao Sawane at P.S. Tadkalas on August 17 at 0700 hours was taking round as per the directions of Police Patil Kishore Marathe. When he reached in front of temple, he had to take shelter from rains inside the temple. Since he entered the sanctum of the temple the people gathered there for singing 'Bhajan' got annoyed ...
>
> ...
>
> [Kachru, hearing his brother's cries at the Hanuman temple]... rushed there and saw aforesaid persons attacking Ambadas with lathis [thick wooden staffs] and stones. Out of fear they ran towards their house and informed of the incident to the father ... [they] went to the spot and found Ambadas lying unconscious in a pool of blood near footsteps of the temple.
>
> ...
>
> It may be mentioned that the accused were saying that Ambadas Mahar entered into their temple and hence they were beating.[11]

This wireless report highlights Sawane's entry as a transgressive act: '[S]ince he entered the sanctum of the temple the people ... got annoyed.' It also offered an upper-caste villagers' perspective on why violence ensued: 'Ambadas Mahar entered into their temple hence they were beating.' Finally, the report drew attention to local caste etiquette that called for Dalits to worship 'from the footsteps of the temple from the outside'.

Where the Parbani wireless relates Sawane's murder with ritual observance of untouchability, the Mumbai PCR cell consistently demanded a more political explanation. Officials in Mumbai, at the top of the chain of command, would re-interpret 'local' information to conclude that Sawane's death was a caste crime.[12] In this they were aided by newspaper reports of long-standing conflict in the village generated by Sawane's desire to install an Ambedkar statue in the village, and those who resisted.[13]

As wireless communication between Mumbai and Aurangabad accelerated, pressure on the police investigation in Parbhani also increased: what was the true cause of Sawane's murder? The response to a report of 30 August 1991, entitled 'Incident of murder of a kotwal belonging to a backward community in Parbhani District', sent to the additional chief secretary of the home department, state of Maharashtra, by the additional director general of police (law and order) elicited a harsh response. In a series of handwritten notes on the margin of this report, the home department commented:

(1) Press note seems to have been clumsily prepared, and contains material that need not have been there.
(2) No indication whether deceased had taken a leading part in installation of Ambedkar bust and whether this was resented by caste Hindus.
(3) Whether such resentment manifested into altercations, or otherwise generated tension.
(4) Were office bearers like sarpanch, police patil, etc. involved?
(5) When was village last visited and didn't police official come to know of differences/tensions?
(6) SP's comment that the incident blew up after 10 days—apparently there was some whispering campaign from both sides.[14]

Like the newspaper reports castigating police mishandling of the case, this home department memo changed the course of the inquiry. It counterposed Ambadas's death on the steps of the temple against accounts of his political activism. Sawane's attempt to install an Ambedkar statue in the village became a crucial piece of information that rendered Sawane's murder legible as an act of symbolic–political violence. Thus, even as local enmity and political corruption were focalized, politicized publicity helped disembed Sawane's murder from locality.

The national commissioner of scheduled castes and scheduled tribes, Ram Dhan, was the person most responsible for associating atrocity with political violence. He wrote to Chief Minister Sudhakarrao Naik about a visit he had made to Pimpri Deshmukh on 3 September noting:

> A sensational news item appeared in the *Times of India* dated 28.8.91 to the effect that a Scheduled Caste (Mahar) Police Kotwal of village Pimpri-Deshmukh in Parbhani district was stoned to death by upper-caste residents on 16.8.91 for standing on the steps of a Hanuman temple in the village. That such an incident should have taken place in the year of the birth centenary of Dr Babasaheb Ambedkar is a matter of extreme shame to the Indian society.[15]

Ram Dhan associated Ambadas's murder on the Hanuman temple steps with Ambadas's position as 'a young and upcoming leader of the Mahars',[16] and argued that Ambadas was murdered for trying to install an Ambedkar statue in the village.

Newspapers picked up on this association between political militancy and the symbolic charge of Sawane's murder on the temple steps. The *Indian Express* reported that caste Hindus had stopped a procession celebrating Ambedkar's birthday on 14 April, and noted that the sarpanch had prevented Ambadas from installing an Ambedkar statue in the village even after he had collected money for the statue.[17] Political parties got involved. The BJP led a delegation to the chief minister's office to press him to visit the village, while the Republican Party of India (Athavale) staged a demonstration in front of the district collectorate in early September.

If the state government consistently downplayed the Ambedkar statue matter, Ram Dhan worked to publicize the murder as a caste atrocity framed as retribution for the Dalits' political self-representation. Ram Dhan's report emphasized the geography of violence and the contest over public space. Arguing that Ambadas's murder had been preceded by a struggle over the social signification of space, he suggested that efforts to claim 'public' space had invited retributive violence and reproduced the spatial segregation that defined untouchability. Ram Dhan also historicized these tensions by asserting that the public commemoration of Ambedkar had become symbolically potent since the *namaantar* agitation.[18] Thus Ram Dhan's report provided a *political* explanation of the atrocity-event, connecting this discrete instance of caste crime with a more generalized upper-caste resentment of the Dalits' militancy.

By then, Sawane's murder had assumed national proportions. The Lok Sabha discussed the issue of atrocities against the scheduled castes and scheduled tribes on 19 August 1991, well before news of Sawane's homicide reached the press.[19] On 31 September, the prime minister wrote to all chief ministers, requesting them to monitor atrocities' cases.[20] The Committee on the Welfare of the Scheduled Castes and Scheduled Tribes noted 'an astounding increase in the number of crimes committed against Scheduled Castes and Scheduled Tribes even after the implementation of the POA Act,' and added that the stringent punishments of the Act encouraged greater cover-up through collusion between state functionaries and upper-caste leaders. The central and state governments were now responsible for addressing how a deterrent measure, the POA Act, was contributing to caste violence. The DIGP–PCR noted the national concern over caste atrocities in a note to the SDPO from Parbhani, on 2 September:

> You are aware that DIGP PCR is looking after this subject and is required to send reports to State Government as well as Central government. It is very disappointing that you failed to send a report to me till it was discussed in the Parliament though you had sent your report to other officials. Explain your failure. All Unit Commanders are again requested to keep this in mind and must endorse copy of their wireless message and reports whenever atrocities are committed on SC/STs. Similar section of PAA must repeat must be applied wherever necessary.[21]

As the state government became involved in Sawane's murder and the case became a state and nationwide scandal, 'locality' also attained new significance. On 3 September 1991, the *Maharashtra Times* and the *Times of India* carried news about the persistence of untouchability in Marathwada's villages. Rajdeep Sardesai noted in the latter that an NGO based in Vasai and the Nirmala Niketan School of Social Work, Mumbai, had conducted a survey between 6 and 26 May 1991. The survey found that over 80 per cent of Dalits did not have the right to enter temples in Marathwada, that they were barred from common water sources, performed defiling labour, and faced political discrimination.[22] Another *Times of India* report (3 September) noted negligence by government functionaries, but focused on the anti-Dalit, anti-Muslim sentiments of Shiv Sena supporters, a majority in the village.[23]

In effect, governmental agencies used journalistic coverage about the atrocity to put pressure on local officials, and it worked![24] A beleaguered note of 19 September from Parbhani, to the Protection of Civil Rights Cell in Aurangabad, acknowledged the scandalous publicity around Sawane's murder:

> The incidence of murder of a Mahar kotwal Ambadas Sawane by caste Hindus at village Pimpri in Parbhani Districton 16-8-91 has attracted huge press publicity and also visits by various V.I.P.s including Social Welfare Minister Ramdas Athwale, Parbhani District Minister Shri Madhukarrao Ghate, Hon. Chief Minister of Maharashtra and Shri Ramdhan, Chairman SC/ST, Government of India, New Delhi followed by the visits of different political parties and social delegations led by Dalit Panther, B.J.P., S.K.P., Shiv Sena, Human Rights Association, 'Rachnatmak Sangarsh Samiti', etc. to the village. I was also present for supervising bandobast and security arrangements. *The press, state associations and even Parliament had brought the village under scrutiny over the above incident.* [Author's emphasis][25]

As the police investigation reacted to, and was framed by publicity, interpretations of Sawane's murder began to coalesce around two perspectives: the first understood Sawane's murder as the consequence of temple-entry, while the second focused on Sawane's efforts to install the Ambedkar statue. Overlaying these interpretations was local political commonsense, which understood that caste relations had altered drastically with the rise of the Shiv Sena in Marathwada.

PRONOUNCEMENT: LEGAL STRUCTURES OF RECOGNITION

The transformation of the raw intelligence gathered by the police into the repetitive structure of the wireless report illuminates how governmental knowledge is vulnerable to (and constituted by) internal and external mechanisms of surveillance, the media, local activists, upper echelons of the police bureaucracy, and state and party functionaries:

police procedure and bureaucratic hierarchies articulated with forms of critical publicity in interpreting Sawane's murder as caste crime. As second order mediation, the jurisprudence of atrocity is implicated in, yet diverges from police knowledge. This section explores the relationship between law and politics, as well as the relative autonomy of the force of law.[26]

In adjudicating Sawane's murder, normalizing judicial–legislative frameworks of the postcolonial state were pressed to recognize a distinct form of subalternity, Dalitness, to redefine Dalit and upper-caste identities as those of victim and perpetrator. The language in which state, policing bureaucracy, and the judge interpreted Sawane's death made it difficult for them to apprehend symbolic–political violence, however. It is precisely this split between recognition of the 'political' ramifications of Sawane's murder, itself the consequence of scandalous publicity, and the impossibility of justice, that was staged in the courtroom. Herein lay the second scandal of Sawane's murder: the depoliticization of the politics of anti-Dalit violence.

The special judge, V.B. Adharkar, passed judgement on Special Case No. 11/91 in the Parbhani sessions court on 18 June 1992.[27] While Adharkar was aware of the symbology of Dalit murder, it is fair to say that he was constrained by laws which assume untouchability as the cause of caste crime, while requiring that judges follow standard judicial procedure in bringing atrocities cases to closure. The way that 'untouchability' was discursively deployed in the courtroom split the recognition of caste atrocity from its possible redress. This bifurcation was evident in Adharkar's judgement, where a history of caste tensions in Pimpri-Deshmukh was disconnected from his reading of intent to murder. This separated aspects of the case that were integrally related to each other.

Adharkar's opened his judgement by describing the social geography of the village, where space was correlated with (caste) power:

As per ancient custom the untouchables reside in a separate Wasti outside the village at a distance of 300 feet towards the North side. The said Wasti was previously known as Maharwada and now as Boudhwada. For the sake of convenience it is referred to as Maharwada. There is a way from the village to the Maharwada running East-West.

The Maharwada is the north side of the road and a house of ... a caste
Hindu (Mali) is to the South of the road. The untouchables decided to
install a statue of Dr. Babasaheb Ambedkar near the house of the said
[Hindu] (3) ...

Later the judge noted that '[t]he said site is not in the Maharwada
but in the village.' (6) Adharkar was in no doubt that the installation
of the Ambedkar statue posed a powerful challenge to the symbolic
division of the village into caste Hindu and Dalit. The sarpanch and
the police patil had opposed the installation of the statue and threatened Ambadas with dire consequences. A group of villagers had as
well tried to bribe the Dalits with 500 rupees if they installed the
Ambedkar statue in the Maharwada. Adharkar thus drew attention
to the (re)signification of space through contending acts of political
commemoration.

Adharkar contrasted the Ambedkar statue with the political geography of the temple, as sacred public space, noting, 'The untouchables
were prohibited from making entry into the temple on the ground
of untouchability. In this way untouchability was observed in the village.' The judge went on to note these spatial exclusions: the upper
castes had denied Sawane entry into the Maruti temple because he
was a Dalit, they had insulted him by calling him *Mahardya*, and they
had assaulted him *on the steps of the temple*. Indeed when asked why
Ambadas was being beaten, the crowd outside the temple is supposed
to have said, 'The temple has been dis-sacred! In our temple Ambadas
Mahar had come and therefore we have been beating him.'[28]

The use of the insulting term, *Mahardya*, is significant, since the
POA Act considers a caste insult to be a psychic wound, approaching the severity of physical assault. When the public prosecutor
emphasized that an insult was a caste crime, the defence had resorted
to an ingenious argument, noting: 'Because the villagers knew that
Ambadas was Mahar by caste, [whether] such person was referred
to as ... "Mahar Ambadas" or only "Ambadas" has no meaning at all.'
In essence, the defence argued that because Ambadas was known to
be a Dalit, verbal confirmation of his identity should not constitute a
criminal act.

Adharkar countered that the substance of the testimony associated Ambadas's caste identity with the desecration of the temple.
Importantly, Adharkar was distinguishing two forms of phenomenal
violence: new violent caste sociality displayed in conflict around the
Ambedkar statue *and* retaliatory counter-violence that reinstated the
Dalits' stigmatized status. In other words, the struggle over installing
the Ambedkar statue had generated counter-violence, which replicat-
ed apparently archaic forms of caste sociality. Adharkar understood
Sawane's murder on the temple steps—and the upper-castes' maintenance of the temple's purity—as a form of retaliatory violence, which
reasserted caste privilege in the face of Dalit militancy.

Though he took the caste insult seriously as a prelude to violence,
Adharkar adjudicated the case by sticking to a narrow interpretation
of intent. Adharkar noted that the villagers had clearly meant to protect the temple from pollution, but that the violence that ensued was
spontaneous. In an earlier instance, during 1985 or 1986, when Dalit
boys who had come to attend a wedding in Pimpri-Deshmukh had
entered the Hanuman temple, they had not been murdered. Temple-
entry was not sufficient cause for murder. Further, the presence of a
crowd made it difficult to find Ambadas's assailant. Adharkar noted,
'[T]he sum and substance of the evidence is that deceased Ambadas
sustained one fatal injury resulting in death but it could not [be]
attributed to a particular accused person in this case.' Though atrocity
legislation was predicated on the collective nature of caste violence,
mob action made it impossible to find the perpetrator. He went further by disregarding evidence of the police patil's involvement in the
crime, since he was not named in the original FIR.

Adharkar's seemingly schizophrenic judgement, at once acknowledging and refusing to include evidence of conflict around the
political symbology of Dalit identity—whether the effort to install an
Ambedkar statue or being killed on the steps of a temple—is exceedingly odd. It is a perversion of justice if we recall that the Prevention
of Atrocities Act explicitly names and describes acts of atrocity—from
humiliation, to economic terror, to ritualized violence. At one level,
perhaps the judge's deliberate and extended search for motive was a
disingenuous response to the enormous publicity around Sawane's

murder. What is more significant is the turn to *mens re* in a case where atrocities' legislation assumes the social fact of Dalit identity as producing vulnerability to violence. In this, Adharkar was enabled by the paradox of atrocities legislation, which acknowledges collective violence and simultaneously individuates it. On the one hand, *all crimes* against Dalits were assumed to be acts of *anti-Dalit violence*. However, the adjudication of caste crime made no *procedural* accommodation for the enmity and mutual fear that was assumed—by atrocities' legislation itself, in fact—as governing everyday sociality between Dalits and caste Hindus. Judgements in atrocity cases, therefore, gave judges great leeway in reproducing precisely the kind of impasse we see in the adjudication of Sawane's murder. The impossibility of justice was built into the model of legal redress.

POLITICS, SYMBOLIC FORM, SACRIFICE, AND COMMEMORATION

A crucial point of entry into the atrocity-event is the performative context from which 'atrocity' gains its intense symbolic charge. And here, Sawane's murder throws into relief a problematic permeability between violent acts that *reproduce* stigmatized existence and violent acts that *prevent* social and political advancement. The double valence of violence derives in part from the specific trajectories of the 'becoming political' of the Dalit subject. Structures of everyday life are politicized as a consequence of creating a new identity for the collective Dalit self through the accelerated symbolization of *Dalit* forms, such as statues of Ambedkar. However, anti-Dalit violence is also enmeshed in a cultural matrix, a set of symbolic codes that devalue *Dalit* bodies. We can neither understand its specificity nor its peculiar intimacy, without considering the semiotic site of political subject-formation. The violent reciprocity between Sawane's involvement with an Ambedkar statue and his murder on the steps of a temple, present caste violence as the doubled effect of the ritual-archaic and the political. Or, we might say that the logic of sacrifice and practices of political commemoration are inter-animated, and that the atrocity-event—because it is a response to the ways in which Dalits have resignified symbolic forms with political charge—becomes that place where we can see them both at work in Dalit subject-formation.

The ritually charged *ves*, the space demarcating the village from the public world, joins the Mahar sub-caste to the task of guarding the village boundary. Living outside the village boundaries, the Mahar *veskar* is the outsider figure, who protects and secures the territory from which he is banished. As kotwal, Ambadas Sawane was vested with responsibility for a modern variant of this practice, calling up symbolic associations between the Mahar's body and the consecrated physical space. For instance, in the medieval Deccan, human sacrifice—often of a Mahar—was a crucial trope through which land grants and *vatandari* rights and patrimonies were either legitimized or challenged. Often, the Mahar was a surrogate for those of higher-caste status or military rank whose claims to sovereignty were understood to be incomplete without human sacrifice to strengthen acts of military incorporation. Mahars were often sacrificed at the foundation of forts or buildings wrested from enemy control in order to appease the gods with an offering imbued with a 'dark polluting magic', though the benefits accrued to the person on whose behalf the Mahar was sacrificed.[29]

The organization of the medieval polity around this victim-figure also became the ground for Mahars' claims to future vatandari rights and duties. These were livelihood claims to maintenance and the right to life, if you will, that positioned Dalits within an old regime *habitus* characterized by performances of distinguishing, demeaning, and subsuming the self that carried across a variety of contexts, from worship to kingship. Sumit Guha relates the case of eighteenth-century Civhe Kolis who advanced claims to vatandari rights to a fort based on a copper-plate inscription from 587 mentioning a Mahar sacrifice. A Mahar surrogate, 'Nathnak, son of Bahirnak Sonnak and Devakai, wife of Nathnak, were buried in the foundations of the tower. Only then could the tower be successfully completed.'[30] Another Mahar claim from 1746–7 noted rival claims to vatandari rights, resurrecting the trope of burial in the foundation of a building or tower. The father of the claimant, one Ramnak, was supposed to have been buried in the 'the Sarja tower … [where] the masonry marker still exists. I am his son.'[31] There are two sides to this act: one is a sacrifice, while the other is a power to claim vatandari rights enabled by a Mahar's burial within a foundational structure. *Both signal the role of the Mahar as a surrogate emissary who transfers impurities from a place or territory through the violent expulsion of sacrificial death*: something is created through the sacrifice of the Mahar body.

This sacrificial logic returns in the Mahars' origin story of the fifty-two *vatandar*'s rights. In an account of Amrutnak from the 1920s, he was said to have castrated himself so that he could escort his queen to safety without imputation of sexual misbehaviour. This was the origin of the charter of the fifty-two rights of the village Mahars, including the guarding of the ves.[32] Both sacrifice and sexuality were connected in Mahar histories of their status as virile protectors; they had virile power *because* they were also sacrificial victims.

Rene Girard's influential discussion describes sacrifice as the ritual-ization of violence. The centrality of sacrifice derives from its status as an act of excessive symbolization that transforms a mimetic doubling of violence into a condensed, singular act. Though the sacrificial act gains salience through its connection to broader contexts of violent enactment, it also transcends them to become a mythic origin point, the pre-history of society or a people, for instance.[33] As Allen Feldman has noted, '[T]he central political problematic of violent reciprocity is the thin membrane of division, reversibility, and doubling that both divides and conflates "legitimate" and "illegitimate" violence.'[34] This describes the Maratha social–political formation perfectly: as Stewart Gordon has argued, here was an emergent polity defined by guer-rilla warfare and the constant transformation of outlaws—including Shivaji himself—into kings.

It is precisely under conditions where the legitimacy of violent acts of expropriation, such as taking a fort by force, had to be retroactively asserted that the 'necessity' for ritual violence, violence placed *outside* the space–time of everyday or political violence, was most pressing. As Feldman notes, 'The search for legitimacy through the search for nonmimetic practice resolves into a new *cultural construction of vio-lence*' (author's emphasis).[36] I would extend this to note that the ritual reconstruction of violence also requires a culturally coded sacrificial victim, the Mahar, who personifies the community's pollution and must therefore be cast out. Sacrifice, like the 'contract' of political theory, *produces* society. In turn society, like caste itself, is organized around an excluded negativity, an abandoned or absent figure—in this case, the Mahar.

The symbolic import of Sawane's murder on the steps of a temple was lost on no one, from the policemen who conducted the initial inquiry to Judge Adharkar. There is a clear formal resemblance between the logic of sacrifice and the murder on the temple steps. Yet the epochal socio-political changes that temporally separated the two sacrificial acts also distorted the aura of sacrality attached to contemporary sacrifice. The sacrifice of a Mahar at the foot of a military fortification was once a ritual act, while the 1991 murder of a Dalit on the steps of a temple was a criminal act. Whereas in the first case, political legitimacy required a sacrificial act, in the second case, a criminal act acquired *symbolic* salience because a Dalit was murdered on the temple steps. In both instances, however, ill-defined boundaries between religious and political space were clarified *through violation of the Dalit's body*. The boundary-enforcing function of the Mahar veskar was intimately tied to this creation of boundaries through the Mahar's physical body.

The archaic imaginary is necessarily limited; it works through repetition and formal resemblance. Sawane's murder on the steps of the temple carried a symbolic charge from the resuscitation of symbolic forms still active in popular memory. These range from the medieval production of an authoritative subaltern history through the narrative signature of Mahar sacrifice, to a twentieth-century Dalit counter-history commemorating Amrutnak's sacrifice.

Although Sawane's murder on the temple steps resonates with the logic of sacrifice, it does not exhaustively define the atrocity-event. The apparent continuities with archaic practice are formal, for Sawane's murder followed from his participation in a project seen as politically militant, namely, commemorating the new Dalit collectivity through the installation of an Ambedkar statue. Since the namaantar movement, many Dalit struggles revolved around new acts of boundary making and destruction, from Dalits' encroachment on to *gayraan zamin* (common grazing land) to the visual icons of B.R. Ambedkar, J. Phule, and E.V. Ramasamy Periyar that began to dot urban and rural landscapes throughout India during the 1990s. Indeed by the

late 1990s, the north Indian state of Uttar Pradesh, under Bahujan
Samaj Party (BSP) leadership, took the lead in such acts of political
commemoration. In 1997 alone, 15,000 statues of Ambedkar were
installed across that state, provoking widespread conflict with caste
Hindus who saw this as a challenge to their hegemony, just as Dalits
on the gayraan zamin brought conflict with a Shiv Sena that had
grown significantly in Marathwada since 1985.

What was the symbolic significance of erecting an Ambedkar
statue and where did the power of its desecration lie? The journalist P.
Sainath has observed, 'Currently, there are more Ambedkar statues in
India's villages than any other leader. His statues are not government
installed—unlike those of the others. The poor put them up at their
own expense.'[37] Ambedkar statues are installed at the cost of the poor
and impoverished. In turn, statue defilements are acts of symbolic
annihilation. Violence to and around the statue links Ambedkar's
symbolization as the origin-point of Dalit history with caste Hindus'
perception of the proliferation of Ambedkar images as acts of sacral-
ization.[38] The particular mode of desecration is significant. Political
desecration of religious icons goes back to the 1920s and 1930s, when
Satyashodak and non-Brahman activists occasionally garlanded
Hindu deities with slippers, though this practice was more common
amongst self-respecters in the south. This turned an act of veneration, garlanding the deity, into an act of desecration through the use
of a defiled object, the slipper made from leather, a defiling substance.
Such garlanding signalled active repugnance toward caste hierarchy
and religious superstition, on par with burning Hindu scriptures and
abusing Hindu gods and goddesses. (This idiom of public desecration has since expanded to include shaming politicians by garlanding
them with slippers, a transliteration from ritual to political registers.)

Erecting an Ambedkar statue imitates acts venerating representations of religious and political figures: but there is a difference.
The proliferation of Ambedkar statues is a claim to space within a
representational economy saturated by deified nationalist icons commemorated by the state, as Sainath notes above. Commodified images
of Ambedkar such as calendars, posters, buttons, and so forth depict
his life in the style of Puranic narratives, where the god's life is told
through a series of ideal–typical events and encounters. There are also

collages of Ambedkar's photographs across time, in which he increasingly resembles the Buddha. The most common three-dimensional representations of Ambedkar, however, portray him in a militant upright pose, dressed in a recognizable blue suit and red tie, holding the Constitution in his left hand, his right arm outstretched to make a point. In this representation, Ambedkar's role as a crucial public figure for independent India merges with his signal importance in producing a new history for the Dalit community and self. On display here is not only his singular individuality, the agentive power of self-determination to remake the Dalit self and thus challenge the social invisibility and humiliation of that community, but also the strong visual connection of Amebedkar to the Constitution of the Indian polity itself.

What I am arguing is that the fact of a Dalit figure at the centre of symbolic exchange does not assume a shared understanding of what the figure means. The desecration of Ambedkar statues by non-Dalits is predicated on assuming a structure of equivalence between Ambedkar and religious icons and symbols. As Dalits experiment with a new regime of signification, their acts and aspirations run the risk of being misrecognized as acts of deification precisely because some idioms of performance resemble acts of veneration. This is ironic because Dalits associate Ambedkar with *refusal* of the representational practices and ideological structures that define caste Hinduism. We must ask whether a political statue imbued with affective charge becomes a 'sacred' object or whether we can find other ways to describe acts of political commemoration that seek to resignify Dalits' resistantance to the cultural and ideational practices of the Hindu order. It is entirely possible to read the response to the desecration of Ambedkar statues not merely as a reaction to defilement but also, and more strongly, as a response to Hindu society's persistent refusal to recognize and respect the acts of symbolization through which Dalit identity is constituted, an enraged response to acts of desymbolization that annihilate (Dalits') individual and community political identity.

In Pimpri-Deshmukh today, there is a bust of Ambadas Sawane next to a statue of Ambedkar. His inclusion within a recognizable tradition of political iconography created a political biography for Sawane: his murder was commemorated as an act of martyrdom.

Sawane's inclusion within this iconography suggests the capacity of semiotic technologies to expand an existing representational field by imputing contiguity between political figures and symbols. The sad irony, of course, is that Sawane's commemoration comes as the result of his own failed attempts to install an Ambedkar statue in Pimpri–Deshmukh.

AFTER ATROCITY: VIOLENCE AND EVERYDAY LIFE

'Atrocity' names legal–bureaucratic forms of protection that have produced new sites of conflict *and* new possibilities for Dalit emancipation. The interpellation of the Dalit subject into regimes of state recognition publicizes anti-Dalit violence *as atrocity* and, in so doing, challenges the postcolonial state's discourses of social welfare and protection. As we have seen, atrocities' legislation is not merely prophylactic. Rather, by embedding agents and social practice in new frames, legal discourse also transforms the perceptual field around categories such as 'untouchability' and identities such as 'Dalit' or 'caste Hindu', provoking new forms of social engagement and interaction. The regulatory–symbolic function of law also allows law to function as a particularly potent form of publicity that creates the exception, the 'case', out of the practices of everyday life. When invisible forms of everyday violence—invisible because they are a structuring violence—are rendered spectacular, as during Sawane's murder, new political struggles organize around the way violence affects the political context.

Political violence unsettles symbolic forms and challenges the deep structure of the caste Hindu order. The resilience of everyday practices of stigmatization, however, also conditions the Dalits' continued quest for social justice and dignity. Sawane's political assertion intensified the field of caste antagonism along the registers of the ritual–archaic and the political. These antagonisms are heightened by legal structures of recognition that emphasize the agonistic nature of caste interaction between victim and perpetrator, violator and violated, often making the Dalits vulnerable to further violence. Rather than a cessation of anti-Dalit violence, efforts to legislate Dalit vulnerability out of existence have instead helped to establish violence as a public mode of recognition between upper castes and the Dalits. The repertoires and targets of violence may be transformed but violent acts responding to new forms of Dalit militancy tend to simultaneously deepen existing patterns of ritual violation and symbolic humiliation. How are we to understand this paradoxical aspect of Dalit emancipation?

A careful reading of the social life of the caste atrocity that was Sawane's murder implicates local state functionaries in the miscarriage of justice. It also implicates the caretaking efficacy of the postcolonial state insofar as legal redress—in this case, the adjudication of murder *as* a caste atrocity—itself re-encodes vulnerability as a crucial axis of Dalit existence. The bifurcation between a definition of caste crime as violence towards a vulnerable collective and adjudication of caste crime through an individuated structure of trial and punishment makes a just social order less possible, even as it becomes all the more urgent.

This is reflected in a further irony: as the targets of anti-Dalit violence become more clearly political—through acts and symbols related to Dalit demands for economic empowerment, education opportunities, jobs, rights to public space—repertoires of retributive violence coalesce around modalities that resonate with the structures through which stigmatization of Dalits has long operated. In the postcolonial period, commemorative political symbology—flags, statues, the namaantar movement, literary work—materially signifies the memory-work through which a new community identity emerges. As these acts of symbolization have drawn new objects and icons into an existing semiotic field, they have also provoked acts of desymbolization by both upper castes and policing functionaries through practices of defilement, dismemberment, and desecration. State functionary participation extends further into the deformation of accepted legal process itself, as we have seen in this chapter, with efforts to protect local officials, such as the patil and sarpanch, and the search for exact but unprovable individual motive.

Acts of symbolization and desymbolization have played a key role in the semiotic density and public salience the term 'Dalit' has acquired across the last century. The public violence of the Worli riots and the namaantar agitation during the 1970s, and the more intimate violence of caste atrocities offer points at which we can historicize the relationship between political violence and symbolic politics in their social and cultural specificity.

By analysing key transformations in Dalit politics through caste violence, we can observe accelerated practices of self-representation and spatialization not merely as a recount of political history, but equally in the semiotics of Dalit life. Is this really political? Yes, because the most powerful axis of Dalit political subject-formation has focused on remaking the caste self and the caste body—the experiential site of stigma—through acts of political re-signification. The demand for rights and social recognition that has defined the Dalit struggle still poses a fundamental challenge to the representational economy of caste Hinduism. Becoming 'Dalit' is the process through which the caste subaltern enters into circuits of political commensuration and the value regime of 'the human'. Because the name and the body and its experience are crucial sites of political subject-formation, political violence must also address this semiotic axis as a space of politics.

NOTES

1. Given the recent occurrence of this atrocity—it was up for appeal at the Aurangabad High Court in 1997, when the police wireless and case documents were procured—the names of individual policemen and the judge have been changed.

2. Giorgio Agamben and Carl Schmitt have each discussed the logic of exception as the practice of sovereignty that exceeds law. For Agamben, sovereignty is defined by the ability to place oneself outside the law. Schmitt's argument is contingently framed around crisis and political emergency, when law must be held in abeyance for the resurrection of political order. Giorgio Agamben, *Homo Sacer: Sovereign Power and Bare Life* (Stanford 1998); Carl Schmitt, *The Crisis of Parliamentary Democracy*, trans. Ellen Kennedy (Cambridge, MA 1988). I suggest that legal exceptionalism is a constitutive feature of colonial and postcolonial law—from legislation to control Thuggee, to racial regulation, and laws containing domestic violence and caste atrocities. For an argument about the colonial exception, see Pierce and Rao, 'Humanitarianism, Violence, and the Colonial Exception,' *Discipline and the Other Body*, 1–35.

3. For a discussion of how debates about the abolition of untouchability were conjoint with the production of laws to prevent caste crime in the period 1951–5, and an analysis of how Dalit identity was associated with vulnerability (to violence), see Anupama Rao, *The Caste Question: Dalits and the Politics of Modern India* (Berkeley, CA 2009), esp. Chapter 4, 'Legislating Caste Atrocity.'

4. A case proceeds as follows: 1) the FIR is filed and receives a CR (Crime Record) number; 2) the police categorize the account into the categories of A (where evidence has not been collected), B (registration of a false case), and C (no offense committed); 3) The charge sheet is filed; and 4) the case receives a CC (Court Case) number once it is sent to the court.

5. No. 5023/DSB/91, 19 August 1991. Superintendent of Police, Parbhani to the Deputy Inspector General of Police, Aurangabad.

6. 'Who Killed Ambadas Savne?' *Illustrated Weekly*, 14 September 1991.

7. In 'Suggestions for Effective Policing in Rural Areas', Onkar Sharma observed that *patils* and *kotwals* were decaying functions, falling prey to political machinations. He writes, 'The present set-up of the Village Police is only nominal and its utility nearly nil. This Village Police agency is not in a position to meet the policing requirements of the villages efficiently and satisfactorily.' Debates about the penetration of the police function into the village explicitly recognize policing as a political issue.

8. Vivek Pandit, *A Handbook on Prevention of Atrocities: Scheduled Castes and Scheduled Tribes* (1995). It was meant to aid activists in the intricacies of the POA Act. In his introduction, Pandit writes, 'On 16 August 1991, Ambadas Savane, a Dalit Kotwal of Pimpri-Deshmukh village in Parbhani district of Marathwada, was stoned to death by the upper castes for taking shelter in the temple premises during a heavy shower. I read a small news item in a local newspaper about this gruesome death. I was deeply affected, and fought for justice on his behalf. I could pursue the case using the SC/ST (Prevention of Atrocities) Act.'

9. The *Enforcement of Untouchability (Offences) Act 1955—A Survey* (1976), and the *Syndicate Study on Implementation of the Protection of Civil Rights* provide regional studies of the Act's effectiveness. The reports reflect the perspective of highly placed administrators who trained and sensitized police officers to respond to caste violence. Both reports offer sociological accounts of untouchability, and represent it as a social evil that has existed 'since time immemorial.'

10. This is also noted in Wireless No. 5023/DSB/91, sent from Parbhani to Dy-IGP, Aurangabad Range, on 19 September 1991.

11. Wireless No. 5023/DSB/91, 19 August 1991, Superintendent of Police, Parbhani to the Deputy Inspector General of Police, Aurangabad.

12. Wireless No. 4372/DSB/91, 19 August 1991.

13. A detailed report appeared of the Sawane murder in *Loksatta* on 28 August 1991, twelve days after the murder, which appears to have accelerated inquiries from Bombay.

14. No. PCR/M-6/Parbhani/91, 30 August 1991, from PCR Headquarters to Addt'l Chief Secretary, Govt. Maharashta. (Notes scribbled on letter.)

15. 'Report on the spot enquiry by Shri Ram Dhan, Chairman, National Commission SC/ST into the killing of a Scheduled Caste Village Police Kotwal in Village Pimpri Deshmukh, Taluka and District Parbhani (Maharashtra) on 16.8.91.'

16. Ibid.

17. Wireless No. 5023/DSB/91 of 19 September 1991, Parbhani to Dy-IGP, Aurangabad Range. It was alleged that Kachru did not mention the installation of the statue and the ensuing tension in his First Information Report, the supplementary information gathered on 30 August 1991, or in his deposition before the Judicial Magistrate First Class on 1 October 1991. These are not available with the court documents, so the allegation could not be verified.

18. 'Report on the spot enquiry by Shri Ram Dhan, Chairman, National Commission SC/ST into the killing of a Scheduled Caste Village Police Kotwal in Village Pimpri Deshmukh, Taluka and District Parbhani (Maharashtra) on 16.8.91.'

19. *Lok Sabha Debates*, vol. 3, 19–22 August 1991, pp. 225–94, 'Motion re. Atrocities Being Committed on the Scheduled Castes and Scheduled Tribes and Other Weaker Sections in the Country.' This debate took about four hours and considered issues ranging from the socio-economic weakness of SC/ST communities to arguments about the persistence of untouchability as a social practice to debates about making laws more stringent and effective. Besides the eclectic speaking styles of some members, what stands out most clearly is the range of 'evidence' they mobilized. It included stories from the Mahabharata about Eklavya's sacrifice of his thumb to illustrate the historic oppression of Dalits to invocations of Ambedkar and Gandhi's arguments against untouchability, social and political evidence of the failure to implement reservations effectively to the destitute conditions under which most SC/STs lived. Speakers consistently highlighted society's 'lack of resolve,' as one member put it.

20. Committee on The Welfare of Scheduled Castes and Scheduled Tribes, 'Tenth Lok Sabha Report on Atrocities on Scheduled Castes and Scheduled Tribes and Patterns of Social Crimes Towards Them,' (1992–3, p. 13). The Prime Minister also convened a meeting of Chief Ministers in October to discuss the atrocities issue.

21. Wireless No. PCR/M-6/Parbhani D/T 2-9-9.

22. The DIG-PCR dispatched special police officers to investigate untouchability in the villages mentioned in the *Maharashtra Times* and *TOI* reports. Wireless No. PCR/M-3/Aurangabad 91 D/T 6-9-91. The note was sent to all police stations in Marathwada (under the ranges of Beed, Latur, Nanded, Osmanabad, Parbhani); to the DIG of the Aurangabad Range; the DySP-PCR in Aurangabad, and the Special IGP (Crime, Pune).

23. *Times of India*, 3 September 1991.

24. Two reports of The Maharashtra State Government's *Anusuchit Jati Kalyan Samiti* (SC Welfare Committee) addressed Sawane's murder in their 1991–2 *Cautha Ahval* (Fourth Report) and 1995–6 *Pahila Ahval*. (First Report) The 1991–2 report noted that the Welfare Committee had conducted a survey of the Dalits (*magasvargiya*, backward class, is the literal term that is used) in Pimpri-Deshmukh on a 'war footing' (*yuddha patalivar*) in order to propose welfare schemes to build their confidence (*athmavishwas vadhavinyasathi*) in government. This report also noted that Ambadas and his brother Kachru had played an

important role in encouraging Muslim residents of Pimpri Deshmukh, who tried to flee the village after the Sena came to power, to remain. (p. 6)

25. No. 5023/DSB/91.

26. This enlarges upon Baxi's critique of the subaltern studies collective's failure to engage rigorously with the work of law. Upendra Baxi, "'The State's Emissary": The Place of Law in Subaltern Studies,' in *Subaltern Studies VII* (Delhi 1992), pp. 247–164.

27. Under the POA Act, the Sessions Court functions as a Special Court for hearing atrocities cases, the Sessions Judge acting as 'Special Judge' for this purpose.

28. The case judgment is in English. I surmise that the term used was *brasht*, polluted, or desecrated.

29. Sumit Guha, 'Recovering Subaltern History in Western India'. I am grateful to Professsor Guha for making this paper available to me and for e-mail exchanges (24–6 July 2007) that clarified some questions regarding Mahar ritual sacrifice. For an early critique of the practice of burying Mahars alive, see *Mahatma Phule Samagra Vangmay*, p. 160.

30. Ganesh Chimnaji Vad, *Selections from the Government Records in the Alienation Office Poona: Sanads and Letters*, ed. Purshotam Vishram and Parasnis Mawjee, D.B. (Poona 1913) pp. 7–8. Cited in Guha, p. 6.

31. *Sivacaritrasahitya Vol. 3*, ed. *Shankar Narayana and Khare Joshi, Ganesh Hari* (Pune 1930) pp. 197–8. Cited in Guha, pp. 14–15.

32. P.A. Gavli, *Pesvekalina Gulamgiri Va Asprisyata: Sammelana Vritta* (1913), p. 96.

33. Rene Girard, *The Scapegoat* (Baltimore 1986).

34. Allen Feldman, *Formations of Violence* (Chicago 1991), p. 258.

35. Ibid.

36. Sacrifice is distinctive precisely because it elaborates a structure of mimetic violence and displays the reversibility of sacred and profane, unlike the place of the contract as a legitimating fiction that works in one direction, recasting violence as law.

37. P. Sainath, 'The Fear of Democracy of the Privileged,' *The Hindu*, 8 December 2006.

38. When an Ambedkar statue was desecrated with a garland of slippers in the Ramabai chawls in the Mumbai suburb of Ghatkopar in 1997, Dalits protested vehemently. Police fire killed ten people, wounded at least twenty-six others, and initiated a government inquiry. S.D. Gundewar Judge Bombay High Court, 'Report of the Committee of Inquiry into Desecration of Dr. Ambedkar Statue Violence, Police Firingon 11th July, 1997 at Ghatkopar, Mumbai', (Bombay 1998).

14

Semiotics of Terror
Muslim Children and Women in Hindu Rashtra*

Tanika Sarkar

A serious inadequacy plagues our known vocabularies of horror. Words like communal violence or carnage or massacre have been overused to describe far too many situations whose horror is minimal, even relatively 'innocent', compared to the last four months in Gujarat [in the year 2002]. The problem is that we naturalize, domesticate, make somewhat bearable and comfortable, Gujarat events when we stretch old words to cover radically new meanings. What is at issue in Gujarat is not simply a recurrence of the perennial communal tension, but a fundamental political transformation: the installation of Hindu Rashtra—the dream of V.D. Savarkar, the vision of a nearly eighty-year-old Sangh. It has been inaugurated with the rituals and rites and sacrifices appropriate to itself. Bystanders and survivors during the days of maximal violence were struck by the festive, carnivalesque aspect of rampaging mobs. Indeed, one such mob looked like a *'barat'*, a wedding band, to unsuspecting Muslims on the fateful morning of 28 February 2002.

* First published in *Economic and Political Weekly Commentary*, vol. 37, no. 20, 13 July 2002, pp. 2872–6. We have retained the aspects of contemporary reportage, academic analysis, and soul-stirring writing represented by this essay.

Gujarat was also a testing ground, a measuring of the tolerance level of the Indian polity, by the fathers of the new nation. There has, indeed, been horrified anguish, protest, sincere relief and rehabilitation efforts from the whole world. Nonetheless, the Modi government continues to enjoy the full support of the centre, the National Democratic Alliance (NDA) holds firm, the Sangh is going to get its chosen president. In a revealing declaration of self-confidence, Vinay Katiyar has been made the Bharatiya Janata Party (BJP) chief in UP, even though the rest of the Sangh combine had so far been careful to publicly distance itself from the Bajrang Dal (BD). Obviously, the Sangh had decided that reticence is no longer necessary. The Vishwa Hindu Parishad's (VHP's) Ayodhya campaign, which was slated for 15 March, had drawn strong protest from sections of the NDA. The [then] forthcoming Ayodhya plan, in contrast, had been received in coy and modest silence by the allies. It seems, then, the Sangh can rely on the emergence of a new moral order, or, rather, on an abrogation of all morality among significant sections of Indians, to risk such telling self-disclosures.

What does the new dispensation look like? State relief and rehabilitation in Gujarat is less than the proverbial fig leaf, and the tawdry relief camps are closing even as Hindu goons are encouraged to kill, intimidate, and terrorize Muslims who attempt to return to their homes. Few arrests have been made of Hindu killers, and none of the political characters has been apprehended. The VHP plans another 'rathyatra' in a ceremony that punctually unleashes violence, counter-violence, and pogroms. The signals seem to be green all along the way, for the Bajrang Dal now holds training camps in combat in far-off states. According to a report in the *Times of India*, Calcutta edition, of 13 June, a ten-day training camp successfully concluded its session in Medinipur in West Bengal, under the guidance of Praveen Togadia.

The irony is that the Indian people, in election after election, gives its mandate against the Sangh. The BJP is the only party that has never been returned twice consecutively to the same state. That only renders the quicker advent of the Hindu Rashtra to replace the democratic polity an urgent necessity for the Sangh. It is a precarious balance of opportunistic allies and inept opposition that keeps it in power. Before a new political constellation emerges, it needs to topple the fundamentals of the democratic constitution. M.S. Golwalkar, the ideologue of the Sangh, was able to fulminate against democracy openly, in the happier days when the Sangh did not have to woo an electorate based on universal adult franchise. In a revealing statement, Vajpayee, in a mild criticism of Gujarat excesses said that 'rajadharma' has been offended: he did not refer to democracy.

If Gujarat is a new landmark in the annals of horror, it is dangerous to overstress its radical emergence. The intrepid journal, Communalism Combat, had predicted the situation at least four years back. Each individual feature of Gujarat has been anticipated and experimented with since the Ramjanmabhoomi movement began: in Meerut, Maliana, Bhagalpur, Ayodhya, Mumbai, Surat, Bhopal, Manoharpur in Orissa and in countless other places. 'After such knowledge, what forgiveness?'

What, then, is radically new in Gujarat? More important than the statistics of loss, is the nature of terror, for violence now consists of public acts of sadism that have been missing from earlier histories of carnage in our country. Looked at dispassionately, we have exceeded the achievements of Nazi terror, Bosnian atrocities, our own Partition violence—if not in scale or numbers, then in the intensity of torture, the sheer opulence and exuberance in forms of cruelty. It is as if the most gruesome elements from all the annals of mass destruction have been pulled together to form a whole that is Gujarat today. However, I would like to argue that what is new about Gujarat can best be exemplified in what happened to Muslim women and children on the days of the long knives. Not just their killings, not just the sadism that effected their killings, but the large symbolic purpose behind the deaths sums up the nature of ethnic cleansing, the shape of Hindu Rashtra. I will return to this point a little later.

THE SANGH PARIVAR'S PENETRATION OF STATE INSTITUTIONS

The facts of Gujarat violence are well known. I will try to locate a few patterns and trends within this violence. My main contention is, it is not the collapse of the state machinery that we are looking at, but the penetration of state and grassroots institutions—from police to hospitals—by the Sangh *parivar*. When talking of Gujarat events, it is very common to use terms like the failure of the Modi government, the weakness of the state, or the limits of the BJP-led coalition at the Centre. I would strongly insist that, on the contrary, the Modi government, as well as the Sangh as a whole, have been spectacularly successful in their agenda. What is happening in Gujarat is not a mark of weakness or inadequacy but a sign of the strength of the Sangh parivar, its firmness of resolve, its ideological consistency. This is the first time in our history that a state is headed by a RSS '*pracharak*'. The state governor, S.S. Bhandari, is a leading light of the Sangh, while the Central government has as its prime minister and home minister two very senior and experienced Sangh leaders. Vajpayee chose to remind us of his basic allegiance in the middle of the carnage during the Goa Conference: 'The Sangh is my soul.' Gujarat's Lokayukta, its chairman of the state public service commission, the vice-chancellor of the Gujarat University, are all old RSS hands. So is Arun Oza, the senior government pleader at the Ahmedabad High Court. Narendra Modi freely used the services of the state radio or Akashvani to put forward his views, and the vernacular press, especially *Sandesh* and the *Gujarat Samachar*, manufactured stories of Muslim violence and freely circulated them.

K.G. Shah, who leads the judicial commission to enquire into Gujarat events, is well known for his Hindutva leanings and his anti-Muslim judgements during the Terrorist and Disruptive Activities (Prevention) Act (TADA) trials. Among senior police officials, Sangh links abound. V.B. Rawal, inspector, Crime Branch, was a '*karsevak*' at the time of the demolition of the Babri Masjid and he proudly displays a photograph to prove his contribution to the cause. DCPs R.D. Makadia and D.G. Patel are close to the VHP general secretary Pravin Togadia, while DCP Parghi is an intimate associate of Haren Pandya, the state home minister, and accused by many of inciting the violence and actively assisting it. We may remind ourselves here that at the time of his election, Pandya had promised to 'wipe out any trace of Muslims of Paldi', Paldi being his constituency, and a site of great violence in recent months. In 1999, Mahen Trivedi, minister of state for home, publicly declared at a police function, 'We told you that we don't want Muslims in controlling posts.' Gujarat, incidentally, has only sixty-five senior Muslim police officers, none of them at present in active field service.

A happy conjuncture for the Sangh parivar, with all contingencies taken care of, all loopholes sealed. As a result, no important member from the entire combine—not even from the Bajrang Dal—has so far been arrested. This, despite the fact that several FIRs had been launched and numerous complaints made by eyewitnesses that not only local BD and VHP office-bearers, but also municipal corporators and MLAs—both men and women—led the mobs. Even BJP ministers have been named by many: Gordhan Zadaphya, home minister; Bharat Barot, food and civil supplies minister; Nitin Patel, finance minister; Ashok Bhatt, health minister; and I . K . Jadeja, development minister. VHP leader Jaideep Patel and Maya Kodnani, BJP MLA, have been explicitly implicated in the gruesome massacres at Naroda Patiya.

Great Solidarity

All the affiliates and the sub-affiliates of the Sangh parivar have displayed great mutual solidarity and protectiveness. BJP supported each of the VHP *bandh* calls that led to massive carnage; as VHP bandhs over the last four years unfailingly had similar results, there was thus sure foreknowledge about what a bandh call would mean. Modi consistently concealed the extent of damage and claimed that things were almost normal even while massacres were happening. The Rashtriya Swayamsevak Sangh (RSS) and the BJP cleared Modi of all blame and responsibility. Vajpayee's explanation for the violence echoed Modi's action–reaction thesis: Godhra led to a spontaneous outburst from all Hindus, Muslims have never lived in peace with non-Muslims anywhere in the world. L.K. Advani had cleared the BD of all charges of violence at the time of the murder of Graham Staines and his children: 'I know these people, they will never do such a thing.' K.K. Shastri, a nonagenarian VHP leader and noted Sanskritist, issued a circular which claimed that a team of fifty lawyers were working to release the arrested and to fight their cases.

It is not accidental that the RSS had described Gujarat as 'the laboratory of the Hindu Rashtra'. The experiments are now showing results. So magistrates sat quietly while the state burned, the police refused help at best, and, at worst, shot, tortured, and raped Muslims. Fire brigades did not come to help, hospitals turned away Muslim victims, Muslim ambulance services were systematically disrupted by the police. FIRs were either not registered, or registered at a collective level which left no room for individual complaints. Arrests were not made and relief came mostly from Muslim, Christian, or non-governmental organizations. There are no rehabilitation plans, compensation claims are impossible to establish, and if established, they are either not paid at all or paid fractionally.

For the last six months [in the year 2002], charges had been made by independent agencies that the BD was holding congregations on Saturday evenings, where tridents and swords were distributed and martial training given. It was also pointed out that systematic lists of Muslim addresses, business concerns, and collaborative ventures with Muslim capital were compiled. The truth of the allegations was borne out in the knowledgeable and sure-footed way in which mobs identified households and residences, selecting Muslim apartments in mixed housing societies, or burning hotels that carried Hindu names but included some amount of invisible Muslim capital. Government departments and their official records had obviously been pressed into service. The pile up of weapons and the training to use new and deadly chemicals to burn houses and bodies, the ability to deftly light and throw burning gas cylinders, the availability of swords which is legally a contraband object—all this proves months of systematic planning and not at all a spontaneous outburst immediately after Godhra.

More sinister is the management of the aftermath of the major flashpoints of violence. Bodies were not just massacred, they disappeared, as did houses, shrines, mosques. Overnight, roads were laid, and Hindu temples were built where Muslim homes used to be. Identities disappeared as well, for refugees in relief camps have neither documents nor identification papers of any sort to prove that they ever had property, jobs, bank balances, land, families, Indian citizenship. How can they legally refute charges, daily made by the Sangh, that camps harbour terrorists? Was the role of the NDA allies also foreknowledge, or was it an inspired guess? Was it anticipated that allies like Fernandes would applaud rape as natural, that the Telugu Desam Party (TDP) would demand the dismissal of the Modi government but would not vote against BJP, that Trinamool would demand president's rule but would vote with the BJP?

Be that as it may, there is no doubt that without a unique conjuncture of events—BJP at the helm in the Centre, an RSS *pracharak* in the state—ethnic cleansing on such a scale could not have been carried out. It was not criminal elements who caused the massacre, nor was it the independent work of lumpen BD activists. At any given time, mobs of thousands were roaming the streets, in as many as sixteen districts, and no state can harbour that large a professional criminal population. Faces in the mob that were recognized by victims included well-known political leaders, teachers, advocates, shopowners and traders, sarpanches, farmers, labourers, tribal, and Dalit groups. The recruitment of widely divergent social groups, the training in combat action, the mobilization of an immense will to violence bespeak tenacious and long-standing political activity within the very pores of civil society.

THE POLITICS OF VIOLENCE

What kind of politics accomplished all this? The BD is the official youth wing of the VHP which, in turn, is the religious wing of the Sangh, established and trained by the RSS. Its top leaders are all RSS members, and many also have BJP membership. The Sangh leaders told us in 1990 that Bajrangdalis were junior members of the parivar, important only during vendettas and scuffles—'during tit-for-tat situations'—but important, nevertheless. Incidentally, on the day of the VHP bandh on 28 February, a group of Akhil Bharatiya Vidyarthi Parishad (ABVP) students ransacked the Delhi University library building. They sported saffron headbands with Jai Shri Ram stamped on them, they carried swords—the typical gear of BD mobs in Gujarat. The ABVP, however, is an official organ of the RSS.

Savarkar had proclaimed in 1923 that Indians were essentially Hindus in their cultural ethos, and all those who had any affiliation with religious or cultural movements outside the land were not Indians. The formula excluded Muslims and Christians from the body politic. Later, the VHP constitution added communists to the list. At one stroke, therefore, citizenship was reserved for Hindus alone and nation and Hindus were made synonymous. In his multi-volume histories of India, Savarkar painted a bleak picture of Muslim tyranny in India, emphasizing especially the alleged abductions of Hindu women. The RSS drew a single corollary from this. All Muslims are a threat to faith and nation, and especially to women at all times, and, therefore, revenge must be taken on present-day Muslims both for historical wrongs and for the future danger that they embody.

So either Hindus avenge themselves or suffer emasculation. Revenge emerged as a mobile concept, as did the figure of the Muslim. For the Muslim of today embodies all past offences and future threats that have been allegedly committed and could be committed. Therefore, revenge may be taken on any Muslim anywhere for anything that any Muslim could do or had done. This is crucial, for it alone explains Modi's action–reaction theory: Muslims of far-away Panch Mahal or Ahmedabad justifiably paying for an action done at Godhra. Or take the notion of Ramjanmabhoomi, for instance. Present-day Muslims must be attacked to avenge an alleged attack on an alleged Hindu temple in the days of Babur. Again, a fifteenth-century Muslim poet's tomb or a twentieth-century Muslim singer's tomb can be smashed to avenge Godhra. Even Muslims of the past must pay for what Muslims of the present are doing, just as Muslims of the present are paying for past sins.

If the motif of infinite, elastic revenge unifies past, present, and future, then the production of an appropriate historical memory is crucial for the generation of the new political culture. History teaching, textbooks, and historical scholarship have been special targets of Sangh attacks. They need to assert their monopoly over historical truth, for there is a strange symmetry between their historical allegations and their present violence. They assert that Muslims broke temples, and then they demolish mosques. They allege forced conversion, and then they command victims to utter the name of Rama or to convert. Legends of rapes of Hindu women abound, and Muslim women are then raped freely.

If the conceptual apparatus is simple, crude, monochromatic, and one-dimensional, the organizational and communicational apparatus is singularly protean, pluralized, innovative, hegemonic. The RSS *shakhas* have ideological and combat training schedules on a daily basis. The training is a blend of physical exercises, martial arts training, speeches and tales, songs and theatre, games and organized sports. Each effort replicates the same message and sense of purpose in a different medium. They also run schools, leisure centres, cultural organizations, welfare societies, tribal- and slum-level educational projects, audio and video stations. They control temple networks, associations of priests and sadhus. They, of course, rule over states.

The cadres and all members of their various mass fronts are taught this message as history, as religion, and as nationalism. Two facts stand out within this ideological formation. One is that both religion and nationalism are being recast as a crusade against Christians and Muslims. At the same time, religion and nation are fused into a single entity whose lifeblood is vindictiveness for alleged past wrongs committed by Muslim rulers. The second is that Hindu unity is based on its antagonism against other Indian religions, which would overrule any engagement with power relations and social abuses of class, caste and gender within the Hindu community. In fact, even a reference to such problems is described as divisive of both religion and nation. The second 'sarsanghchalak' and ideological guru of the Sangh, Guruji Golwalkar, was quite frank in his denunciations of democracy, low castes, and labour agitations. These open statements, however, became covert and muted once independent India adopted a Constitution based on universal franchise and the electoral wing of the RSS needed to broaden its constituency. The new tactic was, therefore, to silence discourses on rights, equality, and social justice by promoting a militant Hindutva and a militaristic nationalism in its place. Savarkar was a staunch supporter of the nuclearizing of India. The Sangh works among exploited social groups to Hinduize and communalize them; it does not tolerate work for social justice.

These are themes that are poured out of RSS shakhas every day, since 1925. A multifarious cluster of numerous mass fronts supplement their dissemination. Narendra Modi is no ordinary politician. He is a Sangh pracharak, a celibate man without any ties of family, job, totally immersed in the work of organizing, teaching, and disseminating Sangh values. He has spent an entire lifetime spreading the message of hate.

SADISM AND HINDUTVA TERROR

There is a dark sexual obsession about allegedly ultra-virile Muslim male bodies and over-fertile Muslim female ones, that inspire and sustain the figures of paranoia and revenge. VHP leaflets, openly circulating in Gujarat, signed by the state general secretary, Chinubhai Patel, promised: 'We will cut them and their blood will flow like rivers. We will kill Muslims the way we destroyed Babri mosque.' This is followed by a poem:

> The volcano which was inactive has erupted
> It has burnt the arse of miyas and made them dance nude
> We have untied the penises that were tied till now
> We have widened the tight vaginas of the bibis.

One of the most spectacular forms of sadism in the recent events had been the way Muslim female and infantile bodies were made to function in the drama of Hindutva terror. There had been earlier anticipations of that. The investigations made by the All India Democratic Women's Association (AIDWA) in 1992–3, especially in Surat and Bhopal, had pointed out several similar features. Women were 'tortured, molested, raped, and then burnt to death'. Sometimes, their children were killed before their eyes. At the same time, more often than not, such atrocities were whispered about and not always confirmed openly. This time, rape victims as well as their male relatives have no inhibition about reporting rape and sexual torture. The police, however, do not admit FIRs on rape. A senior officer claims that mobs have no time for raping, and that Hindus, moreover, do not rape. Fernandes, on the other hand, says that rape is so universally prevalent that Gujarat rapes are not worth talking about. So, either it has not happened, or it happens universally; in either case, it cannot or need not be mentioned.

Women have been killed in very large numbers. At the mass grave that was dug on 6 March to provide burial to ninety-six bodies from Naroda Patiya, forty-six women were buried. Bilkees Beghum from the Godhra relief camp told a tale that seemed to confirm a recurrent pattern in most places, according to survivors' accounts. She was stripped, gang-raped, her baby was killed before her, she was then beaten up, then burnt and left for dead. For variety's sake, other women also had acid thrown upon them, and then burnt in fires. A womens' fact-finding report sums up the usual procedure: 'rape, gang rape, mass rape, stripping, insertion of objects into their body, molestation … a majority of rape victims were burnt alive.' Before they were finally killed, some were beaten up with rods and pipes for almost an hour. Before or after the killing, their vagina would be sliced, or would have iron rods pushed inside. Similarly, their bellies would be cut open or would have hard objects inserted into them. A thirteen-year old girl, Farzana, had a rod pushed into her stomach, and was then burnt. A mother reported that her three-year-old baby girl was raped and killed in front of her, while elsewhere daughters reported on the rapes of their mothers, now dead. Kausar Bano, a young girl from Naroda Patiya, was several months pregnant. Several eyewitnesses testified that she was raped, tortured, her womb was slit open with a sword to disgorge the foetus, which was then hacked to pieces and roasted alive with the mother.

At Fatehpura, young girls were paraded naked. After they were rescued by a Muslim ambulance service, they travelled to the camp without a stitch on them. Other victims arrived naked at camps, too, after acid had been poured upon their clothes, which they tore off in agony from their burning and peeling bodies. Medina Mustafa Ismail Shaikh reported from Kalol camp: 'My daughter was like a flower, still to experience life … The monsters tore my beloved daughter to pieces … the mob was saying, cut them to pieces, leave no evidence … I saw fires being lit. After some time, the mob started leaving. And it became quiet.'

It had become very quiet, for the voices of children could not be heard. A very large number of parents, especially mothers, had to see their children die in excruciating agony before they, too, were tortured and burnt. At the mass grave for ninety-six people, they buried a six-month-old baby. Fatimabibi, who came to Delhi to testify to the violence, kept repeating dementedly: 'Innocent (*masoom*) tender babies were crying for water, they filled them up with petrol and then lit them up.' At Randhikapur village, a young pregnant woman first saw her baby cut to pieces. Then she was raped and her foetus was ripped out and killed. They beat her up and left her for dead. Four-year-old Asif died of 90 per cent burns after several days' of agony. Before he died, the *Hindu* took a photograph of his bandaged face, out of which his large, beautiful, fully aware eyes were blazing out.

Pattern of Cruelty

One can go on narrating the ways in which babies and women were tortured and killed, but the point here is that often the two acts were coupled together. The pattern of cruelty suggests three things. One, the woman's body was a site of almost inexhaustible violence, with infinitely plural and innovative forms of torture. Second, their sexual and reproductive organs were attacked with a special savagery. Third, their children, born and unborn, shared the attacks, and were killed before their eyes.

In readings of community violence, rape is taken to be a sign of collective dishonouring. The same patriarchal order that designates the female body as the symbol of lineage and community purity would designate the entire collectivity as impure and polluted, once their woman is raped by an outsider. Rape, in Gujarat violence, obviously performed that function. But what, then, is the point of the elements of excess, the surplus of cruelty, and its multifarious forms? We need to remember that the Gujarati press invented the murder of eighty Hindu women on the Sabarmati Express at Godhra, who had been raped and had their breasts cut off—a complete invention, since even the Gujarat police denied the story. However, it served to justify rapes and mutilations of Muslim women within the structure of 'action–reaction' discourse. The fact that revenge went far beyond that is not surprising for revenge is not revenge if it does not outstrip the original offence. In Delhi, on 28 February, we heard RSS boys shouting: '*Ek ka badla sau me lenge*' (We will avenge one death with a hundred).

Beyond Godhra are the legends that all boys in the shakhas are bred on: Partition time rapes of Hindu women, rapes of Hindu queens under Muslim rule, abductions of Hindu women all through history by Muslims. There is also the perpetual fear of a more virile Muslim male body that lures away Hindu girls, a kind of penis envy and anxiety about emasculation that can only be overcome by doing violent deeds. Violence, for the Sangh, is both source and proof of maleness. In the 1990s, when communal violence had intensified, bangles were sent to localities where riots had not taken place, to taunt Hindu men with effeminacy. At Jawaharlal Nehru University, a post-Godhra procession of the ABVP chanted: '*Jis Hinduon ka khoon na khola, woh Hindu nahin, woh hijra hain*' (Those Hindus whose blood does not boil, are not Hindus, they are eunuchs'). This identification between killing and masculinity is a strong and uniquely Sangh teaching. In Gujarat, mobs who raped sometimes came dressed in khaki shorts or in saffron underwear, rape being obviously seen as a religious duty, a Sangh duty. In times of violence, Hindu male sexual organs must function as instruments of torture.

But why, then, the deliberate and large-scale killing of children, of babies, most often in the presence of their parents? For generations, anxieties had been whipped up about Muslim fertility rates, of their uncontrolled breeding and imminent outnumbering of the Hindu majority. So coupled with anxieties of a comparatively less potent Hindu maleness, there is a fear of infertile Hindu femaleness, and a drying up of future progeny—the long-standing image of dying Hindus. This is counter-posed to that of vigorously self-multiplying Muslims. Muslim children are a promise of future growth, of community self-strengthening, of survival of the community beyond the pogroms.

Fed on such self-invented self-doubt, Hindu mobs swooped down upon Muslim women and children with multiple but related aims. First, to possess and dishonour them and their men, second to taste what is denied to them and what, according to their understanding, explains Muslim virility. Third, to physically destroy the vagina and the womb, and, thereby, to symbolically destroy the sources of pleasure, reproduction, and nurture for Muslim men, and for Muslim children. Then, by beatings to punish the fertile female body. Then, by physically destroying the children, to signify an end to Muslim growth. Then, by cutting up the foetus and burning it, to achieve a symbolic destruction of future generations, of the very future of Muslims themselves. The burning of men, women, and children, as the final move, served multiple functions: it was to destroy evidence, it was to make Muslims vanish, it was also to desecrate Muslim deaths by denying them an Islamic burial, and forcing a Hindu cremation upon them—a kind of a macabre post-mortem forced conversion.

There were, thus, many layers of signification, of symbolic meanings that went into the act that were repeated by different mobs at different locales, but along fairly identical lines. They can be aligned to Sangh teachings, stereotypes, and fantasies. This also explains why the same female body was subjected to a series of sexual humiliation, torture, mutilation, and obliteration. Conjoined with the bodies of their children, they provided a site where the entire drama of revenge was enacted in its long and complicated sequence.

COMMUNALISM AND THE DENIAL OF CITIZENSHIP

There can be no political implication, no resource for struggle, if we deny the truth claims of these histories of sadism, if we say that such facts need not have a basis in the realm of what actually happened, if we denigrate the search for true facts as mere positivism, a spurious scientism. For the life and death of our political agenda depend on holding on to the truth claim, to that difference with VHP histories, to that absolute opposition to their proclamation that they will make and unmake facts and histories according to the dictates of conviction. There will be a massive effort by the Hindu Rashtra to produce a will to forgetting, to make things that happened disappear from memory, to fill up memory with images of things that had not happened, to generate counterfeit collective memories, amnesias. We need, as a bulwark against this, not simply our story pitted against theirs, but the story of what had indubitably happened.

It is also important to go back to some old but urgent convictions. Survivors in Gujarat unanimously demand the punishment of the guilty. Note that they do not talk of retribution or revenge, the vocabulary of the VHP, but of the restoration of legal processes, of the constitutional order, of their citizenship rights which have been spectacularly cancelled in Gujarat. For they have been killed because they are Muslims and not Hindus, and the fact of their being capitalists or labourers, farmers or artisans, is subordinate to this metanarrative. Their particular socio-economic locations in Gujarat may produce local conjunctures but these invariably flow into a larger frame, which is their religious identity. Muslims and Christians can be tortured and killed at will because they are different, because they stay different, from the majority religious community. It is the secular–democratic constitution that allows them to be different with impunity. As Sudipta Kaviraj recently pointed out in a conference at Pavia, citizenship is the only ground on which cultural difference can be sustained and asserted. We reject this truth as dated, as an old and therefore unusable brand in the marketplace of ideas, at our peril. The only opposite term [category/entity] to equal citizenship rights is unequal citizenship or the denial of citizenship. That is precisely what happened in Gujarat.

COMMUNAL FASCISM AND VIOLENCE

The communal fascism of the Sangh is not simply an ethnic cleansing. The minorities will not be extinguished in a single apocalyptic gesture, but the possibility of extermination at will is going to be displayed and demonstrated again and again, with spiralling sadism. This is a structural necessity for the Sangh. The necessity performs two distinct functions. By producing violence, it holds aloft the threat of Muslim reprisal, terrorism, war. The originary or dominant source of violence is overshadowed by fears of Muslim retaliation to such an extent that further terror against Muslims becomes a perceived necessity in large Hindu circles, especially in places where Muslims had been butchered. For people fear the consequences of the evil that they themselves have done, and, fearing that, they externalize their own deeds as a revengeful Other. As always, the fear of Muslims who have been killed is embodied in the living figures of terrorists and Pakistanis. Once that living shape becomes available, further violence against Indian Muslims is seen as fully legitimate, entirely necessary for the Sangh teaches that each Muslim stands in for all possible Muslims. And, so it goes on.

This breathless climate of terror and counter-terror is the cement that consolidates Hindu unity under Sangh terms. It is a unity that not only ensures perpetual hatred and violence, but also perpetually defers the questions of class, caste, and gender, of the abuses of such power within the community. Not only are abuses of Hindu by Hindu forgotten, all struggles against those power lines can be delegitimized as anti-faith, anti-national, divisive, treacherous. Only on such a ground can patriotism be defined as an act of hatred, of death, not as love for the people of India, not as commitment to the survival and welfare of those who have nothing, not as a protection of the country's environment, rivers, water, and air.

Annotated Bibliography

I. LINKS TO SELECT LEGAL RESOURCES

AltlawForum:
http://www.altlawforum.org/

Anveshi (Hyderabad):
http://www.anveshi.org/

Bangladesh Legal Resource:
http://www.peacemakers.ca/research/Bangladesh/BangladeshPeaceLinks.html

British and Irish Information Institute:
http://www.bailii.org/

Combat Law:
http://www.combatlaw.org/

Gujarat Human Rights Watch Report:
http://www.hrw.org/reports/2002/04/30/we-have-no-orders-save-you

Human Rights Watch:
http://www.hrw.org/

Human Rights Watch, "Broken People", report on caste violence against India's "untouchables", August, 2008:
http://www.hrw.org/reports/2008/08/11/broken-people

Human Rights Watch, "The Anti-Nationals: Arbitrary Detention and Torture of Terrorism Suspects in India:
http://www.hrw.org/reports/2011/02/01/anti-nationals-0

Indian Kanoon:
http://www.indiankanoon.org/

Indian Law Legal database:
http://www.manupatra.com/

Law and Social Sciences Network:
http://lassnet.blogspot.com/

Lawyers' Collective:
http://www.lawyerscollective.org/

Legal Information Institute of India:
http://liiofindia.org/

Majlis (Mumbai):
http://www.majlisbombay.org/index.php

People Unions for Democratic Rights:
http://www.pudr.org/

Privy Council Papers Online:
http://www.privycouncilpapers.org/

Saheli (Delhi):
https://sites.google.com/site/saheliorgsite/

Srikrishna Commision Report:
www.sabrang.com/srikrish/sri%20main.html

Srikrishna Commision Report: Chapter II:
www.hvk.org/specialrepo/skc/skcch2.html

South Asia Legal History Resources:
http://hosted.law.wisc.edu/wordpress/sharafi/research-guide-to-colonial-south-
    asian-case-law/

Women Living Under Muslim Law:
http://www.wluml.org/

II. BOOKS AND ARTICLES

Abrams, Philip. 'Notes on the Difficulty of Studying the State', *Journal of Historical Sociology*, vol. 1, no. 1, 1988: 58–89.

Adam, H.L. *The Indian Criminal*. London: J. Milne, 1909.

Agamben, Giorgio. *Homo Sacer: Sovereign Power and Bare Life*. Daniel Heller-Roazen (Trans.). Stanford: Stanford University Press, 1998.

Agarwal, Rameshwar Dayal and Meenakshi Agarwal. *Commentary on Sexual Offences with Special Reference to Law of Rape*. Bangalore: Premier Publishing Co., 1999.

Agnes, Flavia. 'Interrogating "Consent" and "Agency" Across the Complex Terrain of Family Laws in India', in Lila Abu-Lughod and Anupama Rao (eds) *Social*

Difference Online. Vol. 1, December 2011: (http://www.socialdifference.org/
files/SocDifOnline-Vol12012.pdf).

————. *Family Law.*2 vols. New Delhi: Oxford University Press, 2011.

————. *Law and Gender Inequality: The Politics of Women's Rights in India.*
Delhi: Oxford University Press, 1999.

————. 'Economic Rights of Women in Islamic Law', *Economic and Political
Weekly*, vol. 31, nos 41/42, 1996: 2832–8.

————. 'Hindu Men, Monogamy and Uniform Civil Code', *Economic and
Political Weekly*, vol. 30, no. 50, 1995: 3238–44.

————. 'Protective Legislations: Myth of Misuse', *Economic and Political
Weekly*, vol. 30, no. 16, 1995: 865–6.

Ahmad, Ejaz. *Law Relating to Theft Robbery and Dacoity.* Lucknow: Law Book
Mart, 1965.

Ahuja, Ram. *Crime against Women.* Jaipur: Rawat Publications, 1987.

————. *Female Offenders in India.* Meerut: Meenakshi Prakashan, 1969.

Albemarle, W.C.K. *Speech of the Earl of Albemarle on Torture in the Madras Presidency, Delivered in the House of Lords, 14th April, 1856.* London: J. Ridgway,
1856.

Alam, Javeed. 'State and the Making of Communist Politics in India, 1947–57',
Economic and Political Weekly, vol. 26, no. 45, 1991: 2573–7 and 2579–83.

Alladi, K. (ed.) *Mayne's Treatise on Hindu Law & Usage.* New Delhi: Bharat Law
House, 1993.

Almenas, Lipowsky and J. Angeles. *The Position of Indian Women in the Light of
Legal Reform.* Wiesbaden: Franz Steiner, 1975.

Amin, Shahid. *Event, Metaphor, Memory: Chauri Chaura, 1922–1992.* Berkeley:
University of California Press, 1995.

————. 'Approver's Testimony, Judicial Discourse: The Case of Chauri Chaura',
in Ranajit Guha (ed.) *Subaltern Studies V: Writings on South Asian History and
Society.* Delhi: Oxford University Press, 1985: 166–203.

Anagol, Padma. 'The Emergence of the Female Criminal in India: Infanticide and
Survival under the Raj', *History Workshop Journal*, vol. 53, 2002: 73–93.

Anderson, Clare. *Legible Bodies: Race, Criminality and Colonialism in South Asia.*
London: Berg, 2004.

————. *Convicts in the Indian Ocean: Transportation from South Asia to
Mauritius 1815–53.* London: Macmillan, 2000.

Anderson, Michael. 'Public Interest Perspectives on the Bhopal Case: Tort, Crime
or Violation of Human Rights?' in D. Robinson and J. Dunkley (eds) *Public
Interest Perspectives in Environmental Law.* London: John Wiley and Sons,
1995: 154–71.

————. 'Work Construed: Ideological Origins of Labour Law in British India
to 1918', in Peter Robb (ed.) *Dalit Movements and the Meanings of Labour in
India.* Delhi: Oxford University Press, 1993: 87–120.

————. 'Islamic Law and Colonial Encounter in British India', in David Arnold
and Peter Robb (eds) *Institutions and Ideologies: A SOAS South Asia Reader.*
London: Routledge Courzon, 1993: 165–85.

Anderson, Michael. 'Classifications and Coercions: Themes in South Asian Legal Studies in the 1980s', *South Asia Research*, vol. 10, no. 2, 1990: 158–77.

Anderson, Michael and Sumit Guha (eds) *Changing Conceptions of Law and Justice in South Asia*. New Delhi: Oxford University Press, 1997.

Ansari, Iqbal A. 'Babri Masjid Dispute: Rule of Law and Building Confidence', *Economic and Political Weekly*, vol. 36, no. 51, 2001: 4698–701.

————. *Communal Riots: The State and Law in India*. New Delhi: Institute of Objective Studies, 1997.

Arondekar, Anjali. *For the Record: On Sexuality and the Colonial Archive in India*. Durham, NC: Duke University Press, 2009.

Armitage, David. *The Declaration of Independence: A Global History*. Cambridge, Massachusetts: Harvard University Press, 2007.

Arnold, David. 'The Colonial Prison: Power, Knowledge and Penology in Nineteenth-Century India', in D. Arnold and D. Hardiman (eds) *Subaltern Studies VII: Essays in Honour Ranajit Guha*. Delhi: Oxford University Press, 1994: 147–87.

————. 'Touching the Body: Perspectives on the Indian Plague', in Ranajit Guha (ed.) *Subaltern Studies V: Writings on South Asian History and Society*. Delhi: Oxford University Press, 1987.

————. *Police Power and Colonial Rule: Madras, 1859–1947*. Delhi: Oxford University Press, 1986.

————. 'Rebellious Hillmen: The Gudem and Rampa Risings, 1839–1924', in Ranajit Guha (ed.) *Subaltern Studies I: Writings on South Asian History and Society*. Delhi: Oxford University Press, 1982.

————. 'Industrial Violence in Colonial India', *Comparative Studies in Society and History*, vol. 22, no. 2, 1980: 234–55.

————. 'Looting, Grain Riots and Government Policy in South India, 1918', *Past and Present*, vol. 84, no. 1, 1979: 111–45.

————. 'Dacoity and Rural Crime in Madras, 1860–1940', *The Journal of Peasant Studies*, vol. 6, no. 2, 1979: 140–67.

————. 'The Armed Police and Colonial Rule in South India, 1919–1947', *Modern Asian Studies*, vol. 11, no. 1, 1977: 101–25.

Arun, S.R. *The Peace Keepers: Indian Police Service*. Delhi: Manas Publications, 2000.

Arunima, G. *There Comes Papa: Colonialism and the Transformation of Matriliny in Kerala, Malabar, 1850–1940*. New Delhi: Orient Longman, 2003.

Asad, Talal. 'On Torture, or Cruel, Inhuman, and Degrading Treatment', in Arthur Kleinman, Veena Das and Margaret Lock (eds) *Social Suffering*. Delhi: Oxford University Press, 1998: 285–308.

Austin, Granville. *The Indian Constitution: Cornerstone of a Nation*. Oxford: South Asia Books, 1999.

Bajpai, Anju and Pramod Kumar Bajpai. *Female Criminality in India*. Delhi: Rawat Publications, 2000.

Balchin, C. (ed.). *A Handbook on Family Law in Pakistan*. Lahore: Shirkat Gah, 1994.

Nayar, Baldev Raj. *Violence and Crime in India: A Quantitative Study*. Delhi: Macmillan, 1975.

Bandhyopadhyaya, Mahua. *Everyday Life in a Prison: Confinement, Surveillance, Resistance*. Hyderabad: Orient Blackswan, 2010.

Banerjee, A.C. *English Law in India*. New Delhi: Abhinav, 1984.

Banerjee Dube, Ishita. 'Taming Traditions: Legalities and Histories in Twentieth Century Orissa', in Gautam Bhadra, Gyan Prakash, and Susie Tharu (eds) *Subaltern Studies X: Writings on South Asian History and Society*. Delhi: Oxford University Press, 1999: 98–125.

—————. *Divine Affairs: Religion, Pilgrimage, and the State in Colonial and Postcolonial India*. Shimla: Indian Institute of Advanced Study, 2001.

—————. *Religion, Law and Power: Tales of Time in Eastern India, 1860–2000*. London: Anthem Press, 2007.

Banerjee, S.C. *Crime and Punishment in Ancient India*. Calcutta: Naya Prakash, 1980.

Banerjee, Sumanta. *The Wicked City: Crime and Punishment in Calcutta*. Hyderabad: Orient Blackswan, 2009.

Banerjee, Tapas Kumar. *Background to Indian Criminal Law*. Bombay: Orient Longmans, 1963.

Barlingay, W. *The Hindu Law of Succesion for the Laymen*. New Delhi: All India Congress Committee, 1957.

Basu, Srimati. *She Comes to Take Her Rights: Indian Women, Property and Propriety*. Albany, NY: State University of New York Press, 1999; New Delhi: Kali for Women, 2001.

Baviskar, Amita. 'Urban Exclusions: Public Spaces and the Poor in Delhi', in Bharati Chaturvedi (ed.) *Finding Delhi: Loss and Renewal in a Megacity*. New Delhi: Penguin, 2010: 3–15.

—————. *In the Belly of the River: Tribal Conflicts over Development in the Narmada Valley*. New Delhi: Oxford University Press, 1995.

Baxi, Pratiksha. 'Justice is a Secret: Compromise in Rape Trials', *Contributions to Indian Sociology*, vol. 44, no. 3, 2010: 207–233.

—————. 'Feminist Contributions to Sociology of Law: A Review', *Economic and Political Weekly*, vol. 43, no. 43, 2008: 79–85.

Baxi, Upendra. '"The State's Emissary": The Place of Law in Subaltern Studies', in Partha Chatterjee and Gyanendra Pandey (eds) *Subaltern Studies VII: Writings on South Asian History and Society*. New Delhi: Oxford University Press 1992: 257–64.

—————. *Towards a Sociology of Indian Law*. Delhi: 1986.

—————. 'Discipline, Repression and Legal Pluralism', in P. Sach *et al.* (eds) *Legal Pluralism*. Canberra: Australian National University, 1991: 51–61.

Bayley, David H. *The Police and Political Development in India*. Princeton: Princeton University Press, 1969.

Bayly, C.A. *Recovering Liberties: Indian Thought in the Age of Liberalism and Empire*. Cambridge: Cambridge University Press, 2012.

Bayly, C.A. *Empire and Information: Intelligence Gathering and Social Communication in India, 1770–1870.* Cambridge: Cambridge University Press, 1997.

————. *Indian society and the making of the British Empire.* Cambridge: Cambridge University Press, 1988.

————. *Rulers, Townsmen, and Bazaars: North Indian Society in the Age of Expansion, 1770–1870.* Cambridge: Cambridge University Press, 1983.

Bellasis, A.F. *Reports of Criminal Cases Determined in the Court of Sudder Fauzdari Adawlut of Bombay. Vol. I (1827–1846).* Bombay: Government Press, 1849.

Benjamin, Walter.'Critique of Violence', in Walter Benjamin, *Reflections: Essays, Aphorisms, Autobiographical Writings.* New York: Schocken Books, 1978.

Benton, Laura. *A Search of Sovereignty: Law and Geography in European Empires, 1400–1900.* Cambridge: Cambridge University Press, 2009.

————. *Law and Colonial Culture: Legal Regimes in World History, 1400–1900.* Cambridge: Cambridge University Press, 2001.

Bhadra, Gautam, Gyan Prakash, and Susie Tharu (eds) *Subaltern Studies X: Writings on South Asian History and Society.* Delhi: Oxford University Press, 1999.

Bhargava, Rajeev (ed.) *Politics and Ethics of Indian Constitution.* New York: Oxford University Press, 2008.

———— (ed.) *Secularism and Its Critics.* New Delhi: Oxford University Press, 2005.

Bhargava, Bhawani Shanker. *The Criminal Tribes: A Socio-Economic Study of the Principal Criminal Tribes and Castes in Northern India.* Lucknow: Universal Publishers, 1949.

Bhosle, Smriti. *Female Crime in India and Theoretical Perspectives of Crime.* Delhi: Gyan Publishing House, 2009.

Birla, Ritu. *Stages of Capital: Law, Culture, and Market Governance in Late Colonial India.* Durham: Duke University Press, 2009.

Blackburn, S.H. 'The Kallars: A Tamil "Criminal Tribe" Reconsidered', *South Asia,* ns, vol. 1, no. 1, 1978: 38–51.

Bose, Sugata and Kris Manjapra (eds) *Cosmopolitan Thought Zones: South Asia and the Global Circulation of Ideas.* New York: Palgrave Macmillan, 2010.

Brimnes, Neil. 'Beyond Colonial Law: Indigenous Litigation and the Contestation of Property in the Mayor's Court in Late Eighteenth Century Madras', *Modern Asian Studies,* vol. 37, no. 3, 2003: 513–50.

Briggs, J. 'Account of the Origin, History and Manners of the Race of Men called Banjaras', in *Transactions of the Literary Society of Bombay, Volume 1.* London: Forgotten Books, 2012.

Brown, Mark, 'Crime, Liberalism, and Empire: Governing the Mina Tribe of Northern India', *Social and Legal Studies,* vol. 13, no. 2, 2004: 191–218.

————. 'Ethnology and Colonial Administration in Nineteenth-Century British India: The Questions of Native Crime and Criminality', *The British Journal for the History of Science,* vol. 36, no. 2, 2003: 201–19.

————. 'Crime, Governance, and the Company Raj: The Discovery of Thugee', *The British Journal of Criminology,* vol. 40, no. 1, 2003: 33–56.

Burra, Arudra. 'The Indian Civil Service and the Nationalist Movement: Neutrality, Politics, and Continuity', *Commonwealth & Comparative Politics,* vol. 48, no. 4, 2010: 404–32.

Butalia, Urvashi. *The Other Side of Silence: Voices from the Partition of India.* New Delhi: Penguin 1998.

Buultjens, R. 'Human Rights in Indian Political Culture', in K. Thompson (ed.) *The Moral Imperatives of Human Rights: A World Survey.* Washington, D.C.: University Press of America, 1980.

Cameron, C.H. and D. Eliott. *The First and Second Reports on the Indian Penal Code as Originally Framed in 1837.* Madras: Higginbotham and Co., 1888.

Campbell, G. *Memoirs of My Indian Career.* London: Macmillan, 1893.

Campbell, John. *A Personal Narrative of Thirteen Years Service amongst the Wild Tribes of Khondistan.* London: Hurst and Blackett, 1864. Reprinted London: Stubbe Press, 2010.

Carroll, Lucy. 'Law, Custom, and Statutory Social Reform: The Hindu Widows' Remarriage Act of 1856', *Indian Economic and Social History Review,* vol. 20, no. 4, 1983: 363–88.

Cassandra, B. (ed.) *Muslim Law in Modern India.* Allahabad: Allahabad Law Agency, 1993.

Chakrabarty, Dipesh. 'Domestic Cruelty and the Birth of the Subject', in Dipesh Chakrabarty. *Provincializing Europe: Postcolonial Thought and Historical Difference.* Princeton: Princeton University Press, 2000: 117–48.

————. *Rethinking Working-Class History.* Princeton: Princeton University Press, 2000.

Chakrabarty, Ranjan. *Authority and Violence in Colonial Bengal, 1800–1860.* Calcutta: Bookland, 1997.

Chakravarti, Uma. 'Victims, Neighbours, and *Watan*: Survivors of anti-Sikh Carnage', *Economic Political Weekly,* vol. 29, no. 42, 1994: 2722–6.

Chakravarti, Uma and Nandita Haksar (eds). *Delhi Riots: Three Days in the Life of a Nation.* New Delhi: Lancer International, 1987.

Chande, M.B. *The Police in India.* New Delhi: Atlantic Publishers, 1997.

Chandavarkar, Rajnarayan. *Imperial Power and Popular Politics: Class, Resistance, and the State in India, c. 1850-1950.* Cambridge: Cambridge University Press, 1998.

Chandoke, Neera. *Beyond Secularism: The Rights of Religious Minorities.* Delhi: Oxford University Press, 1999.

Chaterji, Basudev. 'The Darogah and the Countryside: The Imposition of Police Control in Bengal and its Impact (1793–1857)', *Indian Social and Economic History Review,* vol. 18, no. 1, 1981: 19–42.

Chatterjee, Indrani. *Gender, Slavery and Law in Colonial India.* New Delhi: Oxford University Press, 1999.

Chatterjee, Partha. 'Terrorism: State Sovereignty and Militant Politics in India', in Carol Gluck and Anne Loenhaupt Tsing (eds) *Words in Motion: Toward a Global Lexicon.* Durham: Duke University Press, 2009: 240–62.

Chatterjee, Partha. 'Classes, Capital and Indian Democracy', *Economic and Political Weekly*, vol. 43, no. 46, 2008: 89–93.

Chatterji, Roma and Deepak Mehta. *Living with Violence: An Anthropology of Events and Everyday Life*. London: Routledge, 2007.

Chattopadhyay, B. *Crime and Control in Early Colonial Bengal, 1770–1860*. Calcutta: K.P. Bagchi & Co., 2000.

Chattopadhyay, Kunal (ed.) *The Genocidal Pogrom in Gujarat: Anatomy of Indian Fascism*. Vadodara: Rohit Prajapati, 2002.

Chevers, Norman. *A Manual of Medical Jurisprudence in India: Including the Outline of a History of Crime against the Person in India*. Calcutta: Thacker, Spink & Co., 1870.

Chousalkar, A.S. *Social and Political Implications of the Concepts of Justice and Dharma*. Delhi: Mittal Publications, 1986.

Chowdhry, P. *Contentious Marriages, Eloping Couples: Gender, Caste and Patriarchy in Northern India*. Delhi: Oxford University Press, 2007.

————. 'Conjugality, Law, and State: Inheritance Rights as Pivot Control in Northern India', in Srimati Basu (ed.) *Dowry and Inheritance*. London and New York: Zed Books, 2005: 95–116.

————. 'Enforcing Cultural Codes: Gender and Violence in Northern India', *Economic and Political Weekly*, vol. 32, no. 19, 1997: 1019–28.

Cohn, Bernard S. *Colonialism and its Forms of Knowledge: The British in India*. Princeton: Princeton University Press, 1996.

————. *An Anthropologist among the Historians and Other Essays*. Delhi: Oxford University Press, 1990.

————. 'Law and the Colonial State in India', in June Starr and Jane Collier (eds), *History and Power in the Study of Law: New Directions in Legal Anthropology*. Ithaca: Cornell University Press, 1989: 131–52.

————. 'Anthropological Notes on Disputes and Law in India', *American Anthropologist*, ns, vol. 67, no. 6, Part 2: The Ethnography of Law, 1965: 3–32.

————. 'Some Notes on Law and Change in North India', *Economic Development and Cultural Change*, vol. 8, no. 1, 1959: 79–93.

Colebrooke, H.T. *The Law of Inheritance According to the Mitacshara*. Calcutta: Thacker Spink, 1869.

Colebrooke, James E. *Supplement to a Digest of the Regulations and Laws Enacted by the Governor General in Council for the Civil Government of the Territories*. Calcutta, 1807.

Comaroff, Jean and John (eds) *Law and Disorder in the Postcolony*. Chicago: University of Chicago Press, 2006.

Comaroff, John and Simon Roberts. *Rules and Process: The Cultural Logic of Dispute in an African Context*. Chicago: University of Chicago Press, 1981.

Coomer Bose, Arun. *Indian Revolutionaries Abroad, 1905–1922: In the Background of International Developments*. Patna: Bharati Bhawan, 1971.

Cooper, F. and A.L. Stoler. 'Between Metropolis and Colony: Rethinking a Research Agenda', in Frederick Cooper and Ann Laura Stoler (eds) *Tensions of Empire: Colonial Cultures in a Bourgeois World*. Berkeley: University of California Press, 1997: 1–57.

Cossman, Brenda and Ratna Kapur. *Subversive Sites: Feminist Engagement with Law in India*. London: Sage Publications, 1996.

—————. 'Women and Poverty in India: Law, Legal Literacy and Social Change', *Canadian Journal of Women and the Law*, vol. 6, 1993: 278–304.

—————. 'Communalising Gender/Engendering Community: Women, Legal Discourse and Saffron Agenda', *Economic and Political Weekly*, vol. 28, no. 17, 1993: WS35–WS44.

Coulson, N. *Conflicts and Tensions in Islamic Jurisprudence*. Chicago: University of Chicago Press, 1969.

Coward, Rosalind. *Patriarchal Precedents: Sexuality and Sexual Relations*. London: Routledge, 1983.

Cox, Edmund. *Police and Crime in India*. London: S. Paul and Co., 1911.

Crawford, A.T. *Reminiscences of an Indian Police Official*. Westminster: Roxburghe Press, 1897.

Curry, J.C. *Crime in India: with an Introduction on Forensic Difficulties and Peculiarities*. London: Faber & Faber, 1946.

—————. *The Indian Police*. London: Faber & Faber, 1932.

Dale, Stephen F. 'The Mappila Outbreaks: Ideology and Social Conflict in Nineteenth Century Kerala', *Journal of Asian Studies*, vol. 35, no. 1, 1975: 85–97.

Daly, F.C. 'Some Types of the Indian Hereditary Criminal', *The Police Journal: Indian Police Collection*, vol. 1, no. 1, 1928: 105–17.

Dampier, W. *Report on the State of the Police in the Lower Provinces, for the Year 1853*. Calcutta: Thos. Jones, Calcutta Gazette Office, 1855.

Das, Suranjan. 'Behind the Blackened Faces: The 19th Century Bengali Dacoits', *Economic and Political Weekly*, vol. 42, no. 35, 2007: 3573–9.

—————. 'The Goondas: Towards a Reconstruction of the Calcutta Underworld through Police Records', *Economic and Political Weekly*, vol. 29, vol. 44, 1994: 2877–9 and 2881–3.

Das, Suranjan and Basudeb Chattopadhyay. 'Rural Crime in Police Perception: A Study of Village Crime Notebooks', *Economic and Political Weekly*, vol. 26, no. 23, 1991: 129–31.

Das, Rajani Kanta. *Principles and Problems of Indian Labour Legislation*. Calcutta: University of Calcutta, 1988.

—————. *History of Indian Labour Legislation*. Calcutta: University of Calcutta, 1941.

Das, Veena. *Life and Words: Violence and the Descent into the Ordinary*. Berkeley, CA: University of California Press, 2006.

————— (ed.) *Violence and Subjectivity*. Berkeley: University of California Press, 2000.

—————. 'Language and Body: Transactions in the Construction of Pain', in Arthur Kleinman *et al.* (eds) *Social Suffering*. Berkeley: University of California Press, 1997: 67–92.

Das, Veena. *Critical Events: An Anthropological Perspective on Contemporary India*. Delhi: Oxford University Press, 1995.

————— (ed.) *Mirrors of Violence: Communities, Riots, and Survivors in South Asia*. Delhi: Oxford University Press, 1990.

—————. 'Subaltern as Perspective', in Ranajit Guha (ed.) *Subaltern Studies VI: Writings on South Asian History and Society*, Delhi: Oxford University Press, 1989: 310–24.

Dash, Mike. *Thug: The True Story of India's Murderous Cult*. London: Granta Books, 2006.

Datta, K.K. *Biography of Kunwar Singh and Amar Singh*. Patna: K.P. Jayaswal Research Institute, 1957.

Davis Jr., Donald R. 'Hinduism as a Legal Tradition', *Journal of the American Academy of Religion*, 75(2), 2007: 241–67.

—————. 'Intermediate Realms of Law: Corporate Groups and Rulers in Medieval India', *Journal of the Economic and Social History of the Orient*, vol. 48, no. 1, 2005: 92–117.

Day, Terrence P. *The Conception of Punishment in Early Indian Literature*. Waterloo, Ontario: Wilfrid Larner University Press, 1982.

Dawson Mayne, John. 'Native Law Administered in the Courts of the Madras Presidency', *Madras Journal of Literature and Science*, vol. 1, no. 3, 1864: 1–36.

De, Rohit, 'Mumtaz Bibi's Broken Heart: The Many Lives of the Dissolution of the Muslim Marriages Act', *India Economic and Social History Review*, vol. 46, no. 1, 2009: 105–30.

De, Rohit, Leigh Donault, and Eleanor Newbigin (eds) 'Personal Law, Identity Politics, and Civil Society in Colonial South Asia', special issue, *Indian Economic and Social History Review*, vol. 46, no. 1, 2009.

De Certeau, Michel. *The Practice of Everyday Life*. Berkeley: University of California Press, 1988.

Derret, J. Duncan M. *Essays in Classic and Modern Hindu Law: Volume 1, Dharmasastra and Related Ideas*. Leiden: E.J. Brill, 1976.

—————. 'Modes of Sannyasis and the Reform of a South Indian Matha Carried out in 1584', *Journal of the American Oriental Society*, vol. 94, no. 1, 1974: 65–72.

—————. *Religion, Law and the State in India*. London: Faber, 1968.

—————. 'Law and the Social Order in India before the Muhammadan Conquests', *Journal of the Economic and Social History of the Orient*, vol. 7, no. 1, 1964: 73–120.

—————. 'Illegitimates: A Test for Modern Hindu Family Law', *Journal of the American Oriental Society*, vol. 81, no. 3, 1961: 251–61.

—————. 'The Administration of Hindu Law by the British', *Comparative Studies in Society and History*, vol. 4, no. 1, 1961: 10–52.

—————. 'Statutory Amendments of the Personal Law of Hindus Since Indian Independence', *The American Journal of Comparative Law*, vol. 7, no. 3, 1958: 380–93.

Derret, J. Duncan M. *Hindu Law, Past and Present*. Calcutta: A. Mukherjee and Company, 1957.

——————. *Dharmasastra and Juridical Literature (A History of Indian Literature. Vol. 4, Scientific and Technical Literature)*. Wiesbaden: Harrassowitz, 1973.

Desai, A.R. (ed.) *Expanding Government Lawlessness and Organized Struggles*. Bombay: Popular Prakashan, 1991.

Desai, Mahadev. *The Diary of Mahadev Desai, Volume I*. Ahmedabad: Navajivan Publishing House, 1953.

Desai, S.T. *Mulla's Principles of Hindu Law*. Bombay: N.M. Tripathi, 1994.

Devasia, Leelamma. *Female Criminals and Female Victims: An Indian Perspective*. Nagpur: Dattsons, 1989.

Devji, Faisal. *The Terrorist in Search of Humanity: Militant Islam and Global Politics*. New York: Columbia University Press, 2009.

——————. *Landscapes of the Jihad: Militancy, Morality, Modernity*. Cornell: Cornell University Press, 2005.

Dhanagare, D.N. 'Agrarian Conflict, Religion and Politics: The Moplah Rebellions in Malabar in the Nineteenth and Early Twentieth Centuries', *Past and Present*, vol. 74, 1977: 112–41.

Dhagamwar, Vasudha. *Law, Power and Justice: The Protection of Personal Rights in the Indian Penal Code*, New Delhi: Sage Publications, 1992.

Dhareshwar, Vivek and R. Srivatsan. 'Rowdy-sheeters: An Essay on Subalternity and Politics', in Shahid Amin and Dipesh Chakrabarty (eds), *Subaltern Studies IX: Writings on South Asian History and Society*. New Delhi: Oxford University Press, 1996: 201–31.

Dhavan, Rajeev. 'The Ayodhya Judgment: Encoding Secularism in the Law', *Economic and Political Weekly*, vol. 29, no. 48, 1994: 3034–40.

——————. 'Means, Motives and Opportunities: Reflecting on Legal Research in India', *Modern Law Review*, vol. 50, 1987: 725–49.

Dirks, Nicholas. *Scandal of Empire: India and the Creation of Imperial Britain*, Cambridge, MA: Harvard University Press, 2006.

——————. *Castes of Mind: Colonialism and the Making of Modern India*. Princeton, NJ: Princeton University Press, 2001.

——————. 'The Policing of Tradition: Colonialism and Anthropology in Southern India', *Comparative Studies in Society and History*, vol. 39, no. 1, 1997: 182–212.

Diwan, P. *Muslim Law in Modern India*. Allahabad: Allahabad Law Agency, 1993.

——————. *Law of Marriage and Divorce*. Allahabad: Wadhwa & Company, 1988.

——————. *Religion, Law and the State in India*. New York: The Free Press, 1968.

Diwar, Paras. *Modern Hindu Law: Codified and Uncodified*. Allahabad: Allahabad Law Agency, 1979.

Donnelly, Jack. 'Traditional Values and Universal Human Rights: Caste in India', in C.E. Welchand V.A. Leary (eds), *Asian Perspectives on Human Rights*. Boulder: Westview Press, 1990: 55–90.

Donnelly, Jack. *Universal Human Rights in Theory and Practice*. Ithaca and London: Cornell University Press, 1989.

Dreze, Jean and Reetika Khera. 'Crime, Gender, and Society in India: Insights from Homicide Data', *Population and Development Review*, vol. 26, no. 2, 2000: 335–52.

Dreze, Jean, Meera Samson, and Satyajit Singh, *The Dam and the Nation: Displacement and Resettlement in the Narmada Valley*. Delhi: Oxford University Press, 1997.

Dube, Leela. 'Conflict and Compromise: Devolution and Disposal of Property in a Matrilineal Muslim Society', *Economic and Political Weekly*, vol. 29, no. 21, 1994: 1273–84.

————. 'On the Construction of Gender: Hindu Girls in Patrilineal India', *Economic and Political Weekly*, vol. 23, no. 18, 1988: 11–19.

Dube, Saurabh. *Stitches on Time: Colonial Cultures and Postcolonial Tangles*. Durham: Duke University Press, 2004.

————. *Untouchable Pasts: Religion, Identity and Power among a Central India Community, 1780–1950*. New York: State University of New York Press, 1998.

————. 'Colonial Law and Village Disputes: Two Cases from Chhattisgarh', in N. Jayaram and Satish Saberwal (eds), *Social Conflict: Oxford Readings in Sociology and Social Anthropology*. Delhi: Oxford University Press, 1996: 423–44.

————. 'Telling Tales and Trying Truths: Transgressions, Entitlements and Legalities in Late Colonial Central India', *Studies in History*, vol. 12, no. 2, 1996, 171–201.

————. 'Idioms of Authority and Engendered Agendas: The Satnami Mahasabha, Chhattisgarh, 1925–50', *The Indian Economic and Social History Review*, vol. 30, 1993: 383–411.

————. 'Myths, Symbols and Community: Satnampanth of Chhattisgarh', in Partha Chaterjee and Gyan Pandey (eds), *Subaltern Studies VII: Writings on South Asian History and Society*. Delhi: Oxford University Press 1992: 121–56.

Duffield, Ian and Bradley James (eds) *Representing Convicts: New Perspectives on Convict Labour Forced Migration*. London: Leicester University Press, 1997.

Dumont, Louis. *Homo Hierarchicus: The Caste System and Its Implications*, Mark Sainsbury (trans.). Chicago: University of Chicago Press, 1970.

Edwardes, S.M. *Crime in India*. London: Oxford University Press, 1924.

Engineer, Asghar Ali, 'Srikrishna Commission Report: Painstaking Documentation', *Economic and Political Weekly*, vol. 33, nos 33–4, 1998: 2215–16.

Engineer, A.A. and Amarjit S. Narang, *Minorities and Police in India*. New Delhi: Manohar, 2006.

————. 'Ayodhya's Challenge to VHP', *Economic and Political Weekly*, vol. 38, no. 40, 2003: 4217–18.

————. 'Communal Violence and Role of Police', *Economic and Political Weekly*, vol. 29, no. 15, 1994: 835–40.

Ernst, Waltraud. 'Colonial Policies, Racial Politics and the Development of Psychiatric Institutions in Early Nineteenth-Century India', in Waltraud Ernst and Bernard Harris (eds) *Race, Science and Medicine, 1700–1960*. London: Routledge, 1999: 80–100.

Ewick, Patricia and Susan Silbey. *The Common Place of Law: Stories from Everyday Life*. Chicago: University of Chicago Press, 1998.

Fawcett, Charles. *The First Century of British Justice in India*. Oxford: Oxford University Press, 1934.

Fisch, Jörg. *Cheap Lives and Dear Limbs: The British Transformation of the Bengal Criminal Law 1769–1817*. Wiesbaden: Beiträge zur Südasienforschung, 1983.

Foucault, Michel. *The Care of the Self*. Harmondsworth: Penguin, 1990.

—————. *Discipline and Punish: The Birth of the Prison*. London: Penguin, 1977.

—————. *Madness and Civilization: A History of Insanity in the Age of Reason*. London: Tavistock, 1967.

Freitag, Sandria. 'Crime in the Social Order of Colonial North India', *Modern Asian Studies*, vol. 25, no. 2, 1991: 227–31.

—————. 'Collective Crime and Authority in North India', in Anand A. Yang (ed.) *Crime and Criminality in British India*. Tucson: University of Arizona Press, 1985: 140–63.

Fukazawa, H.K. *The Medieval Deccan: Peasants, Social Systems and States*. Oxford: Oxford University Press, 1999.

Fuller, C.J. 'Hinduism and Scriptural Authority in Modern Indian Law', *Comparative Studies in Society and History*, vol. 30, no. 2, 1988: 225–48.

Fyzee, A.A. *Outlines of Mohammadan Law*. New Delhi: Oxford University Press, 1974.

Galanter, Marc. *Law and Society in Modern India*. Delhi: Oxford University Press, 1989.

—————. *Competing Equalities: Law and the Backward Classes in India*. Delhi: Oxford University Press, 1984.

—————. 'The Aborted Restoration of "Indigenous" Law in India', *Comparative Studies in Society and History*, vol. 14, no. 1, 1972: 53–70.

—————. 'Untouchability and the Law', *Economic and Political Weekly*, vol. 4, nos 1–2, 1969: 131–70.

—————. 'The Modernization of Law', in Myron Weiner (ed.) *Modernization*. New York: Basic Books, 1966: 153–65.

Galloway, A. *Observations on the Law, Constitution and Present Government of India*. London: Parbury, Allen and Co., 1832.

Gandhi, M.K. *An Autobiography, or the Story of My Experiments with Truth*. Ahmedabad: Navajivan Publishing House, 1940.

Gayer, Laurent and Christophe Jaffrelot (eds) *Muslims in Indian Cities: Trajectories of Marginalization*. London: Hurst and Co., 2012.

Geetha, V. (ed.) *Ear to the Ground: Writings on Class and Caste: Selected Writings of K. Balagopal*. New Delhi: Navayana, 2011.

Gharpure, J.R. *Rights of Women under Hindu Law*. Bombay: N.M. Tripathi Ltd., 1943.

Ghosh, Durba. 'Household Crimes and Domestic Order: Keeping the Peace in Colonial Calcutta, c. 1770–c. 1840', *Modern Asian Studies*, vol. 38, no. 3, 2004: 598–623.

—————. 'Legal and Liberal Subjects: Women's Crimes in Early Colonial India', *Journal of Women's History*, vol. 22, no. 2, 2010: 153–6.

—————. 'Making and Un-making Loyal Subjects: Pensioning Widows and Educating Orphans in Early Colonial India', *Journal of Imperial and Commonwealth History*, vol. 31, no. 1, 2003: 1–28.

Ghosh, Kaushik. 'Between Global Flows and Local Dams: Indigenousness, Locality, and the Transnational Sphere in Jharkhand, India', *Cultural Anthropology*, vol. 21, no. 4, 2006: 501–34.

Ghosh, Srikanta. *Torture and Rape in Police Custody: An Analysis*. New Delhi: Ashish Publishing House, 1993.

Gilmartin, David. 'Rule of Law, Rule of Life: Caste, Democracy, and the Courts in India', *The American Historical Review*, vol. 115, no. 2, 2010: 406–27

Gilmont, David. 'Cattle, Crime and Colonialism: Property as negotiation in North India', *Indian Economic and Social History Review*, vol. 40, no. 1, 2003: 33–56.

—————. *The Cheese and the Worms: The Cosmos of a Sixteenth Century Miller*. Baltimore: John Hopkins University Press, 1980.

Goonesekere, Savitri. *Violence, Law and Women's Rights in South Asia*. New Delhi: Sage Publications, 2004.

Gopal, S. (ed.) *Anatomy of a Confrontation: The Babri Masjid-Ramjanmabhumi Dispute*. New Delhi: Penguin, 1991.

Gordon, Stewart N. *The New Cambridge History of India, Volume II, Part 4: The Marathas 1600–1818*. Cambridge: Cambridge University Press, 1993.

—————. 'Scarf and Sword: Thugs, Marauders and State-Formation in 18th Century Malwa', *Indian Economic and Social History Review*, vol. 6, no. 4, 1969: 403–29.

Gough, Kathleen. 'Indian Peasant Uprisings', *Economic and Political Weekly*, vol. 9, nos 32–4, Special Number, 1974: 1391–3, 1395–7, 1399, 1401–3, 1405–7, 1409, 1411–12.

Gour, H.S. *Gour's Penal Code of India*. Allahabad: Law Publishers, 1983.

Griffiths, A. *Oriental Prisons: Prisons and Crime in India, the Andaman Islands, Burma, China, Japan, Egypt, Turkey*. London: The Grolier Society, 1900.

Griffiths, Percival Joseph. *To Guard My People: The History of the Indian Police*. London: Benn, 1971.

Guha, Ranajit. 'Discipline and Mobilize: Hegemony and Elite Control in Nationalist Campaigns', in Ranajit Guha, *Dominance Without Hegemony: History and Power in Colonial India*. Cambridge, MA: Harvard University Press, 1997: 100–51.

Guha, Ranajit. 'Chandra's Death', in Ranajit Guha (ed.) *Subaltern Studies V: Writings on South Asian History and Society*. Delhi: Oxford University Press, 1987: 34–62.

————. *Elementary Aspects of Peasant Insurgency in Colonial India*. Delhi: Oxford University Press, 1983.

————. *A Rule of Property for Bengal: An Essay on the Idea of Permanent Settlement*. Paris: Moulton, 1963.

Guha, Ramchandra. 'Adivasis, Naxalites and Indian Democracy', *Economic and Political Weekly*, vol. 42, no. 32, 2007: 3305–12.

Guha, Sumit. 'Wrongs and Rights in the Maratha Country: Antiquity, Custom and Power in Eighteenth Century India', in Michael Anderson and Sumit Guha (eds) *Changing Conceptions of Law and Justice in South Asia*. New Delhi: Oxford University Press, 1997: 14–29.

————. 'An Indian Penal Regime: Maharashtra in the Eighteenth Century', *Past and Present*, vol. 147, no. 2, 1995: 101–26.

Gune, V.T. *The Judicial System of the Marathas*. Poona: Deccan College Post Graduate and Research Institute, 1953.

Gupta, Anandswarup. *The Police in British India, 1861–1947*. New Delhi: Concept, 1979.

————. *Crime and Police in India up to 1861*. Agra: Sahitya Bhavan, 1974.

Gupta, Tilak D. 'Maoism in India: Ideology, Programme and Armed Struggle', *Economic and Political Weekly*, vol. 41, no. 29, 2006: 3172–6.

Haikerwal, Bejoy Shanker. *Economic and Social Aspects of Crime in India*. London: G. Allen and Unwin Ltd., 1934.

Halhed, Nathaniel Brassley. *A Code of Gentoo Laws, or, Ordinations of the Pundits*. London, 1776.

Hallaq, W.A. *History of Islamic Legal Theories: An Introduction to Sunni Usul al-fiqh*. Cambridge: Cambridge University Press, 1999.

————. 'Murder in Cordoba: Ijtihad, Ifta and the Evolution of Substantive Law in Mediaeval Islam', *Acta Orientalia*, vol. 55, 1994: 55–83.

————. 'From Fatwas to Furu: Growth and Change in Islamic Substantive Law', *Islamic Law and Society*, vol. 1, no. 1, 1994: 17–56.

Harlan, Lindsey and Paul Courtright (eds) *From the Margins of Hindu Marriage: Essays on Gender, Religion and Culture*. New York: Oxford University Press, 1995.

Harrington. *An Elementary Analysis of the Laws and Regulations*. Calcutta, 1807.

Hasanat, A. *Crime and Criminal Justice: An Outline of Criminal Sociology, Criminology, Penology, Criminal Jurisprudence and Law, and Criminal Investigation*. Dacca: Standard Library, 1939.

Hay, Douglas. 'War, Dearth and Theft in the Eighteenth Century', *Past and Present*, vol. 95, no. 1, 1982: 117–60.

Hay, Douglas, Peter Linebaugh, and E.P. Thompson. *Albion's Fatal Tree: Crime and Society in Eighteenth Century England*. London: Pantheon, 1975.

Hayne, J.D. *A Treatise on Hindu Law and Usage*. Madras: Higgin Botham and Company, 1906.

Hervey, Charles. *Statistics of the Crime of Dacoite in British Territory and Dependent Native States: 1867, 1868, and 1869.* Calcutta, 1873.

Hervey, H.J.A. *Cameos of Indian Crime.* London: Stanley Paul & Co., 1912.

Hinnells, John R. and Richard King. *Religion and Violence in South Asia: Theory and Practice.* London and New York: Taylor & Francis e-Library, 2007.

Hobsbawm, E.J. *Bandits.* London: Liedenfeld and Nicholson 1969.

————. *Primitive Rebels, Studies in Archaic Forms of Social Movements in the Nineteenth and Twentieth Centuries.* Manchester: Manchester University Press, 1959.

Hollins, S.T. *The Criminal Tribes of the United Provinces.* Allahabad: Government Press, 1914.

Hough, William. *Military Law Authorities.* Calcutta: W. Thacker, 1839.

Hula, Richard C. 'Calcutta: The Politics of Crime and Conflict, 1800 to the 1970s', in Ted Robert Gurr, Peter N. Grabosky, Richard C. Hula. *The Politics of Crime and Conflict: A Comparative History of Four Cities.* London: Sage Publications, 1977: 467–616.

Hussein, Nasser. *The Jurisprudence of Emergency: Colonialism and the Rule of Law.* Ann Arbor, Michigan: University of Michigan Press, 2003.

Ingnatieff, Michael. *A Just Measure of Pain: The Penitentiary in the Industrial Revolution, 1750–1850.* New York: Pantheon Books, 1978.

Jahangir, Asma and Hina Jillani. *The Hudood Ordinances: A Divine Sanction?A Research Study of the Hudood Ordinances and their Effect on the Disadvantaged Sections of Pakistan Society.* Lahore: Rohtas Books, 1990.

Jain, B. *Administration of Justice in Seventeenth Century India (A Study of Salient Conceptions of Mughal Justice).* Delhi: Metropolitan Book Company, 1970.

Jain, M.P. *Outlines of Indian Legal History.* Bombay: N.M. Tripathi, 1966.

Jaising, Indira. 'Women, Religion and the Law', *The Lawyers Collective*, vol. 2, no. 11, 1987.

Jalal, Ayesha. 'The Convenience of Subservience: Women and the State of Pakistan', in Denis Kandiyoti (ed.) *Women, Islam and the State.* London: Macmillan, 1991: 77–114.

Jeffries, Charles Joseph. *The Colonial Police.* London: M. Parrish, 1952.

Jegatheesan P. *Law and Order in Madras Presidency, 1850–1880.* New Delhi: B.R. Pub. Corp., 1987.

Jha, Shefali. 'Secularism in the Constituent Assembly Debates, 1946–1950', *Economic and Political Weekly*, vol. 37, no. 30, 2002: 3175–80.

John, Mary E. 'Alternate Modernities? Reservations and Women's Movement in 20th Century India', *Economic and Political Weekly*, vo. 35, nos 43–4, 2000: WS22–WS29.

Johnston, Valerie J. *Diet in Workhouses and Prisons, 1835–1895.* New York: Garland, 1985.

Jolly, J. *Hindu Law.* Calcutta: Tagore Law Lecture Series (TLLS), 1883.

Joshi, Chitra. 'Fettered Bodies: Labouring on Public Works in Nineteenth Century India', in Marcel van der Linden and Prabhu Mohapatra (eds) *Labour Matters: Towards Global Histories.* New Delhi: Tulika Books, 2009: 3–21.

Joshi, Chitra. *Lost Worlds: Indian Labour and Its Forgotten Histories*. London: Anthem Press, 2005.

Kadam, V.S. 'The Institution of Marriage and Position of Women in Eighteenth-Century Maharashtra', *Indian Economic and Social History Review*, vol. 25, no. 3, 1988: 341–70.

Kane, Pandurang Vaman. *History of Dharmaśāstra: Ancient and Mediæval Religious and Civil Law in India*. Poona: Bhandarkar Oriental Research Institute, 1975.

Kaplan, Martha. 'Panopticon in Poona: An Essay on Foucault and Colonialism', *Cultural Anthropology*, vol. 10, no. 1, 1995: 85–98.

Kasturi, Malavika. 'Rajput Lineages, Banditry, and the Colonial State in Nineteenth Century British Bundelkhand', *Studies in History*, vol. 5, no. 1, 1999: 75–108.

—————. *Embattled Identities: Rajput Lineages and the Colonial State in Nineteenth-century North India*. New Delhi: Oxford University Press, 2002.

Katznelson, Ira and Partha Chaterjee (eds) *The Anxieties of Democracy: Tocquevillean Reflections on India and the United States*. New Delhi: Oxford University Press, 2012.

Kaul, Reema. *Women and Crime*. New Delhi: Omega Publications, 2006.

Kaviraj, Sudipta. *The Imaginary Institution of India*. New York: Columbia University Press, 2010.

—————. 'A Critique of Passive Revolution', *Economic and Political Weekly*, vol. 23, nos 45–7, 1988: 2429–44.

Kaviraj, Sudipta and Sunil Khilnani (eds) *Civil Society: History and Possibilities*. Cambridge: Cambridge University Press, 2001.

Kapur, Ratna. *Makeshift Migrants and Law: Gender, Belonging and Postcolonial Anxieties*. New Delhi: Routledge, 2010.

—————. *Erotic Justice: Law and the New Politics of Postcolonialism*. London: Glasshouse Press, 2005.

————— (ed.) *Feminist Terrains in Legal Domains: Interdisciplinary Essays on Women and Law in India*. New Delhi: Kali for Women, 1996.

Keenan, B. *An Evil Cradling*. London: Hutchinson, 1992.

Kelkar, R. 'Provocation as a Defense in the Indian Penal Code', *Journal of the Indian Law Institute*, vol. 5, no. 319, 1963: 319–55.

Kerawalla, Perin C. *A Study in Indian Crime*. Bombay: Popular Book Depot, 1959.

Kidwai, Mushir Hosain. *Women under Different Social and Religious Laws*. Delhi: Seema Publications, 1976.

King, R.D. *Nehru and the Language Politics of India*. Delhi: Oxford University Press, 1997.

Kishwar, Madhu. 'Codified Hindu Law: Myth and Reality', *Economic and Political Weekly*, vol. 29, no. 33, 1994: 2145–61.

Knox, G.E. *The Criminal Law of the Bengal Presidency, Volume 1*. Calcutta: Thacker, Spink and Company, 1873.

Kodoth, Praveena. 'Courting Legitimacy or Delegitimizing Custom? Sexuality, Sambandham, and Marriage Reform in Late Nineteenth-Century Malabar', *Modern Asian Studies*, vol. 35, no. 2, 2001: 349–84.

Kohli, A. *The State and Development in the Third World*. Princeton: Princeton University Press, 1986.

Kolsky, Elizabeth. *Colonial Justice in British India: White Violence and the Rule of Law*. Cambridge: Cambridge University Press, 2010.

————. 'The Rule of Colonial Indifference: Rape on Trial in Early Colonial India, 1805–57', *The Journal of Asian Studies*, vol. 69, no. 4, 2010: 1093–117.

————. 'A Note on the Study of Indian Legal History', *Law and History Review*, vol. 23, no. 3, 2005: 703–6.

————. 'Codification and the Rule of Colonial Difference: Criminal Procedure in British India', *Law and History Review*, vol. 23, no. 3, 2005: 631–83.

Kothari, Jayna. 'Criminal Law on Domestic Violence: Promises and Limits', *Economic and Political Weekly*, vol. 40, no. 46, 2005: 4843–9.

Kozlowski, Gregory C. 'Personal Law and Political Identity in Independent India', in Robert D. Baird (ed.) *Religion and Law in Independent India*. New Delhi: Manohar, 2003.

————. 'Imperial Authority, Benefactions and Endowments (Awqāf) in Mughal India', *Journal of the Economic and Social History of the Orient*, vol. 38, no. 3, 1995: 355–70.

————. 'Loyalty, Locality and Authority in Several Opinions (Fatāwā) Delivered by the Muftī of the Jami'ah Nizāmiyyah Madrasah, Hyderabad, India', *Modern Asian Studies*, vol. 29, no. 4, 1995: 893–927.

————. *Muslim Endowments and Society in British India*. Cambridge: Cambridge University Press, 1985.

Krishnamurthy, S. *Human Rights and the Indian Police*. Bangalore: R.R. Publishers, 1994.

Kugle, Scott. 'Framed, Blamed and Renamed: The Recasting of Islamic Jurisprudence in Colonial South Asia', *Modern Asian Studies*, vol. 35, no. 2, 2001: 257–313.

Kumar, Kapil. *Peasants in Revolt: Tenants, Landlords, Congress and the Raj in Oudh 1886–1922*. New Delhi: Manohar, 1984.

Kumar, Mukul. 'Relationship of Caste and Crime in Colonial India: A Discourse Analysis', *Economic and Political Weekly*, vol. 39, no. 10, 2004: 1078–87.

————. 'Violence and Political Culture: Politics of the Ultra Left in Bihar', *Economic and Political Weekly*, vol. 38, no. 47, 2003: 4977–83.

Land, Isaac (ed.) *Enemies of Humanity: The Nineteenth Century War on Terrorism*. New York: Palgrave Macmillan, 2008.

Lariviere, Richard W. 'Justices and Panditas: Some Ironies in Contemporary Readings of the Hindu Legal Past', *The Journal of Asian Studies*, vol. 48, no. 4, 1989: 757–69.

Levy, Harold, 'Lawyers Scholars, Lawyers Politicians, and the Hindu Code Bill 1921–1956', *Law and Society Review*, vol. 3, nos 2–3, 1968: 303–16.

Lewin, M. *Torture in Madras*. London: James Ridgway, 1857.

Lee-Warner, Sir William. *The Native States of India*. London: Macmillan, 1910, reprint, 1979.

Linebaugh, Peter. *London Hanged: Crime and Civil Society in the Eighteenth Century*. Cambridge: Cambridge University Press, 1993.

Lingat, Robert. *The Classical Law of India*. J.M. Derret (trans.) Delhi: Thompson Press, 1973.

Lokaneeta, Jinee. *Transnational Torture: Law, Violence, and State Power in the United States and India*. New York: New York University Press, 2011.

Ludtke, Alf (ed.) *The History of Everyday Life: Reconstructing Historical Experiences and Ways of Life*. Princeton: Princeton University Press, 1995.

Macaulay, T.B. *The Complete Works of Lord Macaulay*. London: G.P. Putnam Sons, 1889.

Macaulay, T.B., J.M. Macleod, G.W. Anderson, and F. Millett. *The Indian Penal Code as Originally Framed in 1837, with Notes*. Madras: Higginbotham and Co., 1888.

Macpherson, J. 'Report on Insanity among Europeans in Bengal', *The Indian Annals of Medical Science*, 1854.

Madan, J.C. *Indian Police, Its Development up to 1905: An Historical Analysis*. Delhi: Uppal, 1980.

Madra, A.S. and Parmjit Singh (eds). *Sicques, Tigers, or Thieves: Eyewitness Accounts of the Sikhs (1606–1809)*. Hampshire, UK: Palgrave Macmillan, 2004.

Mahmood, Tahir. *Muslim Personal Law*. Nagpur: All India Reports, 1983.

————. *Civil Marriage Law*. Bombay: N.M. Tripathi, 1978.

————. *An Indian Civil Code and Islamic Law*. Bombay: N.M. Tripathi, 1976.

————. *Family Law Reform in the Muslim World*. Bombay: N.M. Tripathi, 1972.

Major, Andrew J. 'State and Criminal Tribes in Colonial Punjab: Surveillance, Control and Reclamation of the "Dangerous Classes"', *Modern Asian Studies*, vol. 33, no. 3, 1999: 657–8.

Majumdar, N. *Justice and Police in Bengal 1765–1793: A Study of the Nizamat in Decline*. Calcutta: K.L. Mukhopadhyay, 1960.

Malik, P.L. *The Criminal Court Handbook: Containing Three Major Acts, Criminal Procedure Code, Indian Penal Code and Indian Evidence Act*. Lucknow: Eastern Book Co., 1966.

Mallampalli, Chandra. *Race, Religion and Law in Colonial India: Trials of an Interracial Family*. Cambridge: Cambridge University Press, 2011.

————. 'Meet the Abrahams: Colonial Law and a Mixed Race Family from Bellary, South India, 1810–63', *Modern Asian Studies*, vol. 42, no. 5, 2008: 929–70.

Manchanda, S. *Parsi Law in India*. Allahabad: The Law Book Co., 1991.

Mani, L. 'Contentious Traditions: The Debate on Sati in Colonial India', in K. Sangari and S. Vaid (eds) *Recasting Women: Essays in Colonial History*. Delhi: Kali for Women, 1989: 88–126.

Mani, L. *Contentious Traditions: The Debate on Sati in Colonial India*. Berkeley: University of California Press, 1998.

Mantena, Karuna. *Alibis of Empire: Henry Maine and the Ends of Liberal Imperialism*. Princeton: Princeton University Press, 2010.

Masselos, Jim. 'Social Segregation and Crowd Cohesion: Reflections around some Preliminary Data from 19th Century Bombay City', *Contributions to Indian Sociology*, vol. 23, no. 2, 1979: 145–67.

Mayaram, Shail. 'Communal Violence in Jaipur', *Economic and Political Weekly*, vol. 28, nos 46–7, 1993: 2524–41.

Mayne. *A Treatise on Hindu Law and Usage*. C. Sankaran Nair (ed.) Madras: Higginbotham and Co., 1883.

Mazzarella, William. 'Affect: What is it Good for?', in Saurabh Dube (ed.) *Enchantments of Modernity: Empire, Nation, Globalization*. London and New Delhi: Routledge, 2009: 291–309.

Mbembe, Achille. 'Necropolitics', *Public Culture*, vol. 15, no. 1, 2003: 11–40.

Meadows, Taylor. *Confessions of a Thug*. Oxford: Oxford University Press, 1839, new edition, 1986.

Mehta, Nalin and Mona G. Mehta (eds) 'Gujarat Beyond Gandhi: Identity, Conflict and Society', *South Asian Culture and Society*, vol. 1, no. 4, special issue, 2010.

Melcher, C. *The Formation of the Sunni Schools of Law, 9th to 10th Centuries CE*. Leiden: Brill, 1997.

Mendelsohn, Oliver. 'The Pathology of the Indian Legal System', *Modern Asian Studies*, vol. 15, no. 4, 1981: 823–63.

Menon, Nivedita. *Recovering Subversion: Feminist Politics Beyond the Law*. Champaign, IL: University of Illinois Press, 2004.

————. 'State/Gender/Community: Citizenship in Contemporary India', *Economic and Political Weekly*, vol. 33, no. 5, 1998: PE3–PE10.

Menon, Ritu and Kamla Bhasin. *Borders and Boundaries: Women in India's Partition*. New Brunswick, NJ: Rutgers University Press, 1998.

Meron, Y. 'The Development of Legal Thought in Hanafi Texts', *Studia Islamica*, vol. 30, 1969: 73–118.

Merry, Sally Engle. *Colonizing Hawai'i: The Cultural Power of Law*. Princeton: Princeton University Press, 2000.

————. 'Anthropology, Law, and Transnational Processes', *Annual Review of Anthropology*, vol. 21, 1992: 357–79.

Metcalf, Thomas R. *The Aftermath of Revolt: India, 1857–1870*. Princeton: Princeton University Press, 1964.

Mines, Mattison. 'Courts of Law and Styles of Self in Eighteenth-Century Madras: From Hybrid to Colonial Self', *Modern Asian Studies*, vol. 35, no. 1, 2001: 33–74.

Mitra, K. 'Human Rights and Hinduism', *Journal of Ecumenical Studies*, vol. 19, 1982: 77–84.

Mitter, D.N. *The Position of Women in Hindu Law*. New Delhi: Inter-India Publications, 1984.

Misra, B.B. *The Judicial Administration of the East India Company in Bengal, 1765–1782*. Delhi: Motilal Banarsidass, 1961.

Moffatt, E.M. *The Criminal Castes of India*. New York: New York University Press, 1920.

Mohapatra, Prabhu. 'The Hosay Massacre of 1884: Class and Community among Indian Labourers in Trinidad', in Marcel van der Linden and A.N. Das (eds) *Work and Social Change in South Asia: Festschrift volume for Professor Jan Breman*. New Delhi: Manohar-CSH, 2002.

————. 'Restoring the Family: Wife Murders and the Making of a Sexual Contract for Indian Indentured Labourers in the British Caribbean Colonies', *Studies in History*, vol. 11, no. 2, 1995: 227–60.

Monius, A.E. 'Love, Violence and the Aesthetics of Disgust: Saivas and Jains in Medieval South India', *Journal of Indian Philosophy*, vol. 32, nos 2–3, 2003: 113–72.

Moore, Erin P. 'Gender, Power, and Legal Pluralism', *American Ethnologist*, vol. 20, 1993: 522–42.

————. *Gender, Law, and Resistance in India*. Tucson: University of Arizona Press, 1998.

Moore, Lewis. *Malabar Law and Custom*. Madras: Higginbotham and Co., 1900.

Morgan, W. and A. MacPherson. *The Indian Penal Code with Notes*. London: G.C. Hay and Co., 1986.

Moyn, Samuel. *The Last Utopia: Human Rights in History*. Cambridge, MA: Harvard University Press, 2010.

Mukerji, S.C. *Prevention of Offences*. Calcutta: Art Press, 1927.

Mukherjee, Arun. *Crime and Public Disorder in Colonial Bengal*. Calcutta: K.P. Bagchi and Co., 1995.

————. 'Scarcity and Crime: A Study of 19th Century Bengal', *Economic and Political Weekly*, vol. 28, no. 6, 1993: 237–43.

Mukherjee, Mridula. 'Peasant Resistance and Peasant Consciousness in Colonial India: "Subalterns" and Beyond', *Economic and Political Weekly*, vol. 23, no. 4, 1988: 2109–20.

Mukherjee, Rudrangshu. *Spectre of Violence: The 1857 Kanpur Massacres*. Delhi: Penguin Books India, 1998.

Mukhopadhyay, A. *Behind the Mask: The Cultural Definition of the Legal Subject in Colonial Bengal (1775–1911)*. Oxford: Oxford University Press, 2006.

Mukhopadhyay, M. 'Between Community and State: The Question of Women's Right and Personal Laws', in Z. Hasan (ed.) *Forging Identities: Gender, Communities and the State*. New Delhi: Kali for Women, 1994: 108–29.

Mullaly, F.S. *Notes on Criminal Classes of the Madras Presidency*. Madras: Govt. Press, 1892.

Nader, Laura. *Harmony Ideology: Justice and Control in a Zapotec Mountain Village*. Stanford: Stanford University Press, 1991.

Nagla, Bhupendra Kumar. *Female Criminality: An Empirical Study in Andhra Pradesh*. Delhi: Eastern Book Co., 1987.

Nair, Janaki. *Women and Law in Colonial India: A Social History*. Columbia, Missouri: South Asia Books, 1996.

——————. 'Dangerous Labour: Crime, Work and Punishment in Kolar Gold Fields, 1890–1946', *Studies in History*, vol. 13, no. 1, 1997: 19–61.

Nelson, J.H. *Prospectus for the Scientific Study of Hindu Law*. London: Kegan Paul and Co., 1881.

Nelson's Indian Penal Code, Vol. II, 7th edition, revised by S.N. Mulla and L.G. Gupta, Allahabad: Law Book Co., 1983.

Nehru, Jawaharlal. *Selected Works of Jawaharlal Nehru*. New Delhi: Orient Longman, 1973–5.

——————. *An Autobiography*. London: Bodley Head, 1936.

Nicolson, D. 'Telling Tales: Gender Discrimination, Gender Construction and Battered Women Who Kill', *Feminist Legal Studies*, vol. 3, no. 2, 1995: 185–206.

Nicolson, D. and R. Sanghvi. 'Battered Women and Provocation: The Implications of R v Ahluwalia', *Criminal Law Review*, 1993: 728–38.

Nigam, Sanjay, 'Disciplining and Policing the "Criminals by Birth", Part 1: The Making of the Colonial Stereotype—the Criminal Tribes and Castes of North India', *Indian Economic and Social History Review*, vol. 27, no. 2, 1990: 131–64.

——————. 'Disciplining and Policing the 'Criminals by Birth', Part 2: The Development of a Disciplinary System, 1871–1900', *Indian Economic and Social History Review*, vol. 27, no. 3, 1990: 257–87.

Noorani, A.G. *Indian Political Trials, 1775–1947*. Delhi: Oxford University Press, 2007.

O'Brien, Patricia. 'Crime and Punishment as Historical Problem', *Journal of Social History*, vol. 11, no. 4, 1978: 508–20.

O'Hanlon, Rosalind. 'Issues of Widowhood: Gender and Resistance in Colonial Western India', in Douglas Haynes and Gyan Prakash (eds) *Contesting Power: Resistance and Everyday Social Relations in South Asia*. Delhi: Oxford University Press, 1991.

——————. *Caste, Conflict and Ideology: Mahatma Jotirao Phule and Low-Caste Protest in Nineteenth-Century Western India*. Cambridge: Cambridge University Press, 1985.

Owen, Nicholas. *The British Left and India: Metropolitan Anti-Imperialism, 1885–1947*. Oxford: Oxford University Press, 2007.

Pandey, Gyanendra. *Remembering Partition: Violence, Nationalism, and History in India*. Cambridge: Cambridge University Press, 2002.

Pandian, Anand. 'Pastoral Power in the Postcolony: On the Biopolitics of the Criminal Animal in South India', *Cultural Anthropology*, vol. 23, no. 1, 2008: 85–117.

Parashar, A. *Women and Family Law Reform in India*. New Delhi: Sage Publications, 1992.

Parker, Kunal M. 'A Corporation of Superior Prostitutes: Anglo-Indian Legal Conceptions of Temple Dancing Girls, 1800–1914', *Modern Asian Studies*, vol. 32, no. 3, 1998: 559–633.

Parker, Kunal M. 'The Historiography of Difference', *Law & History Review*, vol. 23, no. 3, 2005: 685–95.

Parry, Jonathan. 'Ankalu's Errant Wife: Sex, Marriage and Industry in Contemporary Chhattisgarh', *Modern Asian Studies*, vol. 35, 2001: 783–820.

—————. 'The Marital History of a Thumb Impression Man', in David Arnold and S. Blackburn (eds) *Telling Lives: South Asian Life Histories*. New Delhi: Permanent Black, 2004: 281–318.

Patra, A.C. 'An Historical Introduction to the Indian Penal Code', *Journal of the Indian LawInstitute*, vol. 3, 1961: 351–66.

Paterson, A. *Report on the Prevention of Crime and the Treatment of the Criminal in the Province of Burma*. Rangoon: Superintendent, Government Printing and Stationery Bureau, 1926.

Patra, A.C. *The Administration of Justice under the East-India Company in Bengal, Bihar and Orissa*. London: Asia Publishing House, 1962.

Paul John J. *The Legal Profession in Colonial South India*. Bombay: Oxford University Press, 1991.

Peabody, Norbert. 'Cents, Sense, Census: Human Inventories in Late Precolonial and Early Colonial India', *Comparative Studies of History and Society*, vol. 43, no. 1, 2001: 819–50.

Peers, Douglas M. 'Sepoys, Soldiers and the Lash: Race, Caste and Army Discipline in India, 1820–50', *The Journal of Imperial and Commonwealth History*, vol. 23, no. 2, 1995: 211–47.

—————. 'Torture, the Police and the Colonial State in the Madras Presidency, 1816–55', *Criminal Justice History*, vol. 12, 1991: 29–56.

Peggs, J. *Pilgrim Tax in India*. London: Seely, 1830. [second edition]

Perin, C. Kerawalla. *A Study in Indian Crime*. Bombay: Popular Book Depot, 1959.

Perlin, Frank. 'Protoindustrialization and Precolonial South Asia', *Past and Present*, vol. 98, 1983: 30–95.

Pettigrew, J.M. *The Sikhs of the Punjab: Unheard Voices of State and Guerrilla Violence*. London and New Jersey: Zed Books, 1995.

Pierce, Steven and Anupama Rao. 'On the Subject of Governance', in David Cohen, Fernando Coronil, Julie Skurski, Chandra Bhimull, Edward L. Murphy, Monica Patterson (eds) *Anthrohistory: Unsettling Knowledge, Questioning Discipline*. Ann Arbor: University of Michigan Press, 2011: 240–51.

—————. (eds) *Discipline and the Other Body: Correction, Corporeality, Colonialism*. Durham: Duke University Press, 2006.

Pinney, Christopher. *Camera Indica: The Social Life of Indian Photographs*. Chicago: University of Chicago Press, 1997.

Police Torture and Murder in Bengal: Reports of Two Trials of the Police of the District of Burwan in August and September 1860, confirmed by the Sudder Nizamut. Calcutta: Savielle & Cranenburgh Printers, Bengal Printing Co., 1861.

Pouchepadass, Jacques. 'Delinquance de Fonction et Normalisation Coloniale: Les "Tribus Crimenelles" dans l'Indie Britanique', in *Les Marginaux et les Exclus dans L'Histoire*. Paris: Cahiers Jussieu 5, 1979: 122–54.

Prachand, S.L.M. *Mob Violence in India*. Chandigarh: Abhishek Publications, 1979.

Purkayastha, Sharmila. 'Srikrishna Commission', *Economic and Political Weekly*, vol. 31, no. 9, 1996: 498.

Radhakrishna, Meena. 'The Criminal Tribes Act in the Madras Presidency: Implications for Itinerant Trading Communities', *Indian Economic and Social History Review*, vol. 26, no. 3, 1989: 271–95.

————. *Dishonoured by History: Criminal Tribes and British Colonial Policy*. Hyderabad: Orient Blackswan, 2008.

Radhakrishnan, P. 'Ayodhya Issue and Freedom of Expression', *Economic and Political Weekly*, vol. 37, no. 40, 2002: 4099–100.

Rafael, Vicente L. (ed.). *Figures of Criminality in Indonesia, the Philippines and Colonial Vietnam*. Ithaca: Cornell Southeast Asia Publications, 1999.

Raghavachariar, N.R. *Hindu Law: Principles and Precedents*. Madras: The Madras Law Journal Office, 1980.

Raj Sareen, Tilak. *Indian Revolutionary Movement Abroad, 1905–1921*. New Delhi: Sterling, 1984.

Rajan, Rajeswari Sunder. *The Scandal of the State: Women, Law, and Citizenship in Postcolonial India*. North Carolina: Duke University Press, 2003.

————. 'The Subject of Sati: Pain and Death in the Contemporary Discourse on Sati', *Yale Journal of Criticism*, vol. 3, no. 2, 1990: 1–23.

————. 'Shah Bano', *Signs: Journal of Women in Culture and Society*, vol. 14, no. 1, 1989: 558–82.

Rajgopal, P.R. *Violence and Response: A Critique of the Indian Criminal Justice System*. New Delhi: Uppal Pub. House, 1988.

Rajagopal, Arvind. 'The Violence of Commodity Aesthetics: Hawkers, Demolition Raids, and a New Regime of Consumption', *Social Text*, vol. 19, no. 3, 2001: 91–113.

————. *Politics after Television: Hindu Nationalism and the Reshaping of the Public in India*. Cambridge: Cambridge University Press, 2001.

Ramberg, Lucinda. 'When the Devi Is Your Husband: Sacred Marriage and Sexual Economy in South India', *Feminist Studies*, vol. 37, no. 1, 2011: 28–60.

Ramnath, Maia. *Haj to Utopia: How the Ghadar Movement Charted Global Radicalism and Attempted to Overthrow the British Empire*. Berkeley, CA: University of California Press, 2012.

Rankin, G.C. *Background to India Law*. Cambridge: Cambridge University Press, 1946.

Rao, Anupama. *The Caste Question: Dalits and the Politics of Modern India*. Berkeley, CA: University of California Press, 2009.

————. 'Problems of Violence, States of Terror: Torture in Colonial India', in Steven Pierce and Anupama Rao (eds) *Discipline and the Other Body: Correction, Corporeality, Colonialism*. Durham: Duke University Press, 2006: 151–85.

————. (ed.) *Gender and Caste: Issues in Indian Feminism*. New Delhi: Kali for Women, 2003.

Rao, Anupama. 'Understanding Sirasgaon: Notes towards Conceptualizing the Role of Law, Caste and Gender in a Case of "Atrocity", in Rajeswari Sunder Rajan (ed.) *Signposts: Gender Issues in Post-Independence India*. New Delhi: Kali for Women, 1998: 205–48.

Rao, Narayan Velcheru, David Shulman, and Sanjay Subrahmanyam. *Textures of Time: Writing History in South India*. New York: Other Press, 2003.

Rao, V.D. 'A Note on the Police of the City of Poona', *Journal of Indian History*, vol. 36, 1958: 223–8.

Rao, Venugopala. *Baton and the Pen: Four Decades of Indian Police*. New Delhi: Konark Publishers, 1993.

————. *Victims of Crime*. Bombay: Allied Publishers, 1989.

————. *Perspectives in Criminology*. Shimla: Indian Institute of Advanced Study, 1988.

————. *Crime in Our Society: A Political Perspective*. Delhi: Vikas, 1983.

————. *Dynamics of Crime: Spatial and Socio-economic Aspects of Crime in India*. New Delhi: India Institute of Public Administration, 1981.

————. *Power and Criminality: A Survey of Famous Crimes in Indian History*. Bombay: Allied Publishers, 1977.

————. *Facets of Crime in India*. Bombay: Allied Publishers, 1967.

Ray, Sibnarayan (ed.) *The Story of My Transportation Life*. Bombay: Sadbhakti Publications, 1950.

Reeves, P.D. (ed.) *Sleeman in Oudh*. Cambridge: Cambridge University Press, 1971.

'Recalling Bhagalpur: Aftermath of 1989 Riots', *Economic and Political Weekly*, vol. 31, no. 18, 1996: 1055–9.

Rege, M.P. *Concepts of Justice and Equality in the Indian Tradition*. Pune: Gokhale Institute of Politics and Economics, 1985.

Retzlaff, Ralph. 'The Problem of Communal Minorities in the Drafting of the Indian Constitution', in R.N. Spann (ed.) *Constitutionalism in Asia*. London: Asia Publishing House, 1963.

Richmond Henderson, Charles. 'Control of Crime in India', *Journal of American Institute of Criminal Law and Criminology*, vol. 4, no. 3, 1913: 378–401.

Rocher, Ludo. 'Law Books in an Oral Culture: The Indian "Dharmasastras"', *Proceedings of the American Philosophical Society*, vol. 137, no. 2, 1993: 254–67.

————. 'Can a Murderer Inherit His Victim's Estate? British Responses to Troublesome Questions in Hindu Law', *Journal of the American Oriental Society*, vol. 107, no. 1, 1987: 1–10.

Rocher, Ludo. 'Lawyers in Classical Hindu Law', *Law & Society Review*, vol. 3, nos 2–3, 1969: 383–402.

Roy, Sripati. *Customs and Customary Law in British India*. Delhi: Mittal Publications, 1910, reprinted 1986.

Rudolph, S.H. and L.I. Rudolph. *The Modernity of Tradition: Political Development in India*, Chicago: University of Chicago Press, 1997.

Rudolph, S.H. and L.I. Rudolph. 'Barristers and Brahmans in India: Legal Cultures and Social Change', *Comparative Studies in Society and History*, vol. 8, no. 1, 1965: 24–49.

Sangar, S.P. *Crime and Punishment in Mughal India*. Delhi: Sterling Publishers, 1967.

Sanyal, Kalyan. *Rethinking Capitalist Development: Primitive Accumulation, Governmentality, and Postcolonial Capitalism*. Delhi: Routledge, 2007.

Saksena, N.S. *Law and Order in India*. New Delhi: Abhinav Publications, 1987.

SARAI collective. *Bare Acts*. Delhi: SARAI Media Lab, 2005

Sarkar Shastri, G.C. *A Treatise on Hindu Law*. Calcutta: Book Stall, 1933.

Sarkar, Tanika. *Rebels, Wives, Saints: Designing Selves and Nations in Colonial India*. Calcutta: Seagull Books, 2010.

—————. 'Enfranchised Selves: Women, Culture and Rights in Nineteenth-Century Bengal', *Gender and History*, vol. 13, no. 3, 2001: 546–65.

—————. *Hindu Wife, Hindu Nation: Community, Religion and Cultural Nationalism*. New Delhi: Permanent Black, 2001.

Sathyamurthy, S. *The Rights of Citizens*. Madras: 1919.

Sardesai, G.S. (ed.) *Selections from the Peshwa Daftar*. Bombay: Government Central Press, 1957.

Sastry, K.R.R. 'Hinduism and International Law', *Recueil Des Cours*, vol. 117, 1966: 507–614.

Saxena, Rekha. *Women and Crime in India: A Study in Sociocultural Dynamics*. New Delhi: Inter-India Publications, 1994.

Schact, J. *An Introduction to Islamic Law*. Delhi: Oxford University Press, 1964.

Schama, Simon. *The Embarrassment of Riches: An Interpretation of Dutch Culture in the Golden Age*. New York: Knopf, 1988.

Scott, James C. *Weapons of the Weak: Everyday Forms of Peasant Resistance*. New Haven: Yale University Press, 1985.

—————. *The Moral Economy of the Peasant: Rebellion and Subsistence in Southeast Asia*. New Haven: Yale University Press, 1976.

Semple, Janet. *Bentham's Prison: A Study of the Panopticon Penitentiary*. Oxford: Clarendon Press, 1993.

Sen, Madhurima. *Prisons in Colonial Bengal, 1838–1919*. Calcutta: Thema Books, 2009.

Sen, Sarkar. *Police Today*. New Delhi: Ashish Publishing House, 1986.

—————. *Human Rights and Law Enforcement*. Delhi: Concept Publishing Company, 2002.

Sen, Satadru. 'A Separate Punishment: Juvenile Offenders in Colonial India', *The Journal of Asian Studies*, vol. 63, no. 1, 2004: 81–104.

—————. 'The Female Jails of Colonial India', *Indian Economic and Social History Review*, vol. 39, no. 4, 2002: 417–38.

—————. *Disciplining Punishment: Colonialism and Convict Society in the Andaman Islands*. Delhi: Oxford University Press, 2000.

Sen, Satadru. 'Rationing Sex: Female Convicts in the Andamans', *South Asia*, vol. 30, no. 1, 1999: 29–59.

Sen, Satadru. 'Policing the Savage: Segregation, Labor, and State Medicine in the Andamans', *The Journal of Asian Studies*, vol. 58, no. 3, 1999: 753–73.

Sen, Sudipta. *Distant Sovereignty: National Imperialism and the Origins of British India*. London and New York: Routledge, 2002.

Seth, Hansa. *Juvenile Delinquency in an Indian Setting*. Bombay: Popular Book Depot, 1961.

Sethna, M.J. *Society and the Criminal*. Bombay: Leader Press, 1952.

Schact, J. *An Introduction to Islamic Law*. Oxford: Clarendon Press, 1964.

Schneider, Jane and Peter Schneider. 'The Anthropology of Crime and Criminalization', *Annual Review of Anthropology*, vol. 37, no. 1, 2008: 351–73.

Sharafi, Mitra. *Colonial Parsis and Law: A Cultural History*. Bombay: K.R. Cama Oriental Institute, 2010.

Sharma, R.C. 'Aspects of Public Administration in Northern India in the First Half of the Seventeenth Century', *Journal of Indian History*, vol. LVI, part 1, 1976.

Sharma, R.S. *Material Culture & Social Formations in Ancient India*, Madras: Macmillan India Ltd., 1983.

Shakespeare, John, 'Observations regarding Badheks and T'hegs', *Asiatic Researchers*, vol. XIII, 1820: 282–92.

Silvestri, Michael. *Ireland and India: Nationalism, Empire, and Memory*. New York: Palgrave Macmillan, 2009.

Singh, Mridula. *Displacement by Sadar Sarovar and Tehri: A Comparative Study of Two Dams*. New Delhi: Multiple Action Research Group, 1992.

Singh, Indra Jeet. *Indian Prison: A Sociological Enquiry*. Delhi: Concept Publishing Company, 1979.

Singh, Prabhash P. *Political Violence in India*. Delhi: Amar Prakashan, 1989.

Singh, Pritam. *Victims or Criminals? A Study of Women in Colonial North-Western Provinces and Oudh, India, 1870–1910*. Middleton, New Jersey: Caslon, 1996.

Singh, Ujwal Kumar. *The State, Democracy, and Anti-Terror Laws*. New Delhi: Sage Publications, 2007.

——————. *Political Prisoners in India*. Delhi: Oxford University Press, 2001.

Singha, Radhika. 'Passport, Ticket, and India-Rubber Stamp: The Problem of the Pauper Pilgrim in Colonial India ca. 1882–1925', in Harald Fischer-Tine and Ashwini Tambe (ed.) *The Limits of British Colonial Control in South Asia*. London and New York: Routledge, 2008.

——————. 'Colonial Law and Infrastructural Power: Reconstructing Community, Locating the Female Subject', *Studies in History*, vol. 19, no. 1, 2004: 87–126.

——————. 'Settle, Mobilize, Verify: Identification Practices in Colonial India', *Studies in History*, vol. 16, no. 2, 2000: 151–98.

——————. *A Despotism of Law: Crime and Justice in Early Colonial India*. New Delhi: Oxford University Press, 1998.

Singha, Radhika. 'No Needless Pain or Unintended Pleasures: Penal Reform in the Colony'. *Studies in History*, vol. 11, no. 1, 1995: 29–76.

303

Singha, Radhika. 'Providential Circumstances: The Thuggee Campaign of the 1830s and Legal Innovation', *Modern Asian Studies*, vol. 27, no. 1, 1993: 83–146.

—————. 'The Privilege of Taking Life: Some "Anomalies" in the Law of Homicide in the Bengal Presidency', *Indian Economic and Social History Review*, vol. 30, no. 2, 1993: 181–214.

Sinha, C.S. *The Indian Civil Judiciary in the Making, 1800–1833*. New Delhi: Munshiram Manoharlal, 1971.

Sinha, Mrinalini. *Spectres of Mother India: The Global Restructuring of an Empire.* Durham: Duke University Press, 2006.

Sinha, Nitin. 'Mobility, Control and Criminality in Early Colonial India, 1760s–1850s', *The Indian Economic and Social History Review*, vol. 45, no. 1, 2008: 1–33.

Sinha, N.K. and A.K. Dasgupta (eds) *Selections from Ochterlony Papers (1818–1825) in the National Archives of India*. Calcutta: University of Calcutta, 1964.

Skuy, David. 'Macaulay and the Indian Penal Code of 1862: The Myth of the Inherent Superiority and Modernity of the English Legal System Compared to India's Legal System in the Nineteenth Century', *Modern Asian Studies*, vol. 32, no. 3, 1998: 513–57.

Slate, Nico. *Colored Cosmopolitanism: The Shared Struggle for Freedom in the United States and India*. Cambridge, MA: Harvard University Press, 2012.

Sleeman, W.H. *Journey through the Kingdom of Oudh in 1849–50*. New Delhi: Asian Educational Services, 1995.

—————. *Rambles and Recollections*. Cambridge: Cambridge University Press, 1844, revised, annotated edition, 1915, reprint, 1980.

Smart, Carol. *Feminism and the Power of Law*. New York: Routledge, 1989.

Smith, Graham and Duncan Derrett. 'Hindu Judicial Administration in Pre-British Times and Its Lesson for Today', *Journal of the American Oriental Society*, vol. 95, no. 3, 1975: 417–23.

Smith, Richard Saumarez. 'Rule by Records and Rule by Reports: Complementary Aspects of British Imperial Rule of Law', *Contributions to Indian Sociology*, vol. 19, no. 1, 1985: 153–76.

Sohoni, Neera Kockreja. *Women Behind Bars*. New Delhi: Vikas Publishing House, 1989.

Souryal, S., D. Potts, and A. Al-Obeid. 'The Penalty of Hand Amputation for Theft in Islamic Law', *Journal of Criminal Justice*, vol. 22, no. 3, 1994: 249–65.

Spivak, Gayatari Chakravorty. 'Can the Subaltern Speak?', in Cary Nelson and Lawrence Grossberg (eds) *Marxism and the Interpretation of Culture*. Urbana: University of Illinois Press, 1988: 271–313.

Sreenivas, Mytheli. 'Creating Conjugal Subjects: Devadasis and the Politics of Marriage in Colonial Madras Presidency', *Feminist Studies*, vol. 37, no. 1, 2011: 63–92.

—————. *Wives, Widows, and Concubines: The Conjugal Family Ideal in Colonial India*. Indiana: Indiana University Press, 2008.

Sreenivas, Mytheli. 'Conjugality and Capital: Gender, Families, and Property under Colonial Law in India', *Journal of Asian Studies*, vol. 63, no. 4, 2004: 937–60.

Srivastava, R.C. *Development of the Judicial System in India under the East India Company.* Lucknow: Public House, 1971.

Stanley, Peter. *White Mutiny: British Military Culture in India.* London: Hurst, 1998.

Statham, J. *Indian Recollections.* London: Samuel Bagster, 1832.

Starr, June and Jane Collier (eds) *History and Power in the Study of Law: New Directions in Legal Anthropology.* Ithaca: Cornell University Press, 1988.

Stern, Philip. *The Company-State: Corporate Sovereignty and the Early Modern Origins of the British Empire in India.* New York: Oxford University Press, 2011.

Sternbach, L. *Judicial Studies in Ancient Indian Law.* Delhi: Motilal Banarsidas, 1967.

Stevenson, J.A.R. 'Some Account of the Phansigars, or Gang-Robbers and of the Shudgarshids, or Tribes of Jugglers', *Journal of the Royal Asiatic Society*, vol. 1, 1834: 280–3.

Steele, Arthur. *The Law and Custom of Hindoo Castes within the Dukhun.* London: W.H. Allen, 1868.

—————. *The Hindu Castes: Their Law, Religion and Customs.* Delhi: Mittal Publications, 1826, reprinted 1986.

Stokes, Eric. 'The First Century of British Rule in India: Social Revolution or Stagnation?' *Past and Present*, vol. 58, no. 1, 1973: 136–60.

—————. *The English Utilitarians and India.* Oxford: Clarendon Press, 1959.

Stoler, Ann Laura. *Race and the Education of Desire: Foucault's History of Sexuality and the Colonial Order of Things.* Durham: Duke University Press, 1995.

—————. 'In Cold Blood: Hierarchies of Credibility and the Politics of Colonial Narratives', Special Issue: Imperial Fantasies and Postcolonial Histories, *Representations*, vol. 37, 1992: 151–89.

Sturman, Rachel. *The Government of Social Life in Colonial India: Liberalism, Religious Law, and Women's Rights.* Cambridge: Cambridge University Press, 2012.

—————. 'Property and Attachments: Defining Autonomy and the Claims of Family in Nineteenth-Century Western India', *Comparative Studies in Society and History*, vol. 47, 2005: 611–37.

Sudarshan, R. 'Judges, State and Society', in R. Dhavan, R. Sudarshan, and S. Khurshid (eds) *Judges and the Judicial Power*, Bombay: Sweet and Maxwell, 1985: 268–88.

Suha, B.P. *The Police in Free India: Its Facets and Drawbacks.* Delhi: Konark Publishers, 1989.

Swaminathan, Padmini. 'Prison as Factory: A Study of Jail Manufacture in the Madras Presidency', *Studies in History*, vol. 11, no. 77, 1995: 77–100.

Tanika Sarkar is Professor, Centre for Historical Studies, Jawaharlal Nehru University.

Radhika Singha is Professor, Centre for Historical Studies, Jawaharlal Nehru University.

Anand A. Yang is Golub Professor of International Studies, University of Washington.

Yang, Anand A. 'Crime and Criminality in British India', *Association for Asian Studies Monograph 42*, Tucson: University of Arizona Press, 1985.

——————. 'Linkages Between British Raj and Saran Raiyat: The Development of Local Control Institutions in the Nineteenth and Twentieth Centuries', in Peter Robb (ed.) *Rural India: Land Power and Society under British Rule*. London: School of Oriental and African Studies, 1983: 149–80.

——————. 'Sacred Symbol and Sacred Space in Rural India: Community Mobilization in the Anti-Cow Killing Riot of 1893', *Comparative Studies in Society and History*, vol. 22, no. 4, 1980: 576–96.

——————. 'The Agrarian Origins of Crime: A Study of Riots in Saran District, India, 1886–1920', *Journal of Social History*, vol. 13, no. 2, 1979: 289–306.

——————. 'Guardians of the Raj: The Police in Colonial India, Saran District, 1765–1922', in Walter Hauser and James Manor (eds) *Two Faces of India*. forthcoming.

Zamindar, Vazira Fazili-Yacoobali. *The Long Partition and the Making of Modern South Asia: Refugees, Boundaries, Histories*. New York: Columbia University Press, 2007.

About the Contributors

Padma Anagol is Senior Lecturer, Department of History, Cardiff University.

David Arnold is Professor, Department of History, University of Warwick.

Rajnarayan Chandavarkar was Reader in the History and Politics of South Asia and Fellow of Trinity College, University of Cambridge.

Saurabh Dube is Professor of History, Center of Asian and African Studies, El Colegio de México.

Ranajit Guha is Emeritus Professor, Australian National University.

Sumit Guha is Professor of History, Rutgers University.

Malavika Kasturi is Associate Professor, Modern South Asian History, University of Toronto.

Scott Alan Kugle is Associate Professor, Department of South Asian and Islamic Studies, Emory University.

Sanjay Nigam taught history at Ramjas College, University of Delhi, and is CEO, NDTV, India.

Rajeswari Sunder Rajan is Global Distinguished Professor of English, New York University.

Anupama Rao is Associate Professor of History, Barnard College, Columbia University.

Walzer, Michael. *Spheres of Justice: A Defense of Pluralism and Equality*. New York: Basic Books, 1983.

Wardhaugh, Julia. 'The Jungle and the Village: Discourses on Crime and Deviance in Rural North India', *South Asia Research*, vol. 25, no. 2, 2005: 129–40.

Wash, Cecil. *Crime in India*. London: Ernest Benn Ltd, 1930.

Washbrook, D.A. 'Law, State and Agrarian Society in Colonial India', *Modern Asian Studies*, vol. 15, no. 3, 1981: 649–721.

Webb, Sidney and Beatrice Webb. *English Prisons under Local Government*. London: Longmans, 1921.

Weiner, Martin J. *Reconstructing the Criminal: Culture, Law, and Policy in England, 1830–1914*. Cambridge: Cambridge University Press, 1990.

Welch Jr, C.E., and V.A. Leary (eds) *Asian Perspectives on Human Rights*. Boulder, Co: Westview Press, 1990.

Werner Menski. *Indian Legal Systems, Past and Present*. London: School of Oriental and African Studies Law Department, 1997.

West, R. 'Mohammedan Law in India', *Journal of the Society of Comparative Legislation*, vol. 2, no. 1, 1900: 27–44.

Wilson, Jon E. 'Anxieties of Distance: Codification in Early Colonial Bengal', *Modern Intellectual History*, vol. 4, no. 1, 2007: 7–23.

Wilson, R.W. *An Introduction to the Study of Anglo-Muhammedan Law*. London: W. Thacker, 1894.

Winther, C. 'Chambal Valley Dacoity: A Study of Banditry in North Central India', PhD dissertation, Cornell University, 1972.

Wink, Andre. *Land and Sovereignty in India: Agrarian Society and Politics under the Eighteenth-Century Maratha Svarajya*. Cambridge: Cambridge University Press, 1986.

Whitehead, Judy. 'Bodies Clean and Unclean: Prostitution, Sanitary Legislation, and Femininity in Colonial North India', *Gender and History*, vol. 7, 1, 1995: 41–63.

Wood, Conrad. 'Peasant Revolt: An Interpretation of Moplah Violence in the Nineteenth and Twentieth Centuries', in Clive Dewey and A.G. Hopkins (eds), *The Imperial Impact: Studies in the Economic History of Africa and India*. London: Athlone Press, 1978: 132–51.

Wright Jr, Theodore. 'Muslim Legislators in India: Profile of a Minority Élite', *The Journal of Asian Studies*, vol. 23, no. 2, 1964: 253–67.

Yang, Anand A. 'Bandits and Kings: Moral Authority and Resistance in Early Colonial India', *Journal of Asian Studies*, vol. 66, no. 4, 2007: 881–96.

————. 'Indian Convict Workers in Southeast Asia in the Late Eighteenth and Early Nineteenth Centuries', *Journal of World History*, vol. 14, no. 2, 2003: 179–208.

————. 'Disciplining Natives: Prisoners and Prisons in Early Nineteenth Century India', *Journal of South Asian Studies*, vol. 10, no. 2, 1987: 29–45.

————. 'A Conversation of Rumors: The Language of Popular Mentalites in Late Nineteenth Century Colonial India', *Journal of Social History*, vol. 20, no. 3, 1987: 485–505.

Syeda Hameed *et al. How Has the Gujarat Massacre Affected Minority Women? The Survivors Speak.* Fact-finding by a Women's Panel, sponsored by Citizen's Initiative, 16 April 2002.

Symington, D. *Report on the Condition of Aboriginal Tribes.* Bombay: Government Central Press, 1938.

Talbot, Ian, *Pakistan: A Modern History.* London: Hurst, 2009.

Tambe, Ashwini. *Codes of Misconduct: Regulating Prostitution in Late Colonial Bombay.* Minneapolis: University of Minnesota Press, 2009.

Tarapore, Pheroze Kharsedji. *Prison Reform in India.* Oxford: Oxford University Press, 1936.

Thompson, E.P. *Customs in Common: Studies in Traditional Popular Culture.* New York: New Press, 1993.

—————. *Whigs and Hunters.* Harmondsworth: Penguin, 1977.

Toor, Saadia. *The State of Islam: Culture and Cold War Politics in Pakistan.* London and New York: Pluto Press, 2011.

Trevelyan, C.E. 'The Thugs or Secret Murderers of India', *The Edinburg Review,* vol. LXIV, 1837: 357–95.

Tyagi, D. *Narmada Basin-Land and People: An Anthropological Pilot Study of Madhya Pradesh and Gujarat.* Anthropological Survey of India, Ministry of Human Resource Development, Government of India, Department of Culture, 1998.

Vatuk, Sylvia. 'Islamic Feminism in India: Indian Muslim Women Activists and the Reform of Muslim Personal Law', *Modern Asian Studies,* vol. 42, nos 2–3, Islam in South Asia, 2008: 489–518.

Varady, R.G. 'North Indian Banjaras', *South Asia,* ns, vol. 2, nos 1–2, 1979: 1–18.

Veduckumchery, James. *Police Criminology and Crimes.* New Delhi: Gyan Publishing House, 2002.

—————. *Indian Police and Nexus Crime.* New Delhi: Gyan Publishing House, 2002.

—————. *Third Millenium Police: Take of Trends in India.* New Delhi: A.P.H. Publishing Corporation, 2000.

Vijaisri, Priyadarshini. *Recasting the Devadasi: Patterns of Sacred Prostitution in Colonial South India.* Delhi: Kanishka Publications 2004.

Vincent, Joan. *Anthropology and Politics: Visions, Traditions, and Trends.* Tuscon: University of Arizona Press, 1990.

Visweswaran, Kamala. 'Small Speeches, Subaltern Gender: Nationalist Ideology and its Historiography', in Amin Shahid and Chakrabarty Dipesh (eds) *Subaltern Studies IX: Writings on South Asian History and Society.* Delhi: Oxford University Press, 1996: 83–125.

Wagner, Kim A. *Thuggee: Banditry and the British in Early Nineteenth-Century India,* Cambridge Imperial and Post-Colonial Studies. Cambridge: Palgrave Macmillan, 2007.

Walsh, C.H. *Indian Village Crimes: With an Introduction on Police Investigation and Confessions.* London: Ernest Benn Limited, 1924.

Tanika Sarkar is Professor, Centre for Historical Studies, Jawaharlal Nehru University.

Radhika Singha is Professor, Centre for Historical Studies, Jawaharlal Nehru University.

Anand A. Yang is Golub Professor of International Studies, University of Washington.